# CONTENTS

|  |  |  |
|---|---|---|
| Acknowledgements | iv |
| Introduction | v |
| About the Authors | vi |
| **1** Pregnancy and Birth | 1 |
| **2** Care of the Newborn | 27 |
| **3** Care of the Skin | 57 |
| **4** Sleep, Crying and Teeth | 78 |
| **5** Feeding | 100 |
| **6** The Developing Baby | 125 |
| **7** The Ill Baby | 151 |
| **8** Equipment, Toys and Play | 168 |
| **9** Babies with Special Needs | 187 |
| Appendix: First Aid | 208 |
| Suggested Further Reading | 212 |
| Useful Addresses | 213 |
| Index | 215 |

# ACKNOWLEDGEMENTS

We would like to thank our colleagues in the Child and Social Care programme area of the City and Islington College for their support, help and encouragement in the development of this book.

We would also like to give especial thanks to all the babies who 'allowed' their photographs to be used, and to Brendan O'Donovan for his artwork and computer skills.

*Angela Dare*
*Margaret O'Donovan*

The authors and publishers would also like to thank: the Child Growth Foundation for permission to reproduce the UK growth standards (percentile charts) on pages 130 and 131; and Bubbles/Loisjoy Thurston for the cover photograph.

# A PRACTICAL GUIDE TO
# WORKING IN NURSERIES

## SECOND EDITION

**Angela Dare**
**Margaret O'Donovan**

**Stanley Thornes (Publishers) Ltd**

First published in 1998 by
Stanley Thornes (Publishers) Ltd
Ellenborough House
Wellington Street
CHELTENHAM
GL50 1YW

98  99  00  01  02  /  10  9  8  7  6  5  4  3  2  1

A catalogue record for this book is available from The British Library.

ISBN 0 7487 3635 2

Typeset by Columns Design Ltd, Reading
Printed and bound in Great Britain by Redwood Books, Trowbridge, Wiltshire

# INTRODUCTION

This new and updated edition of the book provides relevant information for students studying all CACHE, BTEC and City and Guilds child care courses. It also provides the underpinning knowledge for NVQ Units C12, C13, and C14 and complements other reading for C17 and C18.

Within each chapter there are a number of Activities. The aim of the Activities, although practically based, is to help you link the theory of child care to your practice. Each Activity should always be followed by a written account or summary of your findings.

At the end of each chapter there are Quick Checks. The aim of Quick Checks is to ensure that you have understood the main points in each chapter.

You should keep all your documentation, including written reports, photographs, baby studies, etc. for inclusion in your portfolio. The portfolio may be used as evidence of your prior learning for entry into other child care courses, for presentation at job interviews and for demonstration of knowledge and understanding for National Vocational Qualification assessment.

Throughout this book we have, of necessity, identified the baby's parents, often the mother, as the prime carer. However, we should stress that consistent, loving care in a stable environment can be provided by other carers, irrespective of sexual orientation or gender.

# ABOUT THE AUTHORS

**Angela Dare**, Cert. Ed., RGN, RHV, FWT, is currently an external verifier for CACHE.

**Margaret O'Donovan**, NNEB Cert., RGN, RM, RHV, FWT, teaches on child-care courses at The Chiltern College, Caversham, Reading.

Both authors have wide experience in health visiting and teaching. They worked together for many years teaching students on child-care courses at City and Islington College, London, and were examiners for the NNEB.

Their book *A Practical Guide to Child Nutrition*, in the same series, was published in 1996. More recently, *Good Practice in Caring for Children with Special Needs* was published in July 1997.

# **1** *PREGNANCY AND BIRTH*

**This chapter covers:**
- Pre-conceptual care
- Conception and pregnancy
- Antenatal care
- Labour and birth
- The postnatal period
- Useful terms

## Pre-conceptual care

Healthy parents tend to have healthy babies. The first 12 weeks of a pregnancy are very important. During that time rapid development takes place as the baby's organs (heart, liver, lungs, kidneys and brain) and body systems are forming. Many babies are conceived with no thought or planning and the woman may be unaware she is pregnant in these early weeks. Any necessary adjustment to her lifestyle will not have been made. Even if she suspects or knows she is pregnant, she may delay seeing her family doctor or attending an antenatal clinic until 12 weeks or later. By this time the developing baby may have been exposed to, perhaps harmed by, infections, drugs, tobacco or alcohol. Pre-conceptual care reduces these risks.

### WHAT IS PRE-CONCEPTUAL CARE?

Pre-conceptual care is medical care and positive health advice offered to a couple before they start a pregnancy, and should begin with the decision to have a baby. It aims to prepare both partners for a healthy pregnancy and ensure they are in the best possible state of health at the time of conception. Pre-conceptual care also includes self-help by continuing, or changing to, a healthy lifestyle.

Family doctors, midwives and health visitors can offer specific care and advice. Family planning clinics, well woman clinics and hospital pre-pregnancy clinics as well as voluntary organisations, such as Foresight, also provide pre-conceptual care. Care is free within the National Health Service. Other agencies may charge a fee.

## TEN STEPS TOWARDS A HEALTHY PREGNANCY

Most babies are born healthy. However, planning and preparing for a pregnancy through these ten steps (see diagram) reduces many of the risks to the unborn and makes the womb a healthy environment in which a baby can safely grow.

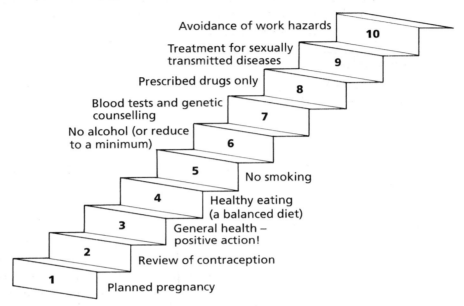

Ten steps towards a healthy pregnancy

### Step 1: A planned pregnancy

Allowing three to six months to plan and prepare for a pregnancy gives a couple time to improve their health, assess their 'readiness to start a pregnancy' and consider the changes that having a baby will bring to their relationship and lifestyle.

Ideally, both partners should want to have a baby and be mature enough to care for a child. While children bring enormous pleasure and satisfaction to their parents and wider family, parenting is a demanding and full-time job that brings many responsibilities. Children have a right to be born and brought up in a secure and stable environment, where they are offered unconditional love and care which meets their physical and emotional needs. They need to feel wanted and valued.

Babies grow rapidly – often into demanding toddlers and, possibly, difficult teenagers – and young people, still teenagers themselves, may lack the maturity and self-confidence to cope with the demands of parenthood and the changes it inevitably brings to their lives.

Parents, today, tend to be more informed about pregnancy and childbirth and both partners often wish to be involved in all decisions relating to the care of the mother and baby. However, pregnancy and childbirth remain unique female experiences and partners may feel alienated at this time, especially as the mother becomes increasingly involved in the baby. Adjusting to a new life together as a family may take time, but a stable relationship will help to overcome any temporary problems. A baby may not cement an uncertain relationship.

## KEY POINT

When babies are born to young, lone parents, those parents particularly need the support of the extended family.

## REMEMBER!

There are many different, equally valid, family units across the whole cultural spectrum.

### Step 2: Review of contraception
The contraceptive pill should be stopped at least three months, and preferably six, before trying for a baby. This allows the natural menstrual cycle to return to normal. Barrier or natural methods of contraception can be used during this time to prevent a pregnancy. The woman's doctor will remove an intra-uterine contraceptive device (IUCD).

### Step 3: General health
Moderate daily exercise, fresh air, rest and sleep will promote a feeling of well-being for both partners. A medical check-up, including blood pressure and weight measurement, is important for a woman. She may gain as much as 12.5 kg (28 lb) or more during pregnancy. Starting her pregnancy as near to ideal weight as possible will reduce the risk of high blood pressure, heart strain, backache and varicose veins. Dental care is essential. A growing baby takes calcium from its mother for bone and tooth growth. Having healthy teeth at the beginning of pregnancy reduces the risk of dental problems for the mother later on. Women with long-term illnesses should discuss the advisability of a pregnancy with their family doctor. A cervical smear test, pre-conceptually, is sensible – abnormal cells present before conception can increase during a pregnancy.

## KEY POINT

High blood pressure in pregnancy can cause problems for the mother and baby.

**Step 4: A balanced diet**

A balanced diet is one that contains a wide variety of the essential nutrients (proteins, fats, carbohydrates, vitamins, minerals, fibre and water). It is an important link with good health for everyone. The proportions of nutrients required varies according to age, sex, occupation and state of health (for example, pregnancy). Food intake must balance the amount of energy (calories) taken in against the energy used up by the body. Excess calories are stored in the body as fat and an 'unbalanced' diet can lead to overweight or underweight.

## KEY POINT

A balanced diet, pre-conceptually, allows a woman to store vital nutrients in her body in readiness for her planned baby.

Dieting to lose weight is inadvisable as important nutrients may be missed out. Dietary and exercise advice can be offered to a woman who is overweight. Especially important is folic acid (folate), a B-group vitamin, which is needed to make foetal cells and for development of the brain and spinal cord. These last two structures form early in foetal life. Inadequate intake of folic acid may be linked to the congenital condition spina bifida. Women should be advised of the foods rich in folic acid, and take 0.4 mg folic acid tablets daily, pre-conceptually, and during the first 12 weeks of pregnancy.

## KEY POINT

A woman who has previously given birth to a baby with spina bifida will be advised by her doctor to take 4 mg of folic acid daily, for the same length of time as above, as a preventive measure.

The basic principles of healthy eating are:
- Eat daily from the four food groups (see the diagram on page 5).
  1 Meat, fish, eggs, poultry, pulses (peas, beans, lentils).
  2 Fruit and vegetables.
  3 Cereals, grains, pasta, potatoes.
  4 Milk and milk products such as cheese and yoghurt.
- Eat fresh food whenever possible.
- Cut down on fatty, sugary and salty foods. Saturated (animal) fat may be linked to heart disease. Polyunsaturates (vegetable and plant sources) are a healthier option. Sugar encourages obesity and dental disease and intake should be reduced to a minimum. A high salt intake is linked to raised blood pressure and should be avoided.

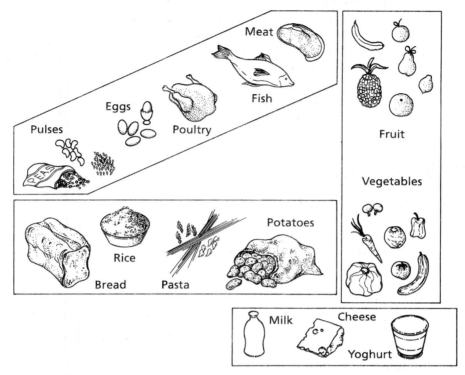

*The four food groups*

**Vegetarian and vegan diets**

Vegetarian diets that include protein foods such as fish, eggs, cheese and milk will provide all the essential amino acids – the important small units from which proteins are made. These, together with a wide selection of fruit and vegetables (excellent sources of vitamins, minerals and fibre) and carbohydrate foods will ensure a balanced, nutritious diet both pre-conceptually and antenatally.

## KEY POINT

■ Vegetarian diets that exclude some of the above protein foods, and vegan diets, which exclude all animal products, can also be adequate but there must be a rich variety of cereals, pulses, nuts and seeds to ensure all the amino acids are available.

Soya milk, and other soya products, are good sources of protein and vitamin B12 (necessary for growth and a healthy nervous system) and should form part of the diet. Again, fruit and vegetables are also important.

Dietary advice is always available from the family doctor, midwife, health visitor or dietician.

### Step 5: Smoking
Smoking can affect the working of the placenta (afterbirth) causing miscarriage, pre-term birth, low birth weight and perinatal death – stillbirth or death in the first week of life (see page 25). Men who smoke may have a low sperm count which can affect their fertility.

Both partners should give up smoking for the sake of their own and their baby's health. Babies continually exposed to cigarette smoke after birth are more likely to suffer from respiratory problems such as asthma.

### Step 6: Alcohol
Moderate drinking (one or two drinks per day) puts a baby at risk of miscarriage and low birth weight. 'Binge' drinking and consistently high levels of alcohol consumption, especially in the early weeks, can cause Foetal Alcohol syndrome (facial, heart and kidney abnormalities and learning delay). Heavy drinking may cause male infertility.

### Step 7: Blood tests and genetic counselling
A simple blood test will indicate whether either partner is anaemic. Dietary advice and prescribed iron tablets should correct anaemia. Blood is tested to check the woman's immunity to the rubella virus. If not immune, she will be offered vaccination and advised against becoming pregnant for at least 3 months.

While the rubella virus may produce only a fleeting rash and a mild feeling of being unwell in the woman, it can seriously affect her unborn baby causing vision, hearing, heart and kidney damage as well as learning delay.

Genetic counselling (usually a hospital-based service) advises on the risk of passing on hereditary disorders such as cystic fibrosis, Down's syndrome, haemophilia and sickle cell condition, to a future baby. This service is of particular help to a couple who already have a child with an inherited condition.

A woman who thinks she may be infected with the human immunodeficiency virus (HIV) may wish to seek professional counselling about being tested for the condition. HIV can be passed to the baby during pregnancy and birth, and through breast milk.

### Step 8: Drugs and medicines

Only prescribed medication should be taken pre-conceptually. Women taking prescribed drugs for conditions such as epilepsy and diabetes must, of course, continue with their medication pre-conceptually and during pregnancy. Many drugs, including addictive ones, can pass from the mother to her unborn baby causing adverse affects. Babies born to drug addicts suffer from withdrawal symptoms at birth and can be seriously ill.

### Step 9: Sexually transmitted diseases

Sexually transmitted diseases (STDs), such as syphilis, gonorrhoea, and genital herpes may adversely affect the unborn baby. If either partner thinks they have been at risk of contracting such a disease, or know they have one, they should seek advice from their doctor or hospital 'special clinic'. Both partners should be seen.

### Step 10: Work hazards

Miscarriages and birth abnormalities may result from working with radiation and some chemicals. Either partner worried about their work environment should seek advice from the family doctor, environmental health officer or works personnel or safety officer.

## Activity

1  In small groups discuss the importance of planning a pregnancy. Think about the phrase 'readiness to start a family'. How might an unplanned, unwanted pregnancy affect family relationships?
2  Choose a representative from your group to contact the voluntary organisation Foresight asking for details of their pre-conceptual care provision. Discuss the care and advice they offer.
3  Find out which foods contain folic acid.
4  Find out about iron deficiency anaemia.
   a)  What are the symptoms of anaemia?

# Conception and pregnancy

Conception occurs when the female egg is fertilised by the male sperm. It takes place in a fallopian (uterine) tube. The fertilised egg splits into two then four, eight and so on as it travels towards the uterus (womb) – a journey of about five days. By now it is a ball of cells that becomes firmly embedded in the wall of the uterus. Then follows the complex process of foetal development and growth. The unborn baby is called a 'foetus' (or 'embryo' in the first eight weeks).

## SUPPORT SYSTEMS

### The placenta

The placenta (afterbirth) is a spongy, red, disc-like structure attached to the wall of the uterus during pregnancy. It is a complex organ able to select from the mother's blood all the substances needed by her developing baby. It provides oxygen and food for the foetus, produces special hormones to keep the pregnancy healthy and transfers antibodies from the mother to the foetus, giving the baby a certain immunity to infection during the first few months of life.

The placenta is rich with both maternal and foetal blood vessels. These lie very close to each other but the actual bloods do not mix.

## KEY POINT

The exchange of substances from mother to foetus and of waste products from foetus back to mother takes place through the thin walls of the blood vessels. This exchange facility of the placenta acts as a barrier to certain micro-organisms (germs) but some are able to cross this barrier and harm the foetus.

### The umbilical cord

The umbilical cord is called 'baby's lifeline'. It links the foetus to the placenta and grows to about 50 cm (20 in) in length. It carries the oxygen and food from the placenta to the foetus and returns waste products and carbon dioxide from the foetus to the mother. The cutting of the cord at birth separates the baby from her mother.

### The amniotic sac

The amniotic sac is a bubble-like structure in which the foetus grows and develops. The sac produces amniotic fluid that gives protection from infection and injury and allows the foetus to move freely. Some time before or during labour this membraneous sac ruptures, a process commonly known as 'the waters breaking'.

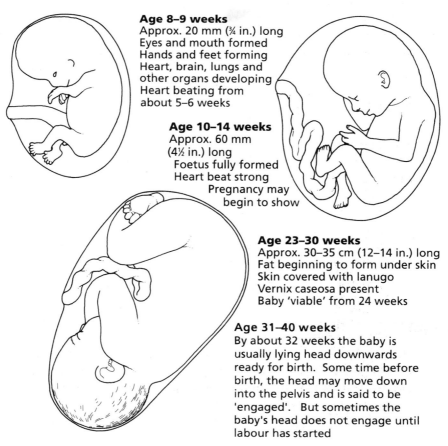

**Age 8–9 weeks**
Approx. 20 mm (¾ in.) long
Eyes and mouth formed
Hands and feet forming
Heart, brain, lungs and
other organs developing
Heart beating from
about 5–6 weeks

**Age 10–14 weeks**
Approx. 60 mm
(4½ in.) long
Foetus fully formed
Heart beat strong
Pregnancy may
begin to show

**Age 23–30 weeks**
Approx. 30–35 cm (12–14 in.) long
Fat beginning to form under skin
Skin covered with lanugo
Vernix caseosa present
Baby 'viable' from 24 weeks

**Age 31–40 weeks**
By about 32 weeks the baby is
usually lying head downwards
ready for birth. Some time before
birth, the head may move down
into the pelvis and is said to be
'engaged'. But sometimes the
baby's head does not engage until
labour has started

*A summary of the stages of foetal growth*

During foetal life:

- Oxygen, food and antibodies pass from the mother to the foetus.
- The nutritional needs of the foetus must be met or growth and development will be affected.
- The risk to the foetus from harmful germs and substances crossing the placental barrier is greatest during the first 12 weeks of pregnancy. Examples include the rubella virus and HIV, various drugs, alcohol and nicotine.
- A large reserve of iron is stored in the foetal liver during the last 12 weeks of pregnancy. Breast milk is low in iron, although it has a relatively high absorption rate. While present day infant formula milks are fortified with iron, the amount of iron available for absorption by the baby may be below her daily needs. The foetal reserve of iron tides the baby over the first 4 to 6 months of life when dietary sources, other than milk, will then provide adequate iron intake.
- Fat is laid down under the skin in the later weeks of pregnancy. This gives the baby a smooth, round appearance at birth and helps to keep her warm.
- Vernix caseosa, a white greasy substance, protects the skin from its watery environment. At birth, vernix is found on baby's body especially in the skin folds. It may be more noticeable in pre-term babies.
- Lanugo (fine hair) covers the face and body. Much of it is lost before birth, the remainder being lost during the first month of life.

## SIGNS AND SYMPTOMS OF PREGNANCY

- Periods stop.
- Nausea and sickness, usually in the mornings and most frequently in the first 3 to 4 months.
- Tingling and fullness of breasts with darkening of the area around the nipples (the areola).
- Tiredness, particularly in early pregnancy.
- Passing urine more frequently, including having to get up in the night.
- A white, mucusy, inoffensive vaginal discharge. This is due to increased hormone levels.

**Pregnancy test**

A special urine test can detect the pregnancy hormone. If the test result is positive a woman is almost certainly pregnant. Testing can be done by the family doctor, hospital, family planning clinic or at home using a pregnancy testing kit. Some chemists also offer this service.

## MINOR AILMENTS OF PREGNANCY

Minor ailments in pregnancy include heartburn, constipation, piles and backache. The doctor or midwife will offer advice and any necessary treatment.

## COMPLICATIONS OF PREGNANCY

High blood pressure and pre-eclampsia (toxaemia of pregnancy) are two common complications of pregnancy. They can be a serious risk to a mother's health and affect the placenta causing poor foetal growth and low birth-weight. Smoking and being overweight can both contribute to high blood pressure. Pre-eclampsia occurs in the second half of pregnancy and is more common with first babies. Signs of pre-eclampsia are:

- high blood pressure
- proteinuria (see page 14)
- swelling of hands, feet, ankles and face
- possible excessive weight gain.

### KEY POINT

If pre-eclampsia cannot be controlled by bed rest and medication to lower the blood pressure then eclampsia, fortunately rare, may develop. It is characterised by epileptic-type seizures and can be fatal for the mother and her baby. Induction of labour or a Caesarean section may be necessary to prevent eclampsia and a poorly baby.

Vaginal bleeding in pregnancy is abnormal and should always be checked by a doctor. Sometimes a pregnancy begins to develop in a fallopian tube. This is called an ectopic pregnancy. At around 6 to 8 weeks the woman will have abdominal pain and vaginal bleeding. An operation is needed and the tube is usually removed. A future pregnancy is still possible provided the other tube is healthy.

# Antenatal care

This is the care given to a mother and her unborn baby. In the United Kingdom it is free as part of the National Health Service provision. Good antenatal care, together with better standards of living and the improved health of the population, continues to play an important part in the reduction in maternal and infant mortality rates (see page 25).

Pregnancy is not an illness, but it makes demands on a woman's body that need sensitive understanding by the professionals looking after her. In particular, women who have had no pre-conceptual care need to be seen as early as possible to alert them to the dangers of poor diet, smoking, drinking, drugs and infections.

## THE AIMS OF ANTENATAL CARE

- To check the progress of the pregnancy and maintain good health of the mother and her baby.
- To prevent, as far as possible, any problems with the pregnancy and provide early treatment and management.
- To ensure the safe delivery of a live, mature, healthy baby.
- To prepare the mother for successful breast-feeding and the integration of the baby into the family.
- To provide health education – parentcraft and relaxation classes; advice on diet, smoking, drinking and general health and help the parents prepare for labour and birth.

The professionals who care for the mother and her partner during pregnancy are:
- obstetricians (doctors experienced in all aspects of pregnancy and childbirth)
- family doctors
- hospital and community midwives.

Health visitors, social workers, physiotherapists, radiographers and dieticians may all have a role in caring for expectant women.

## WHERE TO HAVE THE BABY

Most babies are born in hospital, and care is shared between the family doctor and the hospital. More women are now asking for home births. Their care during pregnancy and birth will be provided by the family doctor and the community midwife. The Domino (Domiciliary In and Out) system may be an option in some areas. This scheme combines the advantages of community care with the facilities of a maternity clinic. Where the baby is born will depend on the mother's previous childbirth history, the type of care available locally, the mother's age, general health and the likely progress and outcome of the present pregnancy.

## PROVISION OF ANTENATAL CARE

Professional care during pregnancy is set out in the diagram on page 14. The first antenatal appointment, the booking visit, should take place as soon as possible after a pregnancy has been confirmed. This is an important hospital appointment with the obstetrician and midwife and will determine whether all antenatal care is with the hospital or shared between hospital and family doctor. If an expectant mother wishes to be seen and examined by a female doctor everything possible will be done to facilitate this.

Mothers having their babies at home will attend for their booking visit at the surgery or health centre and subsequent care will be provided there or in the mother's home. They will be invited to attend hospital for an ultrasound scan at around 18 to 20 weeks. Should any complications arise during the pregnancy they will be referred to hospital to see the obstetrician.

There may be regional differences in the care patterns as described here.

**KEY POINT**

Cultural differences and customs must be recognised and understood by those caring for expectant mothers and their partners. Sensitivity must be shown to women who neither understand nor speak English, and who may find a busy, unfamiliar antenatal clinic both uncomfortable and threatening. They may be reluctant to ask questions, so that queries and anxieties they have about their pregnancies are never resolved. Relatives and friends can act as interpreters and information leaflets in different languages should be readily available. In some inner city areas, interpreters are provided by the local health authority.

## PROFESSIONAL CARE DURING PREGNANCY

**BOOKING VISIT (hospital or surgery/health centre)**

*History taking*
- Past pregnancies
- Present pregnancy (date of last period, expected delivery date)
- Medical history (heart disease, high blood pressure, diabetes can all affect the pregnancy)
- Family history (twins, serious illness)
- Social history (housing, help and support at home)

*Physical examination*
- Heart and lungs
- Blood pressure and weight (give baseline for future comparison)
- Breasts (inverted nipples make feeding difficult)
- Teeth (mother will be reminded of dental care)
- Legs (varicose veins can get worse in pregnancy)
- Internal examination and cervical smear may be offered (women must feel free to say no to these)

*Investigations*
1. Urine test for:
   - proteinuria (protein in urine), a sign of pre-eclampsia and that kidneys not working properly
   - glycosuria (sugar in urine), may be a sign of diabetes
2. Blood test for:
   - blood group and Rhesus factor
   - anaemia (iron and folic acid may be prescribed)
   - rubella immunity (if not immune, mother must avoid contact with virus during pregnancy and be offered immunisation after birth)
   - sickle cell anaemia and thalassaemia where appropriate
   - syphilis (an STD which can affect the unborn baby) **NB** No routine blood testing for HIV or AIDS

**FOLLOW-UP VISITS**
1. Mother seen at regular intervals up to birth, includes:
   - blood pressure, weight, urine test to detect any sign of pre-eclampsia or diabetes
   - checking position of baby
   - listening to baby's heart
   - asking if baby is moving
   - checking for swelling of hands, feet or face
2. Possible blood re-test for anaemia
3. Opportunity for discussion

**SPECIAL TESTS**

Ultrasound scan
Serum alphafetoprotein (SAFP)
Amniocentesis
Chorionic villus sampling (CVS)
(Bart's) Triple blood test – if available

**HEALTH EDUCATION**

Antenatal classes
Breathing and relaxation techniques
These are offered in later weeks of pregnancy

**Discussion**
- Opportunity for mother to ask questions
- Advice on diet, smoking, drinking and general health
- Appointment with dietician or social worker, if appropriate

In partnership with the professionals, mothers can help themselves during pregnancy by following the advice in the diagram, 'Self-care in pregnancy' on page 16.

## SPECIAL TESTS OF PREGNANCY

The following tests may be carried out to check that all is well with the pregnancy or to confirm or discount any concerns the doctor may have about the baby. Expectant mothers have the right to decline the tests.

### Ultrasound scan

An ultrasound scan is an easy and painless procedure. It is offered to expectant mothers at about 18 weeks' gestation (see 'Useful terms', page 25). The ultrasound machine uses high frequency sound waves that are bounced back from the uterus to give a picture of the unborn baby. From the picture it is possible to determine the size and age of the foetus and the position of the placenta. The sex of the baby can also be determined although it is not usually disclosed to the mother. Multiple pregnancies, heart defects and neural tube abnormalities, such as spina bifida and hydrocephalus, can also be detected.

### Serum alphafetoprotein (SAFP)

This is a blood test offered to expectant mothers at 16 weeks' gestation. A raised level of SAFP (a protein normally present in the blood during pregnancy) may indicate the baby has spina bifida, that there is a multiple pregnancy or the pregnancy is further advanced than was thought. A low SAFP in the second three months of pregnancy has been associated with Down's syndrome. When SAFP levels are found to be higher or lower than normal an amniocentesis is usually offered. The SAFP test may be carried out on its own or as part of the triple blood test (see page 17) where available.

### Amniocentesis

Amniocentesis is the withdrawal of amniotic fluid from the uterus by inserting a needle through the abdomen into the amniotic sac. The test is done at or after 16 weeks' gestation and is offered to expectant mothers over the age of 35 years (the risk of Down's syndrome increases with age) or whose SAFP was raised or low. It can detect spina bifida and chromosomal abnormalities such as Down's syndrome and muscular dystrophy.

### KEY POINT

Amniocentesis is a stressful procedure and mothers are under no obligation to undergo the test. There is a slight risk of infection and miscarriage following amniocentesis.

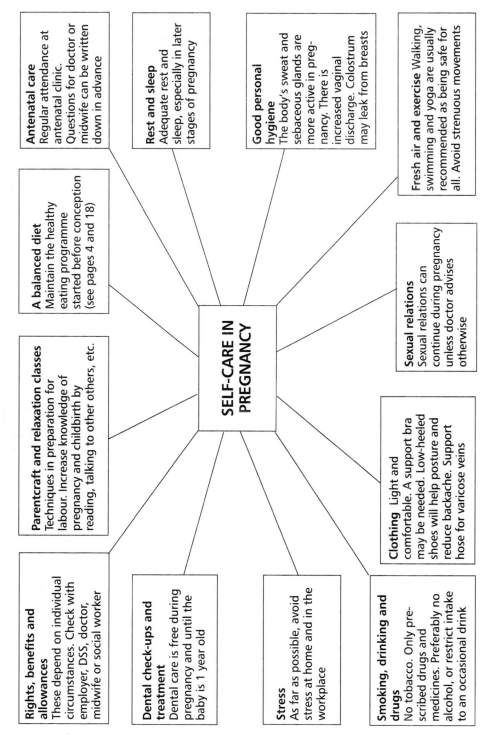

**Antenatal care**
Regular attendance at antenatal clinic. Questions for doctor or midwife can be written down in advance

**Rest and sleep**
Adequate rest and sleep, especially in later stages of pregnancy

**Good personal hygiene**
The body's sweat and sebaceous glands are more active in pregnancy. There is increased vaginal discharge. Colostrum may leak from breasts

**Fresh air and exercise** Walking, swimming and yoga are usually recommended as being safe for all. Avoid strenuous movements

**A balanced diet**
Maintain the healthy eating programme started before conception (see pages 4 and 18)

**Parentcraft and relaxation classes**
Techniques in preparation for labour. Increase knowledge of pregnancy and childbirth by reading, talking to other others, etc.

**SELF-CARE IN PREGNANCY**

**Sexual relations**
Sexual relations can continue during pregnancy unless doctor advises otherwise

**Rights, benefits and allowances**
These depend on individual circumstances. Check with employer, DSS, doctor, midwife or social worker

**Dental check-ups and treatment**
Dental care is free during pregnancy and until the baby is 1 year old

**Stress**
As far as possible, avoid stress at home and in the workplace

**Smoking, drinking and drugs**
No tobacco. Only pre-scribed drugs and medicines. Preferably no alcohol, or restrict intake to an occasional drink

**Clothing** Light and comfortable. A support bra may be needed. Low-heeled shoes will help posture and reduce backache. Support hose for varicose veins

## Chorionic villus sampling

Chorionic villus sampling involves the removal of a small piece of placental tissue via the cervix or abdomen under the guidance of ultrasound. It can be carried out at around 8 weeks of pregnancy making it more acceptable to parents than amniocentesis. The test is used to detect Down's syndrome, sickle cell and thalassaemia conditions and Tay-Sachs disease. It can also be used to determine the sex of a baby if there is a family history of sex-linked disorders such as haemophilia and muscular dystrophy.

## (Bart's) Triple blood test

The full name for this test (first used at St Bartholemew's hospital) is the maternal serum screening test. It measures the levels of three substances in the mother's blood (including the serum alphafetoprotein level) and is designed to identify women whose babies may be at greater risk of having Down's syndrome or spina bifida. It is offered at about 16 weeks' gestation.

See also Chapter 9 page 187 for further reference to these special tests.

## Activities

1 Some expectant mothers are entitled to free milk and vitamins. Find out:
   a) who is entitled
   b) what they are entitled to
   c) how they should claim their entitlement.
2 Why do you think some expectant mothers fail to attend the antenatal clinic? What could be done to encourage these mothers to attend?
3 Find out about parentcraft and breathing and relaxation classes in your own area.
   a) Where are they held?
   b) Who runs them?
   c) Are there any evening sessions?
   d) Are partners invited to attend?
   e) Are there crèche facilities?
   f) What topics are covered in the parentcraft classes?
If possible, obtain a leaflet or handout giving relevant information.

## DIET IN PREGNANCY

■ The healthy eating pattern started prior to conception will meet a mother's health needs, prepare her for labour and breast-feeding and also nourish the developing baby.

- An extra pint of milk daily, cheese or yoghurt will provide calcium for baby's bones and teeth.
- Iron-rich foods are important to guard against anaemia and a possible heavy blood loss during birth.
- Foods containing folic acid are essential.
- Sources of fibre such as fresh fruit and vegetables, whole grain bread, pasta and rice will help to prevent constipation. Bran-enriched cereals and drinks of water will also help.
- The extra calories needed for the growing baby will be provided partly by the diet and partly from naturally conserved energy as mother rests during pregnancy.
- Vegetarian and vegan diets must include protein foods (see page 5).
- Women on low incomes need sensible dietary advice. Milk, eggs, cheaper cuts of meat as well as a wide variety of pulses can be included in the diet. Baked beans, wholemeal bread, cheeses and fresh fruit and vegetables are nutritious and no more expensive than many bought convenience foods.
- Vitamins, iron and folic acid supplements are usually prescribed by the family doctor for women on low incomes and income support as well as those on a restricted diet.

## KEY POINT

- Iron intake must meet the foetal need to store iron in the liver.
- Soft cheese, paté, raw or lightly cooked eggs and meat carry the risk of infections that are harmful to the unborn baby and, if possible, should be avoided. Liver is not recommended because of its high vitamin A content which may be linked to foetal abnormality.

### Activities
1 Explain the basic principles of balanced diet.
2 Make up a 3 day menu of 3 meals a day for the following expectant mothers:
   a) a mother on a low income
   b) an Asian mother
   c) a mother who eats a vegan diet.

## POVERTY IN PREGNANCY AND INFANCY

Antenatal care and support is particularly important for mothers on a low income, or who live below the 'poverty line'. Poor housing, unemployment and a low standard of living have implications for both the mother and her baby. Maternal anaemia is a common result of a poor diet. Attendance at an antenatal clinic may be irregular or non-existent – perhaps because the mother cannot afford transport, does not know or understand the system, or is unaware of the importance of health checks. Some mothers may also lack the confidence to express their needs and concerns to the medical staff and so do not attend the antenatal clinic. As a result, problems may arise later which otherwise might have been prevented.

### KEY POINT

Babies born into poverty or a poor environment tend to be of low birth-weight (see page 48). They are more likely to be bottle fed. Respiratory infections and gastro-enteritis are more common and statistics show a higher incidence of infant mortality. A poor diet in infancy can result in anaemia and failure to thrive. All these factors put baby at a disadvantage right from the start of her life. The health care professionals will be aware of the risks to these babies and preventive health measures, such as health promotion, surveillance and immunisation (see pages 95 and 152), will be a top priority.

### KEY POINT

Some families may suffer discrimination in selection for housing, employment and promotion. This can lead to a lower standard of living with adverse consequences for the health and development of the children.

## Labour and birth

Towards the end of pregnancy the baby moves into position ready for birth. A mother will know labour has started by one or more of the following:

- 'a show' – a blood-stained vaginal discharge
- rupture of membranes, usually called 'the waters breaking'
- regular contractions – movements of the muscles of the uterus that slowly open up (dilate) the cervix at the neck of the womb. They usually start slowly and irregularly with long gaps in between each one. Then they become much stronger and more frequent as labour progresses.

### THE THREE STAGES OF LABOUR

- **Stage 1.** Dilatation of the cervix to allow baby's head to pass through. Most babies are born head first. In a breech birth the baby is born bottom or feet first. The length of time for this stage varies from a few hours up to 24 hours. Throughout the first stage the midwife will monitor the contractions, supporting and encouraging the mother, and listen to the baby's heartbeat.

■ **Stage 2.** The birth of the baby. This is the time when mothers work very hard to push their baby out. Once the cervix is fully open the midwife encourages the mother to push with each contraction until the baby's head is ready to be born. The head is 'panted' out and, shortly after, the baby's body slips out easily (see the diagram below).

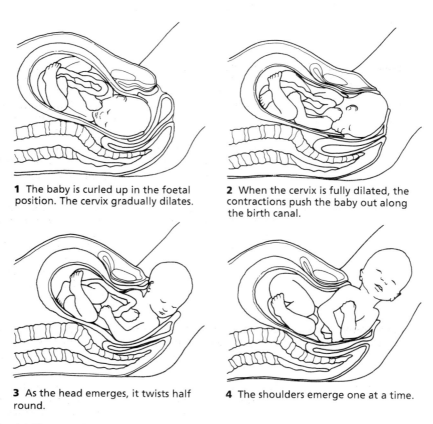

**1** The baby is curled up in the foetal position. The cervix gradually dilates.

**2** When the cervix is fully dilated, the contractions push the baby out along the birth canal.

**3** As the head emerges, it twists half round.

**4** The shoulders emerge one at a time.

*The birth process*

■ **Stage 3.** The delivery of the placenta and membranes. These are always checked to make sure they are complete. If a piece of placenta is left behind in the womb it can cause a serious blood loss. Once the placenta and membranes have been delivered and checked the birth process is complete.

# MANAGING LABOUR

In the early stage of labour the mother will usually be at home. The hospital will advise her when to come in to the labour ward. If she is having a home birth her community midwife and family doctor will now provide all care and support until the baby is safely born.

Women may move around freely in labour for as long as they wish, providing there are no complications and they have not had any pain relieving drugs. As the contractions become stronger some pain relief may be needed (see Table 1.1) although many mothers prefer to manage using only the breathing and relaxation techniques learned at relaxation classes.

**Table 1.1  Pain relief available during labour**

| Pain relief | How it is given | Comments |
|---|---|---|
| Pethidine (most commonly used drug) | By injection | If given late in labour, baby can have breathing problems and may be sleepy |
| Gas and air (oxygen and nitrous oxide) | Breathed in by face mask, particularly used near end of first stage of labour | Takes effect quickly Can cause nausea and light-headedness |
| Epidural anaesthesia | Injection of a local anaesthetic into space around spinal cord Numbs from waist down | May deaden the urge to push, so forceps delivery may be needed Caesarian sections often done under this form of anaesthetic – mother remains awake and able to hold baby immediately Mother cannot move around freely |
| TENS (transcutaneous nerve stimulation) | Electronic blocking of pain using a 'pulsar' control box which mother can adjust as needed | Easy to use by mother No side effects Mother can move around freely |
| Acupuncture | Special needles are inserted into different parts of the body to block pain messages | Not available within the NHS Used with breathing exercises Comments generally favourable |

## KEY POINT

- Emotional support and encouragement from her husband or partner, a close relative or friend can be a great help to the mother during labour.

■ A mother may choose to have her baby squatting, kneeling on a mattress on the floor, or sitting in a 'birthing chair' rather than lying on a
bed. 'Water births' are popular but controversial.

## HELPING THE BIRTH PROCESS

Sometimes the baby needs help to be born. Table 1.2 (page 23) lists the
medical procedures that are commonly carried out in all maternity units.

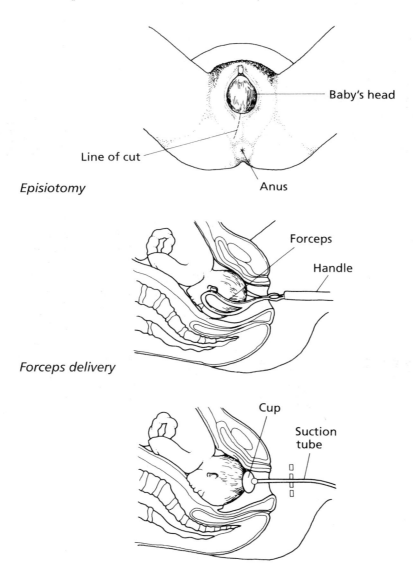

Episiotomy

Forceps delivery

Ventouse or vacuum delivery

**Table 1.2 Procedures available to help the birth process**

| Procedure | Description | Reason for procedure |
|---|---|---|
| Episiotomy | Small cut in the perineum (the tissue between the vagina and anus) to enlarge vaginal opening. Sewn up after delivery under local anaesthetic | To prevent serious tearing<br>To speed up delivery<br>To help the effort of pushing if mother has a medical condition<br>Ventouse extraction or forceps delivery<br>To ease pressure on head of premature baby |
| Induction of labour | Starting labour by artificial means, such as:<br>■ rupturing membranes<br>■ hormonal intravenous drip<br>■ hormonal vaginal pessaries | Pregnancy beyond expected date<br>Maternal conditions, such as:<br>■ pre-eclampsia<br>■ heart conditions<br>■ kidney disease<br>■ high blood pressure<br>■ diabetes |
| Forceps | Special instruments with curved blades which fit and lock around the baby's head. Used only when cervix is fully dilated. Local anaesthetic given. Episiotomy necessary. Gentle traction used | Long second stage of labour<br>Either mother or baby showing signs of distress<br>Medical conditions in mother (as in induction above)<br>To prevent too much pressure on head of a premature baby |
| Ventouse/vacuum extraction | Alternative to forceps. Metal or rubber cap placed on the baby's head and attached to suction pump. Gentle traction used | Same as for forceps delivery. Can be used if cervix not quite fully dilated |
| Caesarian section | Operation under general or epidural anaesthesia. Baby delivered through cut in abdominal wall. Can be elective (planned) or emergency | Baby too big to pass through mother's pelvis<br>Serious bleeding<br>Prolapsed cord<br>Baby in a difficult position<br>Failed induction of labour<br>Baby distressed<br>Serious medical condition in mother |

## IMMEDIATE CARE OF THE MOTHER

The mother will be washed, cleaned up and encouraged to rest. If an episiotomy was necessary, it will require stitching up under local anaesthetic first. Her temperature, pulse and blood pressure are usually taken. Labour is hard work and rest and sleep are important after birth to enable the mother to care for her baby's needs, as well as possibly looking after other children and the home. The length of time spent in hospital depends on the health of both the mother and her baby and the help available at home. If all is well, the hospital stay can be as little as 6 hours.

# The postnatal period

This is the period of 6 to 8 weeks from the time of the birth when:
- the mother recovers from any pregnancy problems and from the birth
- mother and baby bonding takes root and the baby becomes part of the family
- the baby's feeding pattern is established
- postnatal exercises are encouraged to strengthen and tighten all the pelvic muscles which were stretched and slackened during pregnancy and labour

## POSTNATAL EXAMINATION

A postnatal check-up is offered to a mother 6 to 8 weeks after the birth to make sure she has recovered from pregnancy and childbirth and her uterus has returned to its normal size. Her blood pressure will be checked and, if she shows signs of anaemia, her blood haemoglobin level will be tested. A cervical smear may be taken and family planning is usually discussed.

## THE 'BABY BLUES'

Giving birth is a time of heightened emotions, but with the feelings of achievement and elation there is often a sense of anti-climax linked to tiredness, perhaps painful stitches, sore breasts as the milk comes in and alteration in hormone levels. A period of weepiness and sadness, difficult for mothers to explain, is extremely common in the first ten days following birth.

### KEY POINT

The baby blues rarely lasts more than 48 hours but the mother needs reassurance, support and understanding from her partner, family and professionals such as the midwife, family doctor and health visitor during this time.

## POSTNATAL DEPRESSION

This is not uncommon. It is different from the baby blues, usually occurring two to three months after the birth. The mother appears to be tired and exhausted although she may be sleeping quite well. Anxiety and unhappiness are common features and the mother may feel inadequate and unable to care for her baby although baby is obviously well cared for. The mother's relationship with her baby may be affected.

Care and support from the family doctor and health visitor, as well as family and friends, is the mainstay of treatment. Anti-depressant medication may be prescribed. More serious depression may require hospital treatment and care. The Association For Postnatal Illness and the Meet-a-Mum Association (MAMA) (see page 214) can offer help and advice.

> **Activity**
> In what ways can family and friends offer help and support when a mother comes home with her new baby?

# Useful terms

**Gestation** The length of time, or period, of a pregnancy

**Infant mortality rate** The number of deaths of infants in the first year of life (including those occurring in the first four weeks) per 1,000 registered live births

**Infancy** The first year of life

**Low birth-weight baby** A baby weighing 2 kg (5½ lb) or less at birth

**Maternal mortality rate** The number of maternal deaths directly attributable to pregnancy and childbirth per 1,000 registered total births

**Miscarriage** The loss of a baby before 24 weeks of pregnancy

**Neonatal mortality rate** The number of deaths of babies within the first four weeks of birth per 1,000 registered live births

**Neonate** A baby during the first four weeks of life

**Newborn or neonatal period** The first month of life

**Perinatal mortality rate** All stillbirths and deaths in the first week of life per 1,000 total registered births

**Post-term (postmature) baby** A baby born after 41 completed weeks

**Pre-term (premature) baby** A baby born before 37 weeks

**Stillborn baby** A baby born dead after 24 weeks of pregnancy

**Term baby** A baby born between 37 and 41 completed weeks. The average length of a pregnancy is 40 weeks (280 days) calculated from the first day of the last menstrual period

**Viable** Capable of surviving outside the womb – applied to a foetus from the 24th week of gestation

## QUICK CHECK

1   Name the ten steps of pre-conceptual care.
2   What are the dangers to the unborn baby of the mother smoking in pregnancy?
3   At what stage of pregnancy is the unborn baby most at risk from the rubella virus?
4   Name three genetic disorders.
5   Name three functions of the placenta.
6   Which mineral is stored in the foetal liver and why?
7   Name the greasy white substance which protects the skin of the unborn baby.
8   Describe lanugo.
9   Which B-group vitamin is linked to the prevention of spina bifida?
10   Name the nutrients important for growth of the unborn baby's bones and teeth.
11   What is:
   a)  proteinuria
   b)  glycosuria?
12   Describe:
   a)  the signs of labour
   b)  the stages of labour.
13   What effect can pethidine, given to a mother late in labour, have on her newborn baby?
14   What do you understand by:
15   a)  episiotomy
16   b)  induction of labour?
17   What is the postnatal period?
18   How would you recognise the baby blues?
19   What is a pre-term baby?
20   What is the neonatal period?
21   What does the word 'infancy' mean?
22   A baby weighs 3 kg at birth. Is she a low birth-weight baby?

# **2** CARE OF THE NEWBORN

> **This chapter covers:**
> ■ **Immediate care of the newborn baby**
> ■ **Examination of the newborn baby**
> ■ **Neonatal screening tests**
> ■ **Early mother–baby bonding**
> ■ **Keeping the newborn baby warm**
> ■ **Neonatal jaundice**
> ■ **Twins**
> ■ **Low birth-weight babies**
> ■ **Postmaturity**

## Immediate care of the newborn baby

### ESTABLISHING BREATHING

As soon as the baby's head is delivered the midwife or doctor will wipe away any mucus from around the baby's mouth and nose, and check that the umbilical cord is not around the neck. Before birth, the baby's oxygen came from the mother but now the baby's lungs must take in oxygen. Most babies breathe spontaneously within a few seconds of birth. Sometimes mucus and amniotic fluid, which can obstruct breathing and cause lung damage and infection if inhaled by the baby, have to be gently sucked away from the air passages with a soft tube called a mucus extractor. When breathing begins, the baby's colour changes as oxygen is drawn in.

**The Apgar score**
This is the international standard method used to assess the condition of a baby immediately after birth and to identify those who are poorly and need rescusitation.

Five vital signs are observed:
■ heart rate
■ breathing
■ muscle tone
■ reflex response to stimulation
■ colour

**Table 2.1 The Apgar score table**

| Sign | 0 | 1 | 2 |
|---|---|---|---|
| Heart rate | Absent | Slow (below 100 beats per minute) | Fast (above 100 beats per minute) |
| Breathing | Absent | Slow, irregular | Good, crying |
| Muscle tone | Limp | Some movement of hands and feet | Active |
| Reflex response (stimulation of foot or nostril) | No response | Grimace | Cry, cough, sneeze |
| Colour | Blue, pale | Body oxygenated, hands and feet blue | Well-oxygenated |

The heart rate and breathing pattern are the most important signs.

For each sign the baby is given 0, 1 or 2 points (see Table 2.1). The points are added up giving a maximum score of 10.

The baby is assessed at 1 minute and 5 minutes after birth, and the test repeated every 5 minutes until the maximum score of 10 is achieved.

### KEY POINT

The Apgar scoring system was first devised by Doctor Virginia Apgar for white babies. The word 'oxygenated' instead of the original 'pink' embraces all skin colours.

*Interpreting the score*
- **A score of 10** The baby is in the best possible condition.
- **A score of 8–9** The baby is in good condition.
- **A score of 5–7** The baby has moderate asphyxia (breathing problems) and may need further clearing of the airways and some oxygen by face mask.
- **A score of 4 or less** The baby is poorly, has severe asphyxia and needs urgent resuscitation. A tube will be inserted into the windpipe to allow oxygen to flow directly into the baby's lungs. If she still has a low score at 5 minutes there is the possibility of brain damage occurring.

### KEY POINT

- Most healthy babies have an Apgar score of 9, losing one point for the colour of the hands and feet which are not fully oxygenated and remain blue for some hours after birth.
- Pre-term babies, low birth-weight and breech birth babies, and those born by Caesarean section are more likely to need resuscitation.

# THE APPEARANCE OF THE NEWBORN BABY

- The baby will be wet from the amniotic fluid and may be bloodied from her passage through the birth canal.
- Her head is large in proportion to her body and may be misshapen and lopsided from moulding, a caput or cephalhaematoma (see below). Babies born by Caesarean section usually have nicely rounded heads.
- She may look wrinkled and skinny or smooth and plump.
- Vernix is usually present, especially in the skin folds. It will gradually wear off within a few days. Rubbing it off will damage her skin.
- Lanugo may be seen, especially on the back and shoulders of dark-haired and pre-term babies, but it will soon disappear.
- She may have a full head of hair or be quite bald.
- Skin colour varies and depends on her ethnic origin and health. In the first 48 hours blueness of the hands and feet is common due to poor circulation. Black babies appear lighter than their eventual colour because the brown pigment, melanin, has not yet reached its full concentration. A 'mongolian blue spot' – a bluish black area of discolouration, not to be confused with bruising – is commonly found over the base of the spine or the buttocks of babies of Afro-Caribbean, Mediterranean and Asian descent. 'Blue spots' gradually disappear but are always recorded to prevent any future allegations of child abuse.

**Moulding**
This is the altered shape of the baby's head as it makes its way through the birth canal. Overlapping of the skull bones makes the head longer and a bit smaller. The head returns to normal shape within a short time.

**Caput succedaneum**
A swelling appears on the part of the head that was pressing on the dilating cervix during labour. Parents need reassuring it is not harmful to their baby and will disappear within a few days.

**Cephalhaematoma**
A blood-filled swelling on the head, caused by rupture of small blood vessels during labour, appears a little while after birth and may take several weeks to subside. Again, parents should be reassured that there is no danger to the baby's brain.

# Examination of the newborn baby

Immediately after birth a brief examination is carried out by the doctor or midwife to make sure there is nothing obviously wrong with the baby. A detailed examination is carried out 24 to 48 hours after birth.

## DETAILED EXAMINATION

The paediatrician (a doctor caring for children from birth to 16 years) makes a full examination of the baby with the mother present. Fathers, also, are welcome to be present. Babies born at home are examined by the family doctor. The examiner's hands must be clean and warm. The baby is examined from 'top to toe'.

### Heart and lungs
The heart and lungs are examined first, whilst baby is still and quiet. Any heart murmurs or worrying lung sounds will be investigated further.

### Head
The size and shape are noted and the head circumference measured. The mother will be reassured that any marks from a forceps or ventouse delivery will disappear within a few days. The anterior and posterior fontanelles (soft spots) are felt.

*Anterior fontanelle*   The anterior fontanelle is at the front of the head above the brow. It is a diamond-shaped area covered by a tough membrane and its size varies from 1 to 5 cm across. It is slightly depressed and may be seen pulsating. The fontanelle closes between 12 to 18 months of age. A tense, bulging anterior fontanelle may indicate increased pressure around the brain or an infection. A sunken fontanelle may be a sign that the baby is dehydrated.

## KEY POINT

The mother and other carers may worry about touching the fontanelle but normal washing, drying and handling procedures are perfectly safe and baby's the brain will not come to any harm.

*Posterior fontanelle*   The posterior fontanelle is a smaller, triangular shaped area near the crown of the head. It is sometimes closed at birth or closes within the first few months of life.

**Eyes**

Sticky eyes are common in the first 48 hours after birth (see page 76). The eyes are examined for any signs of malformation and for congenital cataract (a cloudiness of the lens), which can be due to rubella or toxoplasmosis infection before birth, or could be a symptom of Down's syndrome.

Wandering eye movements and squinting are normal in the newborn. The baby is unable to use both eyes together until around 2 months old.

Tears are rare until the third or fourth week.

The baby's permanent eye colour is established by 6 weeks.

*Vision*    See pages 132 and 146–9 (Table 6.1).

**Ears**

Differences in position, shape and size can occur, and may be seen in babies with Foetal Alcohol syndrome and chromosome disorders. Any discharge from the ear is abnormal.

*Hearing*    See pages 132 and 146–9 (Table 6.1).

**Mouth**

With a clean finger the roof of the mouth (hard and soft palate) is checked for any evidence of cleft palate. A baby with cleft lip or palate is referred promptly to a plastic surgeon. Sometimes a baby is born with one or more teeth. If the baby has a loose tooth it should be removed to prevent her inhaling it.

**Chest and abdomen**

The doctor will palpate (feel) the baby's abdomen and check the internal organs. It is normal for the abdomen to appear rather large. The umbilical cord will be observed for any sign of infection. It will have already started to shrivel up (see 'Step 5: Umbilical cord', page 65).

Breast engorgement can occur in both girls and boys with sometimes a little leakage of milk. This is due to the mother's hormones which have crossed the placenta during pregnancy, and will subside in a week or so. There is no treatment other than to gently wipe away any leakage, but it is important to reassure the mother.

**Genitalia**

The genitalia of both girls and boys appear rather large.

A whitish or blood-stained vaginal discharge may occur in baby girls soon after birth. Again, this is hormonal. If unexpected, this can cause anxiety for mothers and carers. The discharge will clear within a few days.

The testes are normally in the scrotum at birth – if not, they usually come down in the first month or so. A further check will be made at 8 weeks. Undescended testes can be brought down by surgical operation sometime in the pre-school years.

Baby boys should pass a good stream of urine. A poor stream or difficulty in passing urine should always be investigated.

### Back

With the baby lying prone (face down) the back is checked for any evidence of spina bifida which in its mildest form may only be a dimple or small growth of hair at the base of the spine rarely causing problems. In its most serious form, the bones of the spine have failed to form properly in foetal life, leaving a gap or split in the vertebral column through which the covering of the spinal cord and the cord itself may protrude. Wherever this abnormality occurs on the back, the cord and nerves below it will be affected causing paralysis and loss of sensation.

### Anus

The anus (back passage) is checked to make sure it is normal and that the baby has passed meconium, the greenish-black sticky stool that the baby passes in the first day or two of life. As the baby begins to take milk feeds the colour of the stools becomes greenish brown and then yellowish brown – these are known as changing stoools.

### Hips

All babies' hips are routinely tested for congenital dislocation (see page 38).

### Limbs

Fingers and toes are counted – accessory (extra) digits are sometimes present. Any webbing of fingers or toes is noted.

Foot disorders are common in the newborn baby. Talipes (club foot) needs early treatment and regular checks to prevent permanent disability.

### Skin

Vernix and lanugo may still be present. Small white spots called milia, which are tiny sebaceous glands, are frequently seen around the nose. They soon disappear.

### Birthmarks (naevi)

Red 'stork marks' on the skin are often found on the eyelids, above the nose and at the back of the neck. They fade and disappear.

Other birthmarks, such as moles and 'blue spots', will be checked and noted by the medical staff. Not all birthmarks are present at birth. Some (such as strawberry marks) may appear later and grow rapidly in infancy – parents need reassuring they are harmless and should be left alone.

### KEY POINT

It is always important to check that a newborn baby's bladder and bowels are working normally.

## EXAMINATION OF THE NERVOUS SYSTEM

Examination of the nervous system includes testing a number of primitive or automatic reflexes and observing and evaluating the baby's posture, movements and muscle tone.

### Primitive or automatic reflexes

A reflex action is one that happens without thinking – a prompt and certain response to a specific stimulus. 'Protective' reflexes (which most people have) include sneezing, swallowing, blinking, coughing or the rapid removal of the hand from something too hot.

During the first few months of life babies also have a number of primitive or automatic reflexes. Several primitive reflexes are tested as part of the examination of the nervous system. Reflex responses disappear at different times but by 3 months of age they have mostly been replaced by voluntary, learned responses – for example, the grasp reflex has to disappear before baby learns to hold objects put into her hand.

### KEY POINT

- The baby's reflex responses will depend on the baby's state of alertness at the time of testing
- Reflex responses that last beyond the time they should have disappeared may be a sign of some disorder of the nervous system which may lead to developmental delay.
- While reflex-testing is important in any neonatal examination, their responses must be judged in relation to the more important evaluation of posture, movement and muscle tone.

*Rooting reflex*   If one side of a baby's cheek or mouth is touched gently, she will turn her head in the direction of the touch. This ensures that she will seek the nipple when her cheek is brushed by her mother's breast. This reflex is essential for the successful feeding of the newborn, as are

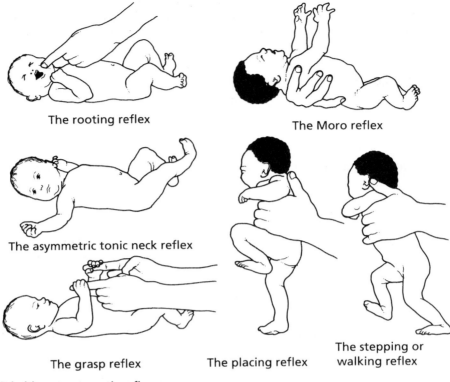

The rooting reflex

The Moro reflex

The asymmetric tonic neck reflex

The grasp reflex

The placing reflex

The stepping or walking reflex

*Primitive or automatic reflexes*

the sucking (placing the nipple or teat into the baby's mouth causing her to suck) and swallowing reflexes.

*Asymmetric tonic neck reflex*   If the baby's face is turned to one side, she will extend (straighten) her arm and leg on that side and flex (bend) her arm and leg on the opposite side.

*Grasp reflex*   A baby will automatically clench her fist if an object is placed in the palm of her hand. If a finger is slipped into each of her palms, she will grasp them so tightly that she can support her own weight. This can also be done with the toes.

*Moro reflex*   The baby's head is held in the doctor's hand and raised a little way off the examination surface before being released quickly. The baby will stretch out her arms with fingers curved before bringing them back over the chest as if in an embrace.

*Startle reflex*   This should not be confused with the Moro reflex. At a sudden, loud noise, or tap on the breastbone, the baby will move her arms outwards with her elbows bent and her hands closed. It is a less exaggerated response than the Moro with a different stimulus.

*Placing reflex*   If the front of the baby's leg is gently brought into contact with the edge of a table, the baby will raise her leg and place her foot on the hard surface.

*Stepping or walking reflex*   If the baby is held upright with the soles of her feet on a flat surface and is then moved forward slowly, she will respond with 'walking' steps.

## KEY POINT

Examination of a baby's primitive reflexes and interpretation of the responses should be carried out only by those trained in this area, for example doctors, midwives and health visitors.

### Posture
The typical postures adopted by a newborn baby when placed in certain positions (see page 36) are outlined below.

*Prone (face downwards)*   The baby's legs are flexed (bent) and drawn up under the abdomen, her pelvis is high, her head turned to the side and her arms are flexed.

*Supine (face upwards)*   Usually the baby's head turns to one side. Her legs are flexed, her knees are apart and the soles of her feet turned inwards.

*Ventral suspension (held horizontally, face downwards)*   The baby's head is held momentarily in line with her body. Her limbs hang down, partly flexed.

### Movements
The movement of the newborn baby's four limbs is jerky and unco-ordinated. Her hands are closed with the thumbs tucked under the fingers but she will open and close her hands when feeding or when you stroke the back of her hand. If pulled to sit, her head will lag (fall back).

### Muscle tone
Muscle tone is the firmness or tension in muscles which allows the body to have normal posture and enables the joints to go through their full range of movements.

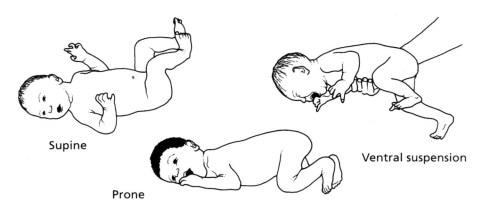

Supine

Prone

Ventral suspension

*Posture*

**Activity**

Observe a new baby. Watch her movements and posture. Look at her skin and gently feel the anterior fontanelle. Describe what you observe, having regard to the information so far in this chapter.

# Neonatal screening tests

Particular screening tests are carried out on the newborn baby to detect problems that can be treated in early life.

## GUTHRIE TEST

A blood test is used to detect the rare inherited disorder phenylketonuria (PKU) which occurs in 1 in 10,000 births. It is caused by an excess of phenylalanine, an amino acid which, due to an enzyme deficiency, cannot be broken down and used in the body. It builds up as a poison and leads to brain damage and learning delay. Six to twelve days after birth (by which time the baby has had several days of milk feeds) a blood sample is obtained by pricking the baby's heel.

A baby with phenylketonuria appears normal at birth but becomes ill within a few weeks. There is no cure but treatment is successful. Early diagnosis is essential.

### Treatment for phenylketonuria

It is important to remember that treatment is dietary and for life.

- Special formula protein foods, available on prescription, form the basis of the diet.
- Prescribed vitamins and minerals are taken with the protein substitute or as medicine.
- Babies require special formula milk. A small feed of breast milk may be given after the formula feed.
- Regular blood tests determine the level of phenylalanine.
- Normal learning can be achieved by keeping to the diet. It may be possible to relax some dietary rules once brain growth is complete.
- A woman with phenylketonuria must maintain a strict low phenylalanine diet during pregnancy to reduce the risk of brain damage to her baby.

## REMEMBER!

- The diet for PKU is restrictive. Family support and encouragement from the doctors, dietician, health visitor and child care workers is important and very necessary, especially when the child is young.
- The National Society for Phenylketonuria and Allied Disorders Ltd (see page 215) provide information and details of the disorder.

## THYROID STIMULATING HORMONE (TSH) TEST

This tests for hypothyroidism, an endocrine disorder, in which reduced function of the thyroid gland results in insufficient thyroxine being produced for normal growth and development. The test is carried out on the sample of blood taken for the Guthrie test.

### Treatment for hypothyroidism

The missing hormone is given in medicine form. It must be continued for life. The dose is adjusted as necessary to ensure normal growth and development. The earlier the treatment starts the better. Support for the parents is important.

# CONGENITAL DISLOCATION OF THE HIP

Congenital dislocation of the hip is more common where there is a family history of the condition. Girls are more often affected than boys. Very large babies and breech birth babies are more at risk.

A dislocated hip means that the head of the thigh bone (femur) is not seated normally in its socket in the pelvis. The hip joint cannot move properly and if untreated will lead to one leg being shorter than the other and the child walking with a limp. There are varying degrees of this disorder and treatment will depend on the actual medical diagnosis.

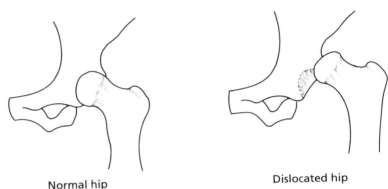

Normal hip                                    Dislocated hip

*Congenital dislocation of the hip*

The modified Ortolani/Barlow manoeuvre is used to detect hip instability at the examination of the newborn and the 8 week check-up. The hips are inspected for signs of dislocation at developmental reviews from 6 to 12 months.

**Treatment for congenital dislocation of the hip**
Treatment is to splint the baby's legs in a frog-like position to keep the head of the thigh bone in place (see the diagram below).

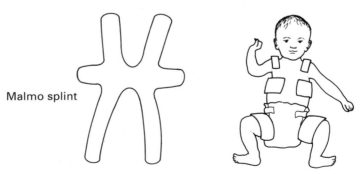

Malmo splint

*Treatment for congenital dislocation of the hip*

Early treatment is very successful. Sometimes an operation is needed followed by several months in plaster. Less serious conditions may be treated by folding an extra nappy between the thighs to keep them apart. X-rays will be taken regularly to check progress.

'Clicky hip' describes the clicking or grating noise of the ligaments around the hip joints sometimes heard when the doctor is examining them.

## KEY POINT

Although the splints may be clumsy and present some problems, they are padded and do not cause the baby pain. Good skin care must be maintained to prevent soreness and rashes. The doctor or health visitor will advise about bathing the baby. Cuddle and care for the baby in the normal way and encourage parents to do the same. The mother may need extra help with breast-feeding.

## OTHER SCREENING TESTS

Screening for sickle cell condition, thalassaemia and cystic fibrosis may be carried out if there is a family history of these disorders. Screening for hearing impairment (around the third day after birth) is routine in some hospitals. Examination to check that both testes are descended in baby boys is routinely done at birth and 8 weeks.

**Activity**
Find out about the weaning diet for a baby with phenylketonuria, particularly noting its restrictions.

# Early mother–baby bonding

A baby is usually delivered onto her mother's tummy, or into her arms, which allows immediate touching and stroking at the time of birth. (Many mothers like to touch their baby's head as soon as it is delivered and actively take part in lifting the baby out and into their arms.) Either the mother or her partner may wish to cut the umbilical cord – a symbolic gesture indicating the start of a new, independent life. Once the cord has been cut, and providing the baby is well, the mother can continue to hold and cuddle her baby. The first moments of holding a new baby are emotional and special, even more so if the baby's father is present as well.

Many women are overwhelmed by the experience of giving birth. Some mothers fall in love with their baby immediately, while for others it is a more gradual process. There is no right or wrong way, and the mother needs to be allowed to proceed at her own pace. What is important, though, is that she has the opportunity to be with her baby as soon as possible after birth. This is the start of getting to know each other in what will be a gradually evolving relationship.

It is well-known that a mother is particularly sensitive to her baby in the immediate newborn period and will spend time looking into her baby's eyes, which are open in the first hour after birth. This eye-to-eye contact is an important part of the bonding process. The mother will talk, and make soothing noises, to her baby and move on to explore the baby's hands and feet, counting fingers and toes.

The mother will be encouraged to offer her baby the breast. The rooting and sucking reflexes are strong in the newborn and although the baby may spend some time just exploring round the nipple she will gradually start sucking. This not only helps the mother-baby relationship but also stimulates the breasts to produce milk.

## KEY POINT

- A mother who has had a long and difficult labour and birth may need to rest before enjoying a prolonged period with her baby.
- It is important to understand that a mother and her baby need to be together. They should not be separated other than for medical reasons. Once the routine procedures of weighing, measuring and cord care have been completed (see Table 2.2 on page 41) the baby should be dressed and placed in a cot beside mother.

### Activity
As a nanny caring for a new baby, how could you help the mother–baby bonding in the early weeks after birth? What factors might influence the bonding process?

# Keeping the newborn baby warm

Keeping a baby warm, but not overheated, is essential. The amount of heat a newborn baby is able to produce depends mainly on her metabolism (how the body uses food) and a store of special brown fat around

**Table 2.2    Important procedures following birth**

| Procedure | |
| --- | --- |
| Labelling the baby with name and hospital number of mother, date and time of birth and sex of baby | This should be done before the umbilical cord is cut. Bracelets should be securely fastened around one wrist and ankle. A 'cot card' also records identification details |
| Cord care | The umbilical cord is clamped and cut after birth. The cord stump, about 2.5 cm (1 in), shrivels and falls off after 5-7 days. Cord hygiene is important (see page 65) |
| Weight | The baby is weighed after birth. The average weight of a term baby is 3.5 kg (7½ lb). Weight is influenced by gestation and the mother's health in pregnancy. Poor diet, smoking, alcohol, drugs and illness can all cause delayed foetal growth, resulting in low birth-weight. A record of birth-weight is kept as a guide for future growth patterns. On average, birth-weight doubles by 6 months and trebles by 1 year |
| Length | The measurement is taken from the top of the head to the heels with the baby in the supine position. The average length of a term baby is 51 cm (20 in). The average length at 1 year is 76 cm (30 in) |
| Head circumference | This should relate to body size. The average head size at term is 35 cm (13¼ in). A very small head can indicate that the baby will have some degree of learning delay. An unusually large head can be due to hydrocephalus (fluid on the brain). The average measurement at 1 year is 46 cm (18 in) |

the back and neck which can be converted into body warmth. Movement and activity also generate heat but the newborn baby does not move a lot and in some cultures remains tightly swaddled.

A newborn baby is unable to regulate her body temperature properly because:

■ her heat regulating centre in the brain is immature
■ she is unable to shiver efficiently
■ she has a relatively large surface skin area in relation to her weight which means she can lose heat quickly especially when exposed to cold air or if her skin is wet, as it is at birth.

The temperature of the outside world is considerably lower than the temperature inside the womb. There is always the danger, therefore, of a baby becoming cold. The baby's temperature should be checked in the first hour after birth.

To prevent chilling:

- the baby should be gently patted dry at birth and wrapped loosely in a warm towel or blanket
- the cot can be warmed by an overhead radiant heater prior to the baby being placed in it. (If the baby is born at home a covered hot water bottle can be used to warm the cot but MUST be removed before the baby is placed in the cot.)
- if necessary, the baby can be warmed up in an incubator for a while
- bathing can be delayed for several hours to prevent the baby becoming cold.

## KEY POINT

A large amount of heat can be lost from the baby's head.

## SAFE PRACTICE

- Always keep the baby in a constantly warm environment of 20–21°C (68–70°F) for the first few weeks. She should not be moved around between rooms with different temperatures.
- Room temperature at night should not fall below 18°C (65°F).
- Physical contact such as cuddling provides warmth.
- All baby care routines such as bathing, topping and tailing, dressing and undressing, which involves baby being naked must be carried out in a warm environment.
- Bath towel and clothes should be warmed before use.
- Layers of loose light clothing will keep the heat in by providing good insulation. Cellular-type blankets are ideal coverings and can be taken off or an extra one put on according to baby's needs.
- The baby should not be taken out in cold or foggy weather.
- In cooler weather, the baby may be taken outside providing she is warm before leaving home and wearing a bonnet to prevent heat loss from her head.
- If the baby sleeps outside in her pram, she must be checked regularly.
- Heat sources such as radiators, gas, electric and open coal fires must be properly guarded, contolled and well maintained.

## REMEMBER!

A baby's ability to maintain her body temperature is dependent on:
- her own individual heat generating capacity
- food intake
- physical contact
- appropriate warm clothing and bedding

- temperature of surroundings (indoors and outdoors), especially in the early weeks.

Hypothermia and overheating (see page 166) are potentially dangerous conditions for a baby.

# Neonatal jaundice

Jaundice in itself is not a disease but a sign that something is wrong. The baby will have yellowing of the skin and whites of the eyes due to an excess of bilirubin in the blood. Bilirubin is formed when red blood cells are broken down. It is normally removed from the bloodstream by the liver. Other signs and symptoms of jaundice can include: dark orange or brown urine, pale stools, vomiting, poor feeding and excessive sleepiness.

A baby with jaundice should always be promptly seen by a doctor. A high level of bilirubin in the blood can be serious and jaundice should never be ignored.

## CAUSES OF JAUNDICE

There are many reasons why jaundice occurs, just three are mentioned here.
- physiological jaundice
- breast milk jaundice
- rhesus blood incompatability.

**Physiological jaundice**
This affects one in three babies in the first few days after birth until the immature liver begins to work properly. The baby may be given phototherapy treatment (daylight fluorescent bulbs are shone directly onto the baby's skin) which helps to remove bilirubin from the skin and superficial blood vessels. The baby is turned at intervals so that the light can reach both her front and back. Special pads protect the baby's eyes from too much light, and the genital area is covered to protect the testes.

A mother may become anxious when her baby is receiving phototherapy. She must be reassured, and encouraged to feed, cuddle and care for her baby as normal.

### Breast milk jaundice

Prolonged jaundice can be associated with breast-feeding. The reason why is not fully understood. Temporary cessation of breast-feeding (and substituting formula milk feeds) results in the level of bilirubin falling, only to rise again when breast-feeding is continued. It may last up to three months but should not cause any ill effects and breast-feeding can continue.

### Rhesus blood incompatability

This is a serious cause of jaundice but much less common today. The mother forms antibodies in her blood which can cause anaemia in her baby. First babies are rarely affected, but to prevent problems for future babies all mothers who are rhesus-negative are given a special injection after the birth.

Infections such as hepatitis can also cause jaundice in the neonate and treatment will depend on the results of investigations.

# Twins

Twinning occurs in about 1 in 90 pregnancies.

*Identical (uniovular, monozygotic) twins* occur when one fertilised egg divides into two and each half becomes a separate baby. They have the same genetic make-up and blood group and are the same sex. Hair and eye colouring are also the same.

*Non-identical (binovular, dizygotic) twins* occur when a woman produces two eggs at ovulation and both are fertilised. The babies may or may not be the same sex and can be as similar or unlike as any two members of a family. Non-identical twins are sometimes called fraternal twins.

A woman's chance of producing twins increases if she herself is a fraternal twin or has blood relatives who are fraternal twins. The more children she already has also increases her chances. A woman's race affects the incidence of twinning with Nigerian women having the highest rates and women from the Far East having the lowest.

### KEY POINT

The use of infertility treatments, such as drugs to stimulate ovulation, and specialist techniques such as *in vitro* fertilisation (IVF) greatly influence a woman's chance of producing twins.

## DIAGNOSING TWINS

Routine ultrasound scanning can diagnose twins (also triplets, quads and more) early in pregnancy, although occasionally one baby 'hides' behind another. A mother expecting twins is likely to be bigger than her dates would suggest with a larger than normal weight gain. A raised serum alphafetoprotein (SAFP) level can indicate the presence of twins but it can also be a sign that there is something wrong with a baby, such as spina bifida, so a correct diagnosis is important in cases of a raised SAFP.

## ANTENATAL CARE FOR TWINS

Antenatal care is the same as for singletons (single babies). The mother will be advised about diet. Vitamin, iron and folic acid tablets are usually prescribed. Anaemia is common. Minor ailments of pregnancy may be more of a problem and breathlessness, tiredness and a large, cumbersome abdomen are usual towards the end of the pregnancy. Rest is important and a stay in hospital may be advised.

## LABOUR AND BIRTH

The babies will be born in hospital. Twins are more likely to be born pre-term (around 36 weeks). Triplets, and the rarer quadruplets and quintuplets, are likely to be very pre-term and small. Breech births and Caesarean section births are more common, although the majority of twins are born normally. Identity labels may be kept on twins a little longer than normal, especially in the case of identical twins.

### KEY POINT

One twin may be much smaller and weaker than the other, because of poor nutrition in the uterus. The closer twins are to a weight of 2.5 kg (5½ lb), the less likelihood there is of complications.

## CARING FOR TWINS

The problems and special needs of low birth-weight twins are the same as for single babies (see pages 49–53).

**Feeding**
Twins can be breast-fed successfully and breast-feeding provides close physical contact with both babies. Whether breast- or bottle-fed, the professional carers will help to establish a feeding routine which makes sure both babies get sufficient milk and are thriving. Much will depend on their size, ability to suck and general health. One twin may have a much

stronger suck than the other. The protection against infection given by breast milk is particularly important as the probability of the babies being pre-term makes them more vulnerable to infection.

## KEY POINT

Breast-feeding both babies at the same time is possible and mothers should be helped to experiment with different positions (see diagram).

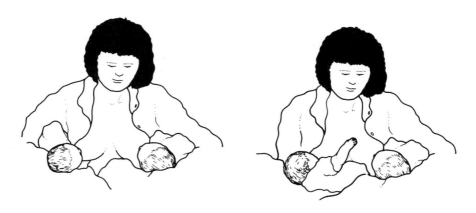

*Comfortable positions for feeding twins*

Bottle-feeding needs much organisation. There will be a lot of work involved in preparing feeds, cleaning and sterilising equipment. The cost of buying formula milk will be high, but bottle feeding has the advantage of the babies' father or another carer being able to help with the feeding.

A night-time feeding routine is necessary so that the parents do not get overtired. Twins will need more frequent night feeds if they are small. If bottle fed, it is advisable to keep a record in the early weeks of how much milk each baby takes.

## REMEMBER!

- Twins are two separate babies, not a pair, but they have the advantage of feeling close to another person from birth.
- Using terms such as 'twinnies' or 'the twins' is not appropriate. Always remember that twins have their own names, personalities and identities. Professional help and advice on caring for them should reflect this.
- Although twins will spend much of their early years sharing (parents, room, pram or buggy), being a twin should not be the most important part of their lives.
- Dressing twins alike should not be done just to draw attention to them.

■ Recognising and meeting the individual needs of each twin is an important part of your role in caring for them.

## DEVELOPMENT OF TWINS

Twins develop at a different rate, and should not be expected to reach their developmental milestones at the same time as each other. Some areas of development, such as sharing, may be in advance of their peers. Other areas may be delayed due to lack of opportunity or stimulation.

Language is commonly an area of developmental delay. For singletons, their role models for speech are usually parents and perhaps older siblings, but for a twin the strongest role model is often the other twin whose language is probably at the same level as their own. It is a mistake to think they are able to help each other with language. Twins often have a 'secret language' (cryptophasia) which only they may understand. Normal language development must take place alongside this special language. Individual time alone with the mother, carer, family members and friends will help language development, as will reading to each twin separately.

### KEY POINT

Although twins may learn early about sharing and have 'common' toys, they also need toys and possessions of their own.

## SIBLING RIVALRY

Older children may be jealous of the attention given to the twins. They may feel left out and displaced by the new arrivals. Friends, relatives and people in the street may be quick to admire 'the twins' while ignoring an older child.

### KEY POINT

If you are caring for a sibling in a day care or education setting she may need extra attention and the opportunity to talk about her twin siblings with you.

## DISABILITY AND BEREAVEMENT

Inevitably some twins will be born with a special need, some will be miscarried or stillborn, while others will die after birth. Remarks such as 'Well at least you've still got the other one' are still encountered by bereaved parents, who in many ways feel the loss of a twin is worse than losing a single baby, as the other twin is there as a constant reminder. The surviving twin may be over-protected by parents who fear he or she may die as well. Twins also suffer from the loss of their brother or sister, and may take a long time to come to terms with being a lone twin. Bereavement counselling is available and a network of support groups, such as the Twins and Multiple Births Association (see page 215), can put parents in touch with others who have suffered in a similar way.

## SUPPORT FOR PARENTS AND CARERS OF TWINS

The community midwife, and later the health visitor, will visit more frequently when the babies come home. Arrangements can be made for weighing and immunisation to be done at home. Extra help at home for a few weeks, from either family, friends or a home help, will enable the mother to concentrate on caring for her babies. Difficulties can arise in the daily routine: who to feed first, who to pick up first if they are both crying, how to manage the sleep routine, how to cope with shopping and using public transport. Talking to others who have been through the same experience is always helpful. Organisations which offer help are listed on page 215. Local twins clubs are also a valuable source of support.

**Activities**
1 Talk to parents of twins and ask them:
   a) What were the areas of greatest difficulty in the twin's first year?
   b) What kind of help would have been appreciated most?
   c) How did other children in the family react to the arrival of the twins?
2 If you are employed as a nanny caring for newly born, bottle-fed twins how would you:
   a) organise the preparation of feeds
   b) decide which baby to feed first
   c) manage night feeding?
3 Approximately how much per week would babies' formula feeds cost?
4 If you are caring for twins under 1 year in a day care setting how could you help them to develop their own identities?
5 Contact the local twins club and ask about its activities.

# Low birth-weight babies

A baby weighing 2.5 kg ($5\frac{1}{2}$ lb) or less at birth, regardless of the period of gestation, is said to be of low birth-weight (World Health Organisation 1961).

Low birth-weight babies are divided into:

- pre-term – babies born before 37 weeks of pregnancy
- light-for-dates – babies born below the expected weight for their period of gestation.

The reasons for low birth-weight are not always known but common causes include: multiple pregnancies, pre-eclampsia and medical conditions in the mother such as high blood pressure, heart disease or diabetes. Reasons which particularly apply to light-for-dates babies are: smoking and drinking in pregnancy, poor maternal nutrition and poor social and economic conditions. Some light-for-dates babies are genetically small. Congenital abnormalities are more common in low birth-weight babies.

## THE PRE-TERM BABY

**Appearance**
Any of the following charateristics may be present – they will be more marked in very small babies and less marked in those born nearer to term:

- less than 51 cm (20 in) long
- shiny, red skin
- lack of fat beneath the skin
- thin limbs
- soft and short nails
- few skin creases on soles of feet
- plenty of lanugo
- little or no vernix
- undescended testes in males
- head unusually large in proportion to body
- soft skull bones and widely spaced sutures and fontanelles.

**Behaviour of the pre-term baby**

- Pre-term babies tend to sleep most of the time.
- They have feeble cries.
- Movements, when they occur, tend to be jerky and frog-like.
- Cough and sucking reflexes, as well as other neonatal reflexes, are poorly developed.

**Problems for the pre-term baby**
For babies born at 32 weeks or more the outlook is generally good. The main problems for the pre-term baby (especially those that are very small) are:

- breathing and feeding difficulties
- poor temperature control
- high risk of infection
- jaundice

*Breathing*   Breathing problems occur because of immaturity both of the lungs and the breathing centre in the brain.

Oxygen can be given by face mask or piped directly into the incubator. The baby can also be 'ventilated' (breathing is done for her through a machine).

The smaller the baby the greater the risk of serious breathing problems.

*Feeding*   A pre-term baby needs frequent, small feeds.

The sucking and swallowing reflexes, which develop around 30 to 34 weeks and are very strong in the term baby, may be weak or absent in a pre-term baby and tube feeding (via the nose to the stomach) with expressed breast milk or special formula milk may be necessary.

Babies born very early may have a problem digesting and absorbing milk, as well as being unable to suck and swallow, and they will be fed special fluids intravenously (through a vein).

## KEY POINT

If a baby is able to suck and swallow she can be offered the breast or bottle. Small babies tire easily, so alternate sucking and tube feeds may be preferable. Breast-feeding should always be encouraged as it is best for the baby and contains antibodies to help against infection.

Pre-term babies lack the store of iron that full-term babies have and are often anaemic. Multi-vitamin supplements are given daily and iron supplement is started at about 4 weeks.

*Temperature control*   The heat regulating centre in the brain is immature in the term baby, but much more so in the pre-term baby. Lack of body fat, especially brown fat, and a large skin surface area in relation to body weight, puts a pre-term baby at risk of hypothermia (see page 166).

A warm environment is provided by an incubator or an 'infant care centre' in which the baby is nursed under a radiant heater.

## KEY POINTS

- If a pre-term baby is big and well enough to be cared for at home, she should stay close to her mother at all times in a constantly warm, draught-free environment. The room temperature should not drop below 20°C (68°F).

■ Her clothing must be light, warm and non-irritating to the skin, allowing her freedom to move and breathe easily.

*Infection*  The risk of infection in the pre-term baby is very great. Her immune system is immature and her ability to make antibodies is poor.

## KEY POINT

Hospital staff, carers and visitors must maintain good personal hygiene practice, particularly hand washing. Anyone with a cough, cold or skin or bowel infection must neither care for nor visit a pre-term baby.

Any sign of infection in the baby will be treated promptly with antibiotics as she can become seriously ill very quickly. A pre-term baby can be immunised against infectious diseases according to the Immunisation Schedule, but whooping cough immunisation should not be given to a baby who has had seizures.

*Jaundice*  Jaundice may be treated with phototherapy (see page 43).

### Care of the pre-term baby
The weight and general health of the pre-term baby at birth will determine where she is cared for. Some pre-term babies may be well enough to be kept near their mothers. Others will be nursed in incubators in a Special Care Baby Unit (SCBU) or, in the case of very sick babies and those with serious breathing problems, a Neonatal Intensive Care Unit.

Incubators are special enclosed cots with the temperature and humidity inside them carefully controlled to resemble as closely as possible the conditions of the womb. Special 'portholes' allow babies to be fed and cared for without being taken out. The baby is usually nursed naked, often lying on sheepskin for comfort and warmth, so that any change in her condition can be easily noticed.

As well as the monitoring procedures in the Special Care Unit, gentle cleansing of the skin, especially the nappy area and parts of the body where tubes are attached with sticky tape, is carried out within the incubator. Bathing is delayed until the baby is big enough and well enough to be transferred to a ward nursery or to go home.

As with term babies, a pre-term baby loses weight at first but regular weighing will allow those caring for baby to be sure she is getting the right amount of food and is able to digest and absorb it. Birth-weight is usually regained in a few weeks.

### Mother–baby bonding
Inevitably, some pre-term babies miss much of the close contact with their mother and other close family that term babies have, but everything

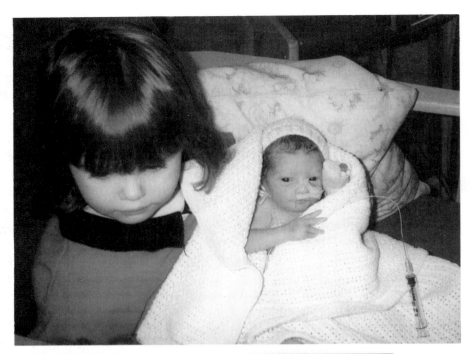

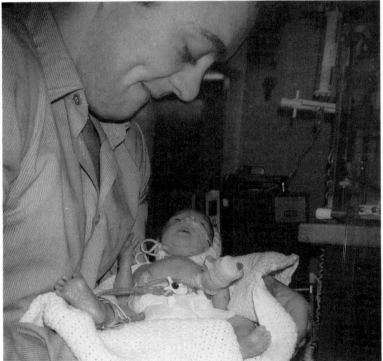

*Babies in a Special Care Baby Unit (SCBU)*

possible is done to limit separation and help a mother to establish a relationship with her baby. It may be possible for the mother to hold baby for a moment immediately after birth. However, breathing problems and the risk of chilling may mean baby is transferred quickly to the Special or Intensive Care unit. The hospital will take a photograph of the baby which the mother can have straight away.

As soon as possible, the mother will be taken to see her baby and be able to touch, stroke and talk to her through the incubator. Depending on baby's size and general condition, she may be able to feed and care for her baby.

## KEY POINTS

- Siblings, as well as parents, are welcome in Special Care Units and are encouraged to touch and hold their new brother or sister after they have washed their hands.
- If the baby has to be left behind in hospital or transferred to a Neonatal Unit some distance from home, this can be stressful for the family. Parents need help and support at this time.

**Going home**

Most pre-term babies can go home when they weigh about 2.5 kg (5½ lb) although, if they are feeding well and the mother is confident about caring for the baby, they are often allowed home at a lower weight.

## KEY POINT

Preparation of parents and siblings for home-coming will lessen anxiety and possible sibling jealousy.

While it is important to guard against infection and keep baby warm and adequately fed, over-concern and special treatment should be avoided as it may lead to behavioural problems later on. Once a small baby is thriving, she can be cared for just the same as other babies.

The baby's progress will be closely followed up by the family doctor and health visitor. Some areas have special Premature Baby Visitors who can visit daily for a while to advise and reassure parents on their baby's care and progress. Progress is linked to the expected, rather than the actual, date of birth and this will be taken into account when plotting growth measurements on the baby's percentile chart and reviewing her development.

## KEY POINT

A pre-term baby will usually 'catch up' by about 2 years of age. Hospital check-ups, as well as reviews at the child health clinic, will continue for some time. The smaller the baby the greater the risk of vision and hearing problems, smaller stature and learning delay.

# THE LIGHT-FOR-DATES BABY

A baby whose birth-weight is below the ninth percentile line for gestational age is said to be light-for-dates, or small for gestational age. This means growth before birth has been limited. Reasons for light-for-dates are not always known but include:

- poor nutrition in the womb
- smoking and drinking in pregnancy
- congenital disorders such as Down's syndrome
- infections in the womb, such as rubella.

## KEY POINT

Often, the babies are small for genetic reasons and are perfectly healthy.

**Appearance of the light-for-dates baby**

- At birth the baby is small, short and she may appear obviously undernourished.
- She may look wizened and old with an anxious expression.
- The skin is often cracked, dry and loose and may be meconium stained. (A baby that becomes distressed in the womb will open her bowels. The meconium mixes with the amniotic fluid and baby's skin, nails and cord are stained green.)
- She will lack body fat and have difficulty in keeping warm.
- She will be prone to infection. However, unless she is also pre-term, she is unlikely to have breathing problems. Most light-for-dates babies spend time in the Special Care Unit where they are observed and cared for in the warmth of an incubator.

The greatest need for these babies is food in order to put on weight. There is usually no problem with the sucking reflex and breast-feeding should be encouraged. The baby's developmental progress depends on how badly her growth pattern has been affected by the time she is born. Some children may later show signs of clumsiness and learning difficulties and may always be smaller than their peers but most catch up by 2 to 3 years of age.

## Activity
A small pre-term baby is in a Neonatal Intensive Care Unit 30 miles from home.
a) What problems might this pose for the baby, her mother and her family?
b) How could some of those problems be alleviated?

# Postmaturity

A baby born at or after 42 weeks gestation is said to be post-term or post-mature. A pregnancy continuing beyond the expected date carries some risks. Post-term, the placenta 'ages' and the baby may not get enough food and oxygen. Once 42 weeks is reached the placenta can fail rapidly causing foetal distress. Inhalation of meconium may occur. This may lead to pneumonia in the early days of life. The incidence of perinatal deaths rises in postmature babies.

When a mother has gone 'past her dates' or there is doubt over the accuracy of her dates, a decision will be made by the obstetrician whether and when to induce labour. An ultrasound scan can accurately date a baby's age, making the decision easier and reducing the risk of the baby being born postmature.

## THE APPEARANCE OF THE POSTMATURE BABY

- The baby is thinner than normal.
- Her skin is dry, cracked and peeling and there may be yellowish green meconium staining of nails, skin and cord. There is usually no vernix present.
- Her face is thin with a worried expression.
- The baby often appears alert, restless and hungry for feeds.
- Her feet may show signs of talipes (club feet).

## CARE OF THE POSTMATURE BABY

The postmature baby may need some time in the Special Care Unit. She will need early, frequent feeding to begin with and should be breast-fed if possible. Antibiotics will be given if there is any sign of chest infection.

## QUICK CHECK

1  a) Name the scoring system for assessing a baby's condition at birth.
   b) Which five vital signs are assessed?
2  Describe:
   a) moulding
   b) a caput succedaneum
   c) a cephalhaematoma.
3  Describe the anterior fontanelle.
4  Why is the inside of a baby's mouth checked during the examination of the newborn?

5 Describe
   a) a mongolian spot
   b) milia
   c) stork marks.
6 When would you expect the umbilical cord to fall off?
7 Describe the grasp reflex.
8 By what age have the primitive reflexes largely disappeared?
9 What do you understand by
   a) prone
   b) supine?
10 Name three screening tests of the newborn baby.
11 What are the signs of neonatal jaundice?
12 What do you understand by the phrase cryptophasia?
13 Which area of development is often delayed in twins?
14 Give the definition of a low birth-weight baby.
15 Name three problems that a low birth-weight baby may have.
16 At what age can a low birth-weight baby start her immunisation programme?
17 Why is a newborn baby unable to regulate its body temperature?
18 What is the ideal temperature for a baby's room in the early weeks after birth?
19 What is meconium?
20 What do you understand by the terms
   a) pre-term
   b) postmature?

# 3 CARE OF THE SKIN

> **This chapter covers:**
> - **Functions of the skin**
> - **Dealing with body fluids in day care**
> - **Bathing**
> - **Topping and tailing**
> - **Nappy rash**
> - **Skin care in the sun**
> - **Common skin conditions and infections**

## Functions of the skin

The skin covers and protects the body. It helps to regulate body temperature and gets rid of waste products through sweat. It is sensitive to touch. In the presence of sunlight the skin synthesises (makes) Vitamin D. Vitamin D works with the minerals calcium and phosphorus to form strong bones and teeth. The skin also produces the brown pigment melanin, which gives colour to the skin and hair. Large amounts of melanin are produced in naturally dark people.

### KEY POINT

A clean, healthy, undamaged skin is one of nature's defences against infection. A newborn baby has little immunity against infection, therefore skin care is very important.

Anyone who cares for a baby is responsible for keeping her clean and comfortable as part of her physical care. Cleaning and refreshing a baby's skin removes germs, as well as sticky milk, urine and faeces, vomit, excess sebum (grease), dust and grime. These are all irritants that make the baby's skin sore.

Skin care routines should be carried out according to:
- the wishes of the parents
- cultural or religious preferences
- medical advice, for example if the baby has eczema, or other skin condition.

- In day care a baby's personal care should be undertaken by her designated carer (see page 142).
- Bathing, 'topping and tailing' and nappy changing routines provide the opportunity for enjoyable and intimate exchanges between the baby and her carer. Remember to maintain eye contact with her, talk to her, tickle her, laugh and sing. Action rhymes and songs which name parts of the body are fun, as well as a learning experience. Allow time for the baby to kick and exercise freely with her nappy off.

### Activity
Make a list of action rhymes and songs particularly suitable for babies during skin care routines.

## SAFE PRACTICE

Because infection can spread rapidly, especially by the hands, carers must pay particular attention to personal hygiene and hand washing routines. In particular, always wash your hands:

- before handling a baby
- before preparing feeds and meals
- after changing a baby's nappy or attending to nasal care
- after cleaning up body fluids
- after using the toilet.

## KEY POINT

Hand washing means washing your hands and scrubbing your nails with soap and water, not just running them under the tap.

# Dealing with body fluids in day care

It is standard procedure in most day care settings to use latex disposable gloves when changing babies' nappies — at bath time, nappy changes and when 'topping and tailing'. Not only does this protect against infection, it prevents discrimination against a baby who has a disclosed blood borne infection. A new pair of gloves should be worn for each individual baby at every nappy change and disposed of safely immediately after use.

Gloves should be removed as soon as nappy changing is complete. Wearing gloves should not diminish the opportunity for interaction between the carer and the baby during these routines.

## SPILLAGES AND SOILED ARTICLES

Put on disposable gloves (and a protective disposable apron) when cleaning up body fluids (blood, urine, faeces or vomit) or dealing with soiled articles. Then:

- Cover the body fluid, and wipe up, with paper towels.
- Clean the soiled area with hot water and household detergent using a disposable cloth.
- Wash the area with a bleach solution made up of 1 part bleach to 10 parts cold water – or a disinfectant of correct strength can be used (check manufacturer's dilution instructions).
- Wash cleaning mops with a bleach solution and allow to dry.
- Blood-stained towelling nappies or clothing should be soaked in cold water, to remove the stain, before laundering. Articles soiled with vomit or faeces should be sluiced in cold water in a lavatory (or in a sink used only for this purpose) and disinfected before laundering in the usual way.

**REMEMBER!**

- Paper towels, cloth, gloves and apron must be sealed in a tie-bag and disposed of according to the setting practice.
- Keep bleach and disinfectants out of the reach of babies.

**KEY POINTS**

- While the use of disposable gloves is widespread in day care, in a private home (where cross infection is less likely), normal high standards of personal cleanliness are usually adopted.
- Cover any cut or wound you may have with a maximum protection waterproof dressing (unless you are allergic to them).
- Wash your hands thoroughly after handling soiled articles or cleaning up body fluids.
- Always know and follow the safe practice routines of your workplace, and the advice of local health and social services authorities in protecting babies and yourself from infections.

# Bathing

## ESSENTIAL PRINCIPLES OF BATHING

■ Remember:
  – *the baby's delicate areas:* eyes, nose, ears, umbilical cord, genitalia
  – *the baby's vulnerable areas:* skin creases.
■ Always wash and dry carefully around the neck, behind the ears, under the arms, behind the knees, in the groins and between the fingers and toes.
■ The skin should be gently patted, rather than rubbed, dry using a warm towel. Make sure sure these areas are dried properly to prevent the baby becoming sore.
■ Nail and hair care are always included in skin care.
■ Use toiletries such as soap, baby-bath preparations, shampoo, oils and moisturisers, and barrier creams that are recommended for a baby's skin.
■ If a baby is allergic to perfumes and additives, simple, unperfumed products, or those recommended by the doctor, should be used.

## KEY POINTS

■ Always discuss with the baby's parents which toiletries to use and how to care for and groom her hair. You may be asked to use a certain kind of shampoo or moisturiser, or a liquid baby bath preparation rather than soap. In day care, parents may wish to bring in particular toiletries and creams for their own baby's use. They may prefer you to use wet wipes to clean their baby's bottom area – check that they do not make the baby sore.
■ Types of toiletries chosen, either by the parents or day care staff, and the different types of gloves used will, inevitably, vary as modern research develops new products and subsequent good skin care practices are advised.
■ Respect for cultural preferences is important. Black skin tends to be dry, and a moisturiser such as cocoa butter or a petroleum jelly preparation is generally applied after bathing. Excessive dryness is common especially in winter and daily massaging with oils (for example, almond oil) can lessen this condition which is sometimes mistaken for eczema. The Afro-Caribbean tradition of combing, plaiting and weaving the hair can be seen even in very young babies. Muslim babies have their heads shaved within the first forty days of birth.

- To prevent accidents whilst carrying or caring for a baby:
  - do not wear bulky, dangling jewellery
  - do wear comfortable, supportive, low-heeled shoes
  - keep your nails clean, trimmed and unvarnished.
- Prepare the room, equipment and clean clothes before attending to the baby. Once you have picked up the baby and started the bathing procedure, you cannot leave her to get something you have forgotten.
- Put the cold water in the bath before the hot water.
- Check the temperature of the bath water with your bare elbow or a bath thermometer – it should feel pleasantly warm or register 37°C (body temperature) on the thermometer. Scalding will cause a baby severe pain and damage her skin, with the consequent risk of infection, and could cause death.
- Cotton buds should not be used on any part of a baby's body. Dry or moistened cotton wool swabs are safer.
- Wet and soiled disposable nappies and used cotton wool swabs from eye, cord and nasal care must immediately be placed in a lidded bucket or bin or secured in a tie-up bag for later disposal. Never flush them down the toilet or leave them lying around. Terry towelling and muslin nappies must be placed in a lidded bucket and laundered either by boiling or soaking in a sanitising solution. Soiled and wet nappy liners can be flushed down the lavatory. Wash and disinfect changing mats after each use. Because of the risk of cross infection these measures are particularly important in a day care setting.
- Never leave a baby alone in the bath. Babies can drown in just 1 cm of water.
- Guard the baby at all times with your body while she is on a changing mat on a raised surface.
- Keep the baby's head well supported during the bathing procedure.

## KEY POINT

The use of talcum powder is not advised. 'Sprinkling' the powder can cause the baby to inhale the powder, which may result in choking and chest infection. Do not use talcum powder on a baby with asthma or other respiratory disorder, she can become seriously ill. If parents particularly wish you to use talcum powder, place a little on your hands and gently smooth it on to the baby's well-dried skin.

A small baby does not have to be bathed every day. Limiting bathing to two or three times a week and 'topping and tailing' (see page 68) on the other days is an acceptable routine.

A very young baby feels insecure when unwrapped and undressed and should be handled gently, with confidence and care. Bathing can be done at any time of the day but immediately after a feed is not a good idea as baby may be sick.

## REMEMBER!

Remember, normal washing and drying over the fontanelle area will not cause any harm.

## KEY POINTS

■ Find out from the baby's parents the best time to bath the baby; how the baby reacts to water; whether she enjoys her bath; whether she minds having her hair washed; and which are her favourite bath-time toys.

■ A carer with diarrhoea and vomiting should not care for a small baby until he or she has recovered.

## PREPARATION OF THE ROOM

The room (or bathing area) must be warm, not less than 20°C (68°F) with the windows closed and no draughts. All the equipment must be to hand. A baby bath placed on its own stand or on a safe, firm surface makes bathing easy. A baby can also be bathed in a basin or sink provided the taps are securely turned off, and covered to prevent her hitting against them or receiving a burn or scald. Operating at ground level by placing the baby bath inside the empty big bath, or putting the baby bath on the floor, are other options.

### Equipment needed

Baby bath; thermometer; chair (if sitting to bath baby); changing mat; waterproof or towelling apron; latex disposable gloves; lidded bins, buckets or tie-bags for used nappy, swabs and clothes; clean clothes and nappy; warmed towel; toiletries; cool boiled water; cotton wool swabs; brush and comb; and nail scissors. If the baby is bottle-fed the feed should be ready for after her bath.

## Activity

a) Before you bath a baby what information will you need to know from her parent or carer?

b) What PERSONAL hygiene and safety precautions would you take BEFORE you bath a baby?

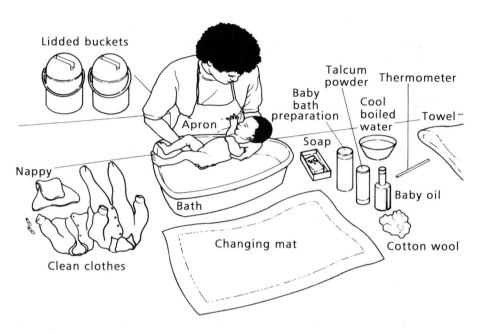

*Equipment for bath time*

## Procedure

■ Having prepared for the baby's bath, put on the apron and wash your hands.

■ Fill the bath, remembering the safety precautions. A liquid baby bath preparation (not bubble bath) can be put into the water, according to the instructions on the container, or baby soap can be used. Undress the baby down to her nappy, either on your lap or on the changing mat, and wrap her in a towel. Place used clothes in a bin, bucket or tie-bag. Follow the steps for bathing baby as shown in the diagram on pages 64–6.

# BATHING BABY: STEP-BY-STEP

**STEP 1: FACE**
- Wipe each eye using separate cotton wool swabs moistened in cool, boiled water. Dry with clean swab.
- Always wipe from inside corner to outer edge of eye in one movement.

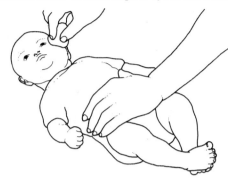

- Wipe around nose with moistened swab, removing any nasal discharge from cold or snuffles. Dry with clean swab.
- Wipe around face and ears using moistened and dry swabs or soft face cloth.
- From 3 months old a soft sponge or flannel can be used to clean a baby's face instead of cotton wool.

**Remember!**
- Do not probe nose or ears with cotton buds.
- Never use the same swab twice – discard each swab after use.

**STEP 2: HEAD AND HAIR**
- Support the baby's neck and shoulders with one hand and tuck her legs under your arm. Hold her head over the bath.
- With your free hand, wet baby's head with bath water. Using a small amount of shampoo or baby soap, wash head and hair. Rinse very thoroughly especially over anterior fontanelle to reduce risk of cradle cap.
- Move the baby back to your lap or changing mat. Dry head and hair gently but thoroughly with corner of towel.

**Remember!**
- Shampoo or soap only necessary two or three times a week. Splash with water at other times.
- Cultural hair care practices.
- Keep shampoo/soap out of the baby's eyes.
- Babies can lose heat from wet head.

**STEP 3: BODY AND SKIN CREASES**
- Unwrap towel, put on gloves, remove nappy and place in bin, bucket or tie-bag.
- Remove any soiling from the baby's bottom with cotton wool, cleaning baby girls from front to back to avoid introducing germs into the bladder or vagina. Remove and dispose of gloves.
- If using soap, make a lather and smooth over the baby's body, including creases of neck, underarms, groin, and between fingers and toes.

- Support the baby's neck, shoulders and upper arm furthest from you with one hand and forearm. With other hand support bottom and legs. Lift her into bath. Release hand supporting bottom and legs and rinse soap from baby's body paying attention to creases.

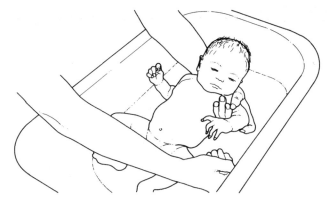

- If using baby bath preparation, wash baby with massage movements, again remembering skin creases.
- Allow a short time for kicking and splashing, but avoid chilling.
- Lift baby out of bath using same manoeuvre as for lifting her in. Wrap her in a warm towel on your lap or changing mat.
- Pat her dry, especially in creases. Remove wet towel.

**Remember!**
Safe practice: water temperature, lift baby correctly, avoid chilling

---

STEP 4: GENITALIA
In baby boys, leave foreskin alone other than to make sure it is dry. Any attempt to pull it back will cause pain, bleeding and possibly infection.

---

STEP 5: UMBILICAL CORD
- Gently dry cord area after bath. Sterile 'wipes' or special cord powder may be provided by midwife.
- Cord must be kept dry and free from irritation of clothing or wet nappy.

**Remember!**
Cord infection can be serious and requires medical attention.

---

STEP 6: OIL, POWDER AND CREAM
- Baby oil or moisturiser may be massaged into skin.
- Do not use talcum powder except at parent's request.
- Barrier cream applied to the baby's bottom will guard against nappy rash.

**Remember!**
Dangers of talcum powder and precautions with use.

STEP 7: DRESSING
- Put fresh nappy on.
- Dress the baby in clean clothes.
- Groom hair.
- Trim nails when necessary, with parent's permission, using blunt-ended scissors. If baby is scratching face, use cotton scratch mittens

**Remember!**
Safe use of nappy pin.

## BENEFITS OF BATHING

Bathing:
- cleans and refreshes the skin
- provides pleasurable contact time and opportunity for meaningful interaction (talking, smiling, eye contact) between the baby and her carer
- gives the baby opportunity to kick and exercise her limbs
- often calms a restless or fretful baby
- affords the carer the opportunity to observe the condition of the baby's skin and to note any rashes, spots, marks or bruises.

## BATHING AN OLDER BABY

At this age (6 months to 1 year), the baby will be spending more time on the floor and making progress with her motor development. She will become grubby and sticky. Topping and tailing in the morning and an evening bath are probably the best routines. At around 6 to 7 months she will progress to the big bath which will give her room to kick and splash. Kneel on the floor rather than bending down, to attend to her. Always be gentle and reassuring particularly if the baby does not seem too keen on the water.

### KEY POINT

Find out from the parent if the baby prefers to sit or lie supported in the water and the procedure for washing her hair. The use of a plastic 'halo', or face mask, during hair washing will keep the water off the baby's face, but if she is still frightened a dampened flannel or sponge can be used to keep her hair clean until she loses her fear.

*By 11 months the baby will have progressed to the big bath*

The principles, and safe practice of skin care mentioned earlier must be followed, with one or two additions.

- A rubber safety mat will help the baby to feel safe and secure.
- Keep the water shallow or the baby will float.
- The hot tap must be securely turned off. Taps are an attraction and should be covered.
- Keep the soap out of reach – it tastes nasty and will sting her eyes.
- Wash the baby's hair with a non-sting shampoo.
- Clean the baby's nails with a soft nail brush.
- Bath time should be fun for both baby and carer. If the baby is frightened by the big bath, continue to use a baby bath or sink, or keep to a routine of an all-over wash until she feels more secure. The baby may be happy in the big bath with an adult.
- Water play with floating and pouring toys (they can be made from safe household objects) will provide enjoyment and stimulation.

As the baby gets older she will become increasingly active, kicking, twisting and trying to stand. Always be ready with a steadying hand and supervise her at all times. NEVER LEAVE HER ALONE IN THE BATH.

- Change a baby's clothes regularly.
- Wash and groom her hair according to parental wishes. Babies must have their own hair brushes and combs which should be washed regularly in hot, soapy water, rinsed well and dried.
- Keep her nails clean and trimmed.
- Clean her teeth daily (see page 91). Toothbrushes must be kept separate in their own holder or mug.
- Make sure a baby has her own towels and face cloths which are changed and laundered after each use. They are a source of cross infection when left lying around or hanging close to each other on individual hooks.
- Continue to dispose of nappies, used swabs and tissues, and latex gloves as before.
- Wash the baby's hands before and after meals.

### Activities
1  Watch a baby being bathed. Observe and write down his or her reactions to bathing.
2  Bath a doll following the procedures set out in this chapter.
3  a) Think about, and write down, the differences between bathing an 8-week-old baby and a 10-month-old baby.
   b) What learning opportunities does bath time provide for a baby?
4  In how many ways do babies 'experience water' in the course of a typical day?

# Topping and tailing

This is the procedure of washing a baby's face, hands and bottom only. It is a simple way of keeping baby clean and fresh without bathing, or between baths. Make sure you are calm, relaxed and unhurried when changing and dressing the baby.

## EQUIPMENT NEEDED

Changing mat; cool boiled water (for eye care in first 3 months); cotton wool swabs; latex gloves; apron; lidded bins or buckets, or tie-bags for soiled nappy, used swabs and clothes; warmed towel; bowl of warm water; soap; creams (if used); clean clothes; and nappy.

**Procedure**
- Wash your hands.
- Remove the baby's clothes down to her vest and nappy. Place them in a bucket or bin if they are to be changed.
- Wrap baby in towel.
- Clean her eyes, nose, face and ears as for bathing.
- Unwrap the towel and wipe and dry baby's hands.
- Put on gloves. Remove her nappy and place it in a bucket or tie-bag.
- Clean her bottom, according to parental wishes, with, for example moist cotton wool swabs, soap and water or baby wipes. Rinse well with cotton wool, sponge or flannel.
- Pat dry, remove gloves and apply cream.
- Put a clean nappy and clothes on the baby.

## NAPPY CHANGING

The routines of personal hygiene and baby's skin care, and the measures for preventing cross infection, are the same for nappy changing as for bathing and topping and tailing. Nappies should be changed whenever the baby is uncomfortable and always checked before and after a feed or mealtime. Make sure the nappy fits well without being tight. 'Boy' and 'girl' disposable nappies offer maximum absorbency. Cream or powder on your hands will prevent the tabs from fastening securely. If you are using towelling nappies make sure the pin is closed properly and the rubber pants fit cosily, but not tightly.

### REMEMBER!

Always thoroughly clean and disinfect the changing mat after each use and wash your own hands well.

### KEY POINTS

- Never show disapproval at a soiled nappy.
- Do not put a baby down to sleep in a wet or soiled nappy.
- If a baby has consistently dry, or only slightly damp nappies, always inform the parents or day care supervisor. It could indicate that the baby is dehydrated or is unwell.

# Nappy rash

Even the best cared for baby can get nappy rash. It is uncomfortable for her, can cause stinging and pain and, if the skin is broken, there is a risk of infection.

The areas affected by nappy rash are: bottom, groins, genital area, upper thighs, lower abdomen and lower back.

## CAUSES OF NAPPY RASH

- Faulty washing technique of bottom and/or nappies.
- Soiled and wet nappies left on too long.
- Diarrhoea.
- Infections such as thrush or chickenpox.
- Eczema and seborrhoeic dermatitis.
- Reaction to creams, detergents, wet-wipes or nappy liners.
- Concentrated urine due to insufficient fluid intake.
- Tightly-fitting plastic pants.

Two particular types of nappy rash are:
- thrush (monilial) dermatitis
- ammonia dermatitis.

### Thrush (monilial) dermatitis

This is a common cause of nappy rash in small babies, especially those who are breast-fed or who have had (or whose mother has had) antibiotics. It is caused by a yeast fungus that lives naturally in many parts of the body including the vagina, and babies may become infected during birth. Dirty feeding bottles and teats are another source of the infection. The baby may have oral thrush at the same time. The nappy rash is pink and pimply and is found in the moist folds of the groin and upper thighs as well as around the anus and genital area.

#### *Treatment*

Prescribed ointment should be applied lightly at each nappy change. The thrush organism thrives on zinc and castor oil barrier cream so it should not be used.

If the baby has oral thrush, a gel or medicine will be prescribed. The mother may be treated as well.

### Ammonia dermatitis

This is the most usual type of nappy rash once the baby is sleeping for longer periods and her nappy is not changed so frequently. It is more common in bottle-fed babies who produce an alkaline stool. The stools of breast-fed babies are acid.

Urine contains waste product urea, while stools contain bacteria: urea + bacteria = ammonia = burning.

The rash starts in the genital area and can spread to the whole nappy area. Because ammonia burns, the skin appears inflamed and ulcerated, and the baby is in pain.

### Treatment

- *Skin care*   Wash the area with warm water and mild soap, gently pat dry and let the baby lie on a nappy with her bottom exposed to warm air. Use a barrier cream or prescribed treatment – make sure the skin is quite dry first. Change the baby's nappy frequently, including at night.
- *Nappy care*   Use a non-biological powder for washing terry towelling nappies. Add vinegar to the final rinsing water to neutralise the ammonia (1 oz vinegar to 8 pints warm water), then wring lightly and hang out to dry.

## PREVENTION OF NAPPY RASH

- Change nappies frequently.
- Wash and dry the nappy area gently, and apply barrier cream to well dried skin.
- Allow the baby time to kick and exercise freely without her nappy on. Make sure the room is warm.
- Use a non-biological washing powder or sanitising powder when laundering towelling nappies. Always rinse thoroughly and dry in the fresh air when possible.
- Identify the cause and treat appropriately.

## ABNORMAL STOOLS

The typical, normal stools of breast- and bottle-fed babies are described on page 116. Some abnormal stools include:

- *Diarrhoea*   This is loose, watery, smelly stools. Never ignore diarrhoea, a baby can quickly become dehydrated and seriously ill (see also page 164, 'Table 7.2 Summary of ailments in babies'). Always let the parents and day care supervisor know if a baby has diarrhoea as the baby will need to be seen by a doctor.
- *Constipation*   This is small, infrequent, hard, greenish brown stools that are difficult and painful to pass. The cause is often incorrect diet and under-feeding. Health visitors and child care workers can help

and advise parents on the types and variety of food their baby should be eating. Other causes will need specialist medical help.

■ *Blood-stained stool* Sometimes, a normal stool is streaked with a little fresh blood. It may indicate an anal crack (fissure) possibly due to constipation and straining. The baby should be seen by a doctor.

## KEY POINTS

■ Some foods and medicines may make the stools a different colour. Reddish stools may be due to rosehip syrup or blackcurrant drinks, or eating beetroot; medicine for threadworms may cause a bright red stool; iron medicine can make the stools black; pale, bulky, fatty, smelly stools may indicate poor absorption of fat in the diet.
■ Always report any concerns about a baby's stools to the parents or day care supervisor.

## TOILET TRAINING

Control of the bladder and bowels is achieved when the nervous system is sufficiently mature to allow a child to recognise the need to use the potty, and the ability to control the appropriate muscles. There is a wide variation of age at which a child is clean and dry. Somewhere around 18 months a child may make the connection between the feeling of wetting and soiling and the actual doing. Around 18 months to 2 years may be the right time to start introducing the potty.

Insisting a baby sits on the potty when she is not ready for the experience will lead to battles that may have long-term effects on the child and ultimately lead to constipation and stool holding.

## KEY POINT

Toilet training is detailed in most child care text books that cover the second and third years.

# Skin care in the sun

A baby's skin can very easily burn, especially on a sunny and windy day when sun can be very hot, so remember:
■ Never expose a baby to direct sunlight.
■ Dress the baby in cool, loose, cotton clothing and a full brimmed sun hat. Make sure the baby's neck, tops of the arms and thighs are covered.

- Use a total sun-block cream for babies on all exposed skin areas.
- Place the baby's pram in the shade (but remember a baby's skin can also burn in the shade), watch as the sun moves around and change the pram position accordingly.
- Use the pram or push-chair canopy when the baby is outdoors.
- Cars can become like ovens on a hot day – make sure there is a cooling draught through the car. Never leave a baby alone to sleep in a car, especially on a hot day. Check the buckles on the baby's car seat, they can get very hot and burn the skin.

**KEY POINT**

To keep a baby cool: keep her indoors when the sun is hottest; do not over-wrap her; open the windows, use a fan; and offer the baby extra drinks of cooled boiled water.

# Common skin conditions and infections

Some common skin conditions and infections are listed in Tables 3.1 and 3.2 (see pages 74–6). If you are at all concerned about the condition of the skin of a baby in your care, always let the parents or day care supervisor know.

**KEY POINT**

When caring for a baby with a skin condition always remember to wash your hands thoroughly before and after carrying out any treatment.

**REMEMBER!**

Remember the importance of:
- personal hygiene of carer, especially hand washing – you are a role model for good practice
- baby's daily skin care routines, including hair, nail and dental care
- daily routines of bathing or 'topping and tailing', and nappy changing
- appropriate toiletries
- parental, cultural and religious preferences and practices
- observation of the skin
- regular clothes and nappy changes
- guidelines of day care setting and local authority for dealing with body fluids
- abnormal conditions (stools, skin, etc)
- care of babies' skin in the sun.

**Table 3.1 Some common skin conditions**

| Condition | Cause | Description | Treatment |
|---|---|---|---|
| Erythema toxicum (Urticaria neonatorum) | Change of environment from womb to outside world | Red, blotchy areas with small central white spots. Appear on face, limbs, trunk. Not infectious. Common in first few weeks | No treatment<br>Clears up in 2–3 days |
| Sweat rash (Miliaria) | Overheating<br>Sweat glands of newborn are immature | Rash of small red spots in areas where sweat glands are numerous, for example, face, chest, skin folds | Remove some clothes<br>Avoid wool next to skin<br>Keep blankets and shawls away from face<br>Bath to refresh skin<br>Apply calamine lotion after drying<br>Avoid over-wrapping baby |
| Chafing (Intertrigo) | Inefficient washing and drying of skin | Inflammation and soreness of skin creases. Usually seen around neck, under arms and in groin | Zinc and castor oil cream or prescribed ointment<br>Prevent by good skin care practice, especially washing and drying |
| Cradle cap (May be seen on its own or as part of seborrhoeic dermatitis) | Build up of sebum<br>Excessive use of shampoo<br>Inefficient rinsing after hair wash | Yellowish-brown crusting on scalp. May be patchy or cover large area. Frequently seen over anterior fontanelle | Soften with olive oil over night<br>Lift off softened flakes with comb, shampoo and rinse well<br>Special shampoos available<br>Prevent by use of shampoo once or twice a week only, and rinse well |
| Infantile seborrhoeic dermatitis | Uncertain | Occurs in first three months. Similar to cradle cap, but spreads to neck, behind ears, shoulders, chest and nappy area. Skin is red, scaly and may weep. Rash is not itchy or infectious. Greater risk of infantile eczema | Medicated shampoo for scalp<br>Mild, unperfumed soap when washing or bathing<br>Prescribed cream for nappy area<br>Care of nappy area |

**Table 3.1** Some common skin conditions *continued*

| Condition | Cause | Description | Treatment |
|---|---|---|---|
| Infantile eczema | An allergic response | Irritating red rash on cheeks and forehead. May spread to whole body, especially skin folds. Scratching causes broken, weeping skin with risk of infection. More common in bottle-fed babies. Usually starts at 2-3 months. Boys affected more than girls. Often family history of eczema, asthma or hay fever. May clear up in first three years. Not infectious. Can cause enormous distress and discomfort | Medical treatment – cortisone or tar ointment applied as directed by doctor Aqueous soap solutions should be used – avoid ordinary soaps and bath preparations Emulsifiers added to bath water prevent skin drying out Sedatives may reduce severe irritation Keep finger nails short, use scratch mittens Use pure cotton or cotton mix fibres – avoid wool Antibiotics may be given for infection and antiseptic solution added to bath water Breast-feeding may delay onset |

**Table 3.2 Infections in the newborn baby**

| Condition | Cause | Description | Treatment |
|---|---|---|---|
| Sticky eyes | a) Blood, amniotic fluid or meconium entering during birth | a) Common in first 48 hours. Yellow crusting or discharge on the eyes or eyelids | a) Bathe eye(s) with saline wipes or cool, boiled water using same technique as in bathing baby to prevent infection being carried to other eye. Lie baby on affected side |
| | b) Blocked tear duct | b) Watery eye. May also be sticky. Tears cannot drain from eye to back of nose | b) Treat as above. Tear duct will normally open without treatment. If condition persists after 6 months, duct may be opened by operation |
| | | | A sticky eye after 48 hours of birth is probably due to a bacterial infection. The baby is isolated and given antibiotics. Hygiene procedure as above to prevent spread |
| Nail bed infection (Paronychia) | Bacterial infection | Inflammation and infection of tissues and skin folds surrounding nail | Gentian violet lotion or antibiotic ointment to dry up infection Cotton mittens Strict hygiene measures |
| Septic spots (Pyoderma) | Bacterial infection | Small septic spots or pustules. Can occur anywhere on baby | Isolate baby Gentian violet lotion or antibiotic ointment to dry up spots Strict hygiene measures |

## Activities

1 Visit your local shops and make notes on the toiletries recommended for babies. Look for:
   - baby bath preparations
   - toilet soaps
   - shampoos
   - baby oils, moisturisers and lotions
   - barrier creams
   - preparations for cradle cap.

   Your research should reflect products for different skin types and different cultural preferences for skin care.

2 Write an essay of between 400 and 500 words on the following title: 'What advice would you give a young mother on caring for the skin of her newborn baby?'

3 If you were caring for a baby on holiday in a hot climate, how would you protect her skin from sunburn?

## QUICK CHECK

1 Name three functions of the skin.
2 Name three irritants which can make baby's skin sore.
3 Why is a healthy, clean, undamaged skin important for a baby?
4 Which are the delicate and vulnerable areas of a baby's body that need special care?
5 Give two methods of checking the temperature of a baby's bath water.
6 What is the danger of 'sprinkling' talcum powder over a baby's body?
7 How would you, in a day care setting, care for a baby's clothes stained with vomit?
8 What is the danger to a baby of diarrhoea?
9 What are the causes of nappy rash?
10 What are the principles of preventing nappy rash?
11 What is cradle cap and how would you advise a mother to treat it?
12 How would you care for a baby with sticky eyes?

# 4 *SLEEP, CRYING AND TEETH*

> **This chapter covers:**
> - **Sleep management**
> - **Why babies cry**
> - **Teeth**
> - **Primary health care**

## Sleep management

The newborn baby sleeps in relatively short spells of three to five hours for a total of around 17 hours out of the 24. By 6 months she is probably sleeping about ten hours a night, with a sleep in the morning and afternoon making up a further four hours or so. By 1 year, she usually sleeps a total of 13 hours, which includes two short spells during the day.

### REMEMBER!

Each baby is an individual with his or her own sleep pattern. Some babies require less sleep than the average, others more. Mothers may have high expectations of how much sleep their baby should have, and often need reassuring that their baby is, in fact, having all the sleep she requires.

No one can make a baby sleep. She may take time to settle into a feeding and sleeping pattern, but she can be made sufficiently comfortable to help her sleep whenever she wants to. She requires frequent feeds, and hunger will wake her up as will pain, feeling cold and the jerking and twitching movements common in the newborn. Household noises should not disturb the baby unless they are sudden and loud. Creeping around trying 'not to wake baby' will lead to unnatural quietness in the home. Many babies quickly adjust to a pattern of sleeping more at night than during the day, and it is important to provide a routine which helps the baby to recognise night as a time for prolonged sleep. She may take a little while to settle, but unless she is obviously distressed there is no need to pick her up. Night feeds should disturb her as little as possible. Once she has been fed and her nappy checked and changed, she should be placed in her cot to settle back to sleep.

From about 3 months a bedtime routine can be established:

- 'top and tail' or bath the baby
- change the baby into night clothes and a clean nappy, talking quietly to her
- feed her without too much stimulation
- check her nappy, wrap her securely, but not tightly, and lay her down to settle in her cot. She may enjoy a music box or wind chimes.

## REST AND SLEEP ROUTINES IN DAY CARE

In day care, babies will need periods of rest and sleep each day. Some babies may have a well established sleep pattern, others may vary from day to day in their requirements. A flexible approach will enable you to match a baby's rest and sleep routine with her home routine and parent's wishes, ensuring continuity of care which will make the baby feel secure.

### REMEMBER!

You will need to find out from the baby's parent or carer:
- the routine which best suits the baby's needs
- if the baby has a comfort object
- the baby's preferred sleep position
- whether the baby enjoys a routine of music, singing, rocking, patting or stroking before settling to sleep
- if the baby likes to be cuddled on waking.

### KEY POINT

Before settling a baby to rest or sleep make sure she is wearing comfortable clothes and has a dry nappy – never put her down in a wet or soiled nappy. Her hands and face may need wiping or washing following a feed, a meal, floor play or messy play.

### Activity
A baby may rub her eyes, yawn or begin to whimper when she is tired. Think of other ways a baby might indicate to you that she is ready for a rest or sleep period.

## WHERE SHOULD A BABY SLEEP?

A new baby needs the security of being close to her mother rather than isolation in a room on her own. During the day this will probably be in a carry cot or pram in whichever room her mother is in. Sleeping in a cradle or cot beside her mother at night means there can be immediate physical contact when needed. Breast-feeding can be achieved quietly, in a dim light, with minimum effort. Taking the baby into the adult's bed to sleep is not recommended as there may be risk of overheating. At about 3 to 4 months the baby may be moved into her own room.

In the early weeks the room where the baby sleeps should be ventilated during the day and kept at a constant temperature of about 20°C (68°F) during the night. The baby should be warm, rather than hot, and chilling must be avoided.

In day care, each baby will have her own cot in a well ventilated (not draughty), warm, safe, 'sleep' room or quiet area. The cots should be spaced at not less than 1 metre apart. This allows air to circulate and lessens the risk of cross infection. It also enables adults to move freely between the cots. A calm, quiet, relaxed atmosphere with at least one adult remaining in attendance to supervise the sleep period, will help the babies to settle and provide reassurance that a familiar carer is near.

Bean bags, large cushions and settees can be used for resting periods for older babies.

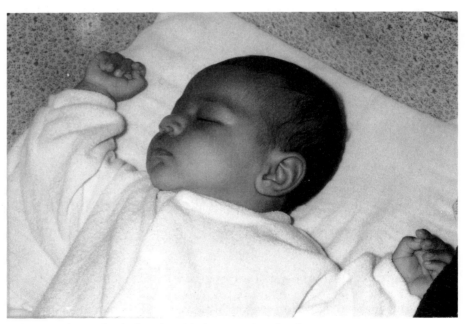

*Safe practice – the baby should sleep on her back*

- See also page 166 'Sudden infant death (Cot death syndrome)'.
- Cots or travel cots, prams and mattresses should meet the British Standards Institution (BSI) safety regulations.
- The Foundation for the Study of Infant Deaths (FSID) recommends the use of firm mattresses which are kept in good condition, clean, dry and well aired to prevent the possibility of bacterial contamination.
- Lie the baby down supine (on her back). If, for medical reasons, a baby needs to lie prone (on her tummy) always check that the bedclothes do not cover her head,
- Cot bumpers, duvets, pillows and baby nests are unsuitable for a baby under 1 year old. She would be unable to lift her head or wriggle free should her face become pressed against or 'buried' in the soft material. There is also the risk of overheating.
- Cotton, rather than nylon, sheets should be used as they allow adequate circulation of air around the baby and absorb perspiration.
- Clothes for sleeping in should be warm and comfortable and allow for freedom of movement.
- Never leave a baby in her pram or cot with a bottle 'propped' in her mouth.
- Babies should not sleep outside in very cold, foggy, or wet weather, nor should they be placed in direct sunlight.
- No one who has taken sleeping tablets or alcohol should take a baby into bed with them. These substances will make them less alert to the baby's movements and needs.

**Day care**

In day care the following principles must be observed.

- Every baby must have her own cot and bedding. Sheets and blankets should be washed weekly, or every time they are wet or soiled, and mattresses regularly aired. The automatic safety catches on cots should work properly and be regularly checked.
- Monitor babies sleeping outdoors every 10 minutes for signs of chilling or becoming unwell. A signed record should be made of all checks.
- Cat nets should be used when babies are sleeping outdoors to prevent cats, other animals and insects from harming the babies.
- Pram brakes, harnesses and anchor points should be checked daily.
- See also page 169 'Sleeping' for care of nursery equipment.

## DIFFICULTIES IN SETTLING TO SLEEP

There are many reasons why a baby may have difficulty in settling to sleep.

- Settling into day care.
- Discomfort – from being too hot or cold, uncomfortable clothes or a wet or soiled nappy.
- Emotionally insecure and unsettled – lacking cuddles and carer interaction.
- Medical conditions – pain, illness, skin irritation such as eczema, breathing problems such as asthma or infestation with threadworms, head lice or fleas.
- Limited accommodation where the baby may share a room with her parents or siblings. Bed and breakfast or hostel accommodation is often poor with little opportunity for a bedtime routine leading to settled sleep.
- Loud, persistent noise within the home or the outside environment.
- Lack of fresh air, exercise and appropriate stimulation during the day as well as a poor diet and hunger.

All these can lead to irritability, discomfort and a poor sleep pattern. In turn, a poor sleep pattern can lead to a miserable, fractious baby during the day.

## SLEEP AND THE OLDER BABY

Make sure the baby has had an interesting and stimulating day and is neither hungry nor thirsty as bedtime approaches. Bathing in the evening is probably better at this age (6 months to 1 year).

Management of bedtime should continue to be calm and enjoyable and the familiar routine and rituals continued. Her cot should be comfortable. Continue to put her down to sleep on her back, but remember, at this age a baby will turn over, wriggle and move around the cot, eventually finding her own sleeping position. The use of an all-in-one sleep suit will prevent her becoming cold. Using a double nappy may reduce the chances of the baby waking up because she is wet, but you should not do this if she has a nappy rash.

### KEY POINT

A poor pattern of care, in which the baby's needs are neither understood nor met will make her miserable and insecure and less likely to sleep. A tense, anxious mother or a mother suffering from postnatal depression can have an adverse effect on her baby's sleeping pattern.

As the baby gets older she may dislike being left alone at bedtime. A dim light, a half open door and household sounds can reassure her. Sleep management programmes can be of great benefit to parents and carers who are exhausted from a constantly distressed baby who does not sleep. Carers of babies as young as 8 months are helped through these programmes which are usually organised and led by the child health clinic team (see page 95).

## COMFORT OBJECTS

A baby will suck what she enjoys and what is available to her from birth. Many babies need more sucking than is derived from feeding. A non-nutritive sucking habit eventually becomes automatic and comforts a baby when she is unhappy, bored or tired. Many babies use a soft toy, or piece of cloth to cling to when they are tired, settling to sleep or separated from their mother as at bedtime or attending day care. These are called comfort objects. They are familiar, important possessions that give the babies a sense of security. They are soft and smooth and develop their own special smell. A baby may cling to or suck a comfort object, rub it against her cheek or just keep it close by. They do no harm and the habit may persist well into the early years with the child eventually growing out of it. However, they do need washing from time to time, and they may also wear out and even get lost. If possible, spare ones should be kept both in the home and in the nursery.

Finger or thumb sucking may develop early or later on. Unlike other comfort objects fingers and thumbs are part of the baby – she can feel and find them at any time and control the sucking – making the habit possibly more difficult to let go of in childhood.

### Dummies

A dummy is frequently used to quieten and comfort a baby. It is under the control of the parent or carer and can be removed at any time. Research suggests a significant relationship between dummy sucking and poor speech development (see page 136 'Language development').

## KEY POINTS

- By 6 months, babies take everything to their mouths. Sucking, mouthing and handling toys and objects provides babies with pleasure and important sensory learning experiences. A baby misses these opportunities if she constantly has a dummy in her mouth.
- There is a link between sugar coated dummies and dental caries (decay), see page 91.

## SAFE PRACTICE

- A baby must have her own individual dummy. Dummies often end up on the floor and need to be kept clean, hygienic and sterilised daily.
- Dummies should have a smooth teat, free from flaws and cracks that could collect germs. Check that they are made of safe, non-toxic material which will not easily disintegrate, with the possibility of the baby choking.
- Parents should be advised to buy dummies which carry a BSI number.
- Never put a baby down to sleep with a dummy in her mouth.
- Adults should not suck a dummy to 'clean' it. Bacteria in an adult's mouth may transfer to the baby who has reduced immunity.

## REMEMBER!

- Periods of rest and sleep are an important part of a baby's daily routine.
- Babies have individual sleep requirements and patterns.
- A baby must feel comfortable when settling to sleep:
  - adequately fed
  - dry nappy
  - warm
  - secure.
- Daily fresh air and developmentally appropriate stimulation and interest will help to promote satisfying sleep.
- Keep a small baby close to her mother or carer.
- Establish a bedtime routine.
- A variety of physical and emotional factors can lead to difficulties in settling to sleep.
- Many babies enjoy a comfort object when settling to sleep.
- Apply the principles of safe practice in relation to sleep.

## Activities

1 Darren is just 1 year old, and you are his key worker at a day nursery. He is a lively, active and happy baby with a good appetite. He seldom sleeps during the day preferring to play and practice his walking skills. In the evening he goes to bed at 6.30pm and is often awake at 5.30am. Darren's father has voiced his concern to you that his son is not getting sufficient sleep.

# Why babies cry

All babies cry. It is their language, a way of communicating their needs. Some babies are naturally calm and content, while others are wakeful, active and need constant attention. It is important to understand the physical and emotional needs of a baby and to be aware of developmental stages in order to interpret and respond to her cries.

*Physical needs*   These include food, warmth, shelter, rest and sleep, fresh air, exercise, cleanliness, and protection from infection and injury.

*Emotional needs*   These include love and security; consistent, predictable care and knowing her needs will be met; sensory experiences and opportunities to explore her environment; encouragement and response to achievement (smiling, clapping); praise and recognition; and exposure to language.

*Developmental stages*   These are discussed in chapter 6 (see page 125).

Crying can mean 'I'm hungry'; 'I'm lonely'; 'I'm in pain'; 'I want to go to sleep'. A quiet, 'good' baby may be ill. Most parents quickly learn to recognise their baby's different cries. Ignoring a baby's cries will make her feel insecure and frightened. Table 4.1 (pages 87–8) details the main causes of crying the role of the carer.

Unexplained crying often responds to the comfort of quick, rhythmical movements such as rocking, either in the carer's arms or in a pram. The speed of rocking (about 60 movements a minute) is thought to imitate the walking pace and heartbeat of the mother that the baby hears while in the womb.

- You cannot spoil a baby in the early months of life by picking her up when she cries.
- Research shows that babies cry less in the later months if carers respond to their cries and meet their needs in the early months.

## CRYING AND THE OLDER BABY

Reasons such as loneliness, pain and illness apply equally to the older baby as to the younger one. Additional causes may be separation from her mother due to illness or hospitalisation of either the mother or her baby.

**KEY POINT**

Strangers and strange environments, such as day care settings, may distress the baby (see also page 145, 'Settling in').

Between 6 months and 1 year the baby is becoming increasingly more mobile and with this stage of development comes frustration and often anger at the restrictions placed on her by adults. A stimulating environment will promote learning and discovery. She may become frustrated trying to learn a particular skill or make a particular toy work. Leaving her to succeed herself may be appropriate but if she is working herself into a rage it is better to help her.

**SAFE PRACTICE**

It is important to provide a safe and secure environment by removing anything dangerous or unstable from the baby's reach.

## PERSISTENT CRYING

Studies show that 1 in 10 babies cry persistently and are difficult to soothe and comfort. A medical check-up is advisable to make sure there is nothing physically wrong with the baby. Sometimes an allergy or infection, or hyperactivity may be discovered but usually the baby is healthy. Most babies will grow out of it but some may grow into demanding toddlers. Persistent crying maybe linked to maternal depression.

**Table 4.1 The causes of crying in babies**

| Cause | Role of the carer |
|---|---|
| Hunger | Milk feed – water will not satisfy<br>Is baby getting enough milk? Check weight<br>Is help needed with feeding technique, for example, fixing correctly at breast, larger hole in teat?<br>Demand feeding<br>Seek advice from health visitor<br>**Remember!** A dummy will not soothe a hungry baby |
| Thirst (especially in hot weather) | Small babies – 30 ml (1 oz) cool, boiled water<br>Older babies – cool, boiled water or well-diluted fruit juice from a cup |
| Discomfort<br>a) Dressing and undressing<br><br>b) Wet/soiled nappy<br><br><br>c) Too hot (damp around neck, face red)<br>d) Cold (whimpering, fretful | a) Babies dislike being dressed and undressed and feeling cold air on skin. Keep disturbance to a minimum and avoid chilling<br>b) Change nappy. Follow guidelines for skin and nappy rash care and treatment and prevention of nappy rash (pages 70–71)<br>c) Remove some clothing/bedding, but avoid chilling. Offer a drink of cool, boiled water as above<br>d) Check hands, feet and abdomen (tummy). Move to a warmer room, cuddle, try a warm feed<br>**Remember!** Hypothermia (see page 166) |
| Loneliness/boredom | Physical contact needed – cuddle, baby sling<br>Talk to baby, play a music box or 'womb' tape<br>Household noises<br>Rythmical movements – rocking, baby bouncer<br>Mobiles, activity centre, 'swipe' objects<br>Put pram under tree or near washing line (do not forget the cat net)<br>Take baby for a walk or car ride<br>**Remember!** Activities appropriate to age |
| Over-stimulation (loud noises, bright lights, too much bouncing, sudden happenings) | Check management<br>Take baby to a quiet place<br>Rhythmical rocking, patting<br>Massage, stroking<br>Sing to baby |
| Jerking and twitching (common movements in newborn babies – can cause them to wake suddenly) | Wrap up more securely, settle back to sleep |
| Colds and snuffles (breathing and feeding difficulties) | Medical care<br>Nose drops<br>Nasal care<br>Drinks of cool, boiled water |

*continued*

**Table 4.1 The causes of crying in babies** *continued*

| Cause | Role of the carer |
|---|---|
| Colic | See page 123 |
| Allergies<br>a) Cow's milk<br><br><br>b) Infantile eczema | Always seek medical help<br>a) Soya formula feed. Breast-feeding<br>mothers reduce intake of dairy products<br>Revision of diet according to medical instructions<br>b) See page 75 |
| Pain and illness<br>(knocks, falls, burns,<br>scalds, fever, diarrhoea,<br>vomiting) | Medical care<br>Safe practice, provision of safe environment<br>Knowledge of illness, infections<br>Knowledge of First Aid<br>Knowledge of workplace procedure<br>See 'Table 7.2' on pages 163–6, and see page 211 |
| Child abuse | Protection of baby, workplace procedure<br>Child protection agencies |

**Effects on parents and carers**

The effects of a crying, unsettled baby on her parents or carer are:

- exhaustion
- lack of confidence in caring for her, expectations may be shattered
- guilt at being unable to make her happy
- depression and anger – resentment of an 'over-demanding' baby
- worry – is something wrong with her? (The majority are perfectly healthy.)
- marriage or partnership affected, family life affected, isolation from friends
- danger of possible physical violence to the baby (studies in America show that child abuse often starts with a crying baby).

*Available help*

Parents and carers should not be afraid of seeking help. Professional advice from the family doctor and health visitor can be helpful.

### KEY POINTS

- Research shows that troublesome crying may be helped by reducing the amount of stimulation the baby receives. Loud music and rattling toys, excessive lifting, patting and winding of the baby should be avoided.
- Holding the baby in a quiet, dimly lit room may settle her. A soft light in the bedroom can have a soothing effect.

Self-help groups, such as Cry-sis and the National Childbirth Trust, put parents in touch with others who have had similar problems with a crying baby. Often just talking to others helps them to understand that they are not alone, and encourages them to try and work out some positive solutions. In some areas there are clinics that help to work out a programme beneficial for both the baby and her carer.

## Activities

1 A member of your group could contact Cry-is and find out about their support network.
   a) How widespread is the network?
   b) How big a need is there for Cry-sis?
   c) How is Cry-sis able to help and support families?
   d) Where would families find information about Cry-sis?
   The information should be brought to the group for discussion.
2 How would you respond to an adult who says: 'Crying is good exercise for a baby's lungs' and 'If you pick a baby up every time she cries you'll spoil her'?

# Teeth

Teeth buds form beneath the gums in the early weeks of pregnancy. They are made of a soft substance called cartilage. At around the fourth or fifth month of pregnancy calcium, phosphorous and vitamin D are laid down on the cartilage in a process known as calcification. The hard bone that develops is called dentine. It forms the bulk of a tooth and is sensitive to touch, temperature, sugar and acids. The inner cavity of a tooth is filled with pulp containing blood vessels and nerves. Enamel, the hardest substance in the body, covers the crown of all teeth. (The crown of a tooth is the part seen in the mouth above the gum.) Enamel does not contain nerve endings.

At birth, the first teeth are present in the jaw and the second teeth are starting to develop. Teeth are used for biting and chewing as well as for speech. They also affect appearance, and sucking a dummy, a thumb or fingers over many years can push the front teeth forward. A baby's first teeth are called 'deciduous' teeth (also known as milk teeth, baby teeth or primary teeth). They start to appear at around 4 to 6 months (see the diagram on page 90). Deciduous dentition is complete by $2\frac{1}{2}$ years. There are 20 teeth in this first set. They are smaller and more widely spaced than the second set of permanent teeth. Although there is a recognised sequence for the appearance of these teeth there is often individual variation. A firmly fixed tooth present at birth can be left alone although it may cause some problems with breast-feeding. A loose tooth will be removed. From the age of about 5 years the roots of deciduous teeth loosen and are absorbed by the body causing the teeth to fall out at intervals. Permanent dentition starts at 6 years. There are 32 teeth in the permanent set.

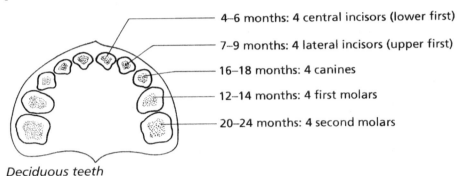

4–6 months: 4 central incisors (lower first)

7–9 months: 4 lateral incisors (upper first)

16–18 months: 4 canines

12–14 months: 4 first molars

20–24 months: 4 second molars

*Deciduous teeth*

*His first teeth – the two lower central incisors*

# CARING FOR TEETH

- Adequate protein, calcium and vitamin D intake by the mother during pregnancy is important.
- A baby's first diet of milk, plus vitamin supplements, provides the essential nutrients for healthy teeth.
- Weaning and family foods should continue to provide calcium, phosphorous and vitamin D and be as sugar-free as possible. Sugar is the main cause of tooth decay and the longer the sugar remains in the mouth the greater the chance of decay. Dental decay is a common condition even among very young children. It is unsightly, causes pain and, often, the affected teeth have to be extracted.
- Dummies dipped in sugar or honey and feeding bottles or soothers of sugar water or sweet fruit drink should not be given as comforters.
- Read the labels on fruit drinks. They may say 'no added sweetening' but may be naturally high in sugar. Always dilute well before giving them to a baby.
- Chewing massages the gums, increases the blood supply and flow of saliva and helps to keep the teeth clean. Foods that encourage the baby to chew can be offered in the second stage of weaning from around 6 to 7 months (see page 122).
- The mineral fluoride guards against tooth decay by protecting the enamel from acid attack. It is found naturally in the drinking water in some areas and in others it has been added by the local water authority. Where there is no fluoridation of water, fluoride drops or tablets may be prescribed or bought. Drops can be given to babies from birth and fluoride treatment can be continued until 16 years of age. However, the dose of any fluoride treatment must always be carefully regulated and advised by the dentist or pharmacist. Too much can cause softening of the teeth, as well as brown staining or white mottling. Many toothpastes now contain fluoride but only small amounts should be used.
- Dental decay is preventable by attention to diet, regularly cleaning the teeth and the use of fluoride. Visits to the dentist should start in the second year.

## KEY POINTS

- Start dental care as soon as the first tooth appears by wiping over the tooth and gum with a clean, non-fluffy cloth or baby's own small toothbrush smeared with a little toothpaste.
- Child care workers are health educators. You can help and advise parents on the importance of dental care and encourage them to ask for sugar-free prescriptions and medicines for their babies.

Babies in day care must have their own toothbrushes that are kept clean and separate from others.

## REMEMBER!

- Teeth buds form early in foetal life.
- There are 20 deciduous teeth and 32 permanent teeth.
- Dental decay is common in young children. It is unsightly and causes pain.
- Professional carers can promote dental care and offer advice to parents and other carers.
- Healthy teeth depend on:
  - mother's diet in pregnancy
  - the baby's diet
  - avoidance of sugary foods, drinks and medicines
  - an appropriate routine of dental care.

## TEETHING

A baby will normally cut her teeth without any problems apart, perhaps, from some swelling of the gum and reddening of the cheek where the tooth is erupting (coming through). Chewing on her hand, thumb or a hard teething ring can be comforting. If she is in obvious distress during teething the family doctor may prescribe a mild analgesic. Teething gels and solutions may give some relief, but check the labels for sugar content. Teething is blamed, wrongly, for many symptoms such as coughs and colds, earache, diarrhoea and nappy rash. It is usually just coincidence that these occur during the teething period. A baby with any of these symptoms should be seen by the family doctor.

### Activities

1 Find out if fluoride has been added to the water in your local area.
2 Collect leaflets and literature from your dentist on caring for children's teeth, including fluoride treatment.
3 Find out about the structure of teeth and about tooth decay.
   a) Draw and study the structure of a tooth.
   b) Make a flow chart to show how dental decay occurs.

# Primary health care

Primary health care is health care and treatment provided IN THE COMMUNITY, as opposed to care and treatment in hospital. It is the basic foundation of community health provision in the National Health Service (NHS). Primary health care is concerned with promoting good health and preventing illness in families and communities.

## THE PRIMARY HEALTH CARE TEAM

Many professionals make up the Primary Health Care team (PHCT). They work together to ensure the best possible health for the community they serve. The core members of the team include family doctors, community midwives and nurses, practice nurses and health visitors. Other health professionals such as community paediatricians, school nurses and doctors, audiometricians, orthoptists and nutritionists, plus administrative staff, are complementary to the PHCT in extending community health care facilities.

The roles of some PHCT members who care for babies and their families are briefly outlined below.

**Family doctors**

Family doctors care for the health of the whole family including sick and unwell babies. They refer babies to hospital (or other community health services) for specialist care and treatment. Many are also practitioners in preventive health care for children and:

■ Care for an expectant mother before, during and after birth, including her postnatal examination at 6 to 8 weeks.

■ Carry out periodic growth and developmental reviews for babies and young children, assesses their health and provide screening and immunisation programmes.

**Community midwives**

Community midwives have specialist training in all aspects of pregnancy and childbirth. They liaise closely with family doctors in caring for mothers both antenatally and postnatally. In particular, they:

■ Monitor the progress of the pregnancy (check blood pressure and weight and test urine); check position of the baby and listen to the heartbeat; offer emotional support; and advise on diet, minor ailments, keeping healthy, and preparing for labour and birth through a programme of relaxation and breathing exercises.

■ Assist with home births.

- Visit mothers and babies (whether a home or hospital birth) at home for at least 10 days after the birth. In particular they advise on feeding (helping to establish breast-feeding), skin and cord care. They take a blood sample for the baby's Guthrie and TSH tests (see page 3), check any abdominal or perineal sutures the mother may have and encourage her to continue with postnatal exercises.

## Health visitors

Health visitors have a background in nursing and midwifery (or obstetric training) and an in-depth knowledge of child health and development. They are members of the PHCT working in the community with people of all ages. However, they have special responsibility towards children under 5 years and their families. In particular they:

- Work with family doctors and community paediatricians in child health promotion and surveillance programmes.
- Visit a mother and her baby soon after the midwife has completed her care, listen to any concerns the mother may have about the baby or herself and offer advice, support and reassurance, particularly to first-time mothers. They will discuss all aspects of baby care (feeding, skin care, sleep pattern and the importance of immunisation) with the parents and ask how the baby is settling into the family.
- Visit the family at home as often as necessary.
- Invite mothers to bring their babies to the child health clinic for periodic developmental and health reviews, screening tests and immunisations.
- Identify mothers who may be exhausted, depressed, unaware of, or unresponsive to, the needs of their babies. They can offer support and advice and bring in other professional help such as the family doctor or social worker.
- Understand, and aim to alleviate, the difficulties experienced by families from different cultures in bringing up their babies and young children, especially those families for whom English is not their first language. They may be able to offer help through an ethnic link worker, cultural support group or information in their home language.
- Screen babies for hearing and vision loss. Early detection is essential. Hearing difficulties can affect normal language development with implications for social, emotional and intellectual well-being. Squinting, although seen in the immediate newborn period, can seriously affect vision if it persists.
- Identify babies and young children with special needs.

# CHILD HEALTH CLINICS

Family doctors practising preventive child health care, together with community paediatricians (see below) and health visitors, have particular responsibility for child health. Families with babies and young children are invited to the child health clinic (usually based in a health centre, but it may be in a village or church hall, or a doctor's premises) and offered a care programme that aims to PROMOTE good health and PREVENT illness and disorders. Parents are helped and supported with feeding, weaning and child care management routines. Health and development reviews, screening tests and immunisations are arranged. Babies attend the clinic for their medical examination at 8 weeks old.

## Community paediatricians

Community paediatricians are part of the Community Child Health Services. Their work in preventive health care for children is similar to that of family doctors although they do not provide an antenatal and postnatal service for mothers.

### KEY POINTS

- Child health clinics are for 'well' babies. If a baby is sick or unwell she will be referred to the family doctor for medical treatment.
- Formula milk (in exchange for milk tokens) and free vitamin drops are available at the clinic for babies under 1 year, for some families receiving certain benefits.

Child health clinics should meet the needs of the families they serve. There should be easy access, convenient opening hours (some are open evenings and Saturday mornings). The premises must be safe with gates and a pram shed.

A warm, welcoming atmosphere and friendly staff make the parents feel comfortable and provide a relaxed meeting place for exchanging news and views and comparing 'baby' notes.

Many have crèche facilities and local information about playgroups, child-minders, baby-sitting services and voluntary organisations displayed on a notice board.

# CHILD HEALTH PROMOTION

Child health promotion has two approaches.

### Encouraging good health (primary prevention)

Good health is encouraged by promoting breast-feeding and supporting mothers who breast-feed; guiding parents in providing a healthy balanced diet for their babies and young children; preventing dental disease (see page 91); immunisations and health education (food hygiene, hand washing, etc.) to protect against infectious diseases – important factors in day care settings; accident prevention (accidents are a common cause of death in children); supporting parents in caring for their children; and offering help, when necessary, to lessen the possibility of emotional or behavioural difficulties in children.

### Health surveillance (secondary prevention)

Health surveillance provides regular growth, development and health reviews; early detection of problems (including emotional and behavioural) and disorders; referral for specialist help; and screening for hearing and vision impairment, dislocated hips and undescended testes

## SCREENING

Screening is a test or examination for a particular disease or disorder that may be cured or treated. Early detection is important in preventing permanent damage and disability. A baby (through her parents) is offered several screening tests in her first year as part of the Child Health Promotion programme. She will be referred for further investigation if there is concern about any result. Screening tests must be carried out and interpreted correctly for them to be of value.

## GROWTH, DEVELOPMENT AND HEALTH REVIEWS

Reviews are offered at certain ages throughout the first year allowing the professionals and parents to assess a baby's progress together. The ages may vary slightly from area to area.

All reviews and assessments should take place in a relaxed and mutually trusting atmosphere. Parents know their baby best and have an important part to play in the exchange of information about her health and development. Any concerns parents may have about their baby should not be ignored.

### REMEMBER!

A baby who is hungry, tired or irritable may not respond appropriately to examination and testing.

Parents should be asked questions relevant to the age and developmental stage of the baby and always given time to answer. Examples include: Do you have any concerns about your baby? How is her feeding/appetite? Tell me what she likes to eat? What is her sleep pattern? How does she respond when you talk to her? What noises/sounds does she make? Does she appear to hear and see normally?

**Typical review and screening tests schedule in the first year**
- **Birth:** growth measurements, neonatal screening tests and 'top to toe' examination, including examination of the nervous system (see page 33). (Neonatal screening test for hearing loss is available in some maternity units.)
- **8 weeks:** repeat growth measurements. Check hips and testes. Discussion with the parents about their baby's progress. Observation of the baby's development and demeanour, and mother–baby interaction
- **8 weeks to 6 months:** opportunities for the family doctor to check the baby when seen for minor ailments and immunisations, and for the health visitor to talk to the parents and observe the baby during home visits
- **6 to 12 months:** growth measurements; examination of heart and lungs; check hips and testes (if undescended); observation of the baby, review of all-round development and emerging skills (gross and fine motor control, vocalisations and social behaviour); discussion with parents, listening to any concerns they may have.

**Vision and hearing assessment:** Do the parents have any concerns? Do they think their baby is seeing/hearing normally?
- **6 to 7 months:** vision screening for squint and other vision problems.
- **8 months:** screening for hearing loss.
There will be a re-test or referral to specialist if there are concerns about the results of either test.

## KEY POINTS

- Growth measurements are plotted on a percentile chart (see page 130). The chart gives a picture of the baby's individual growth pattern in relation to the national average.
- At all times, parents are involved in their baby's screening tests and developmental reviews. They keep their baby's Child Health Record Book in which information relating to her growth, health and development, and immunisation status is recorded.

■ If at any time, parents are concerned about any aspect of their baby's health or development, outside a regular review, they can arrange to see the doctor or health visitor.

## REMEMBER!

■ Primary health care is health care in the community.
■ Family doctors, community paediatricians, community midwives and health visitors have particular responsibility to care for babies and their families.
■ Child health clinics are for 'well' babies.
■ Screening tests aim to detect a disorder at an early age.
■ Health promotion includes encouraging breast feeding and measures to prevent infection such as immunisation, hand washing and food hygiene.
■ Periodic health and developmental reviews are offered during the first year.
■ Parents know their babies best – always listen carefully to their concerns.

## KEY POINT

Health visitors are concerned with the holistic development of the baby. They help parents to promote all aspects of development, with particular emphasis on emotional development and parent–baby relationships.

## Activities

1  In pairs, make an appointment with a health visitor in your area. Ask her:
    a) to explain the statutory duties of a health visitor
    b) to explain how she conducts her first visit to a new baby and her family
    c) at what age developmental reviews are carried out in her area during a baby's first year
    d) what happens if there is concern over a baby' hearing test result.
2  Think of reasons why parents may not take advantage of health and development reviews and immunisation appointments for their baby. How can the Community Child Health Service reach out to these families?
3  Find out about child-rearing in a culture other than your own. Points to consider will be:
    a) childbirth practice

b) the role of the extended family in caring for the baby
c) skin care
d) sleep routine and management.

You will need to use your college resources and local libraries for information. Your local health visitor may be able to arrange for you to visit a family to carry out your research.

## QUICK CHECK

1 Where is the best place for a newborn baby to sleep?
2 List three points of safe practice relating to babies and sleep.
3 Give three reasons why a baby may not settle to sleep.
4 Give three reasons why babies cry.
5 At what age does a baby begin to show frustration at restraints and restrictions put upon her?
6 What are the key points to consider in caring for a baby who is too hot?
7 What effect can a persistently crying baby have on her parent/carer?
8 How many deciduous teeth are there?
9 At what age would you normally expect a baby's first tooth to appear?
10 What is the main cause of tooth decay?
11 What is the name of the hard substance covering the crown of a tooth?
12 What are the functions of the teeth?
13 When is the best time to start dental care?
14 Name the core members of the Primary Health Care team.
15 Which member of this team visits a mother and her new baby for at least ten days after birth?
16 What are the functions of a child health clinic?
17 At what age will:
   a) a baby's hearing be tested for any sign of hearing loss?
   b) a baby's vision be tested for any sign of a squint?
18 In your own words what is:
   a) screening?
   b) a health and development review?

# 5 FEEDING

> **This chapter covers:**
> - **Breast or bottle?**
> - **Breast-feeding**
> - **Bottle-feeding**
> - **Weaning**
> - **Feeding problems**

## Breast or bottle?

The choice between bottle- and breast-feeding is an important one for any would-be parent. It is a decision best made after careful consideration of all the health promotion information available. Pregnancy is an ideal time for information to be given about different feeding methods, research tells us that parents are especially responsive to new information, during the antenatal period. Remember, too, social and cultural factors will also influence choices.

Pressure should never be placed on the parents to choose any particular method. If this happens it could lead, for example, to a mother feeling guilty because she has decided not to breast-feed and this may affect some of her pleasure in the early days of parenthood.

### KEY POINT

The decision on how to feed their baby is for the parents to make, and for carers and health professionals to respect.

### Activities

1 What might influence parents' decisions between breast- and bottle-feeding when considering lifestyle and finance:
   a) Which is cheaper?
   b) How much equipment will be needed for each method?
   c) What is the cost of a packet of formula milk?
   d) How many packets will be required for one year?

# Breast-feeding

Breast-feeding is nature's 'designer food', the milk is specific to each individual baby and although much can be copied in formula milks, the most important parts cannot. Breast milk changes as the baby grows and her needs alter.

## BABIES' NUTRITIONAL NEEDS

Babies need food for energy, growth and repair of body tissues, the maintenance of body temperature, the building of bones and transmission of nerve impulses.

The rate of a baby's growth is greatest in the first year of life, but especially in the first months – a baby will usually double her birth weight by 5 to 6 months and treble it by 12 months. The largest area of growth in these months is the brain. It is, therefore, very important that a baby's nutritional needs are fully met to allow this important development to take place.

### Sources of nutrition

*Proteins, fats and carbohydrates.* These provide energy and promote growth. Proteins are found mainly from animal sources: meat, cheese, eggs, milk and fish. Smaller amounts are found in pulses, rice and nuts. Fats are found in dairy products, as well as in margarines and nuts. Carbohydrates are mainly found in breads, cereals, potatoes and starchy vegetables.

*Vitamins and minerals.* Although they are required only in tiny amounts, vitamins and minerals are an essential part of complete nutrition and allow the baby to use the important nutrients – proteins, fats and carbohydrates – and help the development of the nervous and other body systems. They are found in a wide variety of foods and fruits.

Breast milk is a complete food for the first months of life and no other nutrients are required.

## HOW BREAST MILK IS MADE

The mature breast varies a great deal in size from one woman to another. Sizes of breast, nipple and areola (the surrounding area) are not related to the ability to produce milk successfully.

The important aspect of the nipple is its ability to become erect to allow the baby to attach herself or 'fix' at the breast. The milk does not leave the breast through a single channel at the nipple, but through the lactiferous (milk-producing) ducts leading from each of the lobes (see the diagram below). (There are between 15 and 25 ducts depending on the number of lobes.) The areola also has a number of small glands called Montgomery's tubercles, which become larger and more noticeable during pregnancy. They act like sweat glands and produce a fluid that helps to keep the nipple soft and supple – a natural moisturising cream that shouldn't be removed by washing with any soaps.

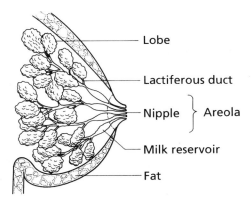

*The lactating breast*

## HOW THE MILK IS RELEASED

Breast milk is released by the 'let-down' reflex (see diagram). Some women find this let-down sensation very strong, while others hardly notice it.

Successful breast-feeding depends on 'supply and demand' – the more the baby feeds, the more milk is made. If this mechanism is broken, for example by giving the baby 'extra' in a bottle, future under-production will result.

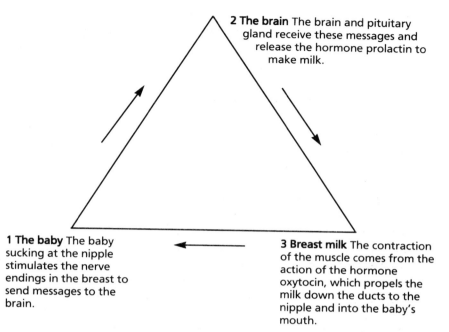

**2 The brain** The brain and pituitary gland receive these messages and release the hormone prolactin to make milk.

**1 The baby** The baby sucking at the nipple stimulates the nerve endings in the breast to send messages to the brain.

**3 Breast milk** The contraction of the muscle comes from the action of the hormone oxytocin, which propels the milk down the ducts to the nipple and into the baby's mouth.

*The let-down reflex*

## THE COMPOSITION OF BREAST MILK

Breast milk is a changing food – it adapts to meet the needs of the growing baby.

**Colostrum**

This syrupy, yellowish substance is the first milk made by the breasts from about the fifth month of pregnancy until about ten days after birth.

The purpose of colostrum appears to be to tide the newborn baby over, from her protected life in the womb, to the more exposed and potentially dangerous existence outside. It has a much higher protein content than later, mature breast milk. This is thought to be because:

- the proteins contain many antibodies which line the baby's intestines and prevent harmful bacteria from entering the blood stream
- the high protein levels ensure that even the small amounts taken in will supply sufficient energy to allow the baby to sleep for long periods in the first days after birth.

For these reasons, even when not intending to continue, mothers are often actively encouraged to breast-feed for the first few days at least. **There is no artificial replacement for colostrum.**

**Mature breast milk**

When milk begins to be made in the breasts and 'comes in' on the second to fourth day, it is still mixed with colostrum and looks rich and creamy. By the tenth day the mature milk looks thin and watery by comparison. The change in appearance does not mean reduced quality. The milk is natural and appropriate to the baby's needs.

By the end of the fourth week, it contains approximately a fifth of the protein of colostrum and more fat and glucose. The milk at the beginning, or 'fore', feed is high in the carbohydrate lactose, for a quick energy boost, and the latter, or 'hind', milk is higher in fat content for longer-lasting satisfaction for the baby. Human milk is almost completely digestible. The proteins are broken down into soft curds and quickly pass through into the small intestine. Water forms the liquid part of the milk.

All milks are poor sources of iron and babies depend on the stores laid down in their livers during pregnancy. These supplies will not be finished until the baby is 4 to 6 months of age. The high concentration of the sugar, lactose, and vitamin C helps in the absorption of iron.

> **Activity**
> a) What special clothing will be required for a mother planning to breast-feed?
> b) Which shops supply this?
> c) What are the comparative prices with everyday clothing?

## MANAGEMENT OF BREAST-FEEDING

A mother breast-feeding her baby will benefit from the support you can give her by explaining and answering her questions. She will be helped by understanding that it may take time for her and her baby to get to know each other and that although breast-feeding is natural, many first-time mothers, especially, need additional support to establish feeding patterns.

It is thought to be important for the baby to be put to the breast as soon after birth as possible. This 'skin-to-skin' contact helps the mother and her baby to develop a loving relationship and, in addition, the sucking helps to release hormones to contract the uterus.

The mother needs a comfortable position when feeding, for example, by lying on her side if her perineum is sore. Pain can lessen the let-down reflex and the flow of milk, so feeding in comfort is important. Chairs should give good support to the lower back, feet can be put on a stool if needed and privacy provided.

### 'Fixing' at the breast

The baby will use the rooting reflex to search for the breast. This can be achieved by stimulating the baby's mouth with the mother's nipple. The baby will then turn to the breast and suck. Take the baby to the breast and never force the breast into the baby's mouth.

The baby is correctly fixed at the breast when she has a mouth full, to include the lower areola – 'chewing' alone on the nipple will cause soreness. When successfully fixed, the baby's mouth will be wide open with her bottom lip curled back and some way from the base of the nipple (see the diagram). If the baby's nose is pressing into the breast and causing her to come off frequently, reposition the baby so that her head tilts slightly backwards. Pressing the breast, to allow the baby to breathe, alters the shape of the nipple and should be avoided.

### KEY POINT

After initially learning how to attach her baby a mother will feel comfortable when she is correctly fixed. This tells her that her baby is feeding in the right position.

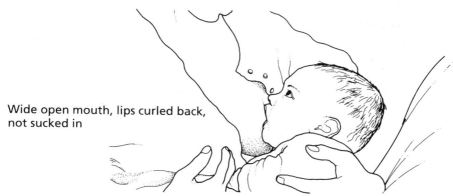

Wide open mouth, lips curled back, not sucked in

*The baby fixed correctly at the breast*

### Taking the baby off the breast

Allow the baby to come off by herself, when she has finished her feed. If necessary, the mother can put her finger into the corner of the baby's mouth to release the suction.

### Frequency and length of feeds

Breast milk production (or lactation) is more easily established if the baby feeds within the first four hours after delivery. Each baby is an individual and it is inappropriate to force her into a feeding routine for an adult's convenience. In the first few weeks of life, a breast-feeding baby often feeds as frequently as every 1 to 2 hours.

Some babies will get all the milk they require within 5 minutes, while others will take longer. It is important to let the baby decide the length of the feed so that she gets the rich, high fat 'hind' milk that will satisfy her for longer. Feeding on demand limits the chances of the breasts becoming engorged or overfull with milk.

It is not necessary for the baby to feed from both breasts at each feed, however offering the other breast at the next feed would seem sensible.

## BENEFITS TO THE BABY FROM BREAST-FEEDING

■ Breast milk is suited to the baby's complete needs and digestion.
■ It is almost germ-free – straight from producer to consumer!
■ The nutritional content of milk contains protective antibodies particularly effective against diarrhoea and vomiting. It is thought to be helpful, also, in the prevention of allergies.
■ A breast-fed baby can get more cuddles from her mother.

## BENEFITS TO THE MOTHER

■ Breast-feeding is thought to aid the mother-child relationship.
■ It is cheap.
■ It is often less work when well-established.
■ It aids in the contraction of the womb.
■ It gives a sense of achievement of 'doing the best.'
■ It is thought to help in the prevention of breast cancer.

## BREAST-FEEDING IN DAY CARE

Many mothers now wish to continue breast-feeding even though they plan to return to work. Being able to breast-feed means a mother can remain close to her baby even when separated for comparatively long periods of time. To allow this to happen may mean one of the following:
■ the mother working close to her baby's carer or nursery so she can come and feed when needed
■ expressing breast milk to be given during her absence
■ partial breast-feeding – breast-feeding at the beginning and end of the day, with bottles of expressed breast or formula milk being given while the mother is at work.

### KEY POINT

This last approach is only possible when lactation is well established. The breasts need regular stimulation to produce adequate supplies of milk, especially in the early days of feeding. See table 5.1 (page 108) for common breast-feeding difficulties.

### Expressing breast milk

Necessary equipment and facilities will include:

- a pump – this works by producing a vacuum and a squeezing action over the areola, in a similar manner to the baby's jaws. Pumps can be hand-, battery- or mains electricity-operated. The breasts must be stimulated in this way regularly during the day and night to maintain the milk supply. Milk can be expressed manually but it will take much longer to produce the necessary amounts for several hours of separation.
- sterile storage containers – sterile bottles, teats, and sterilising equipment
- a vacuum cool bag to carry the expressed milk
- a room, with a lock, that is warm, private, clean and with a comfortable chair
- hand washing facilities and equipment that are nearby
- storage facility for expressed milks – refrigerator or freezer – that is nearby

## REMEMBER!

Wherever a mother feeds her baby or expresses breast milk she needs to feel private, relaxed, comfortable and welcome.

## SAFE PRACTICE

Expressed breast milk must be stored in sterile, covered containers, labelled and dated.

Expressed breast milk must be used within 24 hours if stored in a refrigerator and within three months in a freezer. It should be thoroughly defrosted before use and transported in a vacuum bag. Never keep it warm for bacteria to breed.

Cleanliness and sterility of all equipment are as necessary for expressed breast milk as for formula milk – see 'Preparation of feeds', page 111, and 'Procedure for giving a bottle', page 114.

## KEY POINT

Making a mother feel welcome and giving her privacy and time either to express her milk or feed her baby will make the experience satisfying. Try not to rush her, nor make her feel she is in the way or taking up valuable time or space. If she feels under pressure this may make expressing more difficult, and make both her and the baby anxious if she is breast-feeding.

## BREAST-FEEDING DIFFICULTIES

Table 5.1 lists the common difficulties in breast-feeding.

**Table 5.1 Common breast-feeding difficulties**

| Problem | Cause | Management |
|---|---|---|
| Sore nipples | a) Bad positioning<br>b) Nipples constantly wet<br><br>c) Infections such as thrush | a) Check the baby's position at breast<br>b) Expose nipples to air<br>Change breast pads frequently<br>c) Treatment for both baby and mother |
| Cracked nipples | Failure to manage sore nipples | Discontinue feeding<br>Feed from other breast<br>Keep dry<br>Expose nipples to air<br>Resume feeding |
| Engorgement (breasts overfull and painful) | a) Excess blood supply in early days<br>b) Poor positioning<br>c) Inadequate removal of milk from breasts | a) Baby-led feeding<br>Bathing with hot and cold flannels<br>b) Check feeding technique<br>c) Use of firm bra<br>Possibly manual removal of small amounts of milk |
| Blocked ducts (painful lumps in the breast, mother has no fever) | Poor feeding from baby or poor fixing | Correct fixing of the baby<br>Regular, frequent feeds |
| Mastitis (infection or inflammation in a segment of the breast, possible fever) | Breast becoming overfull; inadequate feeding | Feed from affected side first<br>Feed frequently<br>Extra fluids to mother<br>Bathe breasts with hot and cold flannels<br>Possible treatment with antibiotics |
| Insufficient milk | a) Poor fixing<br>b) Infrequent feeding<br>c) Use of complementary bottles<br>d) Poorly nourished and overtired mother | a) Check positioning<br>b) Baby-led feeding<br>c) No bottles of milk<br><br>d) Support mother, give good diet and sufficient fluids, check amounts of rest |
| Unsettled baby | Wet, tired, abdominal pain; difficulty in fixing | Check physical comfort<br>Additional support at feeding |

**Remember!** What the mother eats will pass through her breast milk. This will include excess alcohol, all drugs and even nicotine.

# Bottle-feeding

Cow's milk is ideal for calves, but it is not the natural food for babies. Unmodified cow's milk, goat's milk and evaporated milk are unsuitable for babies under six months, because:

- they contain high levels of the protein, casein, which cause curds in a baby's stomach that are difficult to digest
- they have high salt contents which are potentially dangerous for small babies with immature kidneys
- the fats they contain have a higher proportion of fatty acids, which are poorly absorbed and can hinder calcium absorption.

Formula milks are essential for all babies who are not breast-fed, preferably up to 1 year old. Milks for new babies are almost all cow's milk-based although if babies have difficulty in tolerating them then soya-based milks are available. All formula milks have been changed by adapting the protein and fat contents and have extra vitamins and minerals added. The addition of iron is particularly important.

## CHOICE OF MILKS

There are many varieties of formula milk available and they are continually being updated. Formula milks are primarily either whey or curd dominant.

Whey dominant formulae contain the protein lactalbumin that is easy for a baby to digest. These milks are particularly suited to the new baby and are nearest in composition to breast milk.

Hungrier babies may be given curd dominant formulae that contain the protein casein. The curds in these milks take longer to digest and the baby feels fuller for longer.

However, there is no difference in the calorie or nutrient content of the two types of milk. Often a baby will come home from hospital having been given a particular brand and unless there is strong reason to change, it is sensible to continue with that brand to allow both the baby's digestion and her taste buds time to adjust.

For 6- to 12-month-old babies 'follow-on' milks have been developed to be used in place of cow's milk. These are less modified than new baby milks but, again, are fortified with extra vitamins, iron and calcium.

### Cow's milk intolerance

Some babies have difficulty in tolerating cow's milk products. This may be due to the specific protein or to lactose (milk sugar). As a result milks have been developed in which proteins from soya bean have been used and the lactose has been changed to glucose. Medical advice should be sought before changing a baby to this type of formula to ensure that any symptoms – normally diarrhoea, rashes and cramp-like pains – are really due to an intolerance.

If a soya-based milk is used, a baby may still develop a sensitivity to the protein. Care must be taken also with dental health as the glucose in soya milk is particularly harmful to teeth – a cup should replace a bottle by 12 months to limit possible damage if a soya-based milk is used.

## Activities

1 a) Visit a chemist shop, or a specialist mother and baby shop, and research the different types of feeding bottles and teats that are available.
   b) Prepare a talk to your group about the advantages and disadvantages of the different equipment you found.
   c) How can a new mother discover easily whether the manufacturers' claims are accurate?

2 Visit the local shops.
   a) What types of formula milk are available?
   b) Do they have age recommendations on them?
   c) Do you think the instructions for making up the feeds are adequate?
   d) Are all the instructions in English or can you find any with instructions in different languages?
   e) Look at the packaging. What might affect a parent's choice between the brands?

## HOW MUCH FEED SHOULD A BABY BE GIVEN?

The calculation for the nutritional needs of small babies is: 75 ml of fully reconstituted feed for every 500 g of a baby's weight ($2\frac{1}{2}$ fl oz per lb) in 24 hours. The total feed is then divided into the number of bottles it is likely the baby will take in that time. For a brand new baby it is usually eight feeds. Remember, however, that every baby is individual and that, like breast-feeding, a schedule should again be 'baby-led' to allow for changes in appetite.

- Inaccuracy in making up feeds is widespread.
- Over-concentration leads to excessive weight gain, too much salt and possible strain on the baby's kidney.
- Cereals and sugars should never be added to bottles.
- Under-concentration is less common, but it can lead to poor weight gain, constipation and a distressed, hungry baby.

## PREPARATION OF FEEDS

### Keeping things clean

Whatever method of sterilisation is chosen, every piece of equipment should be thoroughly clean, including the work surfaces, jugs, knives, and your own hands, nails and clothes. Sterilisation (see the diagram below) is most commonly by a chemical agent. Any sterilising tank or container will need to be thoroughly washed every 24 hours and the correct concentration of solution achieved.

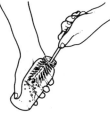

**1** Wash the bottles, teats and other equipment in hot water and detergent. Use a bottle brush for the inside of bottles. **Do not rub salt on the teats.** Squeeze boiled water through the teats.

**2** Rinse everything thoroughly in clean running water.

**3** Fill the steriliser with clean, cold water. Add chemical solution. If in tablet form, allow to dissolve.

**4** Put the bottles, teats and other equipment (nothing metal) into the water. Ensure everything is covered completely by the water, with no bubbles. If necessary, weight down. Leave for the required time according to manufacturer's instructions.

*The procedure for chemical sterilisation*

**Other non-chemical methods of sterilising equipment**

| Method | Efficiency | Costs | Dangers |
|---|---|---|---|
| Steam sterilisation | Up to eight bottles take 8 minutes Very effective | Unit required costs £30 approximately | Dangers of scalding from steam if unit is opened before cycle is complete |
| Microwave sterilisation | Up to four bottles in 10 minutes using effective steam principle | Special unit essential costing approximately £10, plus microwave oven | Not suitable for metal equipment |
| Boiling | Any number of bottles depending on the size of the saucepan All equipment must be fully submerged with no air bubbles for a full 10 minutes with the water at a rolling boil | Cheap with no expensive equipment required | Dangers of handling large quantities of boiling water must be considered carefully |

## KEY POINT

Sterilisation is the complete destruction of all harmful bacteria. Preparing milk feeds for babies requires sterilisation of all equipment used.

## SAFE PRACTICE

It is essential to continue with the sterilisation of all feeding equipment including spoons, measures, jugs, etc. until the baby is 9 months old.

However, as milk is an ideal medium in which harmful bacteria can breed it is safe practice to continue to sterilise bottles and teats, however old the baby, while milk is being given in this way.

### General hygiene

Cleanliness is very important in the preparation of baby feeds. Infections can spread through the air and especially by touch through the hands. Germs live and breed easily in a warm nutritious world, such as milk. High standards of personal hygiene are, therefore, vital.

## REMEMBER!

- Feeds should be prepared in a kitchen away from young children.
- Always check the temperature of the milk on the inside of your wrist, before giving a baby a feed.

**1** Check that the formula has not passed its sell-by date. Read the instructions on the tin. Ensure the tin has been kept in a cool, dry cupboard.

**2** Boil some **fresh** water and allow to cool.

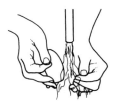

**3** Wash hands and nails thoroughly.

**4** Take required equipment from sterilising tank and rinse with cool, boiled water.

**5** Fill bottle, or a jug if making a large quantity, to the required level with water.

**6** Measure the **exact** amount of powder using the scoop provided. Level with a knife. **Do not pack down.**

**7** Add the powder to the measured water in the bottle or jug.

**8** Screw cap on bottle and shake, or mix well in the jug and pour into sterilised bottles.

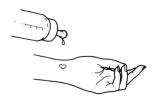

**9** If not using immediately, **cool quickly** and store in the fridge. If using immediately, test temperature on the inside of your wrist.

**10** Babies will take cold milk but they prefer warm food (as from the breast). If you wish to warm the milk, place bottle in a jug of hot water. **Never keep warm for longer than 45 minutes** to reduce chances of bacteria breeding.

**Note** Whenever the bottle is left for short periods, or stored in the fridge, cover with the cap provided.

*Preparing the bottle feed*

- A baby should never be propped up with a bottle and left alone.
- Choking can easily take place.
- Siblings and unsure adults feeding small babies should be supervised at all times.
- Bottles should be used only for milk or cooled, boiled water – never add solids, sugar or use for fruit juices.
- Boiling liquids must never be passed over a small baby.

Note: a microwave oven is unsuitable for the warming of feeds as it can produce unexpected 'hot spots'.

## PROCEDURE FOR GIVING A BOTTLE

- Collect all equipment for the feed, before picking up the baby. Place the bottle on a tray and cover it. Keep it warm in a jug of hot water. Put bib, tissues and any other articles ready as well.
- Change the baby and make her comfortable. Wash your hands.
- Take the baby to the feeding area and sit in a comfortable position. This is a time for talking and cuddling the baby and is an enjoyable time, not to be rushed. Maintain eye contact and hold the baby firmly to give her a sense of security, use a similar position to that for breast-feeding.

*The baby should be held securely, with good eye contact*

- Test the temperature of the bottle against the inside of the wrist.
- Test the size of the teat by turning the bottle upside down. The milk should flow freely at first – several drops per second.
- Stimulate the rooting reflex, by gently touching the baby's lips with the teat and then place the teat over her tongue and into her mouth.

- Check that milk is always present in the teat. This stops the baby becoming frustrated at not receiving feed and sucking on air. Gentle tension on the teat helps her to keep sucking steadily.
- A feed usually takes about 20 minutes with a break after about 10 minutes to bring up the baby's wind. After a feed, let the wind come up again.
- Change the baby again, if necessary, and settle her comfortably.
- Clear away, wash utensils thoroughly and re-sterilise.
- Throw away any unused milk, formula or expressed breast milk.

**Winding a baby**
Many old wives' tales are linked with bringing up a baby's wind.
- Air rises naturally in an upright bottle, so the baby, too, should be held upright, as this helps nature.
- Apply gentle, but firm pressure to the baby's stomach. This can be done by the 'heel' of the hand if the baby is on your lap, or by the front of the body if you are standing.
- Gently rub the baby's back.
  This should result in natural winding.

If winding does not occur within a few seconds, it means that the air has continued on down the gastric tract and will be expelled in the nappy. Babies often expel wind without any help and only become distressed with an adult's efforts.

# BOTTLE FEEDING IN DAY CARE

Many parents and carers are asked to bring their own reconstituted milks for their baby to the nursery or child-minder. If this is the practice in your nursery, check that the bottles are:
- labelled clearly with the child's name to avoid any possible confusion
- transported safely by an insulated carrier bag
- stored at the correct temperature in a clean, regularly defrosted refrigerator.

Make sure that:
- charts are kept of how much milk a baby takes at each feed and the information given at the end of the day to the parent by the baby's key worker
- babies are always fed according to any medical advice and the wishes and cultural preferences of the parents are fully respected.
- procedures for emergency milk supplies are arranged and known by all staff.

## SAFE PRACTICE

When handling milk feeds for babies in group care, hygiene procedures
must be especially rigorous.

Infection is easily transmitted from child to child. Babies with special
medical needs, and low birth-weight and pre-term babies may be particularly vulnerable (see page 49).

## IS THE BABY HAVING ENOUGH FOOD?

This is a question often asked by anxious parents and whether breast- or
bottle-fed. When deciding, consider the following:
- appearance and general behaviour
- weight gain – at first this should be 130–170 g (6–8 oz) per week for
  the first four months (breast-fed babies lose more weight after birth
  than bottle-fed babies, but this is made up by ten to fourteen days)
- alertness when awake, and falling asleep following a period of calm,
  after a feed
- warm and silky skin, firm and elastic to touch
- pink mucous membranes
- abdomen prominent after feeds, but not distended
- urine and stools passed easily without discomfort
- whether the baby moves and kicks well, cries for food (or if cold or
  insecure) but does not have prolonged crying spells
- sleeps well between feeds.

## KEY POINTS

- Bottle-fed babies' stools are putty-coloured, formed and faecal smelling.
- Breast-fed babies' stools are inoffensive, mustard-coloured and very soft.

**Weighing**
While this is an important sign of growth and sufficient food, remember
that babies will have spurts in gaining weight.

Variation in the times of the day when the baby is weighed, accuracy
of the scales, variations between scales, whether the baby is clothed or
naked, whether the baby is weighed before or after a feed, will all play a

part in differences and unexpected changes in weight. See 'Measurement of growth', page 127.

**Failure to thrive**

This is a term used to describe a baby who fails to grow and gain weight. The baby is often listless, shows some developmental delay and falls behind in her milestones – see chapter 6 'The Developing Baby'.

Sometimes the cause is medical, but more often it is due to undernutrition or mechanical feeding problems including:

- sucking difficulties, cleft lip or palate, and pre-term babies (see pages 49 and 205)
- poor absorption of the milk taken in – cow's milk intolerance
- severe illness that causes the baby to be too tired to complete a feed e.g. heart problems, whooping cough.

The cause may be inadequate child care including:

- insufficient or incorrectly made up feeds, over dilution
- difficult mother-baby relationship – poor or delayed attachment
- maternal illness or depression
- poverty.

How a baby, who appears to be failing to thrive, is managed will depend on the cause. The health visitor will be the first line of support and the baby and her family will be referred for medical assessment. Her growth and general progress will be carefully monitored and her weight checked at regular intervals on a percentile chart (see page 130). Families under stress may be offered a priority day care placement and social work support. For extra information see 'Influences on physical development', page 128, and 'Influences on intellectual, emotional and social development', page 134.

# Weaning

When a baby is no longer satisfied with breast or formula milk and is taking large quantities of fluids, weaning (the introduction of solid food) might be considered. Usually this is not wise before 4 months or later than 6 months of age. At under 4 months, a baby's digestive system is too immature to manage a wider diet.

Check that an unsettled baby isn't bored or, perhaps, wants more cuddling, rather than early solid food. There is no evidence to support the idea that early or evening solids help a baby to sleep through the night before they are really ready.

The process of weaning can be a difficult time for parents, carers and the baby. It is very important that it is seen as a gentle on-going process that the baby, parents and carers are learning together, and not as a battle-ground.

## AIMS OF WEANING

- To make the baby less nutritionally dependent on milk. For the baby at the age of 1 year, milk should provide about 40 per cent of the calorie intake. So, it still remains an important food source for the toddler.
- To provide a variety of textures, purees and dices, which will enable the baby to join in family meals, so aiding her social and intellectual development.
- To establish the acceptance of a variety of foods and flavours, setting healthy eating patterns throughout childhood.
- To introduce iron into the diet. Human and unfortified cow's milks are poor sources of this mineral. During the first three to four months an infant has sufficient iron reserves received from her mother. However after 4 months of age, these reserves become run down and foods with good iron contents are needed in the diet.
- To introduce a cup and spoon to the baby.
- To provide and extend the learning experience for the baby, by introducing wider tastes, textures, smells, temperatures, consistencies and to promote fine physical skills and help social development.

### REMEMBER!

Weaning in a day care setting should always take into account a baby's specific medical condition and reflect and complement a baby's cultural, religious and family wishes.

## MANAGING THE WEANING PROCESS

Many mothers worry about this aspect of child rearing, so it is especially important that the carer is calm and confident herself. It helps to remember that the nutritional content of early weaning is less important than the baby beginning to learn about, and to accept, different flavours and textures.

As when experiencing any learning process, the baby should not be too tired or even too hungry. She will not yet realise that the spoon will satisfy her as the bottle or breast does. Milk can be given before a feed to help settle a hungry baby. Allow plenty of time for this new experience to promote a relaxed atmosphere. The morning or early afternoon feeds are good times for introducing something new.

At first, offer a half to one teaspoon of a bland, warm savoury food. The spoon must be sterilised and the best one is plastic with a flat bowl that allows the baby to suck the contents off easily.

Ideally, first weaning foods should be gluten-free, sugar-free, salt-free, and be of a sloppy consistency, for example, baby rice, mashed potato or banana, mixed with milk.

After this initial introduction the same food can be offered the next day – too many new tastes at one time can confuse a small baby and if something upsets her it is easier to discover the cause. Refusal may not mean dislike of the food itself, but of the new experience.

After two to three days when the baby is used to the new flavour and consistency, another food can be tried. If the first chosen weaning food is a baby cereal, the next food could be a puree of fruit or vegetable, for example puree of carrots. Babies appear to enjoy the very bland nature of cereals and there is a risk of a baby becoming overweight if too much is given.

As the quantity of solid food a baby eats increases, the amounts of milk offered may be gradually reduced so that by about the fifth week of weaning one of the milk feeds can be completely replaced by solids. As the milk is reduced, the baby will be thirsty and cool boiled water in a bottle (never sweet drinks that can cause dental decay) might be needed. Diluted pure fruit juices can be offered by a spoon and cup, egg cup, or training beaker.

Babies do not need teeth to cope with more lumpy food as they use their hard back gums to manage lumps, and, from about 7 months, pieces of hard foods such as crusts, peeled apple or a carrot can be given.

## KEY POINTS

- Supervision is important in weaning to limit the dangers of choking.
- Worries over salmonella mean it is no longer recommended that eggs, the white or the yolk, are used as weaning foods and eggs should not now be part of a baby's diet until after 1 year of age.

As the baby becomes more actively involved, let her 'help' by holding a spoon as well. A baby can discover the textures and temperatures of her food with her fingers, as well as learning the co-ordination of getting food into her mouth. Babies enjoy this part of meal times. Inevitably a mess can occur, so plan for this with bibs and protection of carpets, etc. and allow her plenty of time.

## Activities

As a professional carer you will be expected to have wide knowledge to meet the needs of a variety of different families.

1  Make three weaning plans (see Table 5.2) for babies in your care. These plans should be for the first year of life and should demonstrate the changes the baby will encounter during her first year in sucking, chewing, coping with lumps, etc.

    a) One plan for a baby whose parents wish her to be a vegetarian.

    b) One plan for a baby whose parents are from an Asian Muslim family.

    c) One plan for a baby whose parents are Afro-Caribbean.

You will need to widely research the dietary and nutritional requirements of each of these plans. Visit libraries, child health clinics, the health visiting service and community dietician for information.

2  How do you think the foods might differ from the plan in Table 5.2?

3  How suitable do you consider baby foods available in the shops are for a multi-cultural society?

4  Check and comment on the nutritional content of commercial baby foods, from their labels. Take notice of any 'hidden' sugars or salt.

5  Write a report to justify your selection, based on cost, nutritional needs and the cultural and religious needs of the families.

6  Did you find it difficult to meet these needs?

## REMEMBER!

- Is the baby comfortable?
- Wash the baby's hands before and after meals
- Is the baby well-supervised?
- Do not add salt or sugar.
- Test food temperature with a separate sterilised spoon – no blowing or putting your finger in her food.
- Check for bones in fish and pips in fruit.
- Remove bib after meals.

## REMEMBER!

- Not all cultures use spoons and forks when moving babies from milk to solid foods.
- Modified milks should be continued until the baby is 1 year.

Social cleanliness – a high standard of personal and domestic hygiene – is sufficient from 9 months. It is sensible initially for the baby to have all her own bowls, mugs, etc. kept for her own use. They can, though, be washed thoroughly in a dishwasher or sink.

# Feeding problems

Table 5.3 lists the main problems associated with feeding.

**Table 5.3 Problems associated with feeding**

| Problem | Signs and symptoms | Management |
|---------|-------------------|------------|
| Allergies and intolerances | Failure to thrive, diarrhoea and vomiting, infantile eczema/general rashes, wheezing | Liaise with medical advice/dietician<br>Breast-feed if possible<br>Use cow's milk replacement, for example, soya milk |
| Constipation | Small, hard, infrequent stools | Increase fluid intake<br>Ensure feed not too concentrated<br>No laxatives or sugar in feeds<br>If weaned, increase fruit or vegetable intake<br>Check to exclude underfeeding |
| Diarrhoea | Frequent, loose watery stools | Check hygiene of food preparation<br>Give clear fluids and seek medical advice |
| Colic | Babies of (usually) less than 3 months cry and draw legs up appearing to have abdominal pain. Often showing distress at the same time of day – frequently early evening | Cause unknown<br>Feed baby<br>Check teat for size and flow, if bottle-fed<br>Monitor feeding technique<br>Reassure carer that pain is self-limiting<br>Comfort baby with movement and cuddling<br>Seek advice from health visitor |
| Overfeeding | Baby vomits/unsettled, passes large stools, sore buttocks, excessive weight gain | Seek clinic/health visitor advice<br>Check re-constitution of feeds |
| Possetting | Baby frequently vomits small amounts, but gains weight and is happy | Condition self-limiting usually solved when baby is upright and walking<br>Monitor weight |
| Underfeeding | Baby very hungry, wakes and cries; stools small and dark; poor weight gain; vomiting as a result of crying and air swallowing | Ensure feeds are correctly re-constituted<br>If breast-feeding, check technique and mother's diet<br>Increase frequency of feeds, before quantities |

# REMEMBER!

- Diarrhoea and vomiting can be serious in small babies, whatever the reason, and medical advice should be sought.
- A baby's feeding difficulties are stressful for parents and they too will need support.

## QUICK CHECK

1 Explain why goat's milk and milk bought from the milkman are unsuitable for a new baby.
2 What would be the expected weight gain of a baby in the first six months of life?
3 'Milk is a food, not a drink.' Explain what this means.
4 What would you say to a mother when explaining that breast milk is about 'supply and demand'?
5 What is colostrum, and what are its special advantages?
6 How does breast milk change during a baby's feed?
7 What advice might you offer to a mother who says her breast-feeding baby is 'not getting enough milk'?
8 How could you ensure that a baby who is bottle-fed receives clean and safe food?
9 Calculate how much feed a baby of 3.5 kg will need in 24 hours.
10 How do you know whether a baby, breast- or bottle-fed, is receiving enough food?
11 What might be the reason for an apparently healthy and happy baby losing a small amount of weight on a weekly clinic visit?
12 Describe the differences in the stools of babies being breast- and bottle-fed.
13 Why is it important that a baby does not have salt added to her food during weaning?
14 How could you help a baby have a 'total learning experience' when being weaned?
15 Explain the difference between sterilisation and social cleanliness.
   a) When would you move from one to the other?
   b) In what special conditions would you continue to sterilise bottles?

# 6 THE DEVELOPING BABY

> **This chapter covers:**
> ■ **Development**
> ■ **Meeting particular needs in day care**

## Development

Watching a baby grow and develop new skills is an exciting time. 'Signposts' or 'milestones' plot this progress and help carers and professionals to ensure that a baby is developing at the anticipated rate, for example, a baby would be expected to smile by 6 weeks and sit unaided by 8 months. Within these patterns there are wide varieties of 'normal' development, for example black babies usually have stronger muscle control at birth and their physical development remains ahead throughout the first year of life.

Often, babies appear to concentrate their skills in one specific area before moving on to another. A baby attempting to learn to crawl, for example, may 'practise' her speech less at this time. Gaining new skills, too, can often seem to be an uneven process with spurts and lulls. Babies will need the necessary stimulation to be available when they are ready to master something new.

A baby's development is monitored in the following areas:

■ *p*hysical development
■ *i*ntellectual development
■ *l*anguage development
■ *e*motional development
■ *s*ocial development.

This is easy to remember if you take the first letter of each – PILES. Alternatively, from the headings *s*ocial, *p*hysical, *i*ntellectual, *c*ognitive and *e*motional, the word SPICE is used in a similar way to trigger a total view of development.

It is likely that factors are interlinked in the way they can affect a baby. There will be 'outside' influences too: family, culture, health, opportunity, space and freedom.

- One of the most important developmental influences is the consistency and love from the baby's main carer.
- Although babies gain complex skills at different ages, the pattern is the same, for example:
    - head control develops before sitting, crawling and walking (see the diagram below)
    - cooing develops before babbling and single words.

## PHYSICAL DEVELOPMENT

Involuntary reflexes must be lost before controlled movements begin – see page 33, 'Examination of the nervous system'.

In the development of controlled physical movement, gross motor skills come first, starting from head to toe, with large movement arriving before fine movement – the eyes and lips are the exception to this rule.

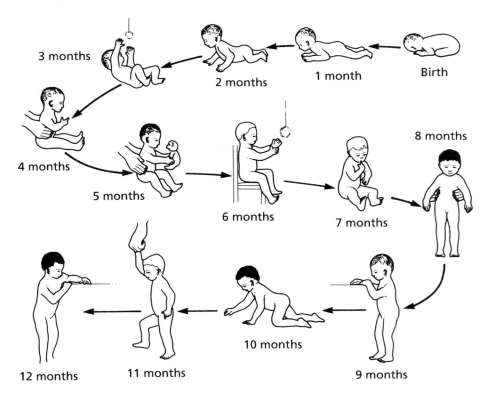

*The development of locomotion*

A baby will gain large and fine movements at the expected times depending on:

■ an undamaged nervous system – brain, nerves and nerve pathways
■ healthy bones and muscles.

See Table 6.1, on pages 146–9, for a summary of the stages of development.

### Growth

Growth – an increase in size, length and weight – is dependent upon a number of factors as shown in the diagram on page 128.

### Measurement of growth

Growth is measured and recorded on percentile charts (see page 131). Accuracy is vital: the baby should be naked and weighed on well-balanced scales, usually in the baby clinic by the health visitor. Three measurements are taken:

■ **weight** – starting with the birth weight
■ **length** – this may be difficult to record accurately in a small baby
■ **head circumference** – especially important in the first six months – a non-stretchable tape is placed around the largest part of the head.

The three measurements are each plotted on a percentile chart (see pages 130 and 131) and growth should follow a steady path on the chart. Each baby will have her own individual pattern. An average-sized baby will generally follow the 50th line (centile), a very large baby the 91st centile and a very small baby the 9th centile or less. There are variations according to a baby's ethnic background, Afro-Caribbean babies, for example, may be slightly above the 50th centile, while Asian babies may be slightly below it.

Percentile charts are an important tool in the assessment and monitoring the progress of babies who are failing to thrive.

Several sets of recordings at regular intervals are needed to give a picture of the growth pattern.

### KEY POINT

All three measurements (height, weight and head circumference) should follow the same line, and if this does not happen further investigation will be needed.

### REMEMBER!

All babies are individuals – Table 6.1 on pages 146–9 and the photos on page 129, are just a guide to steps of development.

INFLUENCES ON PHYSICAL DEVELOPMENT

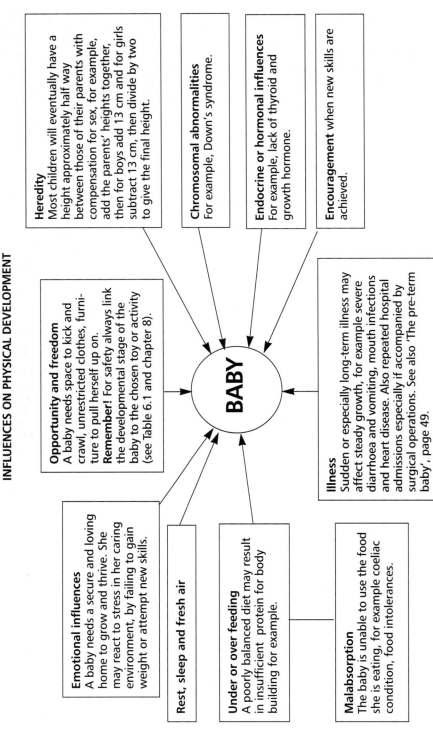

**Heredity**
Most children will eventually have a height approximately half way between those of their parents with compensation for sex, for example, add the parents' heights together, then for boys add 13 cm and for girls subtract 13 cm, then divide by two to give the final height.

**Chromosomal abnormalities**
For example, Down's syndrome.

**Endocrine or hormonal influences**
For example, lack of thyroid and growth hormone.

**Encouragement** when new skills are achieved.

**Opportunity and freedom**
A baby needs space to kick and crawl, unrestricted clothes, furniture to pull herself up on.
**Remember!** For safety always link the developmental stage of the baby to the chosen toy or activity (see Table 6.1 and chapter 8).

**BABY**

**Emotional influences**
A baby needs a secure and loving home to grow and thrive. She may react to stress in her caring environment, by failing to gain weight or attempt new skills.

**Rest, sleep and fresh air**

**Under or over feeding**
A poorly balanced diet may result in insufficient protein for body building for example.

**Malabsorption**
The baby is unable to use the food she is eating, for example coeliac condition, food intolerances.

**Illness**
Sudden or especially long-term illness may affect steady growth, for example severe diarrhoea and vomiting, mouth infections and heart disease. Also repeated hospital admissions especially if accompanied by surgical operations. See also 'The pre-term baby', page 49.

**Key point**  Refer to 'Role of carer' in Table 6.1 on pages 146–9, and 'Toys and play' on pages 179–85

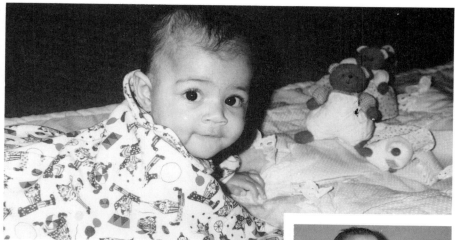

At about 5-6 months, the baby will rest on her forearms and try to get her chest off the ground

At about 8-9 months, the baby is able to crawl and explore by herself

At about 12 months, the baby is able to stand unaided

The birth measurement is an important starting point from which all other recordings are compared. A single measurement of a baby, whether height or head circumference, after six months with nothing to compare it with is meaningless. It cannot indicate any deviation or pattern. There are different charts for girls and boys, for different ages and for each of the three measurements.

### How to record weight on a percentile chart

- The ages of a baby from 0–1 year are indicated at the bottom of the chart in weeks (see 'Percentile chart for girl's weight' on page 130). Find the exact age of the baby. Place a ruler upright into the chart from that point.
- The weights are on the left-hand side of the chart in kilogrammes.

From the weight of the baby place another ruler across the chart.
- Where these two lines cross mark a X and date it at the bottom.
- Consider now where the baby's weight is against her expected curve.

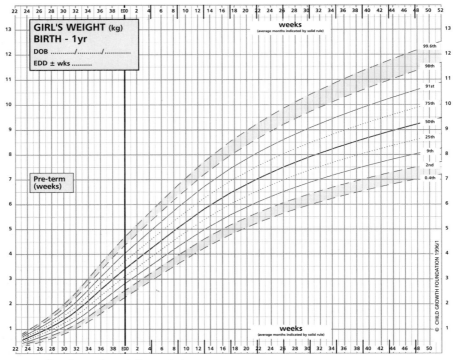

*Percentile chart for girl's weight*

## REMEMBER!

Pre-term babies are charted from their gestational age (weeks spent *in utero*) in the 'Pre-term' section of the chart so adjustments can be made for their lack of growing time. EDD = expected date of delivery.

## Activity
a) On the percentile chart for girl's weight (see above), record:
- birth weight (40 weeks gestation) 3.0 kg
- age 4 months 6.2 kg
- age 6 months 9.0 kg

b) On which line of the percentile chart was the baby at birth?

c) On which line was she at 4 months and 6 months?

What conclusions do you draw from your recordings?

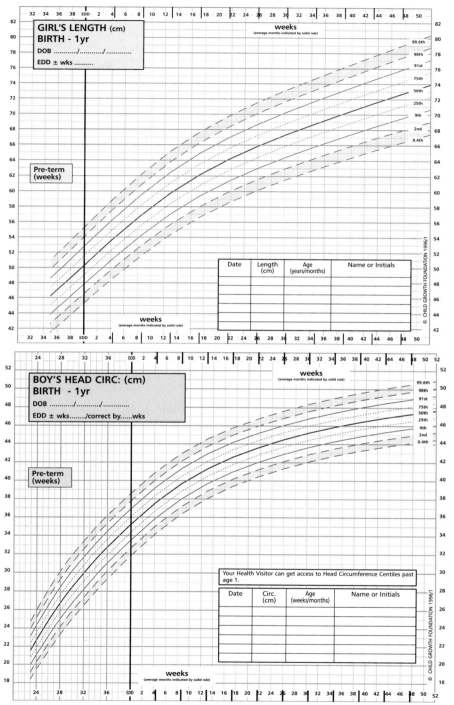

*Examples of percentile charts for girl's length and boy's head circumference*

# THE DEVELOPMENT OF VISION

Babies can see from birth, but focus at about 20 cm – the distance from the baby to her mother's face when breast-feeding.

A newborn baby will turn to a source of light. By 3 months she will watch faces and look around her, and by 4 to 6 months, vision is thought to be similar to that of adults. Babies' eyes should be working together by this age and a squint, or 'lazy eye', must be investigated. Babies appear to respond to red and blue colours more eagerly than others.

## KEY POINTS

Important signs to watch for (if late or missing they may mean developmental delay):
- no eye-to-eye contact, especially with her mother
- does not smile in response to her mother by 6 weeks
- does not follow the human face and bright objects, by 2 months
- does not reach for objects, by 6 to 12 months
- is not mobile and does not avoid obstacles by 1 year.

## REMEMBER!

Always take parents' concerns seriously.


# THE DEVELOPMENT OF HEARING

Hearing ability is difficult to test in the newborn baby. However, a baby should respond to loud noises by blinking or startling. She should turn to her mother's voice or a musical toy by 3 months of age and by 9 months she should be able to find the source of a whisper.

Hearing and the development of speech are linked and babies who are hearing-impaired will make noises similar to any other baby until 6 months of age. Babies whose hearing is impaired are unable to experiment with sounds by practising and listening to their own efforts, so by 6 months they often become silent.

## REMEMBER!

Stimulate a baby's hearing by using different tones in your voice. Make sure she can see your face when you talk to her, especially in the early months. As she begins to vocalise give her time to respond, try not to deluge her with your voice without giving her an opportunity to vocalise in response.

Important signs to watch for (if late or missing they may mean developmental delay):

Infant to 6 months
- does not blink or startle at loud noises
- does not react to household noises such as vacuum cleaner, either by stilling or appearing to listen when they start
- does not smile responsively by 6 weeks – if the baby was born full term.

6 to 12 months
- does not turn to prime carer's voice across the room
- does not babble in conversation – vocalising decreases
- does not respond to own name.

## REMEMBER!

Always take parents' concerns seriously.

## LANGUAGE, INTELLECTUAL, SOCIAL AND EMOTIONAL DEVELOPMENT

These areas of development are all linked making it difficult to separate individual areas – they all influence a range of developmental areas (see page 134, 'Influences on intellectual, emotional and social development', and Table 6.1, 'A summary of the stages of development', pages 146–9).

## THE DEVELOPMENT OF LANGUAGE

Even before birth, a baby is beginning to recognise her mother's voice and immediately after birth will be soothed by this sound. A newborn's cry is a reflex action to a variety of factors such as distress at the sound of sudden noises or hunger and, although this remains so for several weeks, by 3 to 6 weeks her cry will be used in specific situations, for example to show hunger or thirst.

At 8 weeks she can detect human voices and responds differently to human and non-human forms. A baby will begin to coo and use vowels. Carers can help by changing their tone and the volume of their voices when talking to babies.

# INFLUENCES ON INTELLECTUAL, EMOTIONAL AND SOCIAL DEVELOPMENT

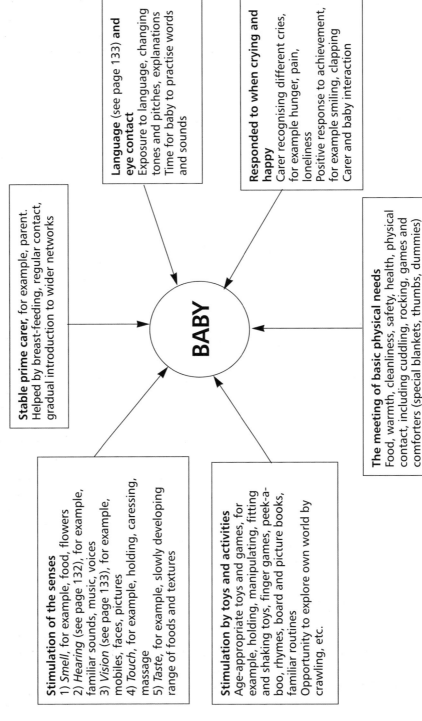

**Stable prime carer,** for example, parent. Helped by breast-feeding, regular contact, gradual introduction to wider networks

**Language** (see page 133) **and eye contact**
Exposure to language, changing tones and pitches, explanations
Time for baby to practise words and sounds

**Responded to when crying and happy**
Carer recognising different cries, for example hunger, pain, loneliness
Positive response to achievement, for example smiling, clapping
Carer and baby interaction

**The meeting of basic physical needs**
Food, warmth, cleanliness, safety, health, physical contact, including cuddling, rocking, games and comforters (special blankets, thumbs, dummies)

**Stimulation of the senses**
1) *Smell*, for example, food, flowers
2) *Hearing* (see page 132), for example, familiar sounds, music, voices
3) *Vision* (see page 133), for example, mobiles, faces, pictures
4) *Touch*, for example, holding, caressing, massage
5) *Taste*, for example, slowly developing range of foods and textures

**Stimulation by toys and activities**
Age-appropriate toys and games, for example, holding, manipulating, fitting and shaking toys, finger games, peek-a-boo, rhymes, board and picture books, familiar routines
Opportunity to explore own world by crawling, etc.

BABY

By 12 weeks the baby will recognise specific sounds, such as a spoon in a cup, and by 4 to 6 months will be using the consonants p, b, m, g, k, f, v, r and l. She will enjoy babbling and listening to the sounds she makes. She will use her sounds to attract attention and will enjoy the responses she gains.

## KEY POINT

Always use everyday care procedures to promote her language. Changing nappies, feeding and bathing are all times when interaction can take place. Tell the baby what you are doing, describe your activity, and reinforce with demonstration – for example talk about and show her the clean nappy; tell her about her toes and tickle them to help her make the link.

By 6 to 7 months the language is becoming even more complicated and the baby is able to change from babbling to cooing, repeating sounds and altering loudness and length. She will enjoy the carer pointing out objects, games of throwing and the beginning of turn-taking. Always give her time to practise her sounds and respond by smiles and praise.

At 8 to 9 months the baby will mimic sounds and in another month repeat and copy sounds (known as echolalia) although they will not be understood. She will learn to point to objects and will be able to respond to simple requests, such as 'Give me the dolly'. She is beginning to link words to meanings so reinforce this by repeating her words back to her.

Finally by 12 months the baby begins to have true speech and can use one or two words with meaning, but understands many more. She will enjoy simple books, with single known objects, and will repeat words spoken to her. The carer can help her develop her language skills by involving the baby in all her care, for example by describing her clothes as she is dressed or explaining what she is having for her new weaning food. It is important to allow the baby time to both listen to the human voice and to practise her own developing skills.

## KEY POINT

A baby will enjoy simple picture books with you for short periods, at quite a young age. Choose books that show familiar objects to gain and keep her interest, represent her own culture to her. Early pleasurable introduction to books can set good habits for childhood.

- Singing, too, promotes language development – introduce songs and rhymes from different cultures.
- A dummy is a comfort object useful in helping a distressed baby to sleep. However, always remove it when the baby is awake to allow her to practise her speech and develop lip and tongue control.

## KEY POINTS

Important signs to watch for (if late or missing they may mean developmental delay):

- mother or carers are not communicating with the child
- severe feeding difficulties
- at 3–6 months baby is silent most of the time even when alone
- limited response to noise, minimal eye contact
- by 6–9 months does not respond to play. Has not babbled or has stopped babbling
- shows lack of rhythm and intonation when babbling
- no consistent response to noise
- by 9–12 months not trying to communicate by vocalising or pointing
- not responding to single words and simple commands
- not using a wide range of different sounds and intonations.

## REMEMBER!

- Always take parents' concerns seriously.
- Language progress is dependent on effective hearing.

## Activity 1

Develop your own personal resource file for songs, finger and action rhymes:

- as you learn a new one write it down, with a description if necessary, for future use
- ask your placement colleagues, peers and friends to help you extend your repertoire
- especially valuable will be the songs and rhymes known by friends and colleagues from different parts of Britain and other countries.

## SOCIAL, EMOTIONAL AND INTELLECTUAL DEVELOPMENT

A baby needs to develop a special bond with her primary care givers – this will give her the security and the confidence to learn, to explore and begin to happily accept new situations and people.

The quality of the relationships a baby makes with her main care givers is seen as very important in the development of her mental health. These relationships are called 'attachments'. Unless a baby makes these attachments it is thought that she will later find difficulty in making and maintaining relationships and this will lead to harmful effects on other developmental areas. Secure attachments give a baby stability and help her develop trust and confidence to explore, develop and learn.

### KEY POINT

It was thought that the only primary attachment a baby made was with her mother, but research now tells us that multiple attachments can take place. However, the quality of these attachments remains vital.

A newborn baby is a social being, responding to a variety of stimulation and needing the company of other humans from birth. She learns quickly to recognise her mother's voice, the way her body moves and even her taste and smell.

The world is an exciting and fascinating place to her even if, initially, she understands little of it.

A baby shows her need to socialise with humans as early as 2–3 months by:

- attempting to imitate facial gestures – even by crying if her mother is distressed or angry
- maintaining eye contact, and increasingly letting her eyes follow her carer around the room
- moving her head to seek a social source
- smiling responsively, from 4 to 6 weeks

- crying
- waving – often somewhat random movements
- making noises of contentment from early weeks, and by cooing and gurgling from 3 months.

The skill and sensitivity with which a carer interprets such pre-verbal signs and responds to them is important in giving a baby confidence and security to try again. A baby who is ignored or handled insensitively is less likely to extend these social and intellectual skills easily. She needs reinforcement and reward for her efforts by you taking notice of her.

A baby in her first three months will respond randomly to a variety of other people, even strangers, but as she develops she shows that she has learnt to recognise specifically just a few special adults and by 6 months is anxious when separated from these known people.

If her mother or prime carer is near she will cry at strangers and reach out to be held by her familiar adult. This fear may not be so obvious if the situation is unfamiliar, the mother is absent and there are several strangers present.

## KEY POINTS

- A baby is said to be attached when she recognises her prime carer and shows anxiety when separated – usually between 6 and 9 months.
- This important sign tells us that the baby has learnt to discriminate and recognise people as separate individuals. Now she can begin to develop permanent meaningful relationships from her safe secure base – the attached adult.

In her early months when an object or person is out of sight the baby thinks they are gone forever. However, towards the end of her first year object-permanence develops. A baby has learnt to understand that objects, although hidden and out of sight, still exist. This is an important intellectual concept for a baby as she now realises that even though her mother may be not immediately visible, for example in another room, she is still near.

### Activity
Visit a parent/carer and toddler group and ask to observe the children at play. If possible watch a baby of about nine months who is crawling.
How confident is he to leave his known adult?
How many times does he return to the adult during a session?
Record any non-verbal signs of anxiety – eyes following, pulling at adults' clothing.

How much vocalisation is taking place?
How much reinforcement is the adult giving the child – what happens if the baby does not earn a response from the adult?

### Meeting emotional, intellectual and social needs

A baby needs opportunities to extend her experiences but she also can only achieve this successfully from a secure base. It is important that a baby is not flooded with large numbers of different people handling her, confusing her and possibly making her anxious. She will respond best by initially getting to know a few people well – her parents, grandparents, sibling and her child care worker.

Respond to the signals she gives:

- smile back at her
- repeat her developing sounds
- name objects you use with her and repeat the words (labelling)
- respond to any distress, by attempting to understand the reason – feeding her, changing her napkin, giving her company and stimulation – and letting her see you while you work (see page 85, 'Why babies cry')
- meet her physical needs, ensure she is warm, dry, comfortable and safe
- check that toys and activities chosen meet her changing developmental needs (see Table 6.1, pages 146–9, 'Role of carer' and pages 179–86, 'Toys and play').

## KEY POINTS

Important signs to watch for (if late or missing they may mean developmental delay):

- not smiling responsively with mother by 6 weeks
- lack of response by prime carers in responding to the baby's needs
- excessive crying
- lethargic and uninterested
- the baby has not shown stranger-anxiety by 6–9 months
- head-banging and rocking at 9–12 months
- failure to thrive (see page 117).

## REMEMBER!

Always take parents' concerns seriously.

## Activity 1

### A long-term baby study

The best way to learn how a baby develops is to observe. Find a friend or relative who will share their baby's progress with you and whom you can easily visit at home. It is best if they are in the final stages of pregnancy and you can discuss the coming birth with them.

■ Plan to record the progress of the baby fortnightly for the first 6 months of life and monthly until 1 year of age.

■ At the first interview record birth weight, length, head circumference and Apgar score (see page 28), as well as anything particular to your chosen baby, for example, the type of delivery and feeding method.

■ At each visit record what the baby is doing.
  – If she is sleeping, describe posture, noises, colour, etc.
  – Try to visit during a bathing session and at a feeding time.
  – As the baby grows, comment on her interaction with mother and siblings, if any.
  – Record types of toys used and whether you feel they were effective at arousing and keeping the baby's interest.
  – Record any periods of illness and the outcome.
  – Try to visit during a clinic development session with the mother and her baby, for example her 6–8 week check or 8-month check. Record what happens and how the baby responds.
  – Ask how the baby's hearing and vision are assessed and observe when the baby begins to locate sounds, follow moving objects and focus.
  – Observe the developing relationships the baby makes within the family.
  – Chart the development of language – the sounds he or she makes. Perhaps record them on tape.

Accuracy is important and it is necessary to record exactly what you see and then compare the progress with Table 6.1 (see pages 146–9).

**Remember:** always share your observations with the mother. Remember you are learning about the development of her baby not judging her child care.

## Activity 2

Whether you are working in a family home or in a day care setting, part of your professional duty as a child care worker is to plan, and deliver, a total learning experience for the babies in your care. After you have carried out your plan you should review how effective you were and record any changes you would make in future schemes.

Remember: your responsibility is to understand:

- the developmental stage and needs of individual babies and how this development can be safely stimulated
- the equipment and materials needed and how to use and present them imaginatively and creatively
- the importance of play as an integral part of a baby's day and how informal routines can be made into fun, learning experiences
- that everyday activities all have potential for learning or promoting aspects of development, especially physical and social development.

Plan a day's play experience for:

a) a baby of 6 months, who is not yet mobile

and

b) a baby of 9 months who is competent in his crawling and keen to practise this skill.

Your plan should stimulate all the baby's developing skills including:

- opportunities to stimulate hand-eye co-ordination and gross motor skills
- the emerging development of language
- intellectual development
- social development
- tactile experiences.

Use chapter 8 for play suggestions that complement a specific developmental stage.

**Remember:** always take care to promote emerging skills – the next developmental stage. This is especially important in a baby who may be delayed in one developmental area (see chapter 9).

# Meeting particular needs in day care

A baby who is cared for away from the home for considerable periods of time will require skilled and sensitive care. Effective liaison and strong links between day care staff and parents will ensure the baby has the best environment in which to develop.

Caring for a baby away from her home means you must have a full understanding of the baby's particular needs. You must know how she expresses these needs by interpreting the signs she gives you.

## KEY POINT

You will also need the maturity and confidence to work closely with parents and create an environment where both parents' and workers' roles are known and valued.

## KEY WORKERS

A key worker is a designated staff member who cares fully for one or more certain babies every session that the babies attend and for the length of their stay in the nursery.

The responsibilities include:

- Planning the baby's day to include her learning programme.
- Monitoring and recording the baby's development.
- Liaising with the baby's parents.
- Meeting all the baby's needs during her stay including always undertaking all personal physical care such as nappy changing, greeting and settling the baby on arrival in the morning, comforting any distress, bottle feeding and returning the baby to the care of her parents at the end of the day, with a report.

A key worker makes separation for a baby from her prime carer easier and promotes healthy emotional development, at a possibly vulnerable time for a baby. The success of a key worker system will, to some extent, depend on all staff appreciating its theory in the promotion of healthy emotional development. Staff understanding of the system will help ensure each baby's needs are responded to by her own particular worker. In a busy environment it may be easier for any member of staff to change an uncomfortable baby, rather than wait for her designated worker to be available but this undermines the system and may confuse and unsettle the baby.

Even when the key worker system is not in practice a nominated member of staff should take especial responsibility for individual babies admitted. Continuity is important for the baby to settle and for her needs to be met. It helps the parents to have a familiar worker in whom they have confidence to talk about their baby and her day, while they are absent. Often this will be an informal discussion, but, increasingly nurseries are using diaries to record the baby's day. These usually include information on feeding, sleeping, play, any minor skin problems or ailments, comments on developmental milestones achieved and records of any distress the baby has had and how it was resolved. This sharing of information promotes a partnership between parents and nursery, helping not only during the crucial initial few weeks of separation but also in setting positive patterns for liaison for parent, baby and nursery staff.

## KEY POINTS

- Always remember, however close you may come, as a worker, to a baby in your care, her stay with you will inevitably be temporary and her parents are her prime carers.
- Nursery policy will need to address issues such as procedures to cover absence of a key worker during illness and holidays.
- Parents must always feel confident their baby will have her physical, social, emotional and intellectual needs met and their cultural and religious wishes respected when she is cared for by substitute carers.
- Always allow sufficient time for sharing information with parents – if you seem rushed they may not feel confident to ask questions or share any worries they may have.

## DAY CARE ADMISSION

Before a day care admission parents need written information about the nursery, its procedures and policies. Many nurseries also offer a home visit, usually by the worker who will be responsible for the baby, for him or her to meet the baby in a known environment and allow the parents to ask questions and share any anxieties. This is a valuable opportunity to explain the role and importance of the key worker in the baby's emotional development, and so addressing the possibility of the worker being seen as a rival to the baby's affections. Such a visit can act as a valuable bridge between home and nursery.

### Information required from parents

Gaining a full picture of a baby and her individual needs means it is necessary, in addition to such basic information as name and address, for parents to complete an admission questionnaire.

Information required from parents should include:
- Baby's feeding, sleeping and settling routines.
- Any special medical requirements, including known allergies.
- Cultural and religious needs.
- Addresses and telephone numbers of: GP, parents' home and work and emergency contact numbers for back-up adult contact.
- The names of the adults permitted to collect the baby at the end of a session.

Signed forms for permission to take the baby out of the nursery on outings and for emergency medical treatment are often obtained at this time.

- This information is personal and must be treated confidentially.
- The information must always be current and relevant.

### Information to be given to the parents

Information to be given to the parents should include:

- Background information about the nursery and its ethos, including its Equal Opportunity Policy and any religious or special cultural affiliation.
- How the nursery is organised – including staff ratio, whether the key worker system operates, if so the name and contact number of the baby's worker.
- How children of specific ages are cared for – whether into age rooms or family units – and the qualifications of the staff. How the baby's progress will be monitored and how parents will be kept informed.
- What parents are required to bring. This may include all the baby's formula milks, even weaning foods and nappies and clothing changes and whether these must be labelled. If the nursery provides weaning foods, how the parents should tell the nursery about special medical or cultural needs.
- The policy of personal possessions for the baby – can a beloved teddy be brought in and what happens if it is mislaid?
- How a baby's day is structured, the learning opportunities provided, and how parents are kept informed about progress.
- The length of the nursery day, the fees and when they must be paid. What happens during holidays and how much notice must be given if a baby leaves.
- What happens if a baby is ill.
- How parental involvement is encouraged.
- The complaints procedures.

## REMEMBER!

Effective communication is a two-way process – always find time to listen to questions and worries as well as asking for information. Nurseries are busy, sometimes noisy places, check that you can provide a quiet, private place for information exchange.

How you communicate is important, so think about the tone and volume of your voice, your facial expression when listening and how you use eye contact and gestures. Think, too, about actual words you use – technical terms may be unfamiliar to some parents and others may not have English as a first language.

## SETTLING IN

Day care is usually organised so babies are kept together and separate from the older children, for at least part of the day. This allows the environment to be specific for this younger age range, and for a higher staff ratio to exist, usually one adult to three babies.

Unlike preparing an older child it is difficult to prepare a baby for separation from her mother so the settling in period is especially important. The time needed for each baby may vary, but a likely timetable for full-time day care is suggested below.

The age at which babies are admitted to day care will vary, sometimes as young as 3 months but more often at 6 months. The younger the baby the easier the separation will appear, as such a young child will not have learnt to discriminate between known and unknown adults. However, she will be distressed by being flooded by a variety of different carers handling her and attempting to understand her needs.

**Likely timetable for settling baby into full-time day care**

| Day | First week – mornings only | Second week |
|---|---|---|
| 1 | Two hour morning. Baby attends with her parent who works with the key worker | Four hour morning. Parent settles baby then leaves. Baby has bottles given and nappies changed by key worker |
| 2 | Two hour morning. As above | Five hour day. Parent settles baby then leaves. Key worker feeds, changes and settles baby for rest |
| 3 | Two hour morning. As above | Full six hour day. Parent settles baby in morning, leaves and returns to collect baby before other children leave |
| 4 | Three hour morning. Parent leaves baby in nursery for an hour then returns to feed her. Key worker changes her nappies | Full six hour day. As above |
| 5 | Four hour morning. Parent leaves baby for two hours. Baby is fed and changed by key worker | Full day, as above, but baby is collected with the other babies |

**Note**   This suggested plan is for a baby who is being bottle-fed, additional adjustments would be needed for a baby who is being breast-fed.

Remember a baby of 6 to 9 months will show separation anxiety – this is part of normal social and emotional development.

---

**Activity**

Contact your local Social Services Department.

a) Find out the staff ratio for babies in their nurseries – compare it to their recommended ratios for children aged 3 to 5 years. Why do you think there is a difference?

b) Does the Department operate a key worker system in their nurseries – why do you think this represents one way of meeting a baby's developing emotional needs?

c) What is the youngest age that babies are admitted to day nurseries?

d) What facilities are provided for parents in the nurseries?

e) Does the Department have a common policy for settling new babies into the nurseries?

---

**Table 6.1 A summary of the stages of development**

| Age | Development | Role of carer |
|---|---|---|
| Birth<br><br>4 weeks | **Physical development**<br>Will fix on faces and objects<br>Eyes follow bright moving objects. Lies supine with head to one side. Drops objects in hands, which are clenched. Reacts to loud sounds<br><br>**Language and social**<br>Throaty noises<br>Interested in faces<br><br>**Learning and emotional**<br>Reflex response, but becomes distressed to discomfort, for example cold.<br>Enjoys feeding and cuddling<br>Great need to suck<br>Quietens when picked up | Talk to baby, change tone, describe events<br>Baby enjoys mobiles and faces (visual range 8–10 in)<br>Hold, touch, fondle<br>Music, gentle movement<br>Use baby's name<br>Introduce to household noises and different rooms<br>Change position of cot<br>Use brightly coloured clothing and linen<br>Hold firmly, talk and sing to baby when feeding<br>Expect no set routine<br>Feed on demand |
| 8 weeks<br>Posterior fontanelle closed | **Physical development**<br>Controlled movement beginning to replace reflex responses. Turns from side to back. Begins to lift head briefly from prone position. Shows eye co-ordination to lights and objects, squinting less obvious. 'Listens' to bell and 'stills' | Use wind chimes and mobiles the baby will see moving from room movement or own activity. Use bright colours in pictures placed in cot<br>Place in supporting infant chair to watch adult's activity, or carry around. Use light rattles, let baby kick without nappies<br>Expose to different textures. Massage, and stroke limbs for example when bathing |

**Table 6.1 A summary of the stages of development** *continued*

| Age | Development | Role of carer |
|-----|-------------|---------------|
| | **Language and social**<br>Begins to respond to adult's voice. Looks for sounds. Begins to coo and squeal with pleasure. Smiles in response to adult. Cries now begin to indicate type of distress | Talk and smile with baby, sing – allow time to respond |
| | **Learning and emotional**<br>Begins to recognise familiar face, more interested in own world. Enjoys sucking | Talk to baby when feeding, hold close<br><br>First immunisation (see page 152) |
| **12 weeks**<br>Primitive reflexes now disappearing | **Physical development**<br>Baby rests on forearms when prone. Basic crawling movements, may get chest off surface. Shows preference for sleeping position. Holds objects in hands brings to mouth, cannot release. Watches hands. Head control improved | |
| | **Social and language**<br>Generally more sociable, smiles readily, babbles and coos. Stops when handled or sees known adult, turns head to follow. Enjoys playing when feeding. Stays awake longer | Encourage smiling, laughing<br>Place on changing mat on floor |
| | **Learning and emotional**<br>Recognises familiar faces and objects. Shows interest in own world and is aware of changes. Enjoys repetition of activities. Continues to enjoy sucking. Routine more settled, especially in sleeping | Continue to widen sound simulation<br>Take on outings well-protected<br>Develop rattle use, stimulate baby to attempt to reach for it and follow with eyes<br><br>Immunisations programme continues |
| **16 weeks**<br>Stepping and rooting reflexes go<br>4-5 months: birth-weight doubled | **Physical development**<br>Eyes focus on small objects. Holds head up when pulled to sitting. Beginning to reach for objects. Turns to familiar sounds. Sits with support. Rolls from back to side. Grasps with both hands. Everything taken to mouth | Show baby mirror and encourage play<br>Give soft squeezy toys of different colours and textures<br>Water play in bath<br>Continue with rattles<br>Pat-a-cake, peek-a-boo games<br>Repeat sounds at varying levels<br>Introduce more gentle 'rough and tumble' |

**Table 6.1 A summary of the stages of development** *continued*

| Age | Development | Role of carer |
|-----|-------------|---------------|
| | **Social and language**<br>Laughs and chuckles socially. Recognises mother, seeks and enjoys attention. Begins to respond to 'no'. Enjoys being propped up | Offer simple picture books, name items<br>**Safety**<br>Watch for toys too small, with loose fittings that might be swallowed |
| | **Learning and emotional**<br>Enjoys attention, becomes bored when alone. Recognises bottle. More interested in mother, shows trust and security. Sleeps through the night, has defined nap time | Completion of primary Triple and HIB immunisations |
| **26 weeks (7 months)** 7–9 months: eye to eye contact Palmar grasp replaced by inferior pincer at 6–7 months Two lower central and lateral incisors appear | **Physical development**<br>Sits alone for a few seconds. Bounces and weight bears when held in the standing position. Transfers objects, and places in mouth with one hand. Enjoys playing with feet. Bangs objects together, rolls over well. Possibly moving by rolling, or squirming | Provide toys to bang, stack and nest (round ones easier)<br>Saucepans, spoons, 'safe' household equipment<br>Continue with peek-a-boo, bye-bye, pat-a-cake<br>Provide opportunities for developing large movement, space, firm furniture |
| | **Social and language**<br>Recognises strangers. Squeals, laughs aloud. Double syllable babbling, starts to say Ma, Da. Talks in 'own' language in conversation with adults | Provide music and movement, simple repetitive rhymes<br>Give pouring and squeezy toys to play with in bath<br>Continue with picture books<br>Extend outings to include animals, for example feeding the ducks<br>Imitate animal sounds |
| | **Learning and emotional**<br>Looks for objects that are out of sight. Curious, handles and looks at objects closely. Knows where sounds originate. Pulls toy with a string. Drops and picks up toys. Continues to 'mouth' and bite. Shows fear of strangers and is upset when mother leaves<br>Continues to explore food. Enjoys sitting in high chair | Let baby copy you – building bricks, etc.<br>Allow time, no hurry<br>Offer cup and extra spoon at mealtimes<br>Strap into high chair, give finger foods but allow to 'play' with own food<br><br>**Safety**<br>Look at wider environment, for example plugs, electrical equipment baby can reach with increasing mobility<br>Encourage achievement |

**Table 6.1 A summary of the stages of development** *continued*

| Age | Development | Role of carer |
|---|---|---|
| **40 weeks (10 months)** Four upper incisors – 9 months | **Physical development** Sits unaided, can regain balance. Manipulates objects with hands. Unwraps objects. Pulls to stand in cot, creeps. Uses finger and thumb to hold objects | Allow baby to make choices in play material<br>Offer balls, dolls, pull and push toys, sand and water trays (well-supervised), building blocks, music |
| | **Social and language** Claps hands when asked. Knows own name, copies facial gestures and sounds. Smiles at self in mirror. Aware of environment, will play alone for considerable periods. Indicates likes and dislikes at meal and bed-times | Teach names of body parts<br>Continue to extend experiences including types of foods, textures and tastes |
| | **Learning and emotional** Begins to imitate. More interested in books. Wishes to be more independent in dressing, feeding, etc. Enjoys achievement | Encourage baby to return affection |
| **12 months** 10–14 months: Anterior fontanelle closing Birth-weight triples Two lower lateral incisors, and four first molars appear by 14 months | **Physical development** Cruises around furniture, begins to stand alone, able to manage stairs. Begins to walk unaided. Turns pages in book. Builds tower of two blocks. Puts ball in box. May use spoon. Can release objects voluntarily. Shows preferred hand. Attempts to throw. Regular bowel movements | Motion toys<br>Enjoys carrying and moving toys<br>Continue with sand, water and music<br>Continue to extend all activities and language |
| | **Social and language** Uses jargon, points to indicate wishes. Enjoys give and take games. Enjoys music, being noticed, having achievement clapped – will repeat for actions | Allow child-directed play in a safe environment |
| | **Learning and emotional** Shows fear, anger, affection, jealousy, anxiety and sympathy. Determined in approach to play, increased concentration and attention. Some idea of space time and effects of own actions | Encourage self-feeding, use of cup and spoon<br>Manage unacceptable behaviour with firm quiet 'no', distract if possible<br>Give and encourage return of affection |

## QUICK CHECK

1 List five major factors that can affect growth.
2 Describe the sounds that a baby of 6 months makes.
3 Explain how you, the carer, can best help the language development of a baby of 9 months.
4 a) What are the charts used to assess growth called?
   b) What three measurements are usually taken?
5 One racial group has advanced physical development – which one?
6 When would you expect a baby's first responsive smile?
7 List six major areas that are vital for social and emotional development in a baby.
8 You suspect that a baby of 7 months is hearing-impaired. Give your reasons.
9 Define 'age appropriate' toys, and say why they are important.
10 There is one overwhelmingly important factor in the total development of a baby – what is it?

# 7 THE ILL BABY

**This chapter covers:**
- **Infection and immunity**
- **Signs and symptoms of the ill baby**
- **Care of the ill baby**
- **Common ailments in babies**

# Infection and immunity

A baby is particularly vulnerable to infection. Before birth she lived in a sterile world, with the placenta and amniotic fluid protecting her from many harmful organisms. In the first 6 months after birth, she will have some protection passed on from her mother through the placenta, called passive immunity and, if breast-fed, from colostrum. However, her own ability to fight infection is immature and when the protection from her mother lessens she will become vulnerable to a wide range of diseases.

## WHAT CAUSES INFECTION?

Germs are all around us living on our skin and in our noses, throats and digestive tracts (stomachs and bowels). Usually they do not cause any harm. However, they can, under certain circumstances, cause outbreaks of common infectious diseases, and sometimes more serious illness.

There are three main types of organism and they are treated in different ways:
- bacteria
- viruses
- fungi.

### Bacteria
These are tiny and many can cause a wide variety of different infections. Others are totally harmless. Harmless bacteria live perfectly happily in our bodies, for example in our throats. Some live in the large bowel and help our bodies to break down food. When these bacteria move to a different part of the body, they may cause infection, though not always.

If harmful bacteria invade the body, the natural defence mechanism produces antibodies which attempt to fight and destroy the bacteria and are ready for future use should the specific bacteria attack the body again. This is called immunity. Bacteria can also be treated with some antibiotic medicines, although not all antibiotics are effective against all bacteria and occasionally the body becomes resistant to certain types of antibiotics.

**Viruses**

These are much smaller than bacteria and enter the cells of the body, changing the way they work. Antibiotics are not effective against them. However, the body can produce its own antibodies against some viruses and prevention through immunisation can be effective against others.

**Fungi**

These can occasionally cause infections, for example nappy rash through thrush (candida albicans). Treatment is by anti-fungal medicine. Antibiotics are not usually effective.

### KEY POINT

It is important for a doctor to know what is causing an infection so that the correct treatment can be given. Clues are provided by the signs and symptoms of the illness and by the taking of samples (for example blood or faeces) or swabs for laboratory investigation.

In addition to modern medicine, nature itself helps protect the small baby:

- the skin acts as a barrier to infection
- the stomach contents are acid and help to neutralise harmful bacteria that have been taken in accidentally
- tears are antiseptic.

As the baby grows, she develops her own active immunity. When her body comes into contact with specific organisms her system begins to recognise them and produces antibodies to fight them. In the process of producing these antibodies she may be ill with an infection that organism is causing, for example measles. However, when recovered, she is able to reproduce these antibodies if she encounters the specific organism again. One antibody is effective against only one specific organism and not a variety.

## IMMUNISATION

We can reproduce active immunity artificially through programmes of immunisation. At 2, 3 and 4 months of age babies are offered a course of immunisation of two doses each month, so for complete protection this will mean the baby will have six injections. The primary course protects against:

- diphtheria, pertussis (whooping cough) and tetanus – the triple immunisation, known as DPT
- poliomyelitis (polio), given by mouth as drops on the tongue
- haemophilus influenzae type B (HIB).
  Artificial immunity is made by giving the baby either a very weakened dose of the specific disease, or by giving her some weakened toxins (poisons) which the disease produces. By giving these mild doses over a period of three months her body is gradually able to build up her ability to produce and reproduce antibodies.

  The HIB immunisation is different from the triple course of injections in that it stimulates the baby to produce antibodies against a bacterium that can cause several illnesses – the most serious being a form of meningitis. It is also effective against forms of blood poisoning (septicaemia), infections in the bones and joints (osteomyelitis) and several other chest conditions.
- Measles, mumps and rubella (MMR) protection is offered to babies between 12 and 15 months in one injection. This is a live vaccine – containing viruses that have been modified so that they no longer cause symptoms, or only a very mild form of the illness, in children.

## KEY POINT

To ensure that the baby is able to produce these new antibodies safely, it is important that she is fit and well at the time of her injections.

If a baby has any reactions to one of her immunisations, if, for example she runs a fever or has a swollen painful lump at the site of a previous injection, then the doctor may postpone further injections. In addition, if there is a history of fits in the baby's family she would not be given the pertussis injections.

A record of the immunisations a baby has received is given to the parent. With so many occurring in early childhood it is easy to forget which immunisations a baby has received.

Table 7.1 on pages 154–5 summarises the main infectious diseases.

## Activity
You are employed as a nanny in a home with a new baby.
a) What professional reasons and arguments might you put forward to the parents as to the benefits of immunisation?
b) Research homeopathic immunisation practices.
c) Discuss the advantages and disadvantages of conventional medicine versus the homeopathic approach with your fellow students.

**Table 7.1** Infectious diseases

| Disease | Cause | Spread | Incubation period | Signs and symptoms | Rash or specific sign | Treatment | Complications |
|---|---|---|---|---|---|---|---|
| Diphtheria | Diphtherus bacillus | Direct contact | 1–6 days | Sore throat, slight temperature, prostration, pallor | Grey membrane in throat | Rest, fluids diphtheria antitoxin, antibiotics, diphtheria toxoid | Paralysis of muscles, throat obstruction, heart involvement |
| Scarlet fever | Haemolytic streptococcus | Direct contact; droplets; indirect contact | 2–5 days | Sudden onset of fever, sore throat, vomiting, 'strawberry' tongue, flushed cheeks, pallor around mouth | *1st or 2nd day:* Bright red rash with raised pinpoint spots behind ears, spreading to trunk, arms and legs, skin peels after 7 days | Rest, fluids, observation for complications, antibiotics | Middle ear infection, kidney infection, heart involvement |
| Tonsillitis | Streptococcus or staphylococci | Direct infection; droplets | | Very sore throat, white patches (pus) on tonsils, swollen glands in neck, aches and pains in back and limbs | No rash | Rest, fluids, medical aid – antibiotics | Middle ear infection |
| Measles | Virus | Direct contact; especially droplets | 10–15 days | Misery, high temperature, heavy cold with discharging nose and eyes, later harsh cough, conjunctivitis | *2nd day:* Koplik's spots – white spots inside cheek *4th day:* dusky red, patchy rash starts behind ears and along hairline, spreads to face, trunk and limbs | Rest, fluids, sponging to reduce temperature, dark room if photophobia | Eye infection, chest infection, middle ear infection, encephalitis |

*continued*

| Disease | Cause | Spread | Incubation period | Signs and symptoms | Rash or specific sign | Treatment | Complications |
|---|---|---|---|---|---|---|---|
| Poliomyelitis | Virus | Direct contact: especially droplets; indirect contact: food or water | 5–14 days | Sudden onset of headache, stiffness of neck and back followed by paralysis | No rash | Rest, medical supervision | Permanent paralysis |
| Rubella (German measles) | Virus | Direct contact; droplets | 14–21 days | Slight cold, sore throat, slight fever, enlarged glands behind ears, pains in small joints | *1st day:* Rash-like sweat rash, bright pink; starts at roots of hair; may last 2-24 hours | Rest if necessary (mild disease) | None unless patient is pregnant woman; virus can seriously affect foetus in first 12 weeks of pregnancy |
| Chicken pox | Virus | Direct contact; droplets | 7–21 days 14–21 days | Slight fever, irritating rash | *1st day:* Red spots with white raised centre on trunk and limbs, mostly very irritating | Rest, fluids, lactocalamine or solution of bicarb. of soda on spots | Impetigo |
| Pertussis (Whooping cough) | Haemophilus pertussis | Direct contact; droplets | 10–14 days | Heavy cold with fever followed by cough | *2 weeks:* Spasmodic cough followed by characteristic cough and vomiting | Rest, supporting during bouts of coughing, feed after bout of coughing | Bronchitis, bronco-pneumonia, haemorrhage due to strain of coughing, prolapse of rectum, mouth ulcers, debility, encephalitis |
| Mumps | Virus | Direct contact | 7–28 days | Fever, headache, swelling of jaw in front of ears, difficulty opening mouth | No rash | Rest, bland fluids through straw | Orchitis (inflammation of testicles), debility, encephalitis (rare) |
| Infective hepatitis (Jaundice) | Virus | Direct contact especially droplets; indirect contact: food or water | 23–25 days | Gradual onset of headache, loss of appetite, nausea, urine dark, faeces pale putty colour | *5th-7th day* Yellow skin, itching, also yellow conjunctiva | Fluids with glucose, fat-free diet, isolation | Liver damage, meningitis |

Source: J. Brain and M.D. Martin, *Child Care and Health for Nursery Nurses*, 3rd edition (Stanley Thornes, 1990)

## WHAT CAUSES INFECTIONS TO SPREAD?

Infections are spread:
- by droplets through the air – coughing, sneezing
- by direct contact – skin to skin, dirty hands
- via the digestive tract – poor personal hygiene, infected food
- by animals – they can carry diseases unharmful to them, but potentially dangerous to humans, for example blindness from toxocara.

### REMEMBER!

The spread of infections is aided by warmth, moisture, food and time.

### SAFE PRACTICE

**Preventing the spread of infections**
- Careful personal hygiene is important in limiting the spread of infection and hands must, therefore, always be washed carefully before handling babies, following nappy changing and before feeding.
- Clean clothing, perhaps helped by the use of aprons, care with covering the mouth when coughing and sneezing, and the maintenance of your own health will all help limit the spread of infection. It is best to discourage visitors who have coughs and colds from contact with very young babies.
- A high standard of cleanliness is important with careful heat regulation by a fixed wall thermometer – temperature maintained at 20°C (68°F). Good air circulation helps to dilute germs and prevent them breeding.
- Disposal of soiled nappies, dirty clothing and dressings into covered bins and sealed bags is necessary. Vomit, excreta and used tissues are effectively managed by flushing down the lavatory (see page 61).

### KEY POINT

Poor hand washing is thought to be one of the major causes of cross infection. The increased use of gloves means that some child care workers do not understand that hands must still be washed before and after using gloves.

# Signs and symptoms of the ill baby

It is an enormous responsibility to care for a baby who is unwell and unable to say where a pain is, or how she feels. The carer who knows a baby well will notice worrying signs and changes in behaviour early (see the diagram on page 157). This is important as babies under 6 months can rapidly become worse and what might, at first, seem a minor illness

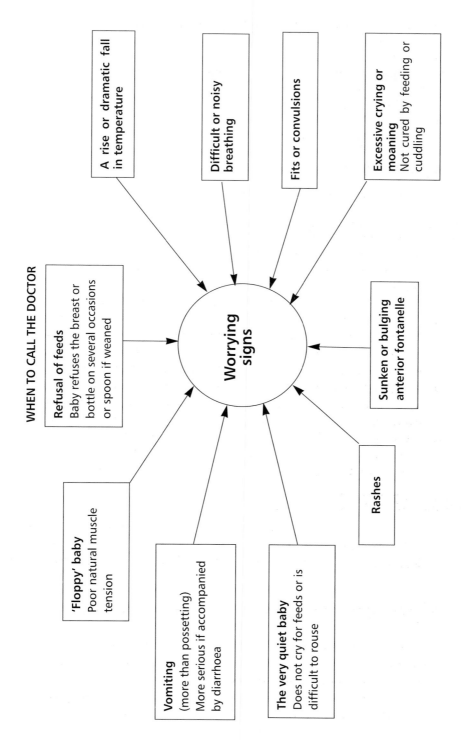

WHEN TO CALL THE DOCTOR

A rise or dramatic fall in temperature

Difficult or noisy breathing

Fits or convulsions

Excessive crying or moaning
Not cured by feeding or cuddling

Refusal of feeds
Baby refuses the breast or bottle on several occasions or spoon if weaned

Worrying signs

Sunken or bulging anterior fontanelle

'Floppy' baby
Poor natural muscle tension

Rashes

Vomiting
(more than possetting)
More serious if accompanied by diarrhoea

The very quiet baby
Does not cry for feeds or is difficult to rouse

could quickly become potentially life-threatening. Generally, the younger the baby, the wiser it is to be cautious.

Telephone numbers to keep to hand in case of an emergency:
- the baby's parents
- the baby's doctor
- the health visitor
- the hospital.

## RAISED TEMPERATURE AND FEVER

The body shows that it is under attack by producing a temperature, raising its body heat, and increasing its heart and breathing rates. Pulse and respiratory rates in a baby are difficult to measure, both are naturally quite rapid and have a wide range of 'normal'.
- Newborn: pulse 70–170; respirations 30–50 per minute.
- 12 months: pulse 80–160; respirations 26–40 per minute.

These rates tells us how hard the lungs and heart are working. It is helpful to practise pulse-taking before attempting it on an ill baby.

### Activity

Practise counting a friend's pulse and respiration.

a) First take the pulse rate – where an artery crosses a bone, use your first and second finger, not your thumb as you have your own pulse there. Try at the base of the thumb in the depression above the wrist, or at the temple.

Using a watch with a second hand, count the beats for a full minute.

Was the beat regular, strong, easy to feel?

b) 'Pretend' to continue taking the pulse, but instead watch the rise and fall of the chest and count each complete breath (in-and-out is one respiration).

Ask your friend if he or she was aware you were counting their breathing and if it affected their ability to act 'normally'.

Remember it is very difficult to obtain accurate measurements of respiratory rates if an adult or older child is aware that they are being recorded.

Temperature recording is probably the most helpful sign of the progress of illness in a baby.

It is thought by some that the raising of the blood heat (or temperature) is an attempt by the body to destroy harmful substances. The heat, or temperature control, mechanism is in the brain and this can appear out of control when a baby is suffering an illness. Small children produce very high temperatures quickly.

Often observation will tell if a baby is feverish, by change in colour (usually increased), but occasionally by pallor. The easiest place to check if a fever is present is to feel the baby's forehead. This is the area of greatest heat loss (the hands are frequently cold even in an ill baby). For a more accurate assessment a thermometer can be used. This is a thin glass rod containing a column of mercury that is sensitive to heat. Measurements are shown on the column (see below). Thermometers are now measured in Centigrade, although occasionally they indicate Fahrenheit as well.

| F = Fahrenheit | C = Centigrade | |
| --- | --- | --- |
| 95 | 35.0 | |
| 96 | 35.6 | |
| 97 | 36.1 | Baby may be |
| 98 | 36.7 | underheating |
| 98.4 | 37 | |
| | | -Normal |
| 99 | 37.2 | |
| 100 | 37.8 | |
| 101 | 38.3 | |
| 102 | 38.9 | Baby overheating |
| 103 | 39.4 | |
| 104 | 40 | |
| 105 | 40.6 | |
| 106 | 41.1 | |

*Measurements on a clinical thermometer*

**How to take a temperature**
The mercury column should be shaken down to well below normal and then placed between two bare skin surfaces. The armpit is ideal. The length of time it should be left there, before accurate recordings are ready, will vary according to the make of the thermometer, but usually one minute is sufficient. It is unsafe for babies to have their temperature taken in the mouth.

**Other methods of measuring temperature**
Increasingly, especially in hospitals, a tympanic thermometer is being used.

The eardrum which is close to the brain, is one of most accurate areas for measuring a baby's temperature. The temperature here can now be measured quickly and safely with an instant tympanic thermometer. This instrument does not contain glass or mercury. A funnel-like attachment is placed gently in the outer ear and the temperature is recorded within a few seconds – a buzzer sounds when the reading is accurate. A disposable filter is attached to the funnel and is changed after use, reducing the chances of cross infection. This method is especially valuable with restless babies as it is quick, safe and very accurate.

Special temperature strips are also available. These are placed across the forehead and are easier to read. However, they are less accurate.

**KEY POINT**

Whatever method is chosen, the result and time when taken, need to be written down.

# Care of the ill baby

## MANAGEMENT OF FEVER

A fever in a baby can occur quickly and in most babies there are no ill effects. However, in a few babies over 6 months a fever may trigger a fit or febrile convulsion. In such a case, the baby becomes stiff, twitches and rolls her eyes, she may go blue and foam at the mouth, and she loses consciousness. It is a frightening experience although not dangerous. Babies who fit with high temperatures usually grow out of them with no harmful effects. It does not mean the baby has epilepsy.

There is little that can be done once a fit is underway except to ensure the baby does not harm herself if she thrashes about. It is dangerous to force anything between the gums to stop the tongue being bitten. Medical advice should be sought. Follow the advice for prevention.

**Prevention of fits**
- Keep the room airy and cool.
- Remove the clothes and gently sponge with tepid, not cold, water. Allow to dry naturally – this will bring down the fever.
- Do not allow her to get too cold and shiver – this will force the temperature up again.
- If medication has previously been prescribed by the doctor, make sure that it is given.
- Observe and supervise the baby carefully.

REMEMBER! If the baby fits she will later need additional comfort.

If you feel the baby is running a high temperature, it is dangerous to wrap her up to keep her warm – this will increase the risk of convulsions.

## ROUTINE CARE OF AN ILL BABY

An unwell baby will feel frightened and will show her distress by changes in behaviour and an unsettled routine. She may regress in social development, for example an ill baby who previously settled well into day care may cling and cry when separated from her parents. At this time it is especially important her care is undertaken by known adults – her parents or key worker.

If her parents are unable to be present during the day they must be kept fully informed of her progress. Always take time to listen to any anxieties; remember the parents know the child best.

While unwell let the baby show how she wishes to be cared for – she may feel the need for extra physical attention, cuddling, etc., or she may appear more settled resting in her own cot and allowing her body to fight the infection. You might find her fractious, wakeful and disrupted in her normal sleeping patterns. Extra supervision will be needed in case her condition worsens, or she vomits unexpectedly. However, it is comforting to remember that babies have the ability to recover quickly from minor illness and usually return to their normal routines speedily.

*An unwell baby may need extra physical attention*

While unwell, a baby will require her usual skin care and although a bath is not essential, it will make her more comfortable if she is topped and tailed, and placed in clean clothes and bedding. Do not force solids onto a previously weaned baby. All she will need is extra fluids, perhaps cooled, boiled water, with the addition of part of the strained juice of a freshly squeezed orange. Babies who have finished breast-feeding often feel the need for this comfort again, if unwell.

Try to keep visitors to a minimum and attempt to stop siblings, or other children wanting to hold and play with her when she is unwell.

If the baby attends day care, the parents may be asked to keep their baby at home until she is recovered. This is to reduce the risk of infection to other children, but also she will feel more comfortable in her own environment.

## KEY POINTS

- Anything unusual in the way of vomit or nappy contents will need to be shown to a doctor.
- Always observe carefully an ill baby.
- Record and chart her temperature if requested.
- Keep parents fully informed of any changes.

Medicines that are prescribed for a baby will almost always be in liquid form and must be given carefully and accurately, according to instructions. Never put medicines into a bottle of milk, it may make the baby refuse a normal feed. Luckily most medication for babies is pleasant tasting and when offered from a spoon is taken readily.

## SAFE PRACTICE

### Medicine
- How often should it be given?
- Should I wake the baby if she is asleep?
- Do I have the correct-sized spoon, sterilised?
- For how long a period should I give the medicine?
- What should I do if the baby is better before the medicine is finished?
- At what temperature should the medicine be stored?
- Should the medicine be given before or after a feed?
- Am I sure the correct baby's name is on the label?
- What are the side effects that I need to look for?
- Can I be certain that other children in the house cannot take the medicine?
- What should I do with any medicine left over?

If you cannot answer all the above questions, seek further advice.

# Common ailments in babies

Table 7.2 summarises the common ailments.

**Table 7.2  Summary of ailments of babies**

| Condition, causes, signs and symptoms | Role of the carer |
|---|---|
| **Colds and snuffles**<br>Viral infection of the lining of the nose, clear discharge is more serious in very tiny babies due to difficulty in mouth breathing – no cure | Small frequent feeds, possible use of nasal drops from doctor to clear nose<br>Gently wipe any discharge from outer nose |
| **Coughs**<br>Viral infections, occasionally bacterial. Often associated with colds. Mucus drains down the back of the throat, cough more at night, may accompany other illnesses, measles for example<br>**Note** A cough is a reflex response to remove irritation from the lung, so a cough might indicate an inhaled object | Keep air moist, for example use steam kettles. Only give prescribed medicines<br>Supervise especially if accompanied by vomiting<br>Seek further advice if baby fails to improve, or if there is any 'noisy' breathing |
| **More serious chest infections:**<br>*Bronchitis*<br>Infection of both upper and lower air passages. Temperature, runny nose, 'rattly' cough, worse at night. Can be viral or bacterial. | As for treatment of cough<br>Observe to ensure condition does not worsen<br>Give prescribed medicine |
| *Bronchiolitis*<br>Initially a viral illness affecting all the tiny air passages in the lungs. More common in winter. Cold-like symptoms. 'Fluid' or 'bubbly' cough. Possible breathing difficulties shown by blueness of lips, etc. | Seek medical help<br>Watch for any breathing difficulties<br>Usually admitted to hospital for oxygen treatment and fluids by tube into stomach or into a vein |

**Table 7.2 Summary of ailments of babies** *continued*

| Condition, causes, signs and symptoms | Role of the carer |
|---|---|
| *Pneumonia*<br>Bacterial or viral infection of the lower air passages, the alveoli, resulting in part of the lung being 'blocked' by infection, reducing air capacity of lung. High temperature, fast noisy or 'grunting' breathing. May or may not have cough | Can be treated at home with antibiotics or more usually in hospital<br>Small, frequent feeds, delay weaning, increase fluids<br>Monitor carefully<br>Follow medical advice |
| *Croup*<br>Babies over 6 months can develop noisy breathing from a spasm of the larynx (upper air passages in the throat). The larynx swells with the spasm and can become narrow, causing a noise as the air tries to get through. Worse at night, baby may become blue as she get less air | Babies usually admitted to hospital, some less serious can be helped by keeping atmosphere steamy with kettles<br>In emergency use bathroom with hot taps turned on<br>Comfort babies, as frightening |
| **Otitis media**<br>Infection of the middle ear. Common in babies as their Eustachian tube (leading from the back of the throat to the middle ear) is short and babies spend more time lying down. Increased risk of food and infection travelling into ear. Baby ill with fever, vomiting, diarrhoea, screaming and crying with pain, possibly pulling at ear if older | Give prescribed antibiotics<br>Comfort baby<br>Ensure follow-up visit to doctor to monitor healing and hearing<br>No swimming with head under water<br>**Note** Commonly confused with 'glue ear' which is less acute and less likely to occur in a 0–1-year-old baby |
| **Vomiting**<br>This is a sign that the stomach is not tolerating food. This may be a minor problem or more serious if associated with diarrhoea (see below) | The amounts the baby is vomiting will have to be judged, as well as colour and how the vomiting occurred. Is the baby still hungry and fit and well? Usually if vomiting alone, it may be a temporary feeding problem (see page 123)<br>The baby's stomach will need to be 'rested' by giving fluids only, for 24 hours – either prescribed solutions or boiled water. Medical advice should be sought |
| **Diarrhoea**<br>Frequent loose stools<br>If accompanied by vomiting, this may indicate an infection and lead to dehydration (loss of fluid) which may be serious, and is indicated by a sunken fontanelle, dry skin and very little urine | Seek medical advice and follow treatment plan<br>Monitor hygiene practice<br>Ensure soiled nappies are disposed of safely<br>Monitor cleanliness of feeding equipment<br>Delay any weaning plans |

**Table 7.2 Summary of ailments of babies** *continued*

| Condition, causes, signs and symptoms | Role of the carer |
|---|---|
| **Colic**<br>Affects many babies. Specific periods of the day, often early evening, baby cries for some time. Pulls legs up onto stomach and appears in pain. Difficult to comfort. Baby thrives in all other respects | No single cure<br>Generally settles by 3 to 4 months<br>Comfort baby by rocking and cuddling<br>Non-nutritive sucking often helps, for example dummy |
| **Pyloric stenosis**<br>Often, but not always, affects male babies of around 6 weeks. Hungry baby, feeds eagerly, but immediately returns feeds, effortlessly and with force – up to several metres in distance. The muscle at the exit of the stomach is thickened and does not allow food to pass. The baby can quickly dehydrate | Report symptoms quickly, with description of type of vomiting<br>Baby admitted to hospital for simple operation to enlarge ring of muscle |
| **Intestinal obstructions**<br>Any condition that stops fluids from going through the digestive tract is potentially very serious. The baby will vomit, may fail to pass urine, and have only a few stools, which are hard and small. The causes may be several, but the main one in a tiny baby is when the gut telescopes inside itself, then swells and causes an obstruction (intussusception) | Observe and report signs and symptoms quickly<br>Baby will be admitted to hospital |
| **Meningitis**<br>A severe infection of the membranes that cover the brain and spinal cord. Causes can be many. The baby may have a fever and be reluctant to feed. The most severe, caused by the meningococcal bacteria, is also accompanied by a rash. This rash does not disappear when a glass is pressed over it. Bacterial meningitis has a dramatic and sudden onset. The condition can be fatal and cause long-term brain damage, hearing and visual problems. If the meningitis is viral in origin the baby may only be ill with flu-like symptoms and will rapidly recover | Good knowledge of the baby will aid early recognition in an unwell fractious child<br>Seek urgent medical help<br>The condition worsens rapidly |

**Table 7.2 Summary of ailments of babies** *continued*

| Condition, causes, signs and symptoms | Role of the carer |
|---|---|
| **Sudden infant death (Cot death syndrome)**<br>A previously fit and well baby is found dead in her cot, with no obvious cause. Usually between 1 week and 2 years of age, the peak time is 3 months. No single cause but certain factors increase risk:<br>a) sleeping prone<br>b) overheating.<br>Also increased risks: winter months, male babies, multiple births, untreated minor ailments, over-concentrated artificial feeds, smoky environments | Ensure baby sleeps supine<br>Do not overheat, use blankets not duvets, no cot bumpers<br>Always place in the *feet to foot* position – baby placed on back with feet at the foot of the cot with the bedclothes over this lower part *only*, so the baby cannot slip under the clothes during the night<br>Never cover baby's head while sleeping<br>Use a firm, flat, mattress that can be kept clean easily<br>Keep thermometer fixed on nursery wall – temperature constant 20°C (68°F) day and night<br>Promote breast-feeding<br>Avoid smoking and smoky atmospheres<br>Promote pre-conceptual health education<br>Support families who suffer such a tragedy<br>Always seek medical advice if the baby is unwell<br>Liaise with health professionals |
| **Neonatal cold injury/Hypothermia**<br>Baby has a false appearance of health with a good colour. Lethargic, runny nose, swollen hands and feet, cold to touch. Usually only happens in early months, pre-term babies more at risk | Prevention important, careful child care practice<br>Keep thermometer fixed on nursery wall – constant 20°C (68°F)<br>Observation<br>If occurs, raise temperature by wrapping baby loosely in warmed blankets and by cuddling<br>*No* direct heat – raise temperature slowly<br>Offer glucose (sugar) feeds<br>Seek medical help urgently |

## *QUICK* CHECK

1 Name the three organisms that can cause illness.
2 How does nature help a baby protect herself?
3 Explain how soiled dressings, vomit, excreta, etc. should be disposed of.
4 List ten worrying signs showing a baby may be unwell and that a doctor is needed.

5 A baby is running a fever. What initially should be done?
6 Explain why diarrhoea and vomiting are so worrying in a tiny baby.
7 Name two factors that are thought to increase the risk of Sudden Infant Death syndrome and describe the recommended sleeping position.
8 Describe how you can limit 'cross infection' in the nursery.
9 What is artificial active immunity?
10 Describe how a baby's behaviour and development might temporarily change with illness.

# 8 EQUIPMENT, TOYS AND PLAY

> **This chapter covers:**
> - **Planning for a new baby**
> - **Basic equipment**
> - **Clothing**
> - **Nappies**
> - **Toys and play**

## Planning for a new baby

There are many things to consider when selecting and choosing equipment for a new baby. This is a time of great importance in the life of any family, and the advice and skill of a child care worker can help in making these decisions. Families are under considerable pressure from many sources and advertising can be very persuasive in attempting to convince new parents of the need to purchase widely and extravagantly.

Consideration of the following points will help to decide priorities.

- **Lifestyle** Choices will be different for a family living in, for example, a flat in a high-rise block where the prime carers will be working full-time and taking the baby to and from day dare. For a family employing a nanny, with a house that has plenty of space and a large, safe garden different equipment may be required.
- **Space** How much is there and of what type? For example, will the baby go straight into her own room? Or will she share with another sibling or with the carer?
- **Cost** How much money can be spent? Are there tight budgetary constraints?
- **First or subsequent baby?** If this is not the first baby, is some equipment still safe, available and suitable?
- **Safety** What safety marks should be looked for? What specific safety equipment should be bought? What if the equipment is secondhand?
- **Flexibility** How long will various pieces of equipment last? Will the baby outgrow them before good use has been made of them? Will the equipment receive enough use to justify buying it?
- **Appearance and comfort** Is the equipment pleasant to look at? Will it visually stimulate the baby? Will it please the carer?

- **Durability** Will the chosen equipment stand heavy use from baby and toddler, and perhaps further children? Is it well-built?
- **Maintenance** Will the equipment be easy to look after? Are replacement parts available?

All of these areas will need to be discussed before buying.

# Basic equipment

A baby needs somewhere to:
- sleep
- bath
- feed
- play
- move around.

## SLEEPING

**The early months**

Tiny babies feel more secure in a close environment and so carrycots or prams are often chosen for the first sleeping place. Cradles and Moses baskets have a short life and are unsuited to a baby weighing much over 4 kg.

Whatever is chosen, it must be sturdy and strong, with washable fabric for ease of cleaning, and matt interiors to limit glare. Prams and carrycots come with a mattress supplied, which will need fitted, waterproof covers. Fitted sheets are preferable and must fully cover the mattress. These, together with blankets should be, light, easily washable and made of natural fibres – cotton or wool and cotton mixture.

For outings, a waterproof top covering is needed.

### SAFE PRACTICE

- Duvets, cot bumpers and baby nests are no longer recommended as they are thought to be linked to overheating and possible cot death (see page 166).
- For safety reasons no pillow is required.

Carrycot stands and transporters are available and can be purchased for the specific model chosen.

The handles of any carrycot transporter must be firmly fixed with the height adjusted to suit the adult who will be using it. If the body of the carrycot is moved by hand, without the transporter, the total weight is usually up to 6 kg.

Many carrycots are insubstantial when a baby is able to sit unsupported and is more active, so care should be taken when buying to check the recommended weight limit for the baby.

### From about 6 months – daytime

When carers are out with the baby a flexible transport system is needed to meet both the developing needs of the baby and the mobility and lifestyle of the carer. There are many new and changing products on the market from which to choose. Many products are now multi-functional, meeting a variety of parents' requirements in one piece of equipment. Parents often no longer need to buy a separate pushchair and pram.

Babies over 6 months can often sleep comfortably for short periods in a semi-reclining position – for example when out shopping.

Transporter combinations now include a conventional type pram or carrycot suitable for a newborn that can adapt as a pushchair for an older baby. They are multi-purpose types of equipment:

- the position can easily be swapped for the baby to face forwards or backwards, as the mother decides
- the 'body' can to be removed so the baby can continue to sleep, without being disturbed
- all come with waterproof coverings, a fixed safety harness and trays for carrying shopping.

Conventional strollers, pushchairs and prams are still widely available.

Twins and children of different ages can use pushchairs where they are kept side by side or one in front of the other.

**KEY POINTS**

- Always check that the weight of the baby matches the recommended weight for the transporter or pushchair you are using.
- Do not look only for the use-by age as the stages of a baby's development will vary.

**SAFE PRACTICE**

Whatever type of pushchair or pram is chosen it is important to remember the following.

- Check the brakes are easy to use and test them regularly.
- Any additional seats for toddlers must not be placed on the less substantial bodies of carrycots.

- If used on pram bodies, toddler seats need to be far back on the body of the pram to prevent toppling over, or used only as recommended by the manufacturer.
- Shopping, if hung from the handles of a carrycot or pushchair, can cause imbalance. It is safer to place shopping on a special tray under the pram and over the wheels.
- Ensure that permanent, fixed harnesses are attached when any pushchair or pram is purchased and are always used when a baby is sitting.
- Cat nets should be used on prams for babies sleeping in gardens, or in homes with a pet cat.

**Cots for longer sleeping periods and night time**

These will be the main sleeping place for the baby, allowing room for growth and movement. They need to be able to withstand several years of hard wear.

### SAFE PRACTICE

**Cots**
- Bars must not be more than 76 mm (3 in) apart.
- Safety catches must be childproof.
- Mattresses must fit snugly with no gaps.
- If it has been repainted, check lead-free paint was used.
- If wooden, check for splinters.
- Check the cot's stability.
- Do not allow toddlers to climb in and out of cots.

### KEY POINTS

- Even if the cot is secondhand it is advisable to buy a new mattress.
- In day care, to limit cross infection, a baby must have her own cot and bedding, clearly identified, for her use alone.

### SAFE PRACTICE

- Change bed clothing frequently (see 'Care of clothing', page 178).
- Keep the cot clean and wash it regularly.

## BATHING

Most new born babies prefer the smaller environment and security of a specific baby bath. This is usually plastic, coloured and easily transported for cleaning and filling. It can be used with the fixed base purchased for the carrycot, or placed in the adult bath or even moved to a warm sitting room.

Some carers prefer to use the adult bath, especially if there is an older sibling and the baby can either be bathed before her sibling, or with them when older. In this case a non-slip mat is a good investment. Some method for checking the warmth of the bathroom is necessary and possibly an additional fixed wall-heater may be needed.

Babies, wherever they are bathed, will need their own towels, face cloths and mild, perfume free toiletries.

Two buckets, with lids, are a sensible buy, one for soiled baby clothes and the other for soiled nappies. See chapter 3 for more information on bath time management and equipment.

## FEEDING

Whether the mother decides to breast- or bottle-feed her baby, certain equipment should be ready for the newborn. Bottles, teats, lids, sterilising equipment are essential not only for giving feeds, if required, but also for cool boiled water to quench thirst and possibly for expressed breast milk too.

If the baby is to be bottle-fed remember that a newborn baby may require ten or more feeds in 24 hours and the number of bottles needs to be bought with this in mind.

If the mother is going to breast-feed her baby, she will have purchased support bras and breast pads to make feeding more convenient. The baby's carer will need a comfortable chair in which to feed, cuddle and talk to the baby (see page 104).

As the baby grows and begins to sit she will need a chair for her mealtimes. Various combinations are available from reclining adjustable low chairs to the more conventional high chairs suitable for a baby who sits securely at about 9 months.

Whatever is chosen, check:
- there is an attached integral harness in good condition – safety standard BS 6684
- the chair can be easily cleaned, with not too many nooks and crannies for food to become lodged
- there is a large, firmly fixed tray attached
- the seating is comfortable
- the chair conforms to the BS 5799 safety standard.

## PLAYING

Initially the most important play for a newborn will be the interaction she has with her parents. Play is discussed in detail on pages 179–86.

## MOVING AROUND

Babies need to be transported safely and that includes their first journey home from hospital. A baby should never be nursed on an adult's lap on the front seat of a car, but must be restrained in a sturdy carrycot with fixed straps on the back seat of the car. Ensure the restraining straps meets the BSI standards for safety and are fitted by someone with special knowledge. If fitted or adjusted wrongly they can be useless in protecting the baby.

When the excess weight limit is reached for babies using a carrycot, or when the carers decide, the safest method of car transportation is thought to be in a baby seat fixed to a rear passenger seat, using the adult safety belt to anchor around it. Again expert advice should be sought about fitting. Baby car seats that can be removed from the car and used to carry the baby about are also available for babies up to 10 kg.

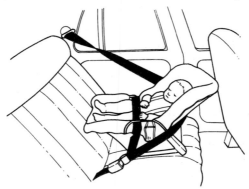

*Secure the baby on the back seat in a recommended baby carrier*

### KEY POINT

Cars with airbags must never have child seats fitted in the front passenger seat.

Baby slings, on the front of the mother's body, are often used in the first few weeks after birth. Their advantage is the close body contact they bring between mother and baby. When the baby begins to gain weight, however, they can put considerable strain on the carrier. Safety must be borne in mind when choosing what activities to undertake when carrying a baby in a sling.

In some cultures babies are carried well into the second year of life on their mothers' backs, giving them a good view of the world, close contact with their mothers and allowing freedom for the mothers to continue their own work. The weight is in a more natural position, causing less back strain.

**Pushchair or pram?**

Parents will have to decide their own priorities when deciding whether to buy a pram or a pushchair or a combination model. Table 8.1 (below) summarises the main points.

Table 8.1 **The advantages and disadvantages of prams, pushchairs and combination models**

| Advantages | Disadvantages |
|---|---|
| *Pram* | |
| Good protection against wind and rain | Expensive |
| Suitable for sleeping comfortably for long periods | Too large for use on public transport |
| Can be used with a toddler seat | Heavy |
| Shopping can be placed underneath | Will need a cat net |
| Often used for several babies, especially in day care | Bulky for storage |
| | |
| *Pushchair* | |
| Baby or toddler has good vision | Baby vulnerable to dogs, etc. |
| Easy to handle. Lighter | Possibly less comfortable |
| Suitable for use on public transport | Not suitable for sleeping for long periods or for a baby under 6 months |
| Less expensive than pram | Only for one child at a time |
| Easier storage | Limited opportunity to carry shopping or extra equipment |
| | |
| *New combination models* | |
| Highly flexible from birth to toddler stage | Expensive |
| Can provide a comfortable, supportive sleeping area | Often not really suitable for use with a toddler seat |
| Baby can be placed face forwards, or face towards carer | Sometimes limited area for carrying shopping |
| Models have different features so parents can choose to suit their own requirements | |

## Activity

Visit a local baby shop or department store and research the variety and types of prams, pushchairs and combination models on sale.

1 Compare prices.

2 What special features do you see that you would consider helpful for:
   a) busy parents
   b) meeting the changing needs of a growing and developing baby?
3 What current developments in safety factors are now included on this type of equipment?
4 Do the cat nets on sale fit snugly all types of prams and pushchairs in which a baby may be left to sleep?

## SAFE PRACTICE

### Prams, pushchairs and combination models
Check the following.
- Are the brakes out of reach of small fingers?
- Do the brakes on pushchairs and combination models with swivel rear wheels work simultaneously?
- Are there two locking devices: one manual, one automatic?

Consider, too, forward planning in safety for the adventurous, mobile baby, such as fixed fireguards, stair gates and highchairs with fixed harnesses.

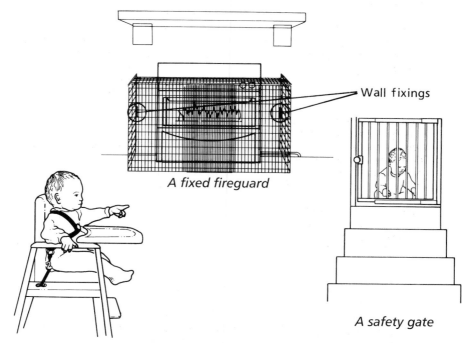

Wall fixings

*A fixed fireguard*

*A safety gate*

*A high chair with fixed harness*

### Other important safety equipment

Other important safety equipment needed:

- non-slip bath mats
- baby monitors
- fixed fireguards and radiator guards
- safety harness for high chairs, pushchairs and prams
- socket covers
- safety glass or safety film for glass for windows and doors
- safety locks and catches for doors, windows, cupboards, fridges and toilets
- corner protectors for tables and low units
- anti-slam door stops
- smoke alarms (always check regularly).

## REMEMBER!

The biggest cause of death of children under 5 years in the home is by fire.

### Activity

Visit a selection of shops. Decide which large pieces of equipment you think are the minimum a new baby will need. Consider: price; quality; safety; comfort/appearance/design; size.

a) Choose one set of equipment suitable for a baby coming to a small home, such as a one-bedroom flat.

b) Choose another set for a home that is spacious and well-equipped with labour-saving devices.

c) Justify your choices to the parents or carers, presenting a list of the costs and the reasons for your decisions.

d) How would you care for and store such expensive equipment?

e) How often would it needed washing, servicing, and brake and stability checks?

f) What advice might you give to help prolong the life of such equipment?

# Clothing

A 'layette' is the first set of clothes bought for a newborn baby. Many baby shops supply complete layettes.

When buying clothes for the newborn remember:

- A newborn will require many changes of clothing in the first months after birth and most babies dislike the necessary dressing and undressing. So clothes for the newborn should be easy to take on and off, not be fussy with bows and buttons and allow for ease of movement.

■ Initially, a baby will need vests, sleeping suits (babygros), jackets, booties, bonnets and gloves depending on the season.

■ If jackets, mittens or bootees are made by relatives check that the tension is firm and does not have a lacy pattern with holes in which small fingers could be trapped.

■ Clothing must be safe for the baby as she grows and becomes mobile.

■ Comfort is best achieved from natural fabrics – cotton or cotton and wool mixtures – that are absorbent,

■ Flame retardant qualities are important – look at the symbols in the clothing – and remember although nylon does not flare it can melt and cause serious burns.

■ The baby will also need protective clothing when she is in her carrycot or pram.

■ Until a baby is walking unaided and sturdily, outside shoes are not necessary. Often, shoes are not essential until the second year of life.

■ Any socks, gloves, or stretch suits or baby slippers should be non-restrictive to the small and delicate bones of the baby's foot.

■ As the baby becomes more mobile it is essential that continual reviews are taken that clothing is of the correct size to allow her to develop skills in crawling and walking safely and with freedom.

## REMEMBER!

Anticipate changes in weather – light layers that trap the air are better insulators than one thick jacket. You can also manage her temperature more easily, preventing under- and overheating.

## DAY CARE

Parents may be asked to bring in changes of clothing for their baby. Check these are suitable and discuss any problems with the parents, for example a dress may inhibit a baby about to attempt to crawl; clothing may be too warm – often, too, the temperature in a day care setting is higher than the home environment and clothing may need to be lighter. Special warmer clothing may be needed for an outing. Any clothing will need to be labelled with the name of the baby.

## REMEMBER!

Respect cultural wishes over specific clothing items.

# CARE OF CLOTHING

The skin of a baby in her first year of life is sensitive and this should be remembered when laundering her clothes and bed linen. They will require above average washing to keep her fresh and comfortable from such things as leakage from her nappy and minor vomiting after feeds. So remember to:

- use non-biological – enzyme free – soap based, washing powders
- always rinse clothing thoroughly
- limit the use of fabric conditioner to the minimum. If a conditioner is used make sure it is perfume free
- soften clothing and bed linen effectively and more gently by tumble drying or line drying in the open air
- check you understand the terms 'flame retardant' and 'flame resistant'
- learn the different laundry symbols on washing powders and compare them with the laundry instructions on the baby's clothes.

## Activities

You need to be aware of the wide range and choices of first clothing available for a baby – the layette.

1  Devise, list and cost a layette.
2  Write a short introduction about a layette and then visit two different shops in your area – preferably one more 'expensive' and one chain-store outlet.
3  Cost the items included in your lists.
4  Compare the total cost of the two shops with comments on quality. Say which layette you consider gave value for money.
5  Write an account in 300 to 400 words of the importance of comfort, safety and design factors of a layette. Remember to include types of materials, ease of laundry and the simplicity of dressing and undressing, including the types of fasteners.
6  Describe how you would launder wool and wool-mixture clothes.
7  Discuss the layout of the two shops you visited and comment on how easy it would be for a parent with a pushchair and toddler to visit.

## REMEMBER!

Choose colours to stimulate the vision and interest of a newborn baby.

# Nappies

Carers will have to decide whether to choose to use the conventional terry towelling nappies, which also require plastic pants, or the modern disposable nappies. Whichever choice is made, remember that a very young baby will need changing many times in a 24-hour period and a considerable amount of money will be spent on this aspect of baby care.

A useful and flexible additional piece of equipment is a baby changing mat – a padded waterproof mat that allows a carer to have a clean and readily available changing surface.

## Activity

You are employed as a nanny. You have been asked your opinion on the merits of disposable nappies against terry towelling nappies. What would you say? You will need to research your answers, including the following questions.

- Consider short- and long-term costs, remembering many children will be using nappies for three or more years. How many should be bought and of what sort?

  In considering costs, include the expense of washing machines, dryers, powders, electricity, etc.

  If the family is living in small accommodation, think about storage of large packets of nappies, and the possible problems of collection, etc.
- Is there a nappy service available? What is it and what are the costs?
- Think of the effects on the environment of both disposable nappies and of the chemicals used in the laundry of terry nappies.
- Which nappies do you think will be most comfortable for the baby?
- Which are the most suitable for the delicate skin of the newborn? Give evidence to support your views.
- Is the lifestyle of the carers more suited to one type of nappy than the other?

# Toys and play

In the first year of life a baby changes more quickly than at any other time of her life. At birth, a baby has random, reflexive, uncontrolled movement, but by 1 year she is sitting, crawling and cruising, and her fine motor development has advanced to allow her to pick up delicate objects between thumb and forefinger and to begin to feed herself (see 'Table 6.1 Summary of the Stages of Development', pages 146–9).

She has made enormous intellectual growth. Toys and play, therefore, must respond and complement these changes.

## BIRTH TO 3 MONTHS

At birth a baby can react to noise, light and touch. However, the richest sensory experience for her will be in the close contact she has with her carer. She will respond to skin-to-skin contact, the sound of her mother's voice (the baby's hearing is acute) and especially to her face, so cuddling, talking and singing to a new baby will be highly pleasurable.

She will enjoy using her developing sight and hearing, through mobiles hung over her cot or changing mat, or attached to her relaxing chair. They should be placed within her field of vision, approximately 20-25 cm from her face. The mobiles should move freely and be of different shapes and colours. Bells and chimes will add to the variety.

Ensure the baby's world is visually changing. Move the cot or changing mat to different areas of the room and use brightly coloured clothing and linen to attract her attention.

*At around three months fingers are interesting and the baby will clasp and unclasp them before her eyes*

### Activity
a) Create a mobile for a new baby using equipment found in the home. Make sure it moves freely. Consider colours and shapes and the noises you could create.
b) Place it over the baby's cot and observe her response and how long it holds her attention.

## 3 TO 6 MONTHS

Reflexive behaviour is slowly being replaced by voluntary movement so the baby will need things to hold as well as to look at. Toys should make sounds to accompany the movement.

The baby will find out about these toys not only from her hands, eyes and ears, but from her highly sensitive mouth, where she receives information about taste, textures, shapes and the hardness and softness of the objects. Rattles are ideal toys at this stage. Variety is important, so toys should be light, safe, easy to hold and move and of different materials too. Small toys strung across a pram allow a baby to try swiping and grasping.

*By 6 months the baby will have discovered her feet, but she will still try to put them in her mouth*

## Activity

a) Find or create a selection of toys that would follow on from the traditional rattle for a baby you know, for example shakers, cotton reels strung and knotted on a ribbon, and toys to 'mouth'.
b) Which toy held the baby's attention for the longest time? Why?

## SAFE PRACTICE

Nothing should be cracked or broken.
Ensure pieces of the toy cannot be torn or broken off.
Everything should be washable or disposable.
Take care with dyes and paints.
Ensure that the filling is non-toxic, and cannot escape and be swallowed.

A baby at this age will enjoy the freedom to lie on a firm, safe surface and explore her developing movements, kicking without a restricting nappy, playing with her fingers and hands and by 6 months her toes and feet.

The baby is developing her communicating skills and will enjoy listening to her own voice and that of her carer. She will continue to enjoy songs and movement in the adult's arms. This is the time too to start interactive games such as 'This little piggy'.

## KEY POINTS

■ Always allow time for her to practise her sounds and developing skills.
■ Show your approval with smiles and gesture.

## 6 MONTHS TO 1 YEAR

The baby will, by now, be sitting with support, progressing to sitting unaided and able to play with her toys around her. She will be moving by rolling, squirming and eventually crawling, cruising and walking. The

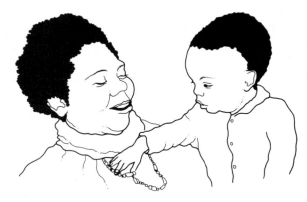

*The baby is attracted by the colours and shapes of the beads around her carer's neck. She is confident in her arms to reach and explore them*

baby will enjoy her bath and the toys and play which go with bath time so reflect this in your choice and planning.

She will enjoy exploring her environment, emptying cupboards, stacking cans, playing with saucepans, etc.

She will begin to 'use' her playthings as well as explore them, for example 'brushing teeth'. She will begin to imitate, not only actions, but also sounds. She will enjoy putting objects in and out of containers and knocking down piles of bricks. Towards the end of the first year she will begin to attempt to build towers with bricks herself.

She will enjoy looking at her reflection in a mirror, familiar photographs and her 'own' possessions, for example a plate with her name on it.

*Water play*

Bath time is an occasion for water play with containers for pouring, floating, sinking and bubble play. A happy bath time enables a baby to become confident in water in preparation for swimming.

At this stage the baby is increasingly interested in the outside world. Outings and visits in the pram or pushchair will enable her to enjoy the changing scenery, see animals, visit shops and parks. The carer should aim to extend the world for the baby, talking and explaining the new experiences to her. She will enjoy repetition of outings to known favourites too, for example feeding the ducks in the park.

As soon as she is a confident crawler, the baby will have much pleasure in crawling for its own sake, reaching toys and interesting things that previously have been out of reach. At this stage of her development, you need to provide stimulating opportunities, as well as constantly watching and monitoring the environment for safety. She will have no concept of danger, and although she may repeat a firm 'no' she will not understand the implications or remember this instruction if something else tempts her curiosity.

## Activity
**Create a treasure basket for a baby who is not yet crawling but who sits steadily when unsupported**

A treasure basket provides an exciting opportunity for a pre-mobile baby to enjoy, explore and learn. It should offer stimulation in all areas but especially in sensory, physical and emotional development.

- Choose a wicker basket – no sharp or jagged edges – that is strong and durable.
- Fill it with about 15 to 20 safe, challenging and stimulating natural articles for a baby – for example an orange, a wooden spoon, a large fir cone, etc.
- Aim for a variety of shapes, textures, weights, colours and materials.
- Aim to provide stimulation for all the baby's senses.
- Allow the baby to play with it on her own, or with a friend.
- As the adult, you should stay near but do not intervene unless she is anxious and needs reassurance.
- Write three observations of the baby playing with the contents.
- Write an evaluation of the activity justifying your choices and comment on any changes you would make when the basket is used again.
- How successful were you in your aims of stimulating and challenging the baby?

If the treasure basket is being used in a day care setting keep other young children away while the basket is in use. Not only will this allow the baby to explore and play unhindered but may prevent some articles becoming unsafe with boisterous toddlers throwing or banging them with force.

**Key point** If the baby's developmental stage means she is insecure in her sitting she will tire easily and lose interest in the basket. She will not have the control to reach, pick up and manipulate objects without toppling over. If, however, she is crawling then she will move away to other interesting and new areas.

For the most effective use of a treasure basket a baby needs to be able to sit securely and confidently for some considerable time, but before she is fully mobile.

## REMEMBER!

A baby learns by discovery, so safety is always important. When purchasing or making toys always consider the following points.

- Toys should not contain small parts which can come loose and be swallowed.
- Materials chosen should be durable, strong and not break leaving sharp edges or splinters.
- Materials must be non-toxic and non-flammable. They should not contain dyes that rub off or toxic paint.
- Take care with toys with small holes to trap fingers, or toys that are hard enough to hurt, if dropped or banged on fingers or toes.
- Toys for the newborn should not have long narrow parts to reach to the back of a baby's throat, and should never be attached around a baby's neck on a string.
- When a baby is playing with paper ensure that she does not chew off small pieces and choke on them.
- See if you can pull toys apart, remove small buttons, etc. Check whether objects can go easily into your mouth. If in any doubt do not give to a baby. Remember everything will be 'explored' through her highly sensitive mouth.
- Look for the BS 5665 standard for toys if unsure.

## KEY POINT

**Supervision is essential**

Your skill is to allow a baby the opportunity to experiment, practise her emerging skills and to discover, within a non-smothering but safe environment. Always consider her developmental stage.

By the end of the first year of life, a baby's play has made enormous strides and by 1 she is enjoying favourite pastimes and rituals, imaginative play with a responsive adult and beginning to demonstrate a sense of humour. Her language will have progressed to a vocabulary of several words but she will understand much more. All play and toys should aim to respond to this rapidly changing development.

## KEY POINTS

- Good playthings are often simple in design, but with a variety of uses.
- A baby needs toys that are easily manipulated so choose toys with large parts.
- Remember to include toys that have tactile properties – warm and pleasant to touch.

### Activity

A baby who is learning to crawl is keen to practise her skills. How can you help?

- Look at her main play area – how might the layout promote her mobility?
- Check the furniture is solid enough for her to pull up on and that floors are non-slip with no loose mats.
- Keep her feet bare to encourage grip and balance.
- Make sure her clothes do not trip her or make movement difficult.
- What exciting safe things can you place within reach – is anything dangerous within grasp?
- What toys are available to promote this area of development – try to find equipment to support her and help her to learn to climb, push, pull, rock and ride.
- Devise a plan of the area and draw it to scale.
- Justify, in writing, the layout, the equipment and the play activities you have chosen.
- What special safety equipment might you need? See page 176.

## REMEMBER!

Your role is to help the baby move to her next developmental stage, when she is ready, by providing appropriate stimulation and encouragement.

## SAFE PRACTICE

Baby walkers are not recommended as they are prone to topple and often enable a baby to reach dangerous areas, especially stairs, in seconds. They also provide a false sense of balance and so may delay walking.

## Activities

1 What do these safety and warning signs mean?

2 How many of the toys and pieces of child care equipment you have researched have had safety marks on them?

3 Do all toys, by law, have to have a recognisable safety standard?

4 How would you ensure that secondhand toys and equipment are safe?

You will need to research in the library and through safety officers at your local town hall and through voluntary bodies.

## *QUICK* CHECK

1 Which bed covering is no longer recommended for babies and why?

2 Describe three safety features you would look for when buying a cot.

3 What advice would you give about transporting a new baby in a car?

4 Describe three safety features you would look for when buying a pram or pushchair.

5 What is a layette?

6 Describe the most important sensory experience a new baby will have.

7 At what age would a baby gain most from a rattle? Why?

8 How can water play easily be offered to a 9-month-old baby?

9 When buying toys, what safety factors would you look for?

10 Describe the main duties of a carer when providing play activities for a mobile baby.

# 9 BABIES WITH SPECIAL NEEDS

**This chapter covers:**
- **Introduction to special needs**
- **Possible causes of special needs**
- **Types of special need**
- **The family – parents and siblings**
- **Meeting the baby's needs**

## Introduction to special needs

The term 'special needs' is used by child care professionals in relation to babies whose development is not following the recognised pattern seen in most babies. Not all babies of similar ages are at the same stage of development. Babies with special needs are simply at different points in the developmental continuum.

All parents wish for, and expect a healthy baby. Pre-conceptual and antenatal care reduce many of the risks to the unborn child. The special tests and investigations during pregnancy (page 15) may identify certain conditions.

### KEY POINTS

- While special tests of pregnancy may identify particular conditions, they cannot alter them. Parents must be supported both in their decision whether to have the test and in their decision whether or not to terminate a pregnancy.
- Parents may wish for information about an inherited condition and the risk of passing it on to children or grandchildren. Genetic counselling can be offered to them (page 6).

## Possible causes of special needs

Special needs may be due to:
- hereditary factors
- antenatal, birth and postnatal developments
- child care and management factors.

## SOME POSSIBLE CAUSES OF SPECIAL NEEDS

**Hereditary factors**

Genetic inheritance — Cystic fibrosis, sickle cell and thalassaemia conditions, phenylketonuria, Tay-Sachs disease and others

Chromosomal inheritance — Down's syndrome, Fragile X syndrome

Sex-linked inheritance — Haemophilia, Duchenne muscular dystrophy

<u>Key points</u>
- Inherited disorders are passed on from parents to their children and are *always present at birth* even if not immediately identifiable
- *One or more* special needs may be present but *one* may predominate

**Prenatal factors** — Substances: drugs, tobacco, alcohol
Maternal infections including: rubella, toxoplasmosis, cytomegalovirus, listeriosis, HIV, some sexually transmitted diseases (STDs)
Threatened miscarriage

**At birth** — Anoxia (lack of oxygen), prematurity, post-maturity, low birth-weight, difficult delivery

**Post-natal developments** — Infections including: bacterial meningitis, measles, mumps, diphtheria, poliomyelitis
Accidents/injuries: particularly those damaging the brain and spinal cord
Childhood cancers: leukaemia, sarcomas, retinoblastoma, Wilm's tumour
Child abuse of any kind
Allergic reactions including: asthma and eczema

**Child care and management factors** — Frequent changes in prime carers during early years
Emotional deprivation
Family stress
Difficulties with parenting

**Unknown factors** — Sometimes it is not possible to identify a clear cause for a special need

<u>Key points</u>
- Conditions present at birth are said to be *congenital.*
- *Congenital* conditions are not necessarily *hereditary*, for example congenital heart disease, congenital dislocation of the hip.
- Special needs may not become obvious until a baby grows and develops, hence the importance of health promotion and developmental review programmes

Sometimes it is not possible to identify a clear cause. The table on page 188 sets out some of the possible causes of special needs.

## RECOGNISING SPECIAL NEEDS

Special needs may be recognised:
- antenatally
- at birth
- through child health promotion and screening programmes
- by follow-up to a parent's observation and concern
- by professional observation in the home and day care settings
- following an accident or serious illness.

The list below, 'Towards prevention and early identification of special needs', sets out measures that may prevent, or identify, special needs at an early stage.

**Towards prevention and early identification of special needs**
- Genetic counselling
- Pre-conceptual care
- High standards of antenatal, perinatal and neonatal care
- Immunisation programmes
- Comprehensive child health promotion programmes and efficient referral systems
- Loving and secure emotional environments in which babies can thrive and be happy
- Healthy and safe environments which lessen the risk of illnesses, infections and accidents

### KEY POINTS

- Throughout infancy, child health promotion and screening programmes are offered (see page 95). Observation of babies by family doctors, health visitors, nursery nurses and parents can identify, at an early age, those who may have special needs. Appropriate help can often limit or reverse the difficulties or delay.
- Immunisation is an effective form of preventive health care for babies. It is offered routinely from the age of 2 months (see page 152). Occasionally there are contra-indications to immunisation.

# Types of special need

There are many types of special need. You will be able to find out from the baby's parents, and other professionals, the difficulties a baby is experiencing. The development charts in chapter 6 on pages 146–9 will help you understand the stages of normal development.

## KEY POINT

Remember that the word 'type' refers to the special need and not to the baby.

You may care for babies with any of the following.
- *Physical conditions*  Cerebral palsy, cleft lip or palate, spina bifida, cystic fibrosis, sickle cell condition, limb deficiencies, and others. These result from damage or injury to the brain and spinal cord, the body and its systems, or the control of movement.
- *Sensory impairment*  Vision and hearing difficulties.
- *Learning delay*  Down's syndrome, Fragile X syndrome and sensory impairment.
- *Emotional difficulties*  While the foundation for emotional difficulties may be partly laid down in the first year of life, the effects may not be evident until later in childhood. The most likely reasons will be separation from, and frequent changes of, primary carers, lack of physical care and affection, and child abuse.

Sometimes it is not possible to clearly identify the particular cause.

## KEY POINTS

- Possible developmental delay may be identified in the first year. More commonly, however, difficulties become more apparent as childhood progresses.
- A baby's special need may affect only a minor part of her life or it may be a major and challenging factor.
- Long-term implications for babies with special needs include physical, intellectual and emotional developmental delay.

## RECOGNISING A SPECIAL NEED

Sometimes a special need is very obvious and clear at, or just after, birth– for example, cleft lip or palate, spina bifida, Down's syndrome (some are also identifiable through a special test of pregnancy). Others such as cerebral palsy, various heart conditions, and vision and hearing impairment may be 'hidden', only becoming apparent in later months when developmental delay is observed in the baby.

## KEY POINT

A baby who is profoundly deaf from birth may initially coo, gurgle and babble as a hearing baby.

# The family – parents and siblings

No parents expect their baby to have developmental delay, require extra help, perhaps intrusive medical procedures, or even to die. The whole sudden experience of having a baby with special needs can be deeply upsetting and isolating.

## PARENTS' REACTIONS

When a special need is recognised, parents need time to understand, adapt and accept; and time to adjust and learn about their baby as an individual with her own personality. Often, the only information parents have about certain conditions is affected by the prejudice of society. Their own experiences may be very limited.

**KEY POINT**

The birth of a baby with special needs may be seen as a tragedy, and friends may offer condolences rather than congratulations because they do not know what to say.

Whether a special need is known at birth, or in later months, many parents will go through the different emotional stages associated with bereavement – grieving for their apparently 'lost' baby – before they are able to accept and adjust. Such reactions are seen across all cultures and social classes. Typically parents experience the following:

- shock, grief, numbness, confusion and an inability to come to terms with or fully comprehend what has happened
- denial of any long-term disabling condition
- feelings of guilt and apportioning of blame, particularly if the baby has an inherited condition, or the mother smoked or drank heavily in pregnancy. Anger and blame may be directed at the doctor for not recognising or preventing the special need antenatally or at birth. Parents may blame themselves, or each other, if their baby's special need is the result of an accident or serious illness
- gradual orientation, acceptance and adjustment. The parents are now able to relate to their baby and take pleasure in her.

**KEY POINT**

There is no time limit to this process of acceptance and adjustment. It may take several years. Parents work through the stages in their own time.

**Parents' adjustment**

In spite of the sadness and stress they feel, most parents learn to love their baby and are aware of the greater degree of dependency and responsibility there is always going to be. Their protective instincts are usually heightened, sometimes to the point of over-protection. Adjusting to the implication that their baby will not 'get better' and striving to provide the care, opportunity and stimulation required (often despite the attitudes of society) can be a challenging process.

### KEY POINT

Some parents find it difficult to cope and may never reach the stage of adjustment. They may be reluctant to share their anxieties with family, friends or professional carers. Some babies with special needs are fostered or adopted.

## QUESTIONS PARENTS ASK

Initially, many questions are asked – 'Why did it happen?', 'What's wrong with her?', 'Why us?', 'Will she die'?, 'Will she learn to walk and talk'? There may be no ready answers. When the cause cannot be determined it often makes the situation harder for the parents to accept, although knowing the cause does not automatically make life easier.

## AREAS OF DIFFICULTY

There are areas of difficulty that may be experienced.

- Mother–baby bonding may be difficult. For medical reasons, the mother and her new baby may be separated from each other, or a mother may be reluctant to hold, cuddle and feed her baby, fearful of yet more powerful emotions should her baby die. Parents may find their baby's physical appearance upsetting. The baby may be rejected.
- Babies with complex and multiple special needs requiring constant care. Feeding difficulties, crying and failing to settle to sleep, and into a pattern consistent with the family routine, cause parents distress and anxiety. This may lead to lack of confidence in their ability to care effectively for their baby's needs.
- Relationships may be strained. Stress and anxiety can lead to irritability and arguments. Separation and divorce are not uncommon, although in some families the relationship grows stronger as they find the energy and determination to find the support and provision their baby needs.

- Social isolation from family, friends and local community (and perhaps in the child health clinic) may be experienced because their baby is 'different' and does not fit in to the normal pattern – many people still have little understanding of special needs.
- There may be financial pressures, perhaps because of a loss of earnings due to caring responsibilities.

## Activity

Imagine you are employed as a nanny caring for a baby, now ten days old, with special needs. The baby's mother is distressed and reluctant to hold, cuddle and care for her baby although she will offer her the bottle.

Think of ways in which you could help and support the mother to get close to and relate to her baby.

## MEETING THE NEEDS OF PARENTS AND FAMILY

Recognition of, and support for, the parents' needs can reduce the length of the grieving process. Support must aim to lessen stress and anxiety and give the parents confidence in their ability to care for the baby.

In particular, parents need the following.

- Information about their baby's condition and the help available. It should be accessible under 'one roof'. Parents have a right to know where to go for help – not knowing, or travelling around from place to place trying to find help, is confusing and stressful.
- Support for their own emotional needs. As their baby reaches the age at which she would have achieved skills such as sitting up, crawling and walking, the sense of loss and sadness frequently re-emerges. Unsupported needs have damaging effects on the whole family. Professional counselling is available, but the support of a loving, caring extended family is often the most positive means of help.
- Practical help in the home from relatives, friends or the social services department.
- Contact and friendship with other parents of babies with special needs through special need support groups or self-help groups. These offer the opportunity to share feelings and concerns which, perhaps, could not be comfortably shared with the professionals.
- Time to be with other members of the family and meet their needs.

- Parents need reassurance that their emotions are normal reactions. Pretending they do not exist does not make them go away.
- Help and counselling are available. A 'special needs' health visitor, or the family's regular health visitor, can be a point of professional contact. A health visitor is outside the family circle so is someone in whom parents may find it easier to trust and confide.

### Link workers

Link workers from black and ethnic minorities should be available from both statutory and voluntary agencies to enable families to obtain the support, information and resources they need. Similarly, parents for whom English is neither their home nor community language, or who have communication difficulties, need interpreters who are skilled in special needs issues, as well as information presented on tapes, in large print and in Braille.

## THE SIBLINGS

The effects on brothers and sisters vary according to their age, birth order and the number of children in the family.

Siblings may experience the following.

- Overprotection or, possibly, neglect.
- Jealousy and resentment at the attention given to their baby brother or sister (over and above what might be considered 'normal' when a new baby arrives).
- A shift in the family balance which means they have to take on a domestic role.
- Worry that they will 'catch' their brother or sister's condition.
- Teasing and social isolation.
- Emotional swings, from being loving and protective to disturbed behaviour such as regression, attention-seeking, moodiness, anxiety, low self-esteem, embarrassment or guilt.

### KEY POINTS

- Not all siblings experience such emotional and social disadvantage. Much depends on individual personality and the bond between them and their brother and sister with special needs. Many remain happy and well adjusted.
- You may care for siblings in a nursery, school or home setting. Observation of their play and behaviour (perhaps in the home corner) or

*Siblings may feel anxious and concerned*

of their drawings, painting and general demeanour, may indicate they are experiencing difficulties. They may exhibit regressive behaviour, resort to temper tantrums or become withdrawn and clinging.

### Meeting the siblings' needs

- Individual attention and reassurance they are loved and valued.
- One-to-one key worker provision for a child in a nursery or education setting.
- Time on their own with their parents.
- Opportunity for older children to express their feelings and be listened to uncritically by parents, carers or professionals.
- Correct information appropriate to their level of understanding.

## REMEMBER!

Always encourage a sibling to care for their brother or sister in small, every-day ways, just as an older child would normally care for a younger member of the family. This includes cuddling, talking, playing and fetching clothes and nappies during bathing and changing routines.

Parents are crucial members of the service team. Every effort should be made to keep babies with special needs at home with their family. This can only be achieved if sustained, flexible, and child-centred services are available that allow families choice and make it possible for the baby to be cared for at home. Each family is unique. Considerable extra help may be needed at particular times and at others a small input of help can make all the difference in keeping the family together. Accessible help and support should be available when needed. This gives parents the confidence and control they need to shape their own lives.

**Statutory services**
The two main statutory service providers for babies with special needs are:
■ the health service
■ social services.

*Health service systems and support*
Usually, the first professionals a baby and her family see are from the health service. The most likely causes of special needs identified through the health service are physical conditions, sensory impairment and developmental delay. Health Service care is likely to be a combination of hospital specialist care, and community care from the Primary Health Care team. The family doctor will care for day-to-day health problems and concerns, and give immunisations. Home nursing care and loans of medical equipment such as suction apparatus, feeding tubes and oxygen are provided by the community paediatric nursing service (not available in all areas). The family health visitor, or a 'special needs health visitor', will visit the family at home offering support, advice and information. Health care provision is set out on page 199.

### KEY POINT

If you have information about a baby's medical condition it must remain confidential and should not be shared with others without permission from the parents.

*Social services systems and support*
Social services support for the baby and her family is provided by social workers employed by local authority Social Services Departments that, under the Children Act 1989, have a duty to provide a range of support services enabling the baby to be cared for at home. Services include: day care provision (nurseries, child-minders), family aide service (to assist with the general running of the home), financial advice and cash grants for specific aids and adaptations to the home (see page 200).

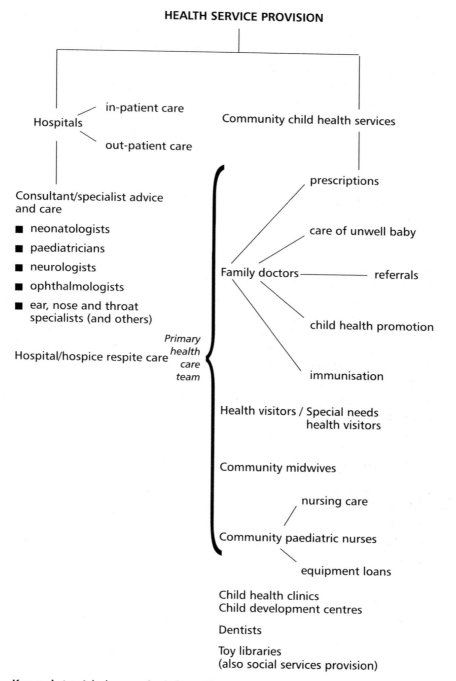

**HEALTH SERVICE PROVISION**

Hospitals
- in-patient care
- out-patient care

Consultant/specialist advice and care

- neonatologists
- paediatricians
- neurologists
- ophthalmologists
- ear, nose and throat specialists (and others)

Hospital/hospice respite care

Community child health services

*Primary health care team*

Family doctors
- prescriptions
- care of unwell baby
- referrals
- child health promotion
- immunisation

Health visitors / Special needs health visitors

Community midwives

Community paediatric nurses
- nursing care
- equipment loans

Child health clinics
Child development centres

Dentists

Toy libraries
(also social services provision)

**Key point**   A baby may be informally assessed during her first year, to determine her need and how best to provide for that need. Formal assessment may be carried out after the age of 2 years (or under 2 years with parental permission).

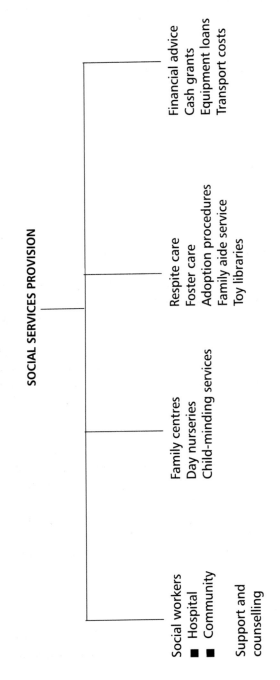

**SOCIAL SERVICES PROVISION**

Social workers
■ Hospital
■ Community

Support and
counselling

Family centres
Day nurseries
Child-minding services

Respite care
Foster care
Adoption procedures
Family aide service
Toy libraries

Financial advice
Cash grants
Equipment loans
Transport costs

Social workers assess babies for day care, respite care and family aide provision. They also offer counselling to parents or carers and have statutory duties towards children being looked after by social services or who are being adopted.

Social services departments also offer family centres, respite care and toy library provision.

*Family centres* These offer a support service to a wide range of families, including those with children with special needs. Family centres can provide:

■ day care and playgroup sessions
■ child health clinics
■ counselling and help with parenting skills
■ toy libraries.

A family centre may operate an 'open door' policy or a family can be referred from health or social services.

*Respite care* This is a period of relief for parents from caring for a baby with profound or complex special needs. The baby may be cared for on a paediatric ward, in a children's hospice, or a home setting with a specialist carer, for a short or longer period of time. Respite care allows the parents time to be together (and with their other children), to rest and recover for a while from their role as full-time carers. An effective system of respite care can mean the difference between a baby remaining in her family, or being looked after by social services. It should be part of the total 'care package' for the baby and her family.

*Toy library provision* This may be organised by social services, health services or voluntary organisations. Toys made of sturdy materials, and suitable for different ages and stages of development, are available for babies and children to play with in a safe setting. Many toys are specifically for use as learning aids for those with special needs. A toy library can be set up in a day nursery, child development centre, health centre or other suitable accommodation. Toy libraries offer a loan service for a small fee.

## DAY CARE PROVISION

Day care settings for babies with special needs include specialist or inclusive day nurseries, or child-minding facilities. Inclusive settings, in which babies and young children with and without special needs are cared for together, are becoming increasingly more common.

An older baby with special needs may benefit from some weekly time in a nursery. All babies require a high quality of care; babies with special needs often require a great deal of extra help and supervision with mobility and physical care routines, and a one-to-one key worker will be important.

## KEY POINTS

- An inclusive day care setting must be the choice of the family. It may not be appropriate for all babies. A specialist setting may more readily meet the baby's needs.
- A child-minder may positively choose to care for a baby with special needs.

A child care worker is part of a multidisciplinary team whose members may include the Primary Health Care team, paediatrician, physiotherapist and speech therapist. Parents are always considered to be valuable members of the team. You need to be aware of your own role, and that of the other members of the team, in caring for a baby with special needs. Always make sure you liaise with the other team members.

## VOLUNTARY PROVISION

Voluntary organisations are a valuable additional source of help for babies with special needs and their families, supporting the work of health and social services. The care and support they offer is flexible and positive.

### The Portage home teaching service

The Portage home teaching service, an early intervention programme, was developed in the town of Portage, Wisconsin USA in the 1960s. It is a valuable early learning resource for children with special needs, providing a home-based daily teaching and learning programme for babies and pre-school children with learning disabilities and physical conditions. For example, a baby with Down's syndrome or cerebral palsy could be helped by Portage, including learning Makaton sign language.

Portage visitors come from a variety of backgrounds such as teaching, nursing, nursery nursing and playgroup work or they may be parents whose own children have grown up. They receive special training and focus on what the baby CAN rather than CANNOT do, believing in the principle of 'one step at a time'.

*Makaton is used to help speech development*

## KEY POINT

■ Portage home visitors work closely with parents who are actively encouraged to implement the programme themselves and, in effect, become their child's teachers with the visitor assuming the role of consultant and supporter. Progress and achievement can be enjoyed by parents, siblings and extended members of the family.

Weekly visits are made to the baby's home. Both the Portage visitor and parents assess the baby's development through a planned programme of constructive activities and play (tasks). The programme particularly concentrates on gross motor and fine manipulative skills, language, cognitive development, self-help skills, stimulation and socialisation. Each task is broken down into stages so that a baby achieves new skills in small steps. Toys and books to develop particular skills are provided through a loan scheme operated by Portage.

## Activity
Invite a Portage visitor to talk about his or her work with babies at a staff development session at your workplace. In particular, ask about their work with babies and the importance of parental participation in the programme and the evaluation process.

*Steven with his Portage visitor, learning to sign*

### Befriending schemes

Volunteer befrienders are well-informed, experienced parents who have been through their own personal experience of having a child with special needs and have faced their own feelings before reaching the stage of acceptance and adjustment. Many families value the support they receive from parent befrienders and eventually become befrienders themselves. Examples of befriending schemes are Face to Face and Homestart.

**KEY POINT**

Part of the initial important bonding process between a mother and her baby is built upon their emerging communications. Eye-to-eye contact may be absent with a baby whose sight is impaired, and smiling may be delayed. Apparent lack of response can cause a parent frustration and undermine confidence. Early involvement for parents with a support agency or group, who have personal experience of such feelings is often helpful.

## STIMULATION, PLAY AND LEARNING

Through her senses, and movement, a baby gathers information to learn about the world around her. Encourage a baby with special needs to use all parts of her body to explore what she touches, smells, tastes, sees and hears. Encourage vocalisation and babbling as you would for any baby and always respond when she attempts to communicate with you.

The principles of good practice in providing sensory stimulation and an interesting and interactive environment apply to ALL babies, with or without special needs, and whether they are cared for at home or in a day care setting (see pages 133–9).

Safe, uncluttered, well-lit spaces, with appropriate equipment, provide the opportunity for babies to develop their motor skills, balance and movement. Positive adult interaction encourages the development of self-confidence and social skills.

## PHYSICAL CARE

Physical care routines provide carers with the opportunity for close personal contact with a baby. Do not rush these times – sensitivity to the baby's feelings is important.

### Feeding and mealtimes

A baby with a cleft lip or palate usually has difficulty in feeding. Specially designed teats may help, or the baby may have to be spoon-fed. Sometimes, a prosthesis (similar to a dental mould), is fitted over the palate during feeds, and removed and cleaned at the end of the feed. Pre-term babies, and those with congenital heart disorders may tire easily when sucking, and alternating breast- or bottle-feeding with tube feeding may be necessary.

- Initially, some babies with cerebral palsy may need to be tube fed. This may lead to difficulty in the baby learning to suck. A mother will require understanding and support at this time. Tensions developing from such a situation are easily passed on to the baby.
- A baby who is 'floppy' needs to be well supported under the ribs to help her keep an upright position and extend her chest.

Mealtimes may take a long time. Encourage the baby to explore her food and take finger foods when she is able to do so, depending on her ability to chew and swallow. Prompt weaning for babies with cerebral palsy helps to develop chewing and tongue control which are important in promoting speech and for healthy teeth and gums, but crumbly foods should be avoided because babies with cerebral palsy often have a poor cough reflex. For safety and stability always use a suction feeding bowl and check it is firmly fixed at each mealtime.

- Introduce new foods very slowly for babies who have chewing or swallowing difficulties.
- Check that your First Aid skills are up-to-date, especially the procedure to use if a baby is choking (see page 211).

## Personal hygiene routines

Carry out personal hygiene routines as you would for babies without special needs. Most babies enjoy water and water play and find these times of close contact pleasurable, feeling reassured by a cuddle or hug from their carer. Special bath seats will support and protect an older baby. Always make sure your practice is safe for both young and older babies (see pages 61 and 67). Change the baby's nappy as often as necessary to keep her clean and comfortable.

Dental care should start as soon as the first tooth appears.

## KEY POINTS

- In any condition where there is loss of movement and sensation it is important to be aware of the danger of pressure sores. A baby with paralysis will feel no pressure or pain and is especially vulnerable to sores. She will not indicate distress even if sores are present.
- Good skin care practice is essential for babies with congenital dislocation of the hip who are wearing a splint or plaster cast.

## Dressing and undressing

Clothes should be easy to put on and take off, allowing the baby as much independence as possible. Mail order catalogues supply clothes that will fit over splints and tubes.

## Sleep routines

Aim to develop a settling sleep routine as for babies without special needs. A baby with cerebral palsy may need moving and making more comfortable in the night to prevent spasms. A special sleeping position may be recommended for her by the physiotherapist.

## Movement and positioning

A baby's muscles and limbs that do not move of their own accord must be exercised by the carer. A physiotherapist will arrange passive exercises for you to undertake for the baby. You will also be advised on how to lift carefully to ensure the baby's comfort and safety. When caring for a baby with a disorder of movement, handle her limbs with care, and never hurry a movement.

The usual baby pushchairs, car seats and body slings will, initially, be suitable for getting around.

## REMEMBER!

- A special need may be present at birth or arise at any time in later months.
- Support for the parents and siblings is essential.
- A baby's special needs should not override her 'ordinary' needs.
- Always use appropriate language, never label a baby by her special need.
- Health and social services are the main statutory care and management providers.
- Offer the baby appropriate stimulation, play and learning opportunities.
- Care sensitively for her physical needs.
- Child care workers are part of the multidisciplinary team.

## QUICK CHECK

1 What do you understand by the term 'special needs'?
2 What post-natal developments can cause a baby to have special needs?
3 Give four ways in which special needs in babies can be prevented or identified at an early age.
4 Describe the different emotional stages parents may go through when they learn their baby has special needs.
5 Describe the difficulties in 'mother–baby bonding' that may occur.
6 For which families would a 'link worker' be particularly beneficial?
7 In a day care setting how might you recognise the difficulties a child may be experiencing whose baby sister has special needs?
8 What are the basic needs of a baby with special needs?
9 Which two statutory services are the main service providers for babies with special needs?
10 What do you understand by the term 'inclusive setting'?
11 Briefly, describe the Portage home teaching service.
12 What feeding aids might help a baby with cleft lip or palate?
13 Why should you avoid offering crumbly foods to a baby with cerebral palsy?
14 Why is skin care so important for a baby with paralysis?
15 Name the professional who would advise you on handling, lifting and positioning techniques for a baby with a disorder of movement.

# APPENDIX: FIRST AID

The carer is responsible for the maintenance of a safe environment for babies in her care. Accidents that happen to immobile babies are the result of a failure on the part of the carer to protect them, either through carelessness or lack of anticipation.

A baby is vulnerable and dependent. When she starts crawling and is able to reach hazards, she will not have the awareness to keep herself safe. You need to link your developmental knowledge to providing a stimulating but safe world for the baby.

First Aid is temporary treatment given before the arrival of more skilled personnel. It should be quick and simple and aimed at preventing the baby's condition from worsening.

## KEY POINT

In day care, all staff should have good current knowledge of First Aid. At least one member of staff should be trained and identified as the designated First Aider of the Nursery.

## REMEMBER!

Priorities in First Aid
1   Remove the baby from immediate danger
2   Maintain breathing and heartbeat
3   Check for and treat severe bleeding
4   Deal with severe burns
5   Place an unconscious baby in the recovery position
6   Seek medical help
Always have parents', hospital's and doctor's telephone numbers prominently displayed.

## Breathing

If a baby is not breathing and her heart has stopped beating, for example due to possible Sudden Infant Death, immediate action must be taken.

**Always think A B C**

**A= Airway** Clear anything immediately obvious at the front of the mouth with a sweep of a forefinger. Do not attempt to scoop anything out from the back of the mouth, as any obstruction may be pushed further down. Look at the chest. Can you see a rise and fall? Place your face near the baby's nose and mouth to feel any breaths. If not, then open the airway by gently pulling the jaw forward and up and flexing the neck back.

**B= Breathing** Place your mouth over the baby's nose and mouth firmly to limit air escape. Puff into the lungs at about 20 breaths per minute, removing your face to allow the exhaled air to escape. Force is dangerous and unnecessary. Watch to ensure the chest is rising and falling, if not then re-check that the airway is still open.

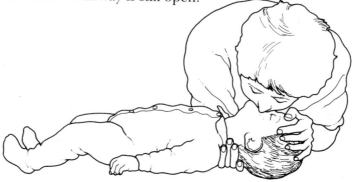

*Artificial respiration*

**C= Circulation** Is the heart beating? Heart massage is dangerous if a beat is present. Try to find a pulse – the arm is suitable – don't use your thumb.

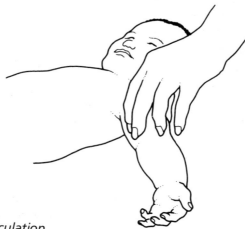

*Check the circulation*

If a pulse is not present, the heart has stopped. It must be stimulated to encourage it to beat. If this cannot be achieved the baby will die and if resuscitation is delayed then brain damage may occur.

Place two fingers at the end of the sternum (breast bone) keeping your arm straight. Gently, with two fingers press down, approximately for 1.5–2.5 cm at a rate of 100 per minute.

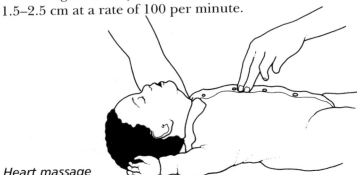

*Heart massage*

Mouth-to-mouth and heart massage should be undertaken at the rate of four to five chest compressions to one ventilation. If two adults are present then both forms should be given at once. Check to monitor if the heart beat returns after one minute and then every three minutes.

Maintain resuscitation until help arrives, if necessary. If the baby begins to breathe and a pulse is felt, place in the recovery position to ensure that the airway remains open.

*The recovery position*

**REMEMBER!**

**The recovery position**
Place baby on her side. You can help keep her in this position by placing a rolled towel down the length of her back, if necessary. Check her airway remains open.

# Bleeding

Minor external bleeding usually clots and heals itself. If the bleeding is severe, treat with direct pressure (a firm bandage, for example) and raise the affected part.

# Burns and scalds

The prime aim of treatment is to cool the affected part quickly. Do not try to remove clothing as this may pull off delicate skin, and in addition the fabric is now sterile.

Immerse the affected area in tepid water, under a running tap or even in a bath, for as long as possible, before medical help arrives.
**Do not apply any ointments, oils or burst any blisters.**

# Choking

If an obvious obstruction is present at the front of the mouth remove it (see 'A= Airway', page 209). Aim to get the head lower than the chest to help gravity move the blockage.

Lay the baby's head downwards, with your forearm supporting the head and chest. Firmly slap the infant between the shoulder blades up to four times.

# Conclusion

Accidents happen often when we are least prepared. Skills and knowledge need constant updating. The St John's Ambulance and the British Red Cross Society both run excellent short courses that are ideal for professional child care workers.

# SUGGESTED FURTHER READING

(Most recent editions have been quoted wherever possible.)

Beaver, Marion; Brewster Jo; Jones, Pauline; Keene, Anne; Neaum, Sally; and Tallack, Jill, *The Development of Babies and Young Children 0–7*, Stanley Thornes, 1994

Bee, Helen, *The Developing Child*, HarperCollins, 1992

Dare, Angela and O'Donovan, Margaret, *Good Practice in Caring for Young Children with Special Needs*, Stanley Thornes, 1997

Goldschmied, Elinor and Jackson, Sonia, *People Under Three*, Routledge, 1995

Hall, David; Hill, Peter; and Elliman, David; *The Child Surveillance Handbook* (2nd edition), Radcliffe Medical Press, 1996

Hilton, Tessa, with Messenger, Maire, *The Great Ormond Street Book of Baby and Child Care*, The Bodley Head, 1993

Hobart, Christine and Frankel, Jill, A *Practical Guide to Working with Young Children*, Stanley Thornes, 1992
*A Practical Guide to Child Observation*, Stanley Thornes, 1994
*A Practical Guide to Activities for Young Children*, Stanley Thornes, 1995
*A Practical Guide to Child Protection*, Stanley Thornes, 1998

Jolly, Hugh, *Book of Child Care*, Unwin Hyman, 1986

Leach, Penelope, *Babyhood*, Penguin, 1991

Lindon, Jennie (ed.), *Child Develcpment from Birth to Eight: A Practical Focus*, National Children's Bureau, 1993

Macfarlane, Aidan; Sefi, Sue; and Cordiero, Mario, *Child Health: The Screening Tests – A Practical Guide*, Oxford Medical Publications

Matheson, Elizabeth (ed.), *This Little Puffin*, Puffin, 1994 (Useful nursery rhymes and songs)

Sadek, Elizabeth and Sadek, Jacqueline *Good Practice in Nursery Management*, Stanley Thornes, 1996

Sheridan, Mary D., *From Birth to Five Years – Children's Developmental Progress* (Revised and updated by Frost, M. and Sharma, A.), Routledge, 1997

# USEFUL ADDRESSES

**Association of Breastfeeding Mothers**, 26 Holmshaw Close, Sydenham Green, London SE26 4TH (0181 778 4769) – offers advice on breast-feeding and local support groups

**Association for Postnatal Illness**, 7 Cowan Avenue, London SW6 6RH (0171 731 4867) – offers advice on postnatal illness

**British Red Cross Society**, 9 Grosvenor Crescent, London SW1X 7EJ

**Cry-sis**, BM Crysis, London WCIN 3XX (0171 404 5011) – offers help and support to parents of babies who cry excessively

**The Equality Learning Centre**, 356 Holloway Rd, London N7 6PA

**Foresight** (The Association for the Promotion of Preconceptual Care), The Old Vicarage, Church Lane, Witley, Surrey GU8 5PN

**Foundation for the Study of Infant Deaths** (Cot Death Research and Support), 15 Belgrave Square, London SWIX 8PS (0171 235 0965/1721) – offers support and information to bereaved parents

**FSID**, 14 Halkin Street, London SW1X 7DP

**HAPA** Play for Disabled Children, Fulham Palace, Bishop's Avenue, London SW6 6EA

**In Touch**, 10 Norman Rd, Sale, Cheshire N33 3DF

**La Leche League of Great Britain**, PO Box BM 3424, London WCIN 3XX (0171 242 1278) – offers advice on breast-feeding

**The Maternity Alliance**, 45 Beech Street, London EC2P 2LX

**Meet-a-Mum Association (MAMA)**, 58 Malden Avenue, South Norwood, London SE25 6HS (0181 656 7318) – offers help and local support groups for mothers

**Multiple Birth Foundation**, Queen Charlotte's and Chelsea Hospital, Goldhawk Road, London W6 OXG (0181 748 4666)

**National Association for Maternal and Child Welfare**, (NAMCW), Stroud House, 46-48 Osnaburgh Street, London NWI 3NP

**National Association of Toy and Leisure Libraries**, 68 Churchway, London NW1 1LT

**National Association for the Welfare of Children in Hospital (NAWCH)**, Argyle House, 29-31 Euston Road, London NWI 2SD (0171 833 2041) – offers support for sick children and their families

**National Childbirth Trust (NCT)**, Alexandra House, Oldham Terrace, London W3 6NH (0181 992 8637) – offers advice on breast-feeding and local antenatal and postnatal support groups

**National Children's Bureau**, 8 Wakely Street, London EC1V 7QE

**National Society for Phenylketonuria and Allied Disorders**, 26 Towngate Grove, Mirfield, West Yorkshire

**Twins and Multiple Births Association (TAMBA)**, 59 Sunnyside, Worksop, Nottingham S81 7LN – offers advice to parents and local Twins Clubs

**Working for Childcare**, 77 Holloway Rd, London N7 8JZ

**World Organisation for Early Childhood Education (OMEP)**, c/o Thomas Coram Foundation, 40 Brunswick Square, London WC1N 1AU

# INDEX

Page references in *italics* indicate illustrations and diagrams, those in **bold** indicate tables

abdomen   31
acupuncture   **21**
afterbirth   8, 9, 20
alcohol   6
allergies   **123**
alphafetoprotein (AFP)   45
ammonia dermatitis   70–1
amniocentesis   15
amniotic sac   8
anaemia   6, 19, 50
antenatal care   11–12
    provision   13–15, *14*
    twins   45
anterior fontanelle   30
anus   32
Apgar scores   27–8, **28**
artificial respiration   209, *209*
asymmetric tonic neck reflex   34, *34*
automatic reflexes   33–5, *34*

'baby blues'   24
back (spine)   32
bacteria   151–2
Bart's triple blood test   17
bathing
    babies with special needs   206
    benefits   66
    equipment   62, **63**, 171–2
    essential principles   60–2
    older babies   66–8
    and play   183
    preparation   62–3, *63*
    step-by-step procedure *64–6*
befriending schemes   204
bereavement and twins   47–8
bilirubin   43, 44

birth *see* labour and birth
birthmarks   32–3
bleeding (first aid)   210
blood pressure, high   11
blood tests
    Bart's triple   17
    before pregnancy   6
'blue spots'   29
bonding *see* mother-baby bonding
bottle-feeding   109, 172
    choice of milks   109–10
    in day care   115–16
    how much feed?   110–11
    preparation   111–12, *111*, **112**, *113*
    procedure   114–15
    twins   46
breast-feeding   101, 102
    benefits   106
    in day care   106–7
    difficulties   **108**
    equipment   172
    management   104–6, *105*
    milk composition   10, 103–4
    milk production   102, *102*
    milk release   102, *103*
    and neonatal jaundice   44
    twins   45–6
breathing
    checking   158
    first aid   209–11
    newborn babies   27
    pre-term babies   50
breech births   19–20, 45
bronchiolitis   **163**
bronchitis   **163**
burns (first aid)   211

caesarian sections **23**, 45
caput succedaneum   29
carrycots   169–70, 173
cars   173, *173*, 174
cephalhaematoma   29
cervix   19, 20, *20*
chafing   **74**
chest infections   **163–4**
chicken pox   **155**
choking (first aid)   211, *211*
chorionic villus sampling   17
clothing   176–8, 206
colds   **163**
colic   **123**, **165**
colostrum   103, 104
comfort objects   83–4
community care *see* primary health
    care
conception   8
constipation   71–2, **123**
contraception   3
contractions   19, 20
cot death syndrome   **166**
cots   80, 81, 171
coughs   **163**
cradle cap   **74**
cradles   169
croup   **164**
crying   86–9, *87–8*
cryptophasia   47

day care   141–2
    babies' clothing   177
    bottle-feeding   115–16
    breast-feeding   106–7
    dealing with body fluids   58–9
    key workers   142–3
    and parents   143–5
    settling in   145–6, **145**
    sleep and rest   79, 80, 81
    special needs   201–2
'deciduous' teeth   89–90, *90*
development   125–6, **146–9**
    and day care   141–6
    and feeding   116–17
    hearing   132–3

intellectual, emotional and social
    133, *134*, 137–9
    language   133–6
    physical   126–31
    reviews   96–7
    special needs   204–5
    twins   47
    vision   132
    *see also* play and toys
diarrhoea   71, **123**, **164**
diet and pregnancy   4–5, 17–18
diptheria   153, **154**
disability   47
    *see also* special needs
doctors, family   12, 93, 198
Domino system   12
Down's syndrome   15, 17
DPT immunisation   153
drugs   7
dummies   83–4, 91, 136

ears and hearing   31, 97, 132–3,
    **164**
echolalia   135
ectopic pregnancies   11
eczema   **75**
embryo   8
emotional development   125,
    133, *134*, 137–9, *146–9*
engorgement, breast   31, **108**
epidural anaesthesia **21**
episiotomy   *22*, **23**, 24
equipment
    bathing   62, *63*, 171–2
    clothing   176–9
    feeding   172
    safety   175–6, *175*
    selection and choice   168–9
    sleeping   169–71
    transportation   170–1, 173–5
    *see also* play and toys
erythema toxicum   **74**
eyes   31, 97, 132
    sticky   31, **76**

failure to thrive   117

fallopian tubes   8, 11
family centres   201
family doctors   12, 93, 198
febrile convulsions   160
feeding
    babies with special needs   205
    bottle-feeding   109–16
    breast or bottle?   100
    breast-feeding   101, 102–8
    equipment   172
    is baby having enough?   116–17
    nutritional needs   101–2
    pre-term babies   50
    problems   **123**
    twins   45–6
    weaning   117–20, **121**
feet   32
fever   158, 159, 160
fingers   32
fireguards *175*, 176
first aid   209–11
fits   160
fluoride   91
Foetal Alcohol syndrome   6, 31
foetus   8
    growth *9*
    support systems   8–10
    viable   26
folic acid   4
fontanelles   30
forceps delivery   *22*, **23**
formula milks   10, 109
    *see also* bottle-feeding
fungi   152

gas and air   **21**
genetic counselling   6
genitalia   31–2, *65*
German measles   6, 153, **155**
gestation   25
grasp reflex   34, *34*
growth   96–7, 127–31
Guthrie test   36

haemophilus influenzae type B
    (HIB)   153

head
    circumference   *41*, 127, *131*
    newborn babies   29, 30
health care *see* antenatal care;
        primary health care; special
        needs
health visitors   94, 198
hearing   97, 132–3
heart   30
heart massage   210, *210*
HIB immunisation   153
high-chairs   172, *175*
hips, congenital dislocation   38–9,
        *38*
hypothermia   **166**
hypothyroidism   37

illness
    common ailments   **163–6**
    effect on growth   *128*
    management of fever   160–1
    routine care   161–2
    signs and symptoms   156–7
    temperature and fever
        158–60
    when to call the doctor   *157*
    *see also* infections
immunisation   152–3
immunity   152
incubators   51
induction of labour   **23**
infections   151
    causes   151–2
    common ailments   **163–6**
    infectious diseases   **154–5**
    pre-term babies   51
    spread of   156
    *see also* illness
intellectual development   125,
        133, *134*, 137–9, **146–9**
intertrigo   **74**
intestinal obstructions   **165**
intolerances   109–10, **123**
iron   10, 50, 104, 118

jaundice   43–4, 51, **155**

key workers 142–3

labour and birth 12, 19, 21
   care of mother after *22*, 24
   pain relief **21**
   procedures to help *22*, **23**, 24
   three stages of 19–20, *20*
   twins 45
lactalbumin 109
lactation 102, 105
language development 47, 125,
   133–6
lanugo 10, 29, 32
layettes 176
learning *see* intellectual
   development
length **41**, 127, *131*
'let-down' reflex 102, *103*
light-for-dates babies 54
link workers 194
locomotion, development of *126*
low birth-weight 25, 48–9
   light-for-dates babies 54
   pre-term babies 49–53
lungs 30, 50

mastitis **108**
mealtimes 119, 205
   *see also* feeding
measles 153, **154**
meconium 32
medicines 7, 162
meningitis **165**
microwave ovens **112**, 114
midwives 12, 93–4
milia 32
miliaria **74**
milk 10, 102–4, 109–10
   *see also* feeding
milk teeth 89–90, *90*
minerals 101–2
miscarriages 25
MMR immunisation 153
'mongolian blue spots' 29
Moro reflex 34, *34*
mortality rates 25

Moses baskets 169
mother-baby bonding 39–40
   pre-term babies 51–3
   special needs babies 192
moulding (babies' heads) 29
mouth 31
movement 35, 126–7, *126*, 206–7
mumps 153, **155**
muscle tone 35

naevi 32–3
nail bed infection **76**
nappies 61, 179
nappy changing 58, 69, 206
nappy rash 70–1
neonatal period 25
   *see also* newborn babies
nervous system 33–6
newborn babies 25
   Apgar scores 27–8, **28**
   appearance 29
   clothing 176–7
   examination of 30–3
   immediate procedures 27,
     **41**
   jaundice 43–4
   keeping warm 40–3
   low-birth-weight 48–54
   mother-baby bonding 39–40
   nervous system 33–6
   postmature 55
   screening tests 36–9
nipples 102, **102**, 105, **108**
nutritional needs 101–2

otitis media **164**
overfeeding **123**, *128*

paediatricians 30, 95
parents
   and babies with special needs
     191–4, 197–8
   and day care admission 143–5
   mother-baby bonding 39–40,
     51–3, 192
paronychia **76**

percentile charts    127, 129–31, *130, 131*
pertussis    153, **155**
pethidine    **21**
PHCT (primary health care teams)    93–5, 198
physical development    125, *146–9*
  growth measurement    127–31, *130, 131*
  influences on    127, *128*
  movement    126–7, *126*
PKU (phenylketonuria)    36–7
placenta    8, 9, 20, 55
placing reflex    *34*, 35
play and toys    179–80
  0 to 3 months    180
  3 to 6 months    180–1
  6 to 12 months    181–4, 185–6
  safety    184
  special needs    201, 204–5
pneumonia    **164**
poliomyelitis    153, **155**
Portage home teaching    202–3
possetting    *123*
posterior fontanelle    30
postmature babies    25, 55
postnatal period    24
  'baby blues'    24
  postnatal depression    25
  postnatal examination    24
posture    35, *36*
poverty    18–19
prams    169, 170–1, 174, **174**
pre-conceptual care    1–7
pre-eclampsia    11
pre-term babies    26, 49–53, 130
pregnacy tests    10
pregnancy    1, 25–6
  antenatal care    11–12, 13–15
  complications    11
  diet in    17–18
  foetal growth *9*
  foetal support systems    8–10
  minor ailments    11
  postnatal period    24–5
  poverty and    18–19

preparing for    2–7
self-care    *16*
signs and symptons    10
special tests during    15–17
where to have the baby    12
premature *see* pre-term babies
primary health care    93
  child health promotion    95–6
  reviews and assessments    96–8
  teams (PHCTs)    93–5, 198
primary teeth    89–90, *90*
primitive reflexes    33–5, *34*
prone posture    35, *36*
proteins    101
pulse rates    158
pushchairs    170–1, 174, **174**
pyloric stenosis    **165**
pyoderma    **76**

recovery position    210, *210*
reflexes    33–5, *34*
respiration *see* breathing
respite care    201
rest *see* sleep
resuscitation    210
rooting reflex    33–4, *34*, 105
rubella    6, 153, **155**

safety equipment    175–6, *175*
SAFP (serum alphafetoprotein)    15
scalds (first aid)    211
scarlet fever    **154**
SCBUs (special care baby units)    51, *52*, 53
screening    36–9, 96, 97
seborrhoeic dermatitis    **74**
septic spots    **76**
sexually transmitted diseases    (STDs)    7
siblings    47, 194–5, *196*
skin
  common conditions    73, **74–5**
  common infections    73, **76**
  functions    57
  nappy rash    70–1
  newborn babies    29, 32

skin care
  bathing   60–8
  nappy changing   58, 69
  routines   57–8
  in the sun   72–3
  topping and tailing   58, 68–9
sleep   78–9
  babies with special needs   206
  comfort objects   83–4
  day care routines   79
  difficulties in settling   82
  equipment   169–71
  older babies   82–3
  where should baby sleep
    79–80
slings, baby   173–4
smoking   6
snuffles   **163**
social development   125, 133,
    *134*, 137–9, **146–9**
social services   198–201, *200*
special care baby units (SCBUs)
    51, *52*, 53
special needs   187, 197
  day care   201–2
  health and social services
    197–201, *199*, *200*
  parents and   191–4, 197–8
  physical care   205–7
  possible causes   187, *188*
  recognition   189, 190
  siblings and   194–5, *196*
  stimulation   204–5
  types   189–90
  voluntary organisations   202–4
speech *see* language development
spina bifida   15, 17, 32
spine   32
startle reflex   35
STDs (sexually transmitted
    diseases)   7
stepping reflex   *34*, 35
sterilisation of feeding equipment
    111, *111*, **112**
sticky eyes   31, **76**
stillborn babies   26

stools, abnormal   71–2
'stork marks'   32
strollers   170
sudden infant death   **166**
sunburn   72–3
supine posture   35, *36*
sweat rash   **74**

talcum powder   61
teeth   31, 89–91, *90*
teething   92
temperature   *166*
  baths   61
  in illness   158, 160
  keeping babies warm   40–3,
    **166**
  measuring babies'   158–60
  pre-term babies   50–1
TENS (transcutaneous nerve
    stimulation)   **21**
term babies   26
tetanus   153
thermometers   159
thrush dermatitis   70
THS (thyroid stimulating
    hormone) test   37
toes   32
toilet training   72
toiletries   60
tonsilitis   **154**
topping and tailing   58, 68–9
toy libraries   201
toys and play *see* play and toys
twins   44–8
tympanic thermometers   159–60

ultrasound scans   15
umbilical cord   8, 31, 39, **41**, *65*
underfeeding   **123**, *128*
urticaria neonatorum   **74**
uterus   8

vacuum extraction   *22*, **23**
vegetarian and vegan diets   5
ventral suspension posture   35,
    *36*

ventuouse extraction   *22*, **23**
vernix caseosa   10, 29, 32
viruses   152
vision   97, 132
vitamins   101–2
vomiting   **164**

walking reflex   *34*, 35

weaning   117–20, **121**
weight   **41**, 116–17
  growth measurement   127,
    129–31, *130*
  pre-term babies   51
whooping cough   153, **155**
winding a baby   115
womb   8

## Praise for Elly Griffiths

'Griffiths has written an excellent murder mystery,
peopled with credible characters, and enhanced
by a masterly depiction of landscape, history and
atmosphere . . . her work is proof that it is often the
lightest of touches which pierces the deepest'
*Crime Fiction Lover*

'If you like your crime to have a whiff of the arcane
about it and you like your heroines to be as engaging and
likeable as forensic archaeologist, Dr Ruth Galloway, then
it's a wonder that you haven't discovered Elly Griffiths yet'
*Red magazine*

'Griffiths always provides a clever mystery and a wealth
of historical detail. But it's her complex characterizations
that put her in the forefront of the current mystery field'
*Kirkus Reviews*

'Like any good writer of detective fiction [Griffiths] always
has something to say about the complexity of the human
condition and this very enjoyable novel is no exception'
*Shiny New Books*

'What makes this series such a draw is that you can
absolutely imagine knowing the people who
sprawl across the page'
*Crime Review*

**Elly Griffiths** was born in London. She worked in publishing for many years. Her bestselling series of Ruth Galloway novels have three times been shortlisted for the Theakston's Old Peculier Crime Novel of the Year, and twice for the CWA Dagger in the Library. Her new series is based in 1950s Brighton. Elly lives near Brighton with her husband, an archaeologist, their two children and her cat.

## Also by Elly Griffiths

### THE RUTH GALLOWAY MYSTERIES

*The Crossing Places*
*The Janus Stone*
*The House at Sea's End*
*A Room Full of Bones*
*Dying Fall*
*The Outcast Dead*
*The Ghost Fields*

### THE STEPHENS AND MEPHISTO MYSTERIES

*The Zig Zag Girl*
*Smoke and Mirrors*

and coming soon
*The Blood Card*

ELLY
# Griffiths
# The
# Woman
# in Blue

A Dr RUTH GALLOWAY MYSTERY

Quercus

First published in Great Britain in 2016 by Quercus
This paperback edition published in 2016 by

Quercus Editions Ltd
Carmelite House
50 Victoria Embankment
London EC4Y 0DZ

An Hachette UK company

A CIP catalogue record for this book is available
from the British Library

PB ISBN 978 1 84866 337 4
EBOOK ISBN 978 1 78429 238 6

16

Typeset by CC Book Production
Printed and bound in Great Britain by Clays Ltd, Elcograf S.p.A.

For Giulia

# WALSINGHAM

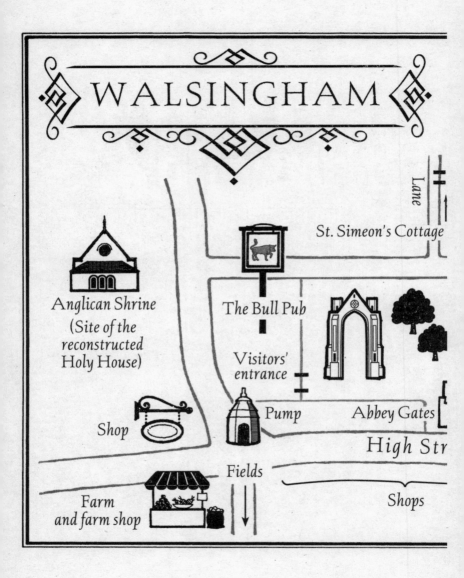

Lane

St. Simeon's Cottage

The Bull Pub

Anglican Shrine
(Site of the
reconstructed
Holy House)

Visitors'
entrance

Pump

Abbey Gates

Shop

High Str

Fields

Farm
and farm shop

Shops

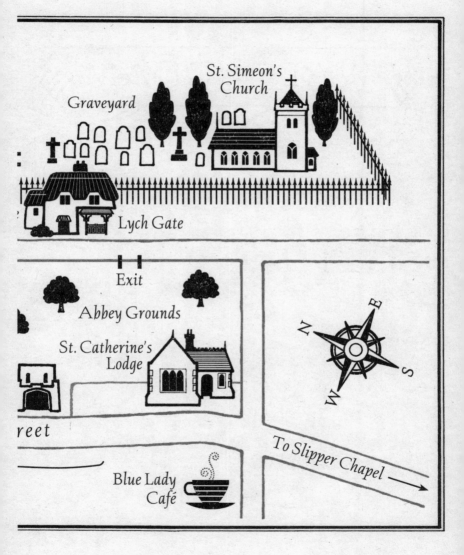

Weep, weep, O Walsingham,
Whose dayes are nights,
Blessings turned to blasphemies,
Holy deeds to despites.
Sinne is where Our Ladye sate,
Heaven turned is to helle;
Satan sitthe where our Lord did swaye,
Walsingham, O farewell!

Ballad of Walsingham, anonymous, sixteenth century

# The
# Woman
## in Blue

# PROLOGUE

*19th February 2014*

Cathbad and the cat look at each other. They have been drawing up the battle-lines all day and this is their Waterloo. The cat has the advantage: this is his home and he knows the terrain. But Cathbad has his druidical powers and what he believes is a modest gift with animals, a legacy from his Irish mother who used to talk to seagulls (and receive messages back). He has a companion animal himself, a bull-terrier called Thing, and has always enjoyed a psychic rapport with Ruth's cat, Flint.

This cat, whose name is Chesterton, is a different proposition altogether. Whereas Flint is a large and lazy ginger Tom whose main ambition is to convince Ruth that he is starving at all times, Chesterton is a lithe and sinuous black creature, given to perching on top of cupboards and staring at Cathbad out of disconcertingly round, yellow eyes. This is Cathbad's third day of house- and cat- sitting, and so far Chesterton has ignored all blandishments. He has even ignored the food that

Cathbad carefully weighed out according to Justin's instructions. He might be living on mice, but Chesterton does not look like an animal who is governed by his appetites. He's an ascetic, if Cathbad ever saw one.

But Justin's sternest admonition, written in capitals and underlined in red, was: DO NOT LET CHESTERTON OUT AT NIGHT. And now, here they are, at nine o'clock on a February evening with Chesterton staring at the door and Cathbad barring the way with his fiery sword. The biblical reference comes to hand because the house is part of an ancient pilgrimage site and is decorated with etchings from the Old Testament. Justin, a custodian of the site, is on a fact-finding trip to Knock, something Cathbad finds extremely funny. He has left the fifteenth-century cottage – and the accompanying cat – under Cathbad's protection.

Chesterton meows once, commandingly.

'I'm sorry,' says Cathbad. 'I can't.'

Chesterton gives him a pitying look, jumps onto a cupboard and manages to slide out through a partially opened window. So that's why he has been on hunger strike.

'Chesterton!' Cathbad lifts the heavy latch and opens the door. Cold air rushes in. 'Chesterton! Come back!'

The cottage is attached to the church, with a passageway through it at ground-floor level forming a kind of lych-gate. Worshippers have to pass underneath the main bedroom in order to get to St Simeon's. There's even a handy recess in the wall of the passage so that pall-bearers can rest their coffins there. The back door of the cottage opens directly onto the churchyard. 'But you won't mind that,' said Justin, 'it's right up your street.' And it's true that Cathbad does like burial grounds, and all places of communal worship but, even so, there's something about St Simeon's Cottage, Walsingham, that he doesn't quite like. It's not the presence of the cat, or the creaks and groans of the old house at night; it's more a sort of sadness about the place, a feeling so oppressive that, during his first evening, Cathbad was compelled to call upon a circle of protection and to ring his partner Judy several times.

He's not scared now, just worried about the cat. He walks along the church path, the frost crunching under his feet, calling the animal's name.

And then he sees it. A tombstone near the far wall, glowing white in the moonlight, and a woman standing beside it. A woman in white robes and a flowing blue cloak. As Cathbad approaches, she looks at him, and her face, illuminated by something stronger than natural light, seems at once so beautiful and so sad that Cathbad crosses himself.

'Can I help you?' he calls. His voice echoes against stone and darkness. The woman smiles – such a sad, sweet smile – shakes her head and starts to walk away, moving very fast through the gravestones towards the far gate.

Cathbad goes to follow her, but is floored, neatly and completely, by Chesterton, who must have been lurking behind a yew tree for this very purpose.

# CHAPTER 1

DCI Harry Nelson hears the news as he is driving to work. 'Woman's body found in a ditch outside Walsingham. SCU request attend.' As he does a handbrake turn in the road, he is conscious of a range of conflicting emotions. He's sorry that someone's dead, of course he is, but he can't help feeling something else, a slight frisson of excitement, and a relief that he's been spared that morning's meeting with Superintendent Gerald Whitcliffe and their discussion of the previous month's targets. Nelson is in charge of the SCU, the Serious Crimes Unit, but the truth is that serious crime is often thin on the ground in King's Lynn and the surrounding areas. That's a good thing – Nelson acknowledges this as he puts on his siren and speeds through the morning traffic – but it does make for rather dull work. Not that Nelson hasn't had his share of serious crime in his career – only a few months ago he was shot at and might have died if his sergeant hadn't shot back – but there's also a fair amount of petty theft, minor drugs stuff and people complaining because their stolen bicycle wasn't featured on *Crimewatch*.

He calls his sergeants, Dave Clough and Tim Heathfield, and tells them to meet him at the scene. Though they both just say 'Yes, boss', he can hear the excitement in their voices too. If Sergeant Judy Johnson were there, she would remind them that they were dealing with a human tragedy, but Judy is on maternity leave and so the atmosphere in the station is rather testosterone heavy.

He sees the flashing lights as he turns the corner. The body was found on the Fakenham Road, about a mile outside Walsingham. It's a narrow road with high hedges on both sides, made narrower by the two squad cars and the coroner's van. As soon as Nelson steps out of his car he feels claustrophobic, something that often happens when he's in the countryside. The high green walls of foliage make him feel as if he's in the bottom of a well and the grey sky seems to be pushing down on top of him. Give him pavements and street lighting any day.

The local policemen stand aside for him. Chris Stephenson, the police pathologist, is in the ditch with the body. He looks up and grins at Nelson as if it's the most charming meeting place in the world.

'Well, if it isn't Admiral Nelson himself!'

'Hallo, Chris. What's the situation?'

'Woman, probably in her early to mid-twenties, looks like she's been strangled. Rigor mortis has set in, but then it was a cold night. I'd say she's been here about eight to ten hours.'

'What's she wearing?' From Nelson's vantage point it looks like fancy dress, a long white robe and some sort of blue cloak. For a moment he thinks of Cathbad, whose favourite attire is a druid's cloak. 'It's both spiritual and practical,' he'd once told Nelson.

'Nightdress and dressing gown,' says Stephenson. 'Not exactly the thing for a February night, eh?'

'Has she got slippers on?' Nelson can see a glimpse of bare leg, ending in something white.

'Yes, the kind you get free in spas and the like,' says Stephenson, who probably knows a lot about such places. 'Again, not exactly the thing for tramping over the fields.'

'If her slippers are still on, she must have been placed in the ditch and not thrown.'

'You're right, chief. I'd say the body was placed here with some care.' Stephenson holds out an object in a plastic bag. 'This was on her chest.'

'What is it? A necklace?'

Stephenson laughs. 'I thought you were a left-footer, Admiral. It's a rosary.'

A rosary. Nelson's mother has a wooden rosary from Lourdes and she prays a decade every night. Nelson's sisters, Grainne and Maeve, were given rosaries for their First Holy Communions. Nelson didn't get one because he was a boy.

'Bag it,' he says, although the rosary is already sealed in a plastic evidence bag. 'It's important evidence.'

'If you say so, chief.'

Nelson straightens up. He has heard a car approaching and guesses that it's Clough and Tim. Besides, he's had enough of Chris Stephenson and his breezy good humour.

His sergeants come towards him. Both are tall and dark and have been described (though not by Nelson) as handsome, but there the resemblance ends. Clough is white and Tim is black, but there's much more to it than that. Clough is heavily built, wearing jeans and skiing jacket. He's looking around with something like excitement and there's a half-eaten bagel in his hand. Tim is taller and slimmer, he's wearing a long dark coat and knotted scarf and could be a politician visiting a factory. His face gives nothing away.

Nelson briefs them quickly. He calls over the local officer, who explains that the body was found by an early morning dog-walker. 'Her little dog actually got into the ditch and was . . . well . . . shaking the deceased.'

'If she's in nightclothes,' says Tim, 'she could be a patient at the Sanctuary.'

The same thought has occurred to Nelson. It was the waffle-patterned slippers that first gave him the idea. The Sanctuary is a private hospital specialising in drug rehabilitation. Because a lot of the patients are famous (though not to Nelson), the place exists in an atmosphere of high walls, secrecy and rumours of drug-fuelled orgies. It is quite near here, about a mile across the fields.

'Good thinking,' he says. 'You and Cloughie can go over there in a minute and ask if any patients are missing.'

'Foxy O'Hara's meant to be there at the moment,' says Clough, swallowing the last of his bagel.

'Who?'

'You must have heard of her. She was on *I'm a Celebrity* before Christmas.'

'You're jabbering, Cloughie.' Nelson turns to Chris Stephenson, who has emerged from the ditch and is taking off his coveralls. 'Anything else for us, Chris? No handy nametapes on the dressing gown?'

'No, but it's a good one. Pricy. From John Lewis.'

'Costs a bit to stay in the Sanctuary,' says Nelson. 'I think that's our best bet.'

'Excuse me, sir.' It's one of the local policemen, nervous and respectful. 'But there's a man asking to see you. Looks a bit of a nutter, but he says he knows you.'

'Cathbad,' says Clough, without looking round.

Clough is right. Nelson sees Cathbad standing beyond the police tape, wearing his trademark cloak. How strange, and slightly unsettling, that Nelson was thinking about him only a few moments before. He strides over.

'Cathbad. What are you doing here?'

'I'm house-sitting in Walsingham.'

'What about Judy? Have you left her alone with a newborn baby?'

'Miranda's ten weeks old and she's an old soul. No, Judy's taken the children to visit her parents.'

'That doesn't explain why you're here, at a crime scene.'

'The woman you've found,' says Cathbad. 'Was she wearing a blue cloak?'

Nelson takes a step back. 'Who says we've found a woman?'

He half-expects Cathbad to say something about spiritual energies and cosmic vibrations, but instead he says, 'I heard the milkman talking about it. Useful people, milkmen. They're up and about early, they notice things.'

'And what did you mean about a cloak? I'm sure the bloody milkman didn't see that.'

Cathbad exhales. 'So it is her.'

'What are you talking about?'

'The cottage where I'm staying, it overlooks the graveyard.' That figures, thinks Nelson. 'Well, last night, I saw a woman standing there, a woman wearing a white robe and a blue cloak.'

'What time was that?'

'About nine.'

Nelson lifts the tape. 'You'd better come through.'

The scene-of-the-crime team have arrived. In their paper suits and masks they look like aliens taking over a sleepy Norfolk village. As Nelson and Cathbad watch, the dead woman's body is slowly winched out of the ditch. The corpse is covered with a sheet, but as the stretcher passes them they both see a length of muddy blue material hanging down. Cathbad crosses himself and Nelson has to stop himself following suit.

'Any idea who she was?' asks Cathbad.

'She was in nightclothes,' said Nelson. 'Your "cloak" was a dressing gown. I'm sending Clough and Heathfield to the Sanctuary.'

'Do you think she was a patient there?'

'It's a line of enquiry.'

The aliens have now erected a tent-like structure over the ditch. The atmosphere has somehow stopped being that of an emergency and has become calm and purposeful.

'Look, Cathbad,' says Nelson. 'I'm going to brief the boys and finish up here. Then I'll come and talk to you about what you saw last night. Where's this place you're staying?'

'St Simeon's Cottage. Next to the church.'

'I won't be long.'

'Time,' says Cathbad grandly, 'is of no consequence.' But he is talking to the empty air.

Ruth Galloway doesn't hear about the body in the ditch until she's at work. She did listen to the radio in the car, but what with the hassle of getting her five-year-old daughter, Kate, to school in time, it all became rather a blur. 'Have you got your book bag?' . . . Here's Gary with the sports news . . . 'Can you see a parking space?' . . . Thought for the Day with the Revd . . . 'Quick, there's Mrs Mannion waiting for you. Love you. See you later.' . . . Icy winds, particularly on the east coast . . . If the dead woman did make it on to the *Today* programme, Ruth missed it altogether. It wasn't until she was at her desk, trying to catch up on emails before her first tutorial, that her head of department, Phil Trent, wandered – uninvited – into her office and asked if she'd heard 'the latest drama'.

'No. What?'

'A woman found dead in a ditch out Walsingham way. It was on *Look East.*'

'I must have missed it.'

'I thought you had a hotline to the boys in blue.'

Phil is jealous of Ruth's role as a special advisor to the police and sometimes she likes to tease him, dropping hints of high-level meetings and top-secret memos, but this morning she doesn't have the energy.

'I doubt it will have anything to do with me. Not unless there's an Iron Age skeleton in the ditch as well.'

'I suppose not.'

Ruth turns back to her screen, and though Phil hovers in the doorway for a few minutes, eventually he drifts away, leaving her to concentrate on her emails. They are the usual collection of advertisements from academic publishers, departmental memos and requests from her students for extra time to finish their essays. Ruth deletes the first and the second and is settling down to answer the third when she sees a new category of email. The subject is 'Long time no see'. This is either intriguing or worrying, depending on your mood. Ruth is probably fifty–fifty on that. She clicks it open.

> Hi, Ruth,
>
> Do you remember me, Hilary Smithson, from Southampton? Where have the years gone? I understand that you're in Norfolk, doing very well for yourself. I'm coming to Norfolk next week, for a conference in Walsingham, and I wondered if we could meet up? I'd like to ask your advice on a rather tricky matter. And I'd love to see you of course.
> Looking forward to hearing from you.
> All best,
> Hilary

Ruth stares at the screen. It's the second time that Walsingham has been mentioned that morning and, as Nelson always says, there's no such thing as coincidence.

# CHAPTER 2

The Sanctuary is an imposing Victorian edifice, more suited to a sooty city centre than the Norfolk countryside. Even softened by trees and gently rolling hills, it looks like a town hall or a railway station that has somehow planted itself in the middle of a field.

Clough, though, is impressed. 'Look at this place. It's like a stately home.'

'Looks more like a prison,' says Tim.

They have stopped at the electronic gates but, before Tim can speak into the intercom, they open soundlessly.

'Not very good security for a prison,' says Clough.

Tim says nothing. In fact, both have brothers who have been in prison, but they are not in the habit of discussing their families. Tim puts the car into gear and they approach the house via a sweeping gravel drive. Wide steps lead to the front door and, facing them, there's a perfect ring of grass with a stone fountain in the middle. There is not a soul to be seen.

They ignore signs to the visitors' car park and leave the car at the foot of the steps. Tim presses the bell and, this time, a voice answers. He has hardly finished saying the word 'Police' when the double doors open.

Inside it's definitely more like a hotel than a prison – a baronial hall with a monstrous stone fireplace and a round table bearing an arrangement of waxy-looking flowers. A grandfather clock ticks ponderously, and gloomy oil paintings look down from the walls. There's even a reception desk where a woman is flashing her teeth at them.

'How can I help you?'

Tim shows his warrant card. 'Can I speak to whoever's in charge?' They agreed in the car that he should take the lead in the interview. Clough hovers supportively at his shoulder.

The receptionist looks at them nervously. 'That's Doctor McAllister.'

'Can I speak to him then?' asks Tim.

'I'll see if she's free.' The receptionist picks up a phone and Clough murmurs, 'You've got to watch these sexist assumptions, Tim.'

'Bugger off,' says Tim without moving his lips.

Doctor McAllister arrives very quickly. She's an attractive middle-aged woman with short brown hair and narrow intimidating glasses. She ushers them to a leather sofa in front of the fireplace. Tim was going to suggest somewhere more private but as – apart from the receptionist who seems oblivious – the lobby is as empty as the grounds, he subsides.

'What's all this about, officer?' The doctor takes charge

immediately, smoothing her white coat and adjusting her glasses.

'We were wondering if any of your patients were missing?' asks Tim.

'What do you mean, "missing"?'

'It's a simple enough question,' says Clough. 'Are any of your inmates missing?'

'They're not inmates, officer, they're patients,' says Doctor McAllister.

'And *are* any of your patients missing?' asks Tim.

'Our patients are free to come and go. They sign themselves in for treatment.'

'Did anyone sign themselves out yesterday?'

'I don't think so,' she admits.

'So everyone is where they should be?'

'Well, we haven't done the rounds of the rooms yet, so I can't be a hundred per cent sure.'

'The thing is,' Tim says, and leans forward confidentially, 'a body has been found.'

'A body?'

'The body of a woman in her nightclothes. We wondered if she was one of your patients.'

'But that's impossible.'

'I thought people were free to come and go,' says Clough.

'Yes,' says Doctor McAllister and shoots him an unfriendly look. 'But we wouldn't sign anyone out just wearing their nightclothes. And, as I say . . .'

The pocket of her white coat starts to vibrate: they can see a red light flashing under the fabric.

'I think someone wants you,' says Tim.

Doctor McAllister pulls out her phone and has a brief monosyllabic conversation. Then she gets to her feet, saying, 'Excuse me, gentlemen.'

Clough and Tim exchange glances, then get up and follow her.

There's a grand staircase to the right of the fireplace. Doctor McAllister takes the stairs two at a time, with the policemen following her. On the landing she opens a door and immediately the country-house hotel vanishes and they enter a world that is altogether more institutional: numbered doors, hand-gel dispensers; even the carpet looks different. Two men in white coats (nurses? doctors? orderlies?) stand by one of the doors. Doctor McAllister hurries forward to speak to them and Tim hears the word 'missing'. He holds out his warrant card and asks, '*Is* somebody missing?'

The doctor shoots him an irritated look, but says, 'Apparently, one of our patients isn't in her room.'

A white-coated man pushes open door number 12. It's a pleasant but functional room: single bed, table, wardrobe, armchair and a beautiful sash window that is slightly too big for the space.

'The patient's name?' asks Clough briskly.

Doctor McAllister confers. 'Jenkins. Chloe Jenkins.'

'And when was Miss Jenkins last seen?'

One of the white coats replies, 'Last night, at about eight, when I took supper round.'

A covered plate lies on the bedside table. Clough lifts the lid, revealing uneaten shepherd's pie congealing at the edges.

'And after that?'

'No. She didn't ring her bell.'

Tim has opened the wardrobe. 'What would Miss Jenkins have been wearing?'

The orderly replies nervously, 'She was in her nightclothes and a dressing gown.'

'What colour?'

'Blue.'

Tim turns to Doctor McAllister. 'I think you'd better come with us.'

What with one thing and another, it's nearly eleven o'clock when Nelson knocks on the hobbit-sized front door of St Simeon's Cottage. The door is opened immediately, but is held ajar, with only Cathbad's face showing through.

'Quickly,' he says. 'I don't want to let the cat out.'

'Trust you to be looking after a mad cat,' says Nelson, squeezing through the aperture.

'He's not mad,' says Cathbad, showing Nelson into a low-ceilinged sitting room. 'He's disconcertingly sane.'

The slim black cat is sitting by the wood-burning stove. He gets up, shoots Nelson a look of contempt and stalks out of the room.

'Friendly creature,' says Nelson.

'I think he's the reincarnation of my old Latin teacher,' says Cathbad. 'He looks at me with exactly the same expression of disappointment.'

Nelson laughs and then realises that this might not be a joke.

'Why's he not allowed out?' he asks.

'He's allowed out in the day, but not at night,' says Cathbad. 'But I've got twitchy about letting him out of the front door. I keep thinking that he'll get run over just to spite me.'

'When's the owner of the house back?'

'Tomorrow. Thank the gods.'

'It's an interesting place,' says Nelson, though privately he thinks that all those beams and uneven floorboards would get him down after a while. There doesn't seem to be a straight line in the whole place. To his surprise, though, Cathbad shudders. 'It's got bad energies,' he says. 'Oppressive. Can't you feel it? I've had a headache all the time I've been here.'

'It's probably just because you keep hitting your head on doorposts.'

Cathbad laughs. 'Probably.'

'So, tell me about this woman you saw last night.'

'I'll show you.'

Cathbad leads Nelson through a door and into a narrow stone passageway. The cat is waiting by the door at the end of it.

'I'll let you out, Chesterton,' says Cathbad, 'if you promise to come back.'

The cat ignores him.

The back door opens directly onto the graveyard. Some of the stones are almost as big as the low house; others lean towards it in a rather threatening way.

'Blimey.' Nelson follows Cathbad along the path through the graves, saying, 'Talk about dead centre of town.'

'It's a very old church,' says Cathbad. 'Anglo-Saxon. It's older than the priory.'

The word 'Anglo-Saxon' reminds Nelson of Ruth, who is fond of throwing around historical eras as if she is unaware of the fact that Nelson has never worked out whether Bronze Age comes before the Iron Age or who the hell Homo Heidelbergensis is. The Anglo-Saxons he thinks came after the Romans, but that's as far as he's prepared to go.

'Where did you see the woman?'

'Here. By this white tombstone.'

Nelson looks at the grass around the stone. It's slightly flattened, but there are no footprints or any signs of a struggle.

'What time was this?'

'About nine. I'd just rung Judy and I try to do that before nine because she goes to bed early these days.'

'What happened next?'

'She smiled at me. Honest to God, Nelson, she had such a beautiful smile, like an angel. I thought . . .'

'What did you think?'

'Walsingham is a shrine to the Virgin Mary. And she was wearing a blue cloak. Well, I thought it was a cloak at the time.'

'You thought you'd seen a vision of Our Lady?'

'Our Lady. You're still such a Catholic, Nelson.'

'Stop trying to wind me up. What happened next?'

'She turned away and started walking towards the gate. I tried to follow but Chesterton jumped out and tripped me up.'

'Chesterton, the cat?'

'Yes. He's like some malign sprite. I'm sure he did it deliberately. When I got back he was sitting by his bowl in the kitchen as if nothing had happened.'

'Forget the cat for a minute. What happened to the woman?'

'When I got up, she was gone. I went to the gate and looked down the lane but there was no sign of her.'

'Show me.'

They walk through the churchyard. There are a few impressive tombs, with weeping angels and towering crosses, but most graves are simply marked by stones, their edges blurred by time and exposure to the elements. Some gravestones have fallen over and others are lined up against the low brick wall; a few are lying flat, sunk into the grass as if laid out for a macabre game of hopscotch. Nelson tries to avoid treading on them. The gate opens easily and leads into another narrow lane with high hedges. It's a fairly straight road, though. The woman must have been walking fast, thinks Nelson, to have got out of sight so quickly.

He looks at Cathbad, who is examining the inscription on a stone angel. 'You didn't think to tell anyone about your vision?'

'No. What was there to tell? The church and graveyard are free to everyone.'

'Was the church open?'

'No. It's shut when they're not having services there. I don't approve. Churches should be open at all times.'

'I suppose they're worried about burglaries.'

'Yes, but a church should be there for the people. A place of sanctuary. Afterwards I wondered if that's what she was doing. Seeking sanctuary in the church.'

There's not much else to see. Nelson walks the perimeter of the graveyard, still taking care not to step on the dead. Then he says goodbye to Cathbad who sidles into the cottage, careful not to let the cat out. When Nelson gets back to his car, he checks his phone. There's a text from Tim saying that the dead woman has been formally identified as Chloe Jenkins, aged twenty-five, a patient at the Sanctuary.

# CHAPTER 3

'What was she being treated for?'

'Drink and drug dependency, apparently.'

'Does she have any family?'

'Parents live in Surrey. The local police are informing them now. Then they'll be on their way here.'

'Poor sods.' Nelson, Tim and Clough are back at the station. The briefing room has already been prepared for a major incident. Tanya Fuller, an extremely keen Detective Constable (Acting Sergeant, as she tells everyone), has pinned up a map of Walsingham and the surrounding area. There are pads and pencils on every desk and extra phonelines are being put in.

Nelson puts a red pin at the spot where the body was found.

'Have you got a photograph of the victim?' he asks Tim.

'The hospital gave us this.' He offers a passport-sized photograph. Nelson squints at it; he really should get his eyes tested. The unsmiling head-and-shoulders shot gives nothing away.

'But we Googled her,' says Clough. 'Look.' He pushes an open laptop towards Nelson.

'Bloody hell.'

The screen is full of images. A beautiful blonde woman stares out at him, replicated again and again, in swimwear, bridal gowns, prom dresses, gothic black and fishnet tights, covered in artistically placed leaves.

'She was quite a well-known model,' says Tim.

'Bloody hell,' says Nelson again.

'I know,' says Clough. 'Looks a lot like your missus, doesn't she?'

What had struck Nelson at first was that Chloe looked like his elder daughter, Laura. But, of course, Laura resembles her mother, and actually what is staring out at him from the myriad images is a younger Michelle. Nelson's wife, a runner-up for Miss Blackpool 1988, was offered modelling work as a younger woman, but hadn't been interested. 'It was all car shows and strip clubs anyway,' she says, 'nothing glamorous'. Besides, Michelle, though aware of her own beauty, doesn't like having her photograph taken.

'Isn't she the image of Mrs Nelson?' Clough turns to Tim.

'Maybe,' says Tim. 'I don't know.'

'The image of her,' says Clough. 'Twenty-odd years ago.'

'Don't let Michelle hear you say that,' says Nelson. 'She doesn't admit to a day over thirty.'

He keeps his voice light, but he's shaken. Resemblance is a funny thing. Michelle is always saying that the girls look like him but he can never see it. They're girls, for one thing. But this likeness is shocking. Maybe in the flesh it wouldn't be so striking – gestures and voice make up so much of what a person is – but here, pixellated on the screen, the similarity is almost frightening. Chloe Jenkins is looking at him out of a face that he has known and loved for more than twenty years.

'What do we know about this girl?' he asks.

'She's twenty-five,' says Tim, 'been modelling since she was sixteen. Two other sessions in rehab, one when she was just eighteen. Parents, Alan and Julie, live in Weybridge in Surrey. Father's an airline pilot. Chloe lived in London and was in a relationship with an actor and model called Thom Novak. She entered the Sanctuary on 27th January and was apparently making good progress. Last seen last night at about eight when an orderly brought round the evening meal. Her body was identified by Doctor Fiona McAllister, the chief medical officer at the hospital.'

Nelson pulls a pad of paper towards him. 'Well the first thing we need to know is Novak's whereabouts last night.'

'Checked,' says Clough. 'He's in rehab too. In Switzerland.'

'Jesus wept. What a set.'

'Doctor McAllister said that it was impossible to leave the hospital without signing out,' says Tim, 'but from what Cloughie and I saw it would be easy enough. There are plenty of side doors and more than one way out.'

'Any idea what she was doing in Walsingham?'

'No. We don't know if she was ever in the village. The road where she was found was on the way to the Slipper Chapel, the Catholic shrine.'

'She was seen in the village,' says Nelson. He describes Cathbad's sighting of Chloe Jenkins in the churchyard.

'Typical bloody Cathbad,' says Clough. 'Trust him to think it was some religious vision and not contact the police.'

'To be fair,' says Nelson, 'he had no reason to know that she was in danger. There are lots of odd people in Walsingham, pilgrims and the like.'

'Should we go door to door in Walsingham,' says Clough. 'Check if anyone else saw her last night?'

'Yes,' says Nelson. 'Let's track the route she might have taken across the fields too. Get some dog-handlers on the scene. Tim, will you speak to the boyfriend in Switzerland?'

'You should have a lot in common with a male model,' says Clough.

'It's not a joking matter,' says Nelson.

'That wasn't a joke.'

'The parents will be here soon. They've lost a daughter, let's not forget that. Tanya, will you look after them? I'll speak to them too.'

'Yes, boss.' Nelson thinks that Tanya looks slightly disappointed to be left with the soft, family liaison role. But someone has to do it and he needs Tim and Clough elsewhere.

'Clough, you organise the door-to-door. Appeal for witnesses on the road too. Tim, after you've spoken to the boyfriend, get on to Intel. We need to know if there's anyone in Chloe's background who might be a suspect.'

'Yes, boss.'

Nelson is getting into gear now, feeling as if the inquiry is really starting. The first hours are the most important. If they can hit the ground running, they have a good chance of finding out who killed Chloe Jenkins. Nelson thinks of the little body in the nightdress and dressing gown and his resolve hardens.

'Right, let's get going.'

Then Leah, Nelson's PA, puts her head round the door. 'Superintendent Whitcliffe wants to see you.'

Whitcliffe, perma-tanned and smooth, is Nelson's nemesis. He's a local boy, a graduate who sees King's Lynn CID as a stepping stone to greater things. He loves phrases like 'twenty-first-century policing' and 'three-hundred-and-sixty-degree appraisal'. He's passionate about community involvement as long as he doesn't actually have to meet any members of the community. Nelson is a major thorn in his side. Nelson's methods are frequently unorthodox and at heart he's an old-school copper who prefers being out in the field to directing strategic operations (another of Whitcliffe's favourite phrases). Whitcliffe would like to get rid of Nelson and bring in a smart young graduate, someone like Tim, perhaps. But Nelson's team are loyal to him and he seems to get results. Whitcliffe lives in hope that Nelson will one day want to go back to the North, a place as remote and shadowy to Whitcliffe as the north side of the moon. But he prides himself on getting on with everyone, so he greets Nelson heartily.

'Ah, Harry, sit down. Good of you to spare the time. Bad business about this young girl.'

'Chloe Jenkins,' says Nelson, remaining standing. 'I'm in the middle of an investigation. The vital first seven hours.'

'Of course. I gather that the dead girl, Chloe, was a well-known model?'

'Yes.'

'Well, you know what this will mean?'

Nelson says nothing, so Whitcliffe expands on his theme. 'It will mean increased press interest. You know how it works, Harry. A good-looking victim and all the papers will be on it. We'll have to call a press conference.'

'But there's nothing to tell them.'

'It's good PR, Harry. You know how important that is. And we can appeal for witnesses. Would you like Tim Heathfield to do it?'

'No, I'll do it,' says Nelson. 'When?'

'Tomorrow, first thing.'

'I'll be there,' says Nelson. 'And now, if you'll excuse me, I'm expecting Chloe's parents.'

They arrive just after four in an unmarked police car. Watching them approach, Nelson thinks that Alan and Julie Jenkins don't seem suited to tragedy. They're a good-looking couple, probably in their early fifties, smartly dressed even on this occasion. But they are shrunken with grief; Julie has her arms wrapped tightly around her body, Alan – a man clearly born to command – looks lost and somewhat frightened.

Nelson greets them. 'I'm so sorry for your loss.' When did they all start saying that? The police used to say, 'My condolences'. This recent phrase probably comes from American TV shows. At any rate, it doesn't register with the bereaved parents.

'Would you like to see her?'

'Yes, please,' says Julie.

'Would you like me to come with you?'

'No,' says Alan, 'we'll be all right.'

'I'll wait here,' says Nelson, relieved, but slightly ashamed of himself all the same. What can it be like, being asked to view your dead child's body? Nelson tries not to think about his own daughters, but that's impossible as he's been thinking about them all day.

A few minutes later the Jenkins emerge, both crying. Nelson takes them into the quiet room, offers tea and coffee and asks a few simple questions. It's too soon for a proper interview.

'When did you last see Chloe?'

Julie takes a long, shuddering breath. 'A week ago. You're not allowed to see patients for their first few weeks at the Sanctuary. It's meant to purge them of all outside influences, something like that. But Doctor McAllister – she's the doctor in charge – said that we could visit last week.'

'And how was Chloe when you saw her?'

'She seemed well.' Julie looks at her husband for corroboration, but he appears to have been struck dumb. 'I mean, she hadn't been there long, but I could already see a difference. When she went in she . . . she wasn't taking care of herself and she was far too thin. When we saw her last week, well, she was still thin, but her hair was clean and her skin looked better. It was lovely, wasn't it, Alan?'

'We were so happy driving home,' said Alan, his voice hoarse with misery. 'We really thought that she was going to get better. And now . . .' He buries his head in his hands.

'I'm so sorry,' says Nelson, 'but anything you tell me now

might help me find the person who did this. Did Chloe say anything last week that might explain why she was in Walsingham last night?'

'No,' says Julie. 'We didn't think they were allowed out at night. We thought she'd be safe.'

Both of them are crying properly now. Nelson can't bring himself to question them any more.

'The car's outside to take you home,' he says. 'Is it all right if I send an officer down to talk to you on Monday? Just to keep you up to date with the inquiry and to see if there's anything you can add?'

He wishes he could send Judy, but it'll have to be Tim. He's good at this sort of thing too.

'That's OK,' says Julie. 'I can't really think of the days ahead. We'll have to start planning her funeral. Her sister's still in the States. She's coming home today.'

'If there's anything I can do to help,' says Nelson, 'you've got my number.'

'She looked so beautiful,' says Julie Jenkins. 'She wouldn't have suffered, would she?'

'No,' lies Nelson. 'Death would have been almost instantaneous.'

'We had our troubles with Chloe,' says Alan, 'but she was a good girl really.' He looks at Nelson as if it is very important that he understands this.

'I know she was,' says Nelson. 'We'll catch the person who did this. I promise you.'

# CHAPTER 4

It's nearly nine o'clock by the time that Nelson leaves the station. He races through the quiet streets, feeling tense and strung up, as he always does when involved in a murder investigation. The fact that, this time, the victim is a young girl – and, what's more, a young girl who bears a striking resemblance to his oldest daughter – brings the whole thing closer to home. He thinks of Chloe's parents, her father saying, 'she was a good girl really'. His daughter Laura is a good girl. Well, both his daughters are, but Laura always seemed to lay special claim to this title. Laura is beautiful, clever (by his lights, anyway) and sporty. As a child she reminded Michelle of Beth in *Little Women*, sweet and domesticated, happy to help around the house. Not having read the book, Nelson was horrified when he saw the film of *Little Women*. Why had no one warned him that Beth actually dies? He had been forced to leave the room and blow his nose loudly in the hall. Afterwards, he had asked Michelle not to compare Laura to Beth any more. In any case, her late teenage years saw Laura become slightly less sweet and domesticated. She acquired a boyfriend and a penchant for short skirts and late nights. She still managed to get to university, studying marine biology at Plymouth, to Nelson and Michelle's mingled bemusement and pride. Now she's working as a holiday rep in Ibiza. 'A three-year gap year' is how Nelson's younger daughter, Rebecca, describes it. It's not quite what Nelson expected when he attended Laura's degree ceremony in a wind-swept marquee on Plymouth Hoe, but it could be worse. Thinking of Chloe Jenkins, he concedes that it could be a lot worse.

Michelle's car is in the drive when Nelson reaches the house. He's pleased. Over the last few months Michelle has been working later and later at the salon. He knows that the hairdresser's is expanding and that she is assuming a lot of responsibility but, deep down, he's a northern man who likes his wife to be waiting for him at the end of the day. Sure enough, as he opens the front door he can smell cooking and hear the television (*Masterchef*, that's the only downside).

'Hi, love. I'm home.'

'Harry.' Michelle appears in the sitting-room doorway. 'You're late.'

'I did text you. Got a big murder enquiry on. Did you see the news?'

'No.' Michelle's not a great one for the news. When the news jingle comes on the radio she usually switches over to another station.

'Young girl found dead just outside Walsingham.'

'How awful.'

'Yes.' Nelson decides not to tell Michelle about the resemblance to Laura. She'll know soon enough when Chloe's picture is in the papers. In fact, in her TV-watching clothes of baggy jumper and leggings, Michelle herself looks hardly older than Chloe.

Nelson goes into the kitchen and gets a can of lager from the fridge. Michelle goes to the oven. 'I've kept your steak warm. Do you want some salad with it?'

'No thanks.'

'Have you heard from the girls?' he asks.

'Rebecca sent me a text asking for a cupcake recipe.' Rebecca is living in Brighton and working for a training company. It's not very well paid, but at least it's making use of her degree and Rebecca loves her adopted town. She's sharing a flat with three other girls and has recently developed an interest in baking.

'What about Laura?'

'She'll Skype us on Saturday.'

'But have you heard anything today?'

Michelle looks surprised. 'She put a picture on Facebook. She was in a club with Andre.'

Nelson breathes a sigh of relief. That was the way of the world now. You rely on Facebook to tell you that your daughter's alive and well, even if she's in the company of Andre, a public schoolboy who thinks he's an American gangster DJ.

'Are you OK, Harry?'

Nelson adds ketchup to his steak and chips. 'I'm fine. It's just this case.'

'I hope you catch whoever did it,' says Michelle, but she

says it vaguely, as if she's more interested in who won *Masterchef*. They've been married for twenty-five years; she's used to murder.

Ruth is trying to write. Kate is in bed (after a seemingly endless reading from *Josie Smith at School*) and Ruth is at her desk with a brain-boosting packet of chocolate biscuits to hand. Three years ago she wrote a book called *The Tomb of the Raven King* about a dig in Lancashire. Rather to her surprise, she acquired a publisher, an editor and something called a 'two-book deal'. Now she is desperately trying to write the second book, about a Bronze Age dig in Norfolk which became inextricably tangled up with the discovery of a body from the Second World War. The first book came easily, partly because no one was waiting to read it (Ruth dreads the cheery 'Hi there' emails from her editor, Javier), and partly because it was a story that ended with a satisfactorily juicy discovery. The new book, *The Shadow Fields*, is proving much more difficult, the story is fractured and complicated and the archaeologists involved are still some way off a final discovery. Ruth is trying to work on her book for an hour a night. If she writes a thousand words a day, she calculates, she will have the book finished in eighty or ninety days. So far she has written 15,000 words.

Ruth stares at the screen. Surely it wouldn't hurt to check her emails. Maybe there will be one from Frank, the American academic with whom she had . . . What? An affair sounds too steamy, a fling too casual. But, for some weeks last year, she had almost believed that she and Frank might have a future together. Frank was going to come to England. He too was writing a book. They were going to write, go on dates, have sex, spend weekends together. Maybe they would even move in together . . . Frank could be a stepfather to Kate, who adored him. Only one thing had stopped them. Ruth, for some stupid reason, couldn't get Nelson out of her head. Nelson with whom she has spent precisely two nights. Nelson, the father of her daughter. Nelson, who is married. It seemed that Ruth couldn't embark on a future with Frank whilst Nelson remained in the background. That's the trouble with Nelson, he never seems to stay in the background. He's always there, annoying her, nagging her about Kate, yet making it impossible for her to contemplate life with another man. Ruth clicks to open up her emails.

The first word she sees is 'Walsingham'. Flint jumps onto the desk and tries to sit on the keyboard. Ruth pushes him off. She is looking at another email from Hilary Smithson.

Hi, Ruth!
Wondered if you'd got my last email? I'm arriving in Walsingham on Sunday. Perhaps we could meet on Monday for a coffee at the Blue Lady? Say 11? I really would like to see you. Hilary x

What does she remember about Hilary, this woman who signs herself with a kiss? She was another graduate student at Southampton. Where had she studied before? Somewhere impressive like Oxford. Ruth's first degree and her MA are from University College London, impressive enough, but somehow real life as opposed to ivory tower. Hilary had been earnest, she remembers, but with a surprisingly good sense of humour. Their PhD advisor had been the great Erik Anderson, a charismatic Norwegian archaeologist of whom Ruth was much in awe. Hilary, she remembered, admired Erik, but sometimes used to tease him in a daringly iconoclastic way. She remembers Erik talking about sacred landscape, how the same particular stretch of ground was important to different peoples over hundreds and thousands of years, and Hilary saying, 'Or it could just be coincidence'. She can still see the dangerous flash of Erik's light-blue eyes before he had answered, 'And it could just be coincidence, Miss Smithson, which is another word for serendipity.'

Is this a coincidence, two mentions of Walsingham in one day? And isn't Cathbad in Walsingham at the moment, house-sitting for one of his mad, religious friends? That's three things and, as Cathbad is always saying, bad news comes in threes.

Despite living near the famous shrine, Ruth has never visited it. Religion is not her thing, probably the result of being brought up by evangelical Christian parents. Mind you, her parents view shrines and pilgrimages with extreme suspicion. Anything Catholic or Anglo-Catholic is almost worse than Satanism (although at least a Satanist will offer you a good fight, with the chance of talking in tongues and probably an exorcism too). But Ruth tries to avoid anything to do with churches. Kate goes to a secular primary school and though she had both pagan and Catholic christening ceremonies (to please her godfather, Cathbad, and her actual father, Nelson), Ruth is determined that her child will have no religious indoctrination whatsoever. Christmas is about presents, Easter is about chocolate and she's hoping that birth, sex and death will wait a few years before rearing their ugly heads.

She Googles Walsingham (anything to avoid going back to the book), and finds that it was once two villages, Little Walsingham and Great Walsingham and that it is famed for its religious shrines in honour of the Virgin Mary. Confusingly, the bigger village that contains the ruined priory is actually Little Walsingham. Another site tells her that the 2001 census recorded a population of 864 in 397 households. She scrolls down, looking for references to archaeology and finds one to a dig in 1961 which excavated the site of the original holy house. The holy house, built on what is now the abbey grounds, was panelled in wood and contained a statue of the Virgin and – apparently – a phial of her breast milk. For years Walsingham was a centre of pilgrimage. Many kings, from Henry III onwards, trod the pilgrim path to Walsingham. Henry VIII paid a visit to celebrate the birth of a son to Catherine of Aragon, but the little prince died and eventually, of course, Henry destroyed the English monasteries. Walsingham Priory at first escaped the dissolution of the monasteries thanks to the abbot, Richard Vowell, doing some serious crawling to Thomas Cromwell. However, the sub-prior, Nicholas Milcham, protested against the destruction of the smaller monasteries and, in 1537, was executed for his pains. In 1538 the priory was dissolved and a private mansion built on its ruins. The abbey's treasures were sent to London and the statue of the Virgin was burnt.

Ruth skips the next few hundred years and clicks on the link 'Walsingham Now'. She learns that Walsingham is now a centre of both Anglican and Catholic worship. There's the Anglican shrine in the village itself and the Roman Catholic Slipper Chapel a mile away. There's even a Russian Orthodox chapel in an old railway-station booking office. Thousands of pilgrims come to the village every year and there's a Passion Play in the abbey grounds at Easter.

Ruth remembers taking part in a dig near Walsingham a few years ago. They'd hoped to find the site of the original Roman shrine but, in the end, the land had yielded nothing apart from some rather dull pottery shards, some glass and a coin or two. What is this conference that Hilary is attending? Is she still an archaeologist? And what is this 'tricky matter' about which she needs some advice? A very Hilary word, 'tricky', she seems to recall. Ruth's finger hovers over the mouse. Should she send a polite response, regretting that she's not available next week? Delete it? Answer that she'd be delighted to meet, can't wait to catch up, whatever happened to old so-and-so?

As she hesitates another email appears on the screen. It's from Hilary.

> Ruth – did you get my last email? I really would like to see you. I'm in trouble and I think you're the only person who can help me.

Cathbad was right; third time means bad news. Ruth sighs and clicks 'Reply'.

# CHAPTER 5

Cathbad celebrates his last day in Walsingham by having lunch with his friend Janet Meadows. They are eating in The Bull, an old pub in the market square, which is actually an odd rhomboid shape with a brick pump-house in the centre. Cathbad likes The Bull because the walls are a palimpsest of prayer cards, black-and-white photographs and articles from long-forgotten magazines on subjects like the mystical Body of Christ. A sign outside the pub welcomes pilgrims from St Thomas More Church, Tring, and inside a bishop in full regalia is finishing a large ploughman's.

Janet, though, is not impressed. 'Couldn't we go somewhere else?'

'Not in Walsingham,' says Cathbad. 'Anyway, I thought you liked religion.'

He is referring to the fact that not only is Janet a local historian, but she's also a prominent member of her parish church. She often invites Cathbad to Christingle services and harvest festivals. Cathbad, who loves ritual, usually accepts.

'I don't like Walsingham,' says Janet. 'It has a nasty

atmosphere. When Tom was little he had friends here. Perfectly nice people, but whenever I went to pick him up from their house I felt as if I couldn't get him away quickly enough. The whole place seemed to be closing in on us.'

Cathbad is interested by the mention of Janet's son, Tom. He knows that Janet doesn't see Tom, who is now grown up, also that Janet (whose name was once Jan) is not Tom's mother, but his biological father. Janet is open about her gender realignment surgery, but rarely mentions her old life.

'I know what you mean,' he says. 'St Simeon's Cottage is beautiful but, when I sit there in the evenings, I feel as if the ceiling's getting lower and lower. I wake up at night struggling to breathe.'

'Some people say that Walsingham was cursed by the monks who were executed by Henry the Eighth. They swore that darkness would descend on the place and never leave.'

Cathbad shivers. He's always susceptible to a good phrase and this seems particularly chilling. Was it that same darkness that he felt pressing down on him in the cottage?

'What about that woman you told me about?' says Janet. 'The one in the churchyard.'

'Did you see today's paper? They've identified her. She was a young model, a patient at the Sanctuary. Strangled and left for dead. Peace be upon her.'

'I wonder.' Janet gets a book out of her handbag. 'I wonder if that was really what you saw.'

'What do you mean?'

Janet opens the book at a place marked by a dried leaf.

Cathbad's attention is momentarily distracted because the menu arrives at the same moment. He chooses fish pie and looks back at the yellowing pages. '"The Blue Lady of Walsingham,"' he reads out loud. 'What's this?'

'It's a legend,' says Janet, who is still perusing the menu. 'I'll tell you about it in a minute. Is the sole fresh?'

Having interrogated the barman (who disclaims any knowledge of the sole), she turns back to Cathbad. 'You know that Walsingham has been a centre of pilgrimage since the eleventh century?'

'Yes. The priory must have been built at about that time.'

'The priory was established in 1156, but before that there was the holy house. Do you know about that?'

'I've heard of it.'

'The whole thing started in 1061 with a Saxon noblewoman called Richeldis de Faverches. Richeldis had a vision of the Virgin Mary, who told her to build a replica of the Holy Family's house in Nazareth. That's why Walsingham is called England's Nazareth.'

'What happened to the holy house? Was it an actual building?'

'Some legends say that it appeared magically in the night while Richeldis was praying. But there was definitely some sort of structure. It's said to form the basis for the priory. There was an excavation in 1961, and a more recent dig too. Ruth might know something about it.'

'And the Blue Lady is the Virgin Mary?'

'That's what people say. She's appeared to various people throughout the centuries and it occurs to me that St Simeon's must be very near the site of the original structure. After all, it's very old, eleventh century.'

'The cottage isn't so old, though. Fifteenth century. Added on later.'

'I'm sure there are some old graves in the churchyard, though.'

'There are. I love looking at old graves.'

'The thing is,' says Janet, 'when the Virgin Mary appears to someone it's usually because she wants something. Think of Bernadette in Lourdes, those children in Fátima.'

'Yes,' says Cathbad thoughtfully. He remembers his first sight of Chloe, how he had crossed himself, thinking that there was something unearthly about her. He likes the idea that he might have had a holy vision, rather than just a tragic sighting of a murder victim. But then he thinks back to the woman's face, her sweet, sad smile. He felt a connection, but it was a very human connection. He remembers now that the woman reminded him of someone. Someone who is very definitely alive.

'I think I saw the dead girl,' he says. 'And I think she wanted me to help her.'

The morning press conference was, from Whitcliffe's point of view, a moderate success. Nelson, managing to sound fairly civil, informed the press that, no, he hadn't caught the killer yet. Press questions had been respectful and, though Nelson had glowered alarmingly throughout, he had answered them in a concise and professional manner. Tim had been there for back-up. 'You're Whitcliffe's pin-up boy,' Clough had told him, but Tim knows that the superintendent values him simply because he's the only black officer on the team. Still, Tim is ambitious too, so he went along with it, nodding and looking appropriately serious as Nelson told the assembled journalists that there were several ongoing lines of enquiry, please respect the family's privacy and give them time to grieve.

Now Nelson is driving to the Sanctuary. He wants to see the place for himself and to interview the doctor in charge, Fiona McAllister. He hopes that seeing the Sanctuary will help him to re-create Chloe's last journey. So far they have had no sightings after Cathbad's vision in the graveyard. What made a recovering addict – doing well, according to her parents – sneak out at night and walk a mile across several fields to visit a country churchyard? And who did she meet after she left the church? Chloe's body was found near the Catholic shrine, the Slipper Chapel, a good twenty minute walk from Walsingham. Chloe was brought up C of E, according to her parents. 'We don't really go to church,' said her mother, 'but we do believe in God.' Typical Anglicans, Nelson's mother would say. Well, Nelson hopes that, whatever faith they have, it's giving them some comfort now.

Like Clough and Tim, Nelson is impressed with the building, though the outside reminds him of a prison or magistrates' court, places where he's spent rather too much of his adult life. As he waits impatiently in the hall, he looks at the oil paintings, flower arrangements and soft furnishings and tries to work out how much this place costs per week. More than most people can afford, that's for sure. On the other hand, it stops rich drug addicts from cluttering up

NHS wards. It's not that he's not sympathetic – he's seen enough of the misery that drugs can cause – but he can't help thinking that it's almost a lifestyle choice for some people, the sort of people who go on reality TV programmes, the sort of people who come to the Sanctuary.

'Detective Chief Inspector Nelson?'

He turns. A short-haired woman in glasses is holding out her hand. 'I'm Doctor McAllister.' She has a faint Scottish accent and a disconcertingly straight gaze behind the glasses.

'Good of you to see me, doctor.'

She inclines her head, but doesn't say that it's a pleasure or her duty or anything like that. 'Shall we go to my office?'

She leads him up the stairs (more gloomy oil paintings and a stag's head or two), through several doors and finally into a modern office that was once obviously part of a bigger room, the fireplace neatly bisected by a plasterboard wall. She offers coffee, which Nelson politely declines.

'How can I help you, Detective Chief Inspector?'

'Tell me about Chloe Jenkins,' says Nelson. 'How long had she been here?'

'Just over three weeks,' says Doctor McAllister. 'She arrived here on Monday 27th January.'

'Did she check herself in?'

'Her parents brought her, as I recall, but she was self-referred, if that's what you mean.'

'And what sort of treatment would she have had?'

'We offer a mixture of medical and psychotherapeutic treatment.'

'Which means?'

'We can prescribe opioid medications such as methadone or buprenorphine, but we also offer various therapies such as cognitive behavioural therapy or motivational interviewing. Basically, prescribing drug substitutes won't work unless the patient actually wants to change.'

'And did Chloe Jenkins want to change?'

Doctor McAllister is silent for a moment. 'Yes, I think she did. She'd been in rehab before, of course. Not here. I think the first time was in a specialist centre for teenagers and the second time somewhere abroad. But I did sense a real will to get her life together at last. That's what makes it so sad . . .'

Doctor McAllister's voice doesn't break, but she does look momentarily stricken. Encouraged by this first sign of humanity, Nelson says, 'What was Chloe like as a person?'

'You should talk to her personal therapist. She knew her best. But I would say that Chloe was a bright girl. I don't think she had any formal qualifications, but she was a great reader, keen to learn more about the world around her. This sometimes led to rather strange enthusiasms, but basically she just wanted to improve her mind. And she was charming. But a lot of addicts are charming. That's how they persuade friends and family to collude with their addiction.'

'I'd like to speak to her therapist.'

'I'll give you her number. Her name's Holly Barrett.' She scribbles on a Post-it note.

'Did Chloe have any special friends here?'

Is it his imagination or is there a slight hesitation? 'She was friendly with another couple of patients, yes.'

'Could I speak to them?'

'I'll let you have the names.' But, unlike Holly Barrett's, it seems that she doesn't have the names to hand.

'Doctor McAllister.' Nelson tries to sound confiding, the way Judy does, but he has a feeling that it's coming out wrong. Fiona McAllister, at any rate, does not look reassured. 'I know this is a difficult question, but do you have any idea who could have killed Chloe Jenkins?'

The doctor looks surprised. 'But wasn't it just some random madman?'

'Random madmen are rarer than you'd think. Victims usually know their murderers.'

'What are you suggesting?'

'Was there anyone she was scared of? Did she mention someone, maybe in her past, who was threatening her or making her feel uncomfortable? She was a very attractive woman, maybe someone had become obsessed with her or was stalking her.'

'I don't know,' says Doctor McAllister. 'She never mentioned anyone like that to me. But maybe she spoke to Holly or one of the other patients.'

'And have you any idea why Chloe left her room on Wednesday night?'

'No.'

'When was the last time you saw her?'

'That morning. It was a group therapy session. Chloe seemed her usual self, quite bouncy and happy.'

'Bouncy?'

Doctor McAllister twitches impatiently. 'It was how she

was. I didn't mean she was manic or anything.'

Interesting, thinks Nelson. 'What was the group session about?'

'Families. Sometimes we do family therapy too. Often the problems with addiction go back to childhood and the family dynamic.'

'What was Chloe Jenkins' family like?'

'They seemed supportive enough. They visited last week. We try to discourage too many outside influences, but Holly and I felt that a visit from her parents wouldn't do Chloe any harm. And it seemed to go well.'

Nelson remembers Julie Jenkins saying 'She seemed well', and Alan describing the happy journey home, both parents thinking that their child was getting the help she needed.

'I've just met her parents,' he says. 'They seem nice people.'

'Oh yes,' says Doctor McAllister. 'Chloe had a privileged background, nannies, boarding school, pony club etc. No lack of money.'

Nelson thinks of the well-dressed couple in the quiet room. He can imagine them being part of a prosperous, middle-class set. But something in Doctor McAllister's voice makes him feel as if a judgement is being made. Maybe it was just because the Scottish accent became more pronounced.

'What was there a lack of?'

The doctor shrugs. 'I don't know. Time maybe. But the family were very supportive of her problems, they paid for rehab several times, bought her a flat, tried to keep her out of trouble. It's wearing, having an addict in the family.'

'What about the boyfriend, Thom Novak?'

'I never met him. I know he has problems with addiction too.'

'He's in rehab at the moment.'

'It's a real problem when addicts get together. A kind of *folie à deux* situation. They enable each other. For Chloe's rehabilitation to work, I think she would have had to break up with Thom.'

'Did you say that to her?'

'Yes.'

'And what was her answer?'

'She said that she loved him. And I'm sure she did. Sadly, sometimes love isn't enough.' Now she really does look sad. Nelson wonders about Doctor McAllister's background. He can't see a wedding ring; maybe she's married to the job.

He thanks Doctor McAllister for her time and says that he can see himself out. She doesn't seem too keen on this and calls a member of the ground staff to escort him. Even with the man's surly chaperonage Nelson is able to see that Chloe would not have found it difficult to leave the hospital unnoticed. There are several fire exits, presumably unlocked, and, although you need a passcode to open the doors from outside, from inside all you have to do is press a red button marked 'Open'. It's hardly *The Great Escape*.

When he gets back to his car, there's a message from Chris Stephenson saying that he has the preliminary autopsy results. Nelson rings him back and tries not to wince when the pathologist calls him 'chief'. 'It's much what you'd expect, chief. Death by manual strangulation. No sign of recent sexual activity. Deceased had no traces of alcohol or drugs in the bloodstream. One odd thing. We found traces of cleaning fluid on her hands and under her nails. Do they have them scrubbing floors in the Sanctuary?'

No, thinks Nelson. He's pretty sure that's not one of the therapies on offer. Then he thinks back to yesterday and Cathbad pointing out the spot where Chloe had appeared to him. 'Here. By this white tombstone.' The other stones had been grey, covered with lichen and the accumulated grime of the years, but the grave which Chloe had been standing next to was white. As if it had been newly cleaned.

# CHAPTER 6

If Chesterton is pleased to see Justin, he doesn't show it. When his owner arrives the cat stares at him coldly for a moment and then stalks out of the room with his tail in the air.

'Still the same old Chesterton,' says Justin.

'Yes,' says Cathbad. 'I think we came to some sort of understanding, though I wouldn't say we bonded exactly.'

Justin has bought Cathbad a bottle of Irish whisky and a small statue of the Virgin Mary. Cathbad is delighted with both presents and balances the glass figurine on his hand.

'She glows in the dark,' says Justin. 'Very useful if you're lost on a lonely road with only a religious icon to keep you company.'

Cathbad is never quite sure about Justin's religious convictions. He's a layman, but Cathbad knows that he once studied for the priesthood. Now he seems happy being a waspish, slightly cynical presence on many local committees and charities. He's also a guide at the priory and a volunteer at the museum. He's a respected historian too and often gives lectures in London. Cathbad first met Justin when they were both concerned with saving the remains of an anchorite's cell in the grounds of a Norwich church. Justin hadn't minded Cathbad turning up to meetings in his druid's robes and referring to the spiritual energies of the site. Cathbad, for his part, had overlooked Justin's weakness for waistcoats and foppish cravats. The campaign had been successful and, by the end of it, Justin and Cathbad were firm – if respectfully distant – friends.

'I had a religious visitation of my own when you were away,' Cathbad says now.

He tells Justin about seeing Chloe Jenkins in the graveyard and the subsequent discovery of her body.

'So that's why there were all those policemen on the Fakenham Road,' says Justin. 'I had to go the long way round.'

'My friend Janet tried to persuade me that I'd seen a vision of the Virgin Mary.'

'Like good old Richeldis de Faverches? It's possible, I suppose.'

Cathbad looks at his friend. 'Have you ever seen anything in the graveyard? Or in the house?'

Justin smiles and bends to stroke Chesterton, who has come back into the room. 'This is a holy house, did you know that?'

'What do you mean?'

'It was once owned by a holy woman called Dame Judith de Hare. She was an anchoress, like Julian of Norwich. Dame Judith used to see regular visions of the Virgin Mary. She described her as being dressed in blue with a heavenly countenance. It's documented in the parish records.'

'Have you ever seen her?'

'No.' From his tone, Cathbad thinks Justin sounds disappointed.

'I think Chesterton's seen Dame Judith, though. Sometimes he's sitting here with me in the evening and suddenly he stiffens and stands up, his hair standing on end, eyes staring.'

Cathbad wouldn't put it past Chesterton to be putting this on, but he doesn't voice this thought. Instead he says, 'So you haven't seen any ghosts here?'

'No I haven't,' says Justin. 'And I don't suppose even the ghosts will get any rest now with all these policemen flat-footing around.'

'I'm sure they won't bother you.'

At that moment there's a knock on the door. It's Nelson, asking if he can look in the graveyard.

Nelson had intended to go straight into the churchyard via the lych-gate. But then he had seen Cathbad silhouetted in the window of the cottage and thought that he'd call in and ask a bit more about the events of Wednesday night. He hadn't reckoned on the door being opened by a man in a tweed suit and a yellow waistcoat. He has a neat moustache and reminds Nelson of one of the animals in *The Wind in the Willows*, memories of a far-off school adaptation with Rebecca as Ratty.

Nelson introduces himself. The man grins delightedly and says that his name is Justin something double-barrelled.

'My friend and I were just discussing the case.'

'Hi, Nelson.' Cathbad appears at Ratty's shoulder.

'Hallo, Cathbad. Might have guessed that you'd be gossiping.'

Justin Double-Barrelled looks from one to the other. 'Do you two *know* each other?'

'We're old friends,' says Cathbad. 'We've even solved a few crimes together.'

'Starsky and Hutch,' says Nelson. 'That's us.'

Justin stands aside to let Nelson into the house. 'Can I offer you anything to drink, Detective Chief Inspector? I've just returned from a work trip so things are in a bit of a state.' He gestures at the perfectly tidy room, which has a wheelie suitcase in the centre of it.

'No, thank you very much. I'd just like to see the churchyard again.' Nelson despises wheelie suitcases.

The three of them walk through the graves. Although it's only three in the afternoon, it's already getting dark. A fine mist hovers in the air, making the tombstones and the trees merge into a hazy grey backdrop. The grave where Chloe Jenkins was seen stands out like a beacon. Nelson crosses over to examine the stone.

'Doreen Westmondham,' he reads, '1940 to 2002. Beloved wife, mother and grandmother.'

He turns to Cathbad and Justin, who are watching him intently. 'Do you know anything about this woman?' he asks.

'No,' says Justin. 'I only moved here in 2006. It's one of the newest graves. Look how white it is.'

'It's white,' says Nelson, 'because it's recently been cleaned.'

And by the wall, hidden under a holly bush, he finds what he's looking for. A cloth and a bottle of something called 'Deluxe Stone Cleaner'.

# CHAPTER 7

Ruth is late for her meeting with Hilary. She took Kate to school, then had planned to spend a couple of hours at work before heading off to Walsingham for eleven o'clock. But at the university she got caught up first with one of her PhD students anxious about his thesis, then with a colleague who wanted to complain about Phil. Normally this is one of her favourite pastimes but, when she catches sight of the clock, it's ten thirty.

'Sorry, Bob, I've got to go. I've got a meeting.'

Bob's voice follows her plaintively down the stairs: 'And he's even changed the loo paper in the staff bogs.'

She hurries to the car park, book bag bumping on her hip. Her car is parked under a lime tree that drops sticky resin onto the bonnet but this has always been Ruth's spot, and at the university you don't change things unless you really have to. The marks on the paint didn't matter when Ruth had a battered old car, but this one is new, bought last year. It's smart and comfortable, but instead of a key it comes with a whizzy card device that you click to open the doors.

Ruth always had problems finding her car keys, but the card is something else. Now she has to upturn her bag to find it, nestling at the bottom amongst the Polo crumbs and loose tampons. By the time she has inserted the card to start the ignition, the time on the dashboard clock says ten forty-five.

Ruth races through the back roads to Walsingham. This car is faster than her old one, but that doesn't help when she ends up behind a horse trailer for the first mile and then a man in a hat driving a Nissan Micra for the second. When she finally gets to Walsingham she follows signs to the car park and ends up at the top of the hill behind the farm shop. What was the name of the cafe Hilary mentioned? The blue something. Well, it can't be far away. Walsingham seems very small, just a village, really. She passes an odd-looking pump-house with a brazier on top, a pub and a couple of shops selling shrine souvenirs. 'Everything £1', says one, Ruth's first experience of a religious pound shop. She walks down the road, past flint and timbered houses, others painted in delicate pastel shades. Halfway down there's a gateway that's signposted as leading to the abbey grounds. The heavy wooden gates are shut now, apart from a grille showing a tantalising glimpse of green. The gate with its worn stone gargoyles looks odd amongst the picturesque houses, like a grey growth forcing its way through the wattle and daub. Ruth hurries on, looking in the shop windows for signs that one of them might be a cafe in disguise. As she does so she realises that these are very particular retail outlets. One sells priest's vestments, gorgeous shades of green, purple and gold. Another has life-size models of the Holy Family, Mary in blue and white with upturned eyes, Joseph solid in russet red and brown, a disturbingly adult-looking baby Jesus. Aid to the Church in Need, The Pilgrim Shop. This must be where priests and vicars go for a spending spree. But, although the car park had been fairly full, there's not a soul to be seen.

At the bottom of the street she finds the Blue Lady. It's part-cafe, part-bookshop and, at first, this too looks empty. Then she sees a woman browsing the shelves. Could that be Hilary? She's about the right height and shape, but this woman has grey hair, cut in a glossy bob. Ruth has a few white hairs, but they always disappear if she changes her parting. Hilary is about her age, forty-five. Could she have gone completely grey?

The woman turns and all thoughts of hair colour vanish. Because the woman is definitely Hilary and she is equally definitely a priest.

'Hallo, Ruth.'

'Hallo.' For one lunatic moment Ruth wonders if she should address her as 'Reverend'.

Hilary gestures at the dog collar. 'Sorry to spring this on you, but I couldn't think of a way to tell you via email.'

'That's OK,' says Ruth. She wonders if it would be socially acceptable to slip out of the cafe and run back up the high street screaming.

'Shall we sit down?' Hilary indicates a table in the window. 'They do nice cakes in here. Do you fancy a cake? I do. It's not Lent yet.'

Ruth has no idea when Lent is, but she's surprised to hear a vicar sounding so enthusiastic about cakes. Aren't they meant to live on bread and water? She only knows one other member of the clergy and he seems to eat and drink fairly normally. But he's Irish and a Catholic. Her parents' church has elders, ordinary people who are just holier (and smugger) than the rest of them. She doesn't really have any experience of C of E vicars, aside from *Rev* or reruns of *The Vicar of Dibley*.

Hilary orders tea and a slice of carrot cake. Ruth goes for coffee and a chocolate brownie.

'Have you lived in Norfolk long?' Hilary asks her.

'About seventeen years.' Christ, is it really that long?

'And you work at the university? I've looked you up. Very impressive.'

Why? thinks Ruth. Why have you looked me up? Instead she says, 'Are you still working in archaeology? I mean . . . not now obviously . . .' Her voice trails away.

'I worked as an archaeologist for a while,' says Hilary. 'Did some fantastic digs in Sussex. At Boxgrove and Whitehawk. But then . . .' She shrugs. 'I found God.'

Why do people keep doing this? Ruth's parents discovered God when she was ten and her life was never the same again. Why couldn't He just stay hidden?

Feeling she should show an interest, she asks Hilary how long it takes to become a vicar.

'Ages,' says Hilary with a brilliant, ageless smile. 'First there's the discernment period – where you ask yourself if this is really what God wants for you – then there's the training. That took three years in my case. Then I was a curate for four years. Now I'm a parish priest in south London.'

'Where?' asks Ruth. 'I'm from south London originally.'

'I know,' says Hilary, rather worryingly. 'My church is in Streatham. Quite a challenging area, very mixed.'

What does 'mixed' mean in this context, wonders Ruth. Black and white? Rich and poor? Sheep and goats?

'I'm very happy,' says Hilary. 'I love my work and I'm married with a four-year-old son.'

'I've got a five-year-old,' says Ruth. 'A daughter. Kate.'

This is something Hilary doesn't know about her. She beams. 'That's wonderful! I wish we could get them together. What does your partner do?'

'I'm single,' says Ruth. 'I'm not with Kate's father.'

Hilary gives her a compassionate smile. 'Must be hard work.'

'It is, sometimes. But I have a lovely childminder and friends help out a lot.'

'That's good.'

'Yes, it is.'

Their drinks and cakes arrive and Ruth divides her attention between the chocolate brownie and wondering how she can get round to asking why it was so important that they meet and have this fascinating chat about lifestyles. Then Hilary, cutting her cake into tiny cubes, says, 'Are you wondering why I wanted to see you?'

'Well, I . . .'

'The thing is, Ruth . . .' For the first time Hilary's sunny glow falters. She looks older, and afraid. 'The thing is, I've been getting these letters.'

'What sort of letters?'

'The thing is,' says Hilary again, cubing the cubes, 'there are some people who just don't like the idea of women priests.'

Ruth knows. She's read about it in the *Guardian*. Though, to be honest, she usually skips those articles on the way to the TV listings.

'Most women priests get abuse of some kind, people saying things, refusing to come to their services. When I first started getting the letters I didn't think anything of it. A rite of passage, that's what Brian, my husband, says.'

'What does Brian do?' Well, Hilary had asked her.

'He's a priest too.' Hilary smiles. 'Crazy, isn't it? But we met at theological college. He's a school chaplain.'

'So what do these letters say?'

'Well at first it was the usual stuff about all the disciples being men, women not being worthy, women's vocation being motherhood and domesticity. I could ignore all that. You get it all the time. Then, at the end of last year, the tone seemed to change, to become nastier, more sinister. But what worried me most were the references to archaeology.'

'To archaeology?'

'Yes. And that worried me because it was specific to me. The letter-writer must know that I used to be an archaeologist. And recently there are references to Norfolk. He must have found out that I was coming to this conference.'

Ruth notes that Hilary assumes that the writer is male. In her experience misogyny is not always confined to men.

'So I thought,' Hilary goes on. 'I thought, why don't I talk to Ruth? She's in Norfolk and she knows all about archaeology.

And, when I looked you up, I saw you were a special advisor to the police.'

Damn that LinkedIn profile. Ruth says, 'If the letters are threatening, you must go to the police. I'm not a member of the police. I'm just an archaeologist who advises them on buried bones. I can't investigate this for you. I'm not Miss Marple.'

'But if you would just look at the letters . . .'

'Look,' says Ruth. 'I know a policeman. Someone fairly senior. He's a good man. He'll take this seriously. Believe me, I know. Will you talk to him?'

Hilary looks at her squarely. 'If you'll read the letters.'

'Am I being blackmailed by a priest?'

Hilary reaches out to touch her hand. 'No, of course not. It would just be a comfort to me if you would read them. You can pass them on to this policeman if you think it's worth it.'

Ruth sighs. 'All right.'

Hilary reaches into her voluminous backpack and Ruth realises that she had the letters with her all the time. Did she always count on being able to persuade Ruth?

'Thank you, Ruth. And maybe we could meet up again? The conference lasts for a week.'

'What's it about?'

Hilary grins and Ruth sees the first trace of the old Erik-baiting Hilary. 'Preparing for Episcopacy. That should really upset the letter-writer.'

Ruth looks it up later; it's something to do with becoming a bishop.

*

Tim, too, is out of his comfort zone. He is in a room that could almost be the setting for some early evening costume drama: low sofas, a herd of spindly-legged tables, an upright piano, doors leading onto a perfect, landscaped garden. Only the giant TV screen embedded in the Regency wallpaper spoils the illusion. That and the hundreds of condolence cards displayed on the marble fireplace, the bookshelves and many of the little tables. Tim, looking for somewhere to put his coffee cup, can't escape the words: sympathy, sorrow, love, consolation, angel. But, then again, what do you say when someone has died? When he was at school one of his friends lost a brother in a shooting incident (it was that kind of school) and, whilst Tim's mother had had all the words, or at least knew where to find them in the Bible, Tim had found himself avoiding that friend because he didn't know what to say. He had hated himself for it.

Julie Jenkins sees him looking and slides a silver coaster under the cup.

'Thank you.' Tim smiles at her and is encouraged to get a wobbly smile back. 'Be charming,' Nelson had said to him, as if suggesting that he employ the dark arts. 'Some people find you charming, I hear.' Maybe that was a reference to Superintendent Whitcliffe. Even so, the remark had made Tim uneasy.

'Thank you so much for seeing me,' he says now to Julie and Alan, sitting close together on one of the sofas. 'I know how hard this must be for you, but it's very important for us to get a complete picture of Chloe.'

He wishes he hadn't used these words because, over the

fireplace, there is an actual picture of Chloe, an oil painting, presumably of her with her sister. The two faces, both impossibly beautiful, stare sadly down at him.

Julie sees him looking. 'That's Chloe and Lauren. It was painted when Chloe was seventeen and Lauren twenty.'

'It's beautiful.' Tim's no expert but he doesn't think the artist will be winning any prizes – the style is painting-by-numbers crossed with Athena poster – but there is no doubt that the girls themselves are lovely.

'Yes. They were very close.' Julie catches herself using the past tense and her mouth wobbles as the tears begin to flow again.

'Where's Lauren now?' asks Tim, as Alan silently passes his wife a tissue.

'She's a flight attendant,' says Alan. 'Working long-haul. She came home as soon as she heard, but she's with her boyfriend today. I don't think she likes being here.' He gestures at the luxurious room with the flowers and the angels and the messages of condolence.

'Are you in the aviation business too, Mr Jenkins?' Tim knows the answer already but, even if he hadn't, the room would have given him a clue. Apart from the one of the girls over the fireplace, most of the pictures are of planes: biplanes coasting over grey seas, modern jumbos on the runway, uniformed men with wings and gold braid on their caps. But he meant to give the bereaved father something else to think about, and it works. Alan straightens up immediately.

'Yes. I used to be in the RAF, but now I'm a commercial pilot.'

'The whole family are mad about planes,' says Julie. 'Both girls have amateur pilots' licences.'

'Really?' It's hard to imagine Chloe, the glamorous model, flying a plane, but, of course, that's what this interview is for. To see the whole person, not just the murder victim.

'It started when they were young,' says Julie. 'When we were still living on the base. At RAF Skulthorpe.'

This name rings a faint bell with Tim. A bell that seems to speak in the voice of his sat nav.

'Skulthorpe. Is that in Norfolk?'

'Yes.' Julie holds the tissue to her eyes. 'It's very near where she was . . . It's near the Sanctuary.'

This is interesting. As far as he knows, the investigating team have no idea that Chloe was originally from Norfolk.

'When did you leave Norfolk?' he asks.

'When Chloe was eight. She was sad to go. She loved it there. But Alan left the RAF and we needed to be near the big airports.'

'Tell me something about Chloe,' says Tim. 'What sort of a child was she?'

'Very happy,' says Julie. 'Always smiling. Everybody loved her. She was an angel, that's what her childminder said. Her problems . . . well, they didn't start until later.'

Tim waits. 'She was too pretty for her own good,' says Alan. 'She was scouted by a model agency when she was only fourteen. I didn't want her to take it up. I wanted her to have a proper career. She was a very bright girl. She just didn't try at school.'

'I made her wait until she was sixteen,' says Julie, with a

flash of spirit. 'But I couldn't stop her. She wanted to be a model. Her head was quite turned by it all, and no wonder really.'

'At the age of sixteen she was travelling all over the world on assignments,' says Alan. 'Drugs were everywhere. Chloe always found it hard to say no. By the time she was eighteen she had a real problem.'

'That must have been hard for you as parents,' says Tim.

'It was awful,' says Julie. 'At first we didn't realise. We didn't know the signs. But then I actually saw her taking the drugs. Here in her bedroom. Snorting them with a fifty-pound note! I confronted her, Alan confronted her, even Lauren begged her to get help. And, eventually, she agreed.'

'She went to this special rehabilitation place for teenagers,' says Alan. 'It was tough but it worked. She got clean. She was our little girl again. She even started studying for her A-levels.'

'What happened next?' asks Tim.

'She met him,' says Alan. 'Thom Novak.'

This time there is real anger in his voice. Julie looks at her husband apprehensively. 'She went back to modelling,' she explains to Tim. 'We didn't want her to, but they were offering such good money. She met Thom on a shoot. He's an actor and a model too, he's really handsome. Well, he is!' This to Alan, who makes a derisive noise. 'You can't say he's not handsome. And charming too. We liked him at first. You know we did, Alan.'

'He was all right,' says Alan. 'A sight too pleased with him-self, I always thought. Public school type. But he got Chloe back into drugs. He was part of that "in the gossip papers every weekend" set. We were always seeing him and Chloe falling out of some nightclub.'

Tim has seen the pictures too. There are some in the crime file. Chloe, wearing nothing much more than a brilliant smile, clinging on to Thom's arm at red-carpet events. Chloe stumbling out of a taxi. Chloe in dark glasses at the airport. Chloe at a pop festival, flowers in her hair.

'So when did you suspect that she was taking drugs again?' he asks.

'It was Thom himself who told us,' says Julie. 'He rang us one weekend and just said "We need help." He was crying on the phone. We drove to their flat. They had this really nice place in Chiswick. Well, it was a tip. Bins overflowing, empty wine bottles everywhere. Chloe was lying on the bed. I thought she was dead at first. She was so thin, the marks on her arms . . .'

'I phoned the Sanctuary at once,' says Alan, in a voice that suggests he took charge of the situation. 'We drove her there that night.'

'What about Thom?'

'I called his parents. They got him into a rehab place in Switzerland. I suppose he's still there. He wasn't our responsibility.'

Tim remembers speaking to Thom on the day that Chloe's body was found. He had wept then, too.

'How did Chloe get on at the Sanctuary?' he says. 'I understand you went to see her.'

'She seemed to be doing well,' says Alan. 'It was early days, but she liked Holly, her therapist, and the main doctor. She'd made some friends there, she said. Adults, not stupid young models.'

'She looked so much better,' says Julie, 'after only a few weeks. She'd put on weight, her eyes were brighter. She was talking about taking a course. Chloe was always taking courses. It was a sign that she was feeling better.'

'What was she taking a course in?'

'I can't remember,' says Julie. 'Something spiritual. Chloe was very spiritual.'

'The coroner told us that there were no drugs in her bloodstream,' says Alan. 'Sounds strange, I know, but that was a real comfort to us.'

'I can understand that,' says Tim. He looks around the room, at the perfect furniture and the florist's arrangements in muted, funereal colours. Despite the cards and the flowers, he thinks that comfort must be hard to come by.


Ruth rings Nelson as soon as she gets back to the university. He answers on the second ring.

'Ruth. Is anything wrong with Katie?'

Ruth counts to ten. Not only does Nelson always assume she's ringing with bad news, he always insists on calling their daughter Katie when he knows full well that her name's Kate.

'Kate's fine. I'm ringing about something else.'

'Oh?' Ruth thinks that Nelson sounds nervous. Does he think that she's about to demand that he leaves Michelle and marries her? Not likely after all this time. Not least because she knows he'd say no.

Ruth explains about Hilary and the letters. 'I told her to contact you. I hope that's OK.'

Nelson is silent and Ruth wonders whether she has crossed some invisible line. Maybe he thinks it's too trivial a matter for a DCI? Maybe he's just annoyed because she has given his name to a third party.

Then Nelson says, 'Do these letters mention Walsingham?'

'I haven't read them yet. I'm going to do it tonight.'

'When you've read them, can you ring me?'

'OK. Is something up?'

'Have you read about the woman found dead just outside Walsingham?'

'Yes. She was an actress or a model or something, wasn't she?' Ruth seems to remember a lot of pictures in the papers. Easy to get coverage if you're beautiful, blonde and dead.

'It's probably nothing, but if there's some nutter threatening women . . .'

'This guy – if it is a man – seems to be fixated on women priests, though.'

'Yes. There's probably no connection. Tell your friend to give me a ring. There are laws against this sort of harassment now.'

'I will. Thanks.'

'And call me when you've read the letters.'

'I will.'

Nelson puts down the phone, feeling thoughtful. Ruth's letter-writer may have nothing to do with Chloe Jenkins' murder, but it's worrying that there might be two woman-haters focusing on Walsingham. He has learnt to ignore such vitriol at his peril. Equally he knows that it can be fatal to assume that people who write violent letters are always violent themselves. That was the mistake the police made in the Yorkshire Ripper case. And the thought that Ruth actually knows a woman priest is surely the most astonishing aspect of all. They were at university together, says Ruth. Well, you get all types at university (so he's heard; he left school at sixteen), but, even so, he can't imagine Ruth being friendly with anyone overtly religious.

The case is frustrating him. He still has no idea why Chloe was wandering around Walsingham last Wednesday. He has spoken to Chloe's therapist, Holly Barrett, on the phone and she seemed to have no particular insights into her patient's state of mind. Chloe appeared to be making good progress, she was in a 'good place', no she hadn't complained about any stalkers or sinister ex-boyfriends. Maybe Chloe's friends from rehab will be more forthcoming. Nelson is seeing them at the Sanctuary this afternoon.

Even Nelson's hunch about the gravestone is proving inconclusive. Intel have traced Doreen Westmondham. She was a local woman from Houghton St Giles, married with three children and five grandchildren, a former school dinner-lady and, according to tributes following her untimely death from cancer at sixty-two, 'loved by all who knew her'. Doreen and her husband had also fostered over a hundred children. Her funeral at St Simeon's Church was standing room only. What was Doreen's link with Chloe Jenkins, model, socialite and drug addict? It's hard to see the connection.

At one o'clock Tim returns from his trip to Surrey. Nelson accosts him before he has had time to eat his lunchtime salad. Salad! Sometimes Nelson worries about Tim.

'Did you get anything from the family?'

Tim puts down his plastic fork. 'They're still in shock. But they're nice people, very respectable. They seemed to have done their best to help Chloe. They're heartbroken.'

'Did you find anything that might help with the enquiry?'

'Well, they weren't keen on the boyfriend, Thom Novak, but he's got a pretty solid alibi. He was in Switzerland. I spoke to him myself.'

Nelson grunts, trying to work out how long it would take to get from Switzerland to Norfolk. He doesn't believe in solid alibis.

'Anything else?'

'Well, one interesting thing. Did you know they were from Norfolk?'

'No,' says Nelson, 'I didn't.'

'Yes. They lived near here when Chloe was little. Alan was stationed at RAF Skulthorpe. They moved when she was eight.'

'That's interesting.' It could explain, thinks Nelson, how Chloe was able to find her way to Walsingham at night across the fields. Isn't RAF Skulthorpe quite near Walsingham?

'I'm going back to the Sanctuary this afternoon,' he says. 'Do you want to come?'

'OK,' says Tim, turning back to his salad.

'For God's sake,' says Nelson, 'have a burger to go with that. You'll never make a detective inspector living on lettuce.'

# CHAPTER 8

Tim remembers Alan Jenkins saying that Chloe's new friends were 'adults, not stupid young models'. Even so, he is surprised by the two people waiting for them in the television lounge of the Sanctuary. Stanley and Jean are middle-aged and, not to put too fine a point upon it, dowdy. Jean, a food technology teacher, has dyed red hair, grey showing at the roots, and a round placid face. Stanley, who doesn't vouchsafe his occupation, is thin and stooped, fiddling nervously with a Styrofoam cup of coffee. Both are dressed in tracksuits. The boss's face gives nothing away as he makes brisk introductions, but Tim is sure that he too is surprised by the friends Chloe made while having her treatment. Surely she should have palled up with that pop star that Cloughie's always going on about, Foxy something?

'Holly Barrett says that you were particular friends of Chloe Jenkins,' says Nelson.

Tim almost expects the two impostors to deny this, but, instead, Jean says in a voice trembling with emotion, 'Dear

Chloe. I just can't believe she's gone. We loved her, didn't we, Stanley?'

'Yes.' Stanley too looks on the verge of tears. 'We loved her.' He tears a large portion of Styrofoam off his cup and coffee starts dripping onto the carpet.

'Here. Give that to me.' Jean is motherly and capable, tipping the coffee into a plant pot and handing Stanley a tissue (all the rooms in the Sanctuary are equipped with large boxes of tissues). Is this why Chloe liked these people, because they were substitute parents? Maybe more accessible parents than the smart, attractive couple in the room dominated by pictures of airplanes?

'How did you get to know Chloe?' asks Tim.

'We hit it off right away,' says Jean. 'I sat next to her in one of the group sessions and we just started chatting. She was so open and easy to talk to. Not like some of the younger ones here.'

'She was like an angel,' says Stanley.

What had Julie said? That Chloe's childminder had thought she was an angel. There are getting to be too many angels around for Tim's liking.

'I know this is very difficult,' says Nelson, 'but we're looking for any reasons why someone might have wanted to kill Chloe. Did she ever tell you about anyone threatening her? Maybe someone from her past?'

Jean shakes her head. 'She talked about her boyfriend Thom. Poor thing, he sounded like another troubled soul. But she wasn't scared of him, if anything she felt she needed to protect him. She was a very caring person.' She reaches for the tissues.

'Did Thom contact her while she was here?' asks Tim.

'I don't think so. Visitors aren't encouraged. You're meant to purge yourself of all influences. Chloe's parents came once. They seemed a nice couple. Chloe only had good to say about them. A lot of addicts, they blame their parents. I used to do it myself before I went into therapy.'

Jean looks too old to have parents living, let alone culpable for their daughter's lifestyle. Before Nelson can stop her Jean has launched into her life story.

'. . . blamed myself because I was never good enough. My sister was always my mother's favourite. I did everything to win Mum's approval, even becoming a teacher like her. I started drinking at teacher-training college. I coped for years, drinking and taking drugs at the weekend, teaching all week. Then my marriage broke up and it all unravelled. I was coming to work hungover, drinking in my lunch break . . .'

She stops for a sip of coffee, and Nelson takes his chance. 'Can you think of anything else Chloe said or did that might have relevance here? It could be the smallest thing, something that didn't seem significant at the time.'

He is looking at Jean, but it's Stanley who says, 'She was religious.'

'Was she?' says Nelson encouragingly.

'Yes. I don't mean that she was any particular religion, but she was very spiritual. She used to pray. A lot of people here meditate, but she actually used to pray. She'd light candles in the recreation room and pray every night. She said that she thought her guardian angel was looking after her. Turns out he wasn't,' he adds, with sudden bitterness.

'Her mother said that she wanted to take a course,' says Tim. 'Something spiritual, she said. Do you know what that was?'

Jean and Stanley look at each other and smile. 'It was a course in angel therapy,' says Jean. 'You tap into the healing vibrations of the angels.'

More angels. Tim doesn't dare look at Nelson. 'Where did she find this course?' he asks.

'Online,' says Jean. 'You get a certificate and everything.' She obviously thinks some sort of explanation is needed because she says, 'Chloe loved angels. She collected pictures of them. She gave me this beautiful angel brooch. I'll never take it off.' She points at her chest, where a little gold cherub nestles in the grey fleece. 'She was interested in all sorts of spirituality, though. As an ex-teacher I recognised a truly curious mind. She meditated, as Stanley says, she did mind, body and spirit courses and she went to conventional C of E church services.'

'She went to church?' says Nelson. 'Where?'

'St Simeon's in Walsingham,' says Stanley. 'I went with her sometimes. Doctor McAllister drove us, but she never came into the church.'

'That figures,' says Jean. 'Fiona McAllister's an atheist if I ever saw one.'

'Did Chloe ever talk to you about anyone she met at St Simeon's?' asks Nelson.

'She said she used to see her guardian angel there,' says Stanley, in a matter-of-fact voice.

'What do you think she meant by that?' asks Tim.

'She said she'd seen a vision of her guardian angel,' says Stanley, 'in the graveyard.'

'Did you believe her?'

'Oh, yes,' says Stanley. 'She was telling the truth, I'm sure of it. I've learnt to spot true mystics in my line of work.'

'What line of work is that?' asks Nelson.

Stanley gives him a sad smile. 'I'm a priest,' he says.

'Bloody hell,' says Nelson, driving back through the darkening lanes. It's still afternoon, but already the daylight is fading. 'You don't expect to find a priest in a drying-out clinic.'

'I don't know,' says Tim. 'They must come under tremendous strain. People dump all their problems on their ministers. I don't know if they have enough training or counselling to help them to cope. I should imagine it's enough to make you turn to drink.'

It's a characteristic, measured Tim response. 'Is your family religious?' asks Nelson.

'My mum is,' says Tim. 'She goes to church every Sunday. All her social life is bound up in the church too. I don't believe myself, but her faith's got Mum through some very bad times. It's been a real support to her, a real community.'

Nelson wonders what the bad times entailed. Tim never mentions a father – perhaps he died or deserted the family. It's typical of Tim to answer a question in a very open, friendly way and yet not tell you much.

'My mum's religious too,' he says. 'Roman Catholic. We were all brought up as Catholics but none of us practise now.

For my mum, though, it's the centre of her world. She's like your mother, never misses a Sunday.'

She goes on Fridays too, for some obscure reason that Nelson can never remember. Something to do with collecting brownie points for the souls in purgatory. He has a superstitious impulse to cross himself. He remembers Cathbad saying, 'You're still such a Catholic, Nelson.'

'Stanley wasn't a Catholic priest, though,' he says aloud. '"Anglo-Catholic", he said.'

'It's not the same,' says Nelson. 'Anglo-Catholics are still Protestants.' He can still hear his mother criticising her parish priest, Father David, who's a Church of England convert ('He only came over to us because he couldn't stand the thought of female priests'). She'd adored the previous incumbent, Father Damian. Come to think of it, Damian went back to Ireland to recover from a drink problem. Maybe Tim's right: there's more of it around than you think.

He's about to ask Tim what he thought of Stanley and Jean, when his sergeant says, so urgently that Nelson turns to look at him, 'Boss. I've got something to tell you.'

'What?' Nelson swerves to avoid a fallen branch.

'I want a transfer.'

'What?!' Nelson swerves again, causing Tim to say, recklessly, 'Look out!'

'Don't tell me how to drive,' growls Nelson. 'What do you mean, you want a transfer?'

'I want to move. Away from Norfolk.' After a pause Tim adds, 'I'm sorry.'

They have come to the outskirts of King's Lynn. Nelson

slows down, but only slightly. He says, 'You've had a tough few months, what with that business at Blackstock Hall.'

He's referring to the time when Tim shot a man. There has been an inquiry, and Tim was completely cleared (there were extenuating circumstances, like the fact that he saved Nelson's life), but there's no doubt that the whole business was incredibly stressful for everyone involved.

'Take some time off,' says Nelson. 'Think about it.'

'I have thought about it,' says Tim. 'I've really enjoyed working for you, but I think it's time to move on.'

'Where will you go?'

'Maybe back to Essex. To be near my family.'

Nelson understands this. He sometimes feels a real pull to go back to his home, Blackpool, away from Norfolk and its flat, alien fields. But Tim doesn't sound like a man yearning for home. He sounds disconsolate, as if he's got nothing left to look forward to. When Tim first moved to Norfolk Nelson assumed it wouldn't be long before he got himself a girlfriend and settled down. As far as Nelson knows, this hasn't happened, although Tim's a decent-looking boy who keeps himself fit.

'We'll miss you,' he says now. 'Cloughie will have no one to wind up.'

'He'll find someone,' says Tim. But he still sounds depressed.

# CHAPTER 9

Ruth doesn't open the letters until Kate has gone to bed. She feels that they need her full concentration and that's impossible with Kate organising her Sylvanians into Hogwarts houses and insisting that every one of her bath toys takes to the water. There's another reason too. She looks at the letters on her desk: brown envelopes (bad sign), addresses in capitals (ditto), and their appearance of having been read and reread several times. She's reluctant to open them and let the nastiness out. Cathbad would say that it was about bad energy. He would have recommended lighting candles and drawing up a circle of protection, but Ruth takes her own precautions by pouring herself a large glass of red wine and putting on a Bruce Springsteen CD.

Dear Doctor Smithson,
I won't call you Reverend because, as I will elaborate in this letter, you do not deserve the title. I am prepared to call you Doctor because this title you have earned without fear or favour. But I will never accept

your right to call yourself a priest. 'Man and Woman Created He Them' (Genesis 1:27). Men and women are different, Doctor Smithson. Not better or worse. Different. I am not a misogynist, as you women academics would have me. I simply believe that men and women have different tasks in the world. Women have the privilege of bearing children. Men are the appointed protectors of the family. And Jesus appointed men to be the protectors of his church. Yes, all the disciples were men and to these men was given the gift of the Holy Spirit and the task of spreading the word of God. You and your fellow harpies are bringing this holy church into disgrace. It is obscene to see a woman on the altar, her hands on the Blessed Chalice. Our Blessed Lord said, 'Anyone who has seen me has seen the Father' (John 14:9). Priests are in His image. The Father, not the Mother. The imagery of the scriptures is entirely masculine. A male priest symbolises the power, the masterfulness, of our Saviour. In the church, as in the family, the man has the authority, the guardianship, the duty of care. A women's sphere is motherhood and domesticity, not arguing from a pulpit. 'I do not permit a woman to teach or to have authority over a man' (1 Timothy 2:12). I will pray for you.

There's no signature.

Flint jumps on to the table and tries to sit on the letters. Ruth moves him gently. In the background Bruce Springsteen sings about a wreck on the highway. She thinks about the letter-writer. Is he a priest? A theologian? The painstaking biblical notations certainly seem like the work of someone with biblical knowledge, or at least someone who wants to seem learned. Maybe he's a thwarted academic? The reference to 'you women academics' sounds bitter and personal. Maybe he has been passed over for promotion by a woman. Ruth takes a sheet of paper and starts noting the biblical references. The Genesis quotation sounds as if it comes from an old translation. The writer is obviously the sort of person who likes archaic syntax. She's willing to bet that he's a Tolkien fan. Is the writer definitely a man? It's certainly someone who believes that men should have 'authority' over women, but plenty of women believe that too. Ruth has heard similar arguments in her parents' church, all about what a relief it is to have someone to make all the decisions, it's so *peaceful*. Well, so is a prison cell peaceful, after a fashion. And isn't there something of the submissive woman about the emphasis on God's 'masterfulness'? Not that Ruth knows any submissive women. She's proud to say that she hasn't even read *Fifty Shades of Grey*.

The letters aren't dated, but someone (Hilary presumably) has written the date they were received on the envelopes. The next two letters are sent a few months apart and more or less reprise the arguments of the first: the disciples were men, God is a man, men and women are different. With the fourth letter there is a distinct change of tone. According to the note on the envelope this letter was received on the first of November. Kate's birthday. All Saints' Day.

Dear Doctor Smithson,

You haven't replied to my letters. [Difficult to do, thinks Ruth, when there's no return address.] I fear you are mired in sin and in the wrongness of your ways. Do you follow the True Cross? 'I warn you, repent, for the Kingdom of Heaven is near at hand' (Matthew 4:12). 'He will put the sheep on his right hand and the goats on his left' (Matthew 25:33). You and your fellow she-devils are the goats, make no mistake about that. 'The Son of Man will send forth His angels, and they will gather out of His kingdom all stumbling blocks, and those who commit lawlessness, and will throw them into the furnace of fire; in that place there will be wailing and gnashing of teeth' (Matthew 13:42).

The last letter was received on 27th December, which probably meant that it had been sent just before Christmas. The writer had obviously decided on a new salutation.

Dear Jezebel,

They dug in Walsingham but they did not find the True Treasure. Nor will you find the Truth there. You may have borne a child (O sacrilege that anyone calling themselves a priest should do so!), but you have not suckled from the Virgin's breast. She stands before you, clad in blue, weeping for the world.

*Weep, weep, O Walsingham,*
*Whose dayes are nights,*

*Blessings turned to blasphemies,*
*Holy deeds to despites.*
*Sinne is where our Ladye sate,*
*Heaven turned is to helle;*
*Satan sitthe where our Lord did swaye,*
*Walsingham, O farewell!*

Beware, Doctor Smithson, for the Lord knows your ways and His eye follows you wherever you go.

Yours in Christ —

Ruth Googles Jezebel and learns that she was the wife of Ahab, who encouraged him to worship false gods. Her punishment was to be eaten alive by dogs. Ruth takes a thoughtful sip of wine. Bruce is still singing about driving and highways and the treacherous lure of his home town. Flint purrs loudly, wanting to be noticed, and Ruth strokes him with her spare hand. She can see why these last letters so disturbed Hilary. There are the threats of hellfire and damnation, but, worse still, the mention of her child and the implication that the letter-writer, as well as the Lord, will be watching Hilary wherever she goes. And the letter-writer knows that Hilary will be in Walsingham. Well, maybe that's not too difficult to find out. Presumably Hilary is listed as attending the conference on preparing for bishopness, or whatever it's called. The phrase 'They dug in Walsingham' is interesting. Hilary thought it referred to an archaeological dig, and Ruth knows that there were some excavations in the sixties. She must look them up.

She looks at her list.

## BIBLICAL

'Man and woman created He them' (Genesis 1:27)

'Anyone who has seen me has seen the Father' (John 14:9)

'I do not permit a woman to teach or to have authority over a man' (1 Timothy 2:12)

Jezebel

'Repent, for the Kingdom of Heaven is near at hand' (Matthew 4:22)

'He will put the sheep on his right hand and the goats on his left' (Matthew 25:33)

'The Son of Man will send forth His angels . . .' (Matthew 13:42)

## HISTORICAL

The True Cross

'Weep, weep, O Walsingham' (Where is this from?)

## ARCHAEOLOGY

They dug at Walsingham.

She remembers making a similar list, years ago, on the case where she first met Nelson. The thought of that case, and the places where it led, makes her feel suddenly uneasy. She has been sitting by the window. Outside all is blackness, but she knows the marshes are there, with their secret paths and treacherous waterways, miles of grassland and sand leading to the sea. Ruth gets up and pulls the curtains. Flint jumps off the table with a thud. Ruth switches on the television, wanting the noise and distraction. It's the ten o'clock news. She had promised to ring Nelson when she'd read the letters, but is it too late now? She decides it is; besides, she never likes ringing him at home.

But, just as she settles down in front of the TV, he rings her.

'Ruth. Have you read the letters?'

'Yes.'

'I thought you were going to ring me.'

'I was, but then it seemed a bit late . . .'

'Bollocks. It's not late. Michelle's still out at her book group.' (Why tell me that? thinks Ruth. But she's interested, nonetheless. Michelle has never struck her as much of a reader.) 'Anyhow, is there anything in the letters? Have we got another madman on our hands?'

'I don't know,' says Ruth, 'but they certainly read like the work of someone disturbed. What sort of person sends anonymous letters in the first place? And there's lots of stuff about death, judgement and hell. Plus a nasty reference to Hilary and her child.'

Nelson is silent for a moment. Ruth thinks she can hear him thinking. 'Can you bring them in to the station tomorrow?' he asks. 'They sound like they're worth looking into. Anything else?'

'I've made a list.'

'Good girl.'

Ruth hates being called a girl, but she can't help smiling. A love of lists is one of the few things she and Nelson have in common.

'The letter-writer obviously has a real problem with women,' she says.

'Haven't we all?' says Nelson.

'He's even worse than you. Actually, I'm not even sure it is a man.'

'A female woman-hater?'

'They do exist, believe me.'

There's another silence and then Nelson says, 'Tim's leaving.'

'What?'

'Tim says he wants a transfer. He wants to go back to Essex.'

'Because of what happened before Christmas? The shooting and everything?'

'I asked him that. He just says it's time to move on. I've said he should take some more time to think about it. I've even offered him counselling.'

Nelson sounds aggrieved. Ruth knows that it will have cost him a lot even to say the word 'counselling'.

'You'll miss him,' she says.

But Nelson seems to regret confiding in her. 'Plenty more police officers where he came from,' he says, before ringing off with a brusque injunction not to forget the letters tomorrow.

Ruth stares unseeingly at the news for a few minutes, then she gets up and pours herself another glass of wine. She feels unsettled and not just by the letters. Last year, before Christmas, she saw Michelle and Tim together in the car park of the sports club. They were locked in a passionate embrace, an image that somehow Ruth cannot delete from her mental inbox. Were they having an affair? *Are* they having an affair? Ruth doesn't know, but, in the light of the car park kiss, Tim's request for a transfer seems to make a kind of sense. He is removing himself from temptation and taking the threat to Nelson's marriage away with him. So, although Nelson is obviously aggrieved at Tim's defection, Ruth, as his friend, should be pleased for him. But is she?

Ruth takes a long drink of wine and considers whilst, on the television, the weather forecast promises sunny spells and warns of squally showers. Ruth wants Nelson to be happy, of course she does, and, much as she sometimes hates to admit it, for him happiness probably means a solid marriage and a home to which his daughters can return whenever they feel like a dose of family life. So, if Tim disappears into the wilds of Essex, the Nelson marriage is saved for the nation. The only problem is, when she saw Michelle and Tim together, Ruth – the loyal family friend – suddenly saw an image of herself married to Nelson and, much as she tries to press that delete button again, the idea has imprinted itself on her imagination. Does she want to be married to Nelson? On the face of it, no. Ruth has never wanted to be married to anyone. Once she shared this house with her boyfriend Peter, but, after Ruth ended the relationship, she vowed never to live with anyone again (except her cats). But then Kate came along and now she is knitted into the very fabric of Ruth's life. A man would change (spoil) everything: giant shoes on the stairs, alien books on her shelves, a heavy body in her bed. This last image, she has to admit, is also slightly exciting.

But, even with Frank, though she did imagine living with him, she never thought of marriage. She considered him as a potential stepfather, not as a potential husband. Why then these shamefully retro thoughts of a white dress, a registry office (even in her fantasies she doesn't go as far as a church) and Kate dressed up as a bridesmaid. Is it because of Kate? If Ruth married Nelson, then Kate could live with her actual father. Wouldn't that be neat? No – as the seemingly end-less local weather forecast continues ('Areas of low pressure spreading eastwards') – Ruth has to admit it. Somewhere, deep down, she is still in love with Nelson.

Warnings of thundery weather ahead.

# CHAPTER 10

Ruth has agreed to meet Hilary in the abbey grounds at ten.

'We can go for a walk and see the snowdrops,' she had said.

'Snowdrops?' For the moment Ruth thought she was referring to some strange religious sect.

'Flowers, Ruth.' Hilary laughed, in that slightly patronising way that was becoming familiar all over again. 'They're famous. Don't tell me you've never seen the snowdrops in February?'

'Somehow the abbey's not on my usual route.'

On her way to work Ruth drops the letters into King's Lynn police station with a note for Nelson. The desk sergeant, a grey-haired man who looks like Captain Birdseye, greets her with alarming friendliness.

'Hallo there, stranger. How are things?'

'Fine. Thank you.' She can't remember the man's name, but she knows that she has met him before. How come they are on 'Hallo there, stranger' terms? Does he just remember her as the archaeologist who helped on earlier cases, or is it something else? She never knows how much the other police officers know about her relationship with Nelson.

'How's your little girl?'

'She's fine. She's five now.'

'Five! I can't believe it. She must be at school then.'

'Yes. She's in Reception.'

'Where? At St Faith's?' He names a local private school.

'No.' She gives him a look. 'At Bridge Street Primary.'

'That's a nice little school. My niece used to be a TA there.'

'Yes, it's a lovely school. Can you see that DCI Nelson gets this package?'

'Will do. Shall I call him down? He'll be starting the briefing in a minute.'

'No. Don't worry. If you could just give him the package . . .'

Ruth doesn't think she could stand greeting Nelson in front of the sergeant's benevolent grin. She doesn't know what's worse; him suspecting that Nelson is Kate's father or him thinking that she would send her daughter to a private school.

It's still early when she gets to the university. The corridors are deserted, but, when she gets to her office, she sees that Phil's door is open. Her head of department is at his desk.

'Have you got a minute, Phil?'

'Yes, of course.' Phil looks surprised, but immediately composes his face. Maybe he's hoping that she's come to resign.

'It's about the 1961 Walsingham excavation.'

'Rather before my time, Ruth.'

'I know that,' says Ruth patiently. 'I was wondering if you knew where the finds are. Would they be at the museum?'

'I suppose so. There was a rather beautiful figure of

Mercury, I remember, and a bust of a strange three-horned god. But the rest was just the usual medieval pilgrim relics. Pilgrim badges and ampullae for carrying oil and holy water. That sort of thing.'

'Is there a write-up somewhere?'

'There'll be a list of finds at the museum, I suppose. Why this sudden interest in Walsingham, Ruth? Not getting religious in your old age, are you?'

'No, a friend of mine was looking at funding for a dig.' Ruth is pretty sure that Phil won't bother to check this story. Besides, if there was any funding going, he would have devoured it years ago.

'I doubt they'll get an English Heritage grant,' he says. 'Anything good has been excavated years ago. They think they found the site of the original holy house, but, as it was made of wood, there was nothing much left. You did a dig near Walsingham a few years ago, didn't you?'

'Yes,' says Ruth. Phil was meant to be involved too, she remembers, but he had left for a coffee break on the first morning and never reappeared. 'We were hoping to find the site of the original pagan shrine, but it was rather disappointing. The land had been really broken up by ploughing. All we found were some coins, a few pottery shards and some glass.'

Phil is busy straightening the objects on his desk: stapler, hole-punch, pens in a British Museum mug, stone paperweight. His in-tray contains just one sheet of university-headed paper. How the hell has he managed that? Ruth's in-tray regularly overflows onto the floor.

'There was one interesting find,' he says. 'A sort of cross-shaped reliquary. The chaps at UCL thought that it might have been made to hold a fragment of the True Cross.'

'The True Cross?' Wasn't there a reference to the True Cross in the letters? Ruth tries to remember.

'Yes. It's one of those crazy religious things. You know, as if Christ's cross managed to find its way to medieval Norfolk. But they believed anything in those days.'

Phil always sounds as if bygone generations were a completely different species. In Ruth's opinion, humans haven't really changed that much. We're just as credulous now, she thinks, except about different things.

'I'll let my friend know,' she says, standing up. 'Maybe she should visit the museum and see what they've got there.'

'There's no money in medieval relics these days,' says Phil, straightening the single sheet of paper. 'It's all about dead kings. I blame Richard the Third.'

Ruth hadn't really been expecting much from the snowdrops but, when she and Hilary walk through the gates, she actually catches her breath in wonder. Nothing much is left of the priory at Walsingham, just the arch and a few free-standing walls. But stretched out between them is a carpet of white, as if the church has risen again in all its finery. Trees rise up like organ pipes and, far above them, a skylark is singing.

'It's amazing,' says Ruth. 'Is there still an abbey here?'

'The Prior's lodging was converted into a private house which is now called The Abbey,' says Hilary, 'but the medieval priory was destroyed. This is all that remains of it. There was a friary too, you can see the remains of that behind St Simeon's Church. I can't believe you've lived in Norfolk seventeen years and never been here.'

'I'm not religious,' says Ruth. 'You must remember that about me.'

Hilary laughs and takes her arm. Ruth stiffens. She's not keen on people holding on to her. Apart from Kate, who doesn't count, she can't remember the last time she held another person's hand. Maybe it was Max, an archaeologist with whom she had a brief relationship a few years ago. Max liked holding hands, going out for meals, watching television together; all the coupley things. Maybe that was why Ruth had ended the relationship. She just couldn't act the part convincingly. It feels odd, having to adjust your pace to someone else's. As soon as possible, she stops and disentangles herself.

'This must be where the original holy house stood,' she says.

There's a wooden sign saying: 'Site of the 11th-century, Anglo-Saxon shrine of the holy house of Nazareth (excavated 1961)'. But, of the original structure, there's no trace at all, just smooth grass studded with white flowers. The only marker is a small cross fixed into the ground.

'Did you look up the 1961 excavation?' asks Hilary. It's the first time either of them has mentioned the letters, even obliquely.

'I talked to my head of department this morning,' says Ruth. 'He said there are some finds at the museum, a figure of Mercury, for example. You know that they think Walsingham was once a shrine to Mercury?'

Hilary ignores this information about Walsingham's pagan past. 'I went to a talk at King's Lynn Museum once,' she says. 'They have quite a lot of artefacts there, mostly medieval, but a few Roman ones too.'

'Yes. Phil mentioned some pilgrim badges and ampullae. I took part in a dig near Walsingham a few years ago and we found some Roman coins and pottery. But it was pretty disappointing on the whole. My boss did mention something interesting, though.'

'What?' Hilary takes her arm again.

'It was a cross-shaped reliquary. The experts thought it might have been made to hold a fragment of the True Cross.'

'The True Cross,' repeats Hilary, dropping Ruth's arm. '"Do you follow the True Cross?" That's what the letter-writer said.'

'Do you know what that could have meant?'

'Well, there's meant to be a relic of the True Cross at the Anglican shrine.'

'Do they really believe that it's *the* cross?' asks Ruth. 'The one Jesus died on?'

'You sound very doubting,' says Hilary.

'Well, it's not very likely, is it? What's the provenance?'

'That doesn't matter,' says Hilary. 'What matters is that people believe that it was the True Cross. Do you see?'

'Not really,' says Ruth. They carry on walking, across the grass pitted with the remains of walls and odd flat squares of ground where fragments of paving can be seen. Eventually they reach parkland and a picturesque bridge over a fast-flowing river. They stand on the bridge, watching the water rushing between the grassy banks. It's a beautiful day, bright but cold, the sky high and palest blue. Ruth says, 'The letter-writer says: "They dug in Walsingham but they did not find the True Treasure".' She had read the letters again after her discussion with Phil. 'What do you think he meant?'

'I don't know. I thought it was a reference to the Holy Spirit, the true treasure in men's hearts. That sort of thing.'

'Men's hearts,' says Ruth. 'Not women's.'

Hilary sighs, lifting up her face to the sun. Her hair gleams almost white, but otherwise she looks ageless, her skin unlined and her eyes clear.

'It's very wearing,' she says. 'How much some people hate us.'

'Why do you carry on then?' says Ruth. 'Why not do a job where people don't hate you just for being a woman?'

Hilary gives Ruth her sibylline stare, eyes wide and haunted. 'Because God's love is for everyone. We're all made in God's image, not just men. Besides there aren't enough priests to go round. Without women, the priesthood would die out.'

Ruth doesn't really see why that's a bad thing, but she doesn't voice this thought. Instead she says, 'What about the other women on your course? Have any of them received letters?'

'I don't think so,' says Hilary. 'I haven't asked, though.'

'It's just, if they have, it might prove that the link's Walsing-ham, rather than you.'

'That's true.' Hilary gives her a more considering look, the sort of look that she used to give Erik in lectures. 'But I was getting letters before I even booked to come on this course.'

Ruth thinks that Hilary sounds slightly reluctant to consider that she might not be the letter-writer's only target.

'It might be worth asking them all the same,' she says.

'You sound like a detective,' says Hilary. 'Have you spoken to your policeman friend about the letters?'

'He's not . . .' begins Ruth and then she stops. How can she possibly explain her relationship with Nelson to Hilary? 'Yes,' she says. 'I dropped the letters into the police station this morning. You said I could,' she adds, as she thinks that Hilary looks slightly annoyed.

'Yes, I know. I'm very grateful.'

'You said you'd talk to him too. About being threatened.'

'Do you think the letters are anything to worry about?' asks Hilary. 'Or is it just some nutcase with a grudge against women priests?'

'I don't know,' says Ruth. 'It's probably nothing, but there was a nasty tone to the later letters. The mention of your child, for one thing.'

'I'm not scared,' says Hilary. 'I have complete trust in God. Plus –' she grins suddenly – 'I have a black belt in taekwondo.'

'I'm impressed,' says Ruth. 'Shall we go and get a cup of tea? I've got about half an hour before I have to get back to work.'

'Good idea,' says Hilary. They walk quickly back through the grounds, passing an almost complete section of the priory, a chamber with four walls, windows and a door, although with a roof open to the skies.

'They say this was the crypt,' says Hilary, pointing to a sign set into the grass, 'but I don't think it was. There are the remains of a vaulted ceiling and there's a fireplace too.'

'It must have been a magnificent place,' says Ruth. The grounds are filling up. A flock of nuns passes by, excited as schoolgirls, their veils flying in the wind. They pass a walled garden with gardeners at work on the flowerbeds. Ruth points out silvery shapes in the newly turned soil. 'Oyster shells. Those monks lived well.'

'Yes,' says Hilary. 'There are all sorts of tales about riotous living at the priory in the old days. There was a report in 1514 that mentions the "scandalous life of the monks". Mind you, this priory wasn't suppressed until 1538, two years after the dissolution of the monasteries. I think that's because the abbot was very quick to swear allegiance to Henry the Eighth.'

Ruth supposes that Hilary, as a good Protestant, would approve of the suppression. She has mixed feelings herself. She's no fan of monks and nuns, but she always thinks there's something grand, something illogically heroic, about the pre-Reformation Church. And didn't the monks look after the poor, too, as well as feasting on oysters?

'The verse in the last letter,' says Hilary, 'it was part of an anonymous sixteenth-century ballad lamenting the dissolution of the monasteries. I was wondering if it meant that the writer was a Catholic.'

'I thought the same thing,' says Ruth. 'There's a lot about the Virgin Mary too. That suggests Catholicism.'

Hilary laughs and waves her hand, encompassing the

white lawns, the ruined priory, the blue sky above. 'Look at all this. It's a shrine to the Virgin Mary and both Catholics and Anglicans come here. England has always had a special devotion to Mary. That's why it was called "Mary's dowry".'

Ruth doesn't like Hilary's tone, which she thinks is both patronising and unpleasantly fervid. 'There's a lot of scripture quoting in the letters, though,' she says. 'That's not a particularly Catholic thing. Or am I wrong about that too?'

Hilary takes her arm again and squeezes it in apology. 'No, you're absolutely right. It's a bit different now, but Catholics used not to be encouraged to read the scriptures. And some Catholics – and some Anglo-Catholics for that matter – would still like the Bible to be in Latin, as if Martin Luther had never existed.'

If he had never existed, thinks Ruth, would this priory still be standing, its vaulted roof in place? But maybe it's more beautiful this way, the building becoming landscape, its aisle and nave filled with snowdrops. Gently, she disengages her arm from Hilary's.

'So you think the writer might be a Catholic?'

'I don't know,' says Hilary. 'He mentions the "Blessed Chalice". If it was a Catholic surely he'd say something about the chalice containing the Blood of Christ?'

It all sounds rather horrible to Ruth, but then many religions do, including the gentle paganism practised by Cathbad. She wonders how Cathbad enjoyed his stay in Walsingham. She must ring him tonight. She notes that Hilary knows the letters by heart; also that she's convinced the writer is a man.

They are almost back at the great arch, standing on its own by the entrance. Looking at it, Ruth is reminded of a building site in Norwich, where an arch was the only thing remaining of the original house. Under the arch, which once framed a doorway, Ruth had found a child's bones. The memory makes her feel anxious and slightly dizzy. She hurries through the archway and bumps into a priest. That's the problem with Walsingham. There are priests everywhere.

'I'm so sorry,' she says.

'My mistake,' says the man courteously in an Irish accent. Then 'Ruth? Is it you?'

It's as if Ruth's thoughts have conjured up the past. Because there in front of her is Father Patrick Hennessey, the priest involved with the ruined house in Norwich. They have kept in touch sporadically over the years – it was Father Hennessey who baptised Kate – but now, to see him here, in Norfolk, under another archway, seems almost like a miracle.

'Father Hennessey! What are you doing here?'

Is it her imagination or does the priest look slightly embarrassed, almost furtive? 'Just a private pilgrimage, Ruth. Just a private pilgrimage. But how are you and your lovely baby?'

'She's not a baby any more. She's five and at school. Oh, sorry . . .' Ruth is suddenly aware of Hilary standing beside her, looking extremely curious. 'This is my friend Hilary Smithson.'

'The Reverend Smithson, I see.' Father Hennessey doffs his hat, an old-fashioned trilby. 'Delighted to meet you.'

'Delighted to meet you too.' Hilary seems rather confused to be receiving so much respect from the elderly clergyman.

She puts her hand up to her clerical collar, as if surprised to find it there.

'We're just going for a cup of tea,' says Ruth. 'Would you like to come?'

'Thank you, no,' says Father Hennessey. 'I've only got a few minutes before Mass. Just time for a quick look at the snowdrops. I'm sure we'll meet again.' And he raises his hat again and disappears through the archway like the White Rabbit.

Nelson is preparing for the morning team meeting. Sometimes these briefings can be fairly perfunctory affairs – Nelson reading through the logbook while Clough eats a McDonald's breakfast – but, with a major incident under way, the team meeting is crucial. Nelson will need to make sure everyone is up to speed on all developments, assign lines of enquiry and answer idiotic questions from Roy (Rocky) Taylor, the slowest policeman in the country. So, when there's a knock on his door, Nelson makes his most discouraging noise and hopes that the visitor is going to go away.

To his annoyance, the caller mistakes the sound for 'Please come in'.

'Boss, can I have a word?'

It's Tim. For one moment, Nelson thinks that he's come to tell him to forget the whole transfer conversation, that he's reconsidered and is happy to stay in Norfolk. This thought makes him sound unusually welcoming.

'Of course. What is it?'

'It's about Chloe Jenkins.'

'What about her?'

'It was something her mother said. That, when she was little, Chloe's childminder had said that she was like an angel.'

'Everyone seems to be talking about angels. Chloe was seeing angels here, there and everywhere, going on courses to feel their vibrations and what have you.'

'The same thought struck me,' says Tim seriously. 'Anyway, I thought it might be worth talking to the childminder, especially if she's local. So I rang the parents last night and asked for her number.'

'Good thinking. Are you going to go and see her?'

'That would be difficult,' said Tim. 'She died in 2002. She's buried in the graveyard at St Simeon's.'

He looks at Nelson, who slowly gets the message.

'Good God. So Chloe's childminder was . . .'

'Doreen Westmondham. Julie, Chloe's mother, says that Chloe was devoted to Doreen. She was devastated when the family left Norfolk, and they had to say goodbye. She never forgot her.'

'You can say that again,' says Nelson, 'if she was sneaking out at night to clean the woman's grave. Fiona McAllister said that Chloe had been in a family therapy session on the day before she died. Maybe that's what put Doreen into her mind.'

'I looked up the Westmondhams,' says Tim. 'Doreen had three sons, as well as lots of foster children. They all still live locally.'

'What do they do?'

'Steven's a plumber, lives in Fakenham. Married with two daughters. Kevin's divorced and lives in Holt with his new partner. But Larry, the youngest son, is the interesting one.'

'Why?'

'He's the vicar at St Simeon's.'

Nelson thinks of the church which didn't provide sanctuary to Chloe Jenkins, of the overgrown graveyard and the one white stone, so lovingly tended.

'You'd better go and see him,' he says.

Ruth and Hilary are back in the Blue Lady tea rooms. Ruth has virtuously refused a brownie, but accepts half of Hilary's scone. It's a well-known fact that shared food doesn't contain calories.

Hilary chats brightly about her course.

'Everyone's so friendly. It's a real tonic. We went to a service at St Simeon's last night. It was really beautiful. And then Larry, the vicar, invited us back to his house for lasagne.'

'Did the vicar cook for you all?'

'Well, his wife did. She was charming.'

Ruth reflects that vicars still have charming wives who do the cooking. She wonders whether Hilary's husband could rustle up a lasagne.

'What sort of people are on the course?'

'All women priests. Most of them are like me and have been in post several years. So we're ready for the next step.'

'Which is becoming a bishop?'

Hilary smiles modestly. 'I wouldn't say I was ready, personally, but we're hoping that the General Synod will give its approval to women bishops in July. It's as well to be prepared.'

'Who's running the course? A woman priest?'

Hilary looks slightly embarrassed as she says, 'No, it's a theologian called Robin Rainsford. He's very well respected, though, and a big supporter of the cause. I went on another course that he ran last year.'

Ruth rather envies Hilary all these courses. She wanted to go on a course a couple of years back – something to do with DNA-dating techniques – but Phil had flatly refused. 'We just don't have the budget, Ruth.' This before disappearing on a weekend fact-finding trip to Padua.

'The other women seem lovely,' Hilary is saying. 'So supportive and friendly. In fact . . .' She looks speculatively at Ruth.

'What?'

'Well, we're going out for a meal tomorrow night. You should come. I know they'd love to meet you.'

Why? thinks Ruth. Why should they want to meet me and why should I want to meet them? She takes refuge in her usual excuse. 'I'll have to see if I can get a babysitter.'

'Of course.' Hilary is looking supportive again. 'It must be hard when you're on your own.'

'I'm sure it's hard with both of you working,' counters Ruth. 'Especially with you and your husband both being priests. It's not exactly a nine-to-five job, is it?'

Hilary doesn't seem to want to discuss her domestic arrangements.

'Who was that priest you introduced me to?' she says. 'Is he a friend of yours?'

Ruth hesitates – is Father Hennessey her friend? She liked him from the first, he's clever and funny and surprisingly non-judgemental. But can a priest be a friend? Then again, here she is sharing a scone with her old university friend Hilary, who is also a priest.

'He's called Father Patrick Hennessey,' she says. 'I met him when I was working on a case in Norwich.'

'A police case?' says Hilary.

'Yes. The field archaeology team found some bones buried in a house that was about to be demolished. The house used to be a children's home. Father Hennessey ran it.'

'Oh.' Hilary looks as if she has some more questions, but, to her credit, she doesn't ask them. Instead she says, 'What's going to happen to the letters now?'

'I think Nelson . . . the police . . . just want to look at them to see if there's anything . . . suspicious.'

Hilary looks at her shrewdly. 'There's something you're not telling me.'

That's the trouble with Hilary. She always was sharp, even in the old days. Ruth sighs. 'You know there was a murder here last week?'

'Yes. Some poor drug addict. I read about it in the papers.'

'Well, Nelson thinks there's a possibility – just a possibility, mind you – that there's a link.'

'Between my letters and the murder of that poor girl?'

'It's just a theory. He has to explore every lead. I probably shouldn't have told you this much.'

'Is that why you asked me if any other women priests had had letters?'

'I suppose so.'

For some reason Hilary is smiling. 'I was right. You have become a detective.'

'No I haven't.' Ruth is feeling rather stupid, an emotion she realises that Hilary often engenders in her.

'You have. You really must come out with us tomorrow night. Do some sleuthing.'

Ruth is about to reply – to recall some vital prior engagement – when she sees a dark figure hurrying past. It's Father Hennessey. She's about to tap on the window to invite him in, but there's something about the black-clad figure that makes her hesitate. Father Hennessey looks like a man on a mission. And not a particularly divine one either.

# CHAPTER 11

Even without Tim and Clough, the briefing room seems full. Tanya is sitting at the front, glasses glinting. Rocky Taylor is at the back. He has his notebook open, though Nelson notices that he has neglected to take the cap off his pen. Officers from other stations take the remaining seats, most of them trying not to look excited. This is the biggest case most of them will have seen.

Nelson runs through the investigation so far.

'Chloe Jenkins left the Sanctuary at approximately eight p.m. on Wednesday 19th February.' He points at the map. 'A woman answering her description was seen by Michael Malone, commonly known as Cathbad, in the graveyard of St Simeon's Church, Walsingham, at about nine o'clock. Chloe's body was found by a dog-walker the next morning. Her body was in a ditch, about a mile outside Walsingham on a road known as the Pilgrim Route to the Slipper Chapel, the Catholic shrine. Chloe had been strangled. No sign of sexual assault. She was still in her nightclothes: white nightdress, blue dressing gown. No underwear was found. A rosary was also found in the ditch. It had hand-carved wooden beads and a silver cross. We've followed it up and it's a design sold both at the Walsingham Shrine shop and the Slipper Chapel. The pathologist puts the time of death at between ten o'clock and midnight on the Wednesday night. So we are looking for any sightings between eight o'clock and midnight.'

'What was Chloe doing when this Malone saw her?' The question comes from a young officer from another district. Anyone from King's Lynn would know Cathbad.

'She was standing by a gravestone. I've got reason to believe that she'd been cleaning it. There were traces of cleaning fluid on her fingers and cleaning equipment was found hidden in the undergrowth nearby. The grave belonged to one Doreen Westmondham, who died in 2002. It turns out that Doreen was also Chloe's childminder when the family lived in Norfolk.'

Tanya says, 'So Chloe was visiting the grave of her old nanny? That's very sad.'

'I don't think she was a nanny as much as an occasional babysitter,' says Nelson, 'but I want to find out more about her. Heathfield and Clough are interviewing Doreen's son Larry now. He's the vicar at St Simeon's. Chloe was making good progress at the Sanctuary, according to her doctor, Fiona McAllister. I've also spoken to her personal therapist Holly Barrett, and Heathfield and I have interviewed her closest friends amongst the other guests.'

'Are they models?' asks Rocky hopefully.

'No, they're a middle-aged couple. A retired teacher and a retired vicar. Fuller . . .' He turns to Tanya, who sits up even straighter. 'Chloe was doing an online course. Something to do with angels. Can you follow it up? Find out a bit more about it?'

'Yes, boss.' Tanya sounds less than enthusiastic to be given the angel brief. Nelson decides to cheer her up. 'But first you can go to Walsingham and co-ordinate the scene-of-the-crime search. They're concentrating on the area where Chloe's body was found.'

Tanya brightens immediately. Co-ordinating is almost as good as being in charge.

'Chloe had a boyfriend called Thom Novak,' continues Nelson. 'He's also in rehab, in Switzerland. Heathfield spoke to him on Thursday and he seemed very shaken by Chloe's death. He's got an alibi for Wednesday night, but nevertheless we should keep an eye on him. I don't need to tell you that the killer is usually someone close to the victim. Miller and Cannivan –' he turns to two DCs from Norwich – 'you look into Novak's history. See if there's anything we need to know about. If you need to speak to the family, go through DS Heathfield.'

'We need to trace Chloe's footsteps on Wednesday night,' says Nelson. 'I simply don't believe that no one saw a young girl in her nightdress wandering through the fields. We could do a reconstruction. Her sister might be willing to play Chloe's part. Taylor –' he turns to Rocky who is chewing his pen lid – 'You make sure there are signs on all the roads leading in and out of Walsingham, asking for witnesses.' Surely Ricky can't mess this up?

'Yes, boss,' says Rocky. 'Witnesses to what?'

\*

Tim and Clough arrive just as the morning service is finishing and have to endure an excruciating few minutes listening to the Reverend Larry Westmondham praying aloud to a congregation of three old ladies and a sleeping man who looks as if he might be homeless.

When the old ladies leave they look at the two policemen curiously.

'Good morning,' says Clough.

The women move closer together as if for safety.

'Good morning,' whispers one. And they scuttle out through the church porch. The homeless man sleeps on.

Larry Westmondham comes to greet them. He has taken off his vestments and is dressed in a black clergyman's suit with white dog collar. He's an affable-looking man of about forty. He's almost completely bald, but, curiously, this has the effect of making him seem young rather than old.

'DS Heathfield, DS Clough.' They shake hands and Tim thinks that Westmondham has a typical vicar's handshake, firm and controlling.

'You said you wanted to see me.' Larry Westmondham then ushers them to a pew near the front of the church. There aren't that many pews, although the church is a vast, cavernous space. To Tim it seems very bare after his mother's place of worship; no children's posters or colourful tapestries, just grey stone and a high altar that's almost invisible. There are some statues around the outside wall, but they are grey too and seem to blend into the stone. It's a cold place – physically cold too. Tim and Clough both keep their coats on.

'Thank you for seeing us,' says Tim. 'It's about the young woman who was murdered just outside Walsingham last week. Her name was Chloe Jenkins. Did you read about the case?'

'Yes.' Larry passes a hand over his smooth head. 'Such a terrible thing to happen. She was a patient at the Sanctuary, wasn't she?'

'She was,' says Tim. 'But it seems that she also had a link to your family.'

'To my family?' Larry casts a worried glance at the altar as if wondering exactly which family is being mentioned here.

'Yes. It seems that your mother, Doreen Westmondham, was Chloe's childminder. Did you know about this?'

At the mention of his mother's name, something seems to happen to Larry's face. The contours relax and he even smiles, a rather sweet, reminiscent smile.

'I didn't know, but Mum looked after so many children. She was a school dinner-lady – all the pupils loved her – and she was a foster mother. She must have fostered over a hundred children. Lots of them came to her funeral and said such lovely things about her.'

'She sounds like a wonderful woman,' says Tim, meaning it. 'So you didn't know Chloe Jenkins personally?'

Larry's brow furrows again. 'I don't think so. How old was she?'

'Twenty-five.'

'There you are. I'm forty-four. I was probably at university or working by the time Mum looked after her. The house was always full of children. My brothers and I said that, as soon as we left home, she moved some more foster children into our rooms.'

Did they resent that? wonders Tim. There's nothing in Larry's face to suggest as much, but he supposes that priests – like policemen – become adept at disguising their true emotions.

'We also believe that Chloe attended services here,' says Tim. 'Do you remember speaking to any patients from the Sanctuary?'

'I don't know,' says Larry. 'I try to speak to everyone after Sunday services, but I wouldn't know where they came from unless they told me.'

'Here's a picture,' says Clough. In deference to Larry's holy orders they have selected the least provocative of Chloe's modelling pictures. It shows her in a demure white dress, standing in a field of buttercups. She is turning, laughing, towards the camera, one hand holding back her long blonde hair.

Larry blinks and, indeed, the picture, so golden and sundrenched, seems to glow like a beacon in the gloomy church.

'Do you recognise her?' prompts Tim.

'Yes,' says Larry. 'I think so. I remember . . . I think I remember seeing her at services.'

I bet you do, thinks Tim. From what he has seen of Larry's congregation, Chloe would definitely stand out.

'Did you ever speak to her?' asks Clough.

'I may have done,' says Larry. 'Just hallo and goodbye. As I say, I try to have a word with everyone.'

'Can you tell us where you were on the evening of the 19th February?' This is Clough, in his role as bad cop.

Larry doesn't seem unduly fazed by the question, though.

'That was a Wednesday, wasn't it? There's no Evensong on a Wednesday. My wife has a knit and natter group at the house so my job is usually keeping the kids out of her hair.'

'How many children do you have?' asks Tim, good cop.

'Four,' says Larry. 'Girls aged ten, eight and six and a baby boy, eighteen months old.'

'You must have your hands full.'

'Well, my wife does really. It's a full-time job running this place. I've got three other parishes as well.'

'Really?' Clough is surprised out of his hard-boiled persona. 'I thought vicars only had one church.'

'That was in the good old days of the Vicar of Dibley,' says Larry. 'These days vicars in rural communities have three or four parishes each. And these big old churches cost a bomb to keep up.' Larry's eyes wander to the giant thermometer propped up by the back wall labelled 'Parish Improvement Fund'. Judging by the level achieved so far, the patient is critical.

'So you were at home all evening on Wednesday?' says Tim.

'Yes. I supervised the girls' homework and bath time. When the children were in bed Daisy and I watched television.'

'What did you watch?'

'*Rev*,' says Larry with enthusiasm. 'It's our favourite programme.'

'That's a comedy, isn't it?' says Clough.

'It's both comic and tragic,' says Larry. 'Like life.'

'Chloe was seen in the graveyard of St Simeon's on the night she died,' says Clough. 'Do you know anyone who would have been near the church then?'

'No,' says Larry. 'The church is locked and the verger lives in Great Walsingham, a few miles away. Justin, who lives in the cottage, was away then. He had a friend house-sitting. A charming chap, very interested in church history.'

That sounds like Cathbad, who is interested in everything. Still, it appears that Larry doesn't have anything to add about Chloe Jenkins, and he has an alibi for the night of the 19th (though that will have to be checked).

'If anything else occurs to you,' says Tim, 'here's my card. Don't hesitate to be in touch.'

'I will,' says Larry, pocketing the card without looking at it. 'Goodbye. God bless you.'

As they leave, the homeless man is still snoring in one of the back pews.

When he gets back to his office, Nelson sees a yellow sticky note on his desk: 'Ruth Galloway called. She left a package for you.' He goes downstairs and finds Tom Henty, the doughty desk sergeant, holding several envelopes tied together with string. 'Ruth left these,' he says. 'She's looking well. Can't believe her little girl is at school.' Nelson looks at Tom suspiciously. He never knows how much the staff at the station guess about Kate's parentage. His team know, but the subject is never mentioned unless Nelson raises it first. He grunts something non-committal and heads back to his office, taking the stairs two at a time.

At first he skims through the letters, pausing only to wonder how people can get so upset about a subject like this. He has no problem with the idea of women priests – or married priests for that matter – though he's sure that his mother would have something to say on the subject. But Maureen would never buy into all this a woman is not to 'teach or to have authority over a man' nonsense. As far as Nelson can see his mother has preached to everyone all her life, and she's the most authoritative person he knows.

But when he gets to the last letter his expression changes. He reads it again, frowning. Then he picks up the phone.

'Ruth. It's Nelson.'

'I know.' She sounds irritated. He dimly realises that this might not be a convenient time to call.

'Sorry. Are you teaching? Lecturing?'

'No. I'm just getting into the car.'

'Late start?'

'No. I met my friend in Walsingham.'

'Is that the friend who received these letters?'

'Yes. Is something the matter? It's just that I've got to get back to the university. I've got a tutorial in half an hour.'

'There's something in the letters that worries me. Have you spoken to Cathbad recently?'

'No. I was going to call in on him and Judy on the way home tonight.'

'Well, on the night that Chloe Jenkins was murdered, Cathbad was house-sitting in Walsingham. He was staying at a cottage attached to the church, St Simeon's. Anyway, he went out at about nine to call the cat in and he saw a woman standing in the graveyard. A woman wearing a white dress and a blue cloak.'

'What? Oh . . . There's something in the letters about a woman wearing blue.'

'"She stands before you, clad in blue, weeping for the world",' quotes Nelson. 'It's a bit of a coincidence isn't it? When Chloe was found she was wearing a white nightdress and a blue dressing gown. Keep that bit of information to yourself, though.'

'She was a patient at the Sanctuary, wasn't she? That much was in the papers.'

'Yes. Poor kid. I don't like coincidences, as you know. I think I need to talk to your friend.'

'But the letters were all written before Christmas. How could the writer know about Cathbad's vision? I bet Cathbad thought it was a vision, didn't he?'

'Of course he did. But what I'm thinking is that there may be this madman wandering about Walsingham, incensed about women in general, obsessed with the Virgin Mary. The sight of a woman dressed in blue might have driven him over the edge.'

'But why would he kill her? Wouldn't he be more likely to fall on his knees and worship her?'

'Madmen do mad things, Ruth, as we both know.'

'Yes.'

'I'd like to speak to your friend. What's her name?'

'Hilary Smithson. She's staying at the conference centre.'

'What's the conference about?'

'Women wanting to be bishops.'

'Jesus wept.'

'Yes, very probably.'

'I can't see you being friends with a priest somehow.'

'Really? I'm going out with them tomorrow night. Just me and seven women priests.'

'I'll send Clough to give you some police protection.'

'Please don't.'

There's a short silence, and then Ruth says, 'Nelson? I saw Father Hennessey just now.'

'Really? Where?'

'Here. In Walsingham.'

'I suppose priests go there all the time. Pilgrimages and what have you.'

'Yes, but I thought he seemed a bit odd. Have you spoken to him recently?'

'Just a card at Christmas. He didn't sound odd on the card but then no one does, do they?'

'I suppose not. I don't send Christmas cards.'

'Well, Michelle does ours.'

Another silence.

'Well, I just thought I'd tell you. I'd better go now. I need to get back to work.'

'All right, Ruth. Take care of yourself now.'


'He recognised her all right,' says Clough, as they drive back to the station.

'She's hard to miss really,' says Tim.

'Weird how much she looks like Michelle, isn't it?' says Clough, then, when Tim is silent – 'You know, the boss's missus. You have met her, haven't you?'

'Yes, I've met her.'

'She's a cracker. Not a patch on Cassie, though.'

'I can't think what Cassie sees in you.'

'It's my charm,' says Clough. 'Can you look in the glove compartment? I'm sure I've got some crisps in there.'

Tim looks and comes up with a half-eaten bar of chocolate, which he passes to Clough.

'Thanks.' Clough shoves it into his mouth.

'You should be the size of a house,' says Tim. 'The amount of crap you eat.'

'I exercise,' says Clough thickly. 'I burn it off.'

Tim doesn't like to ask what form this exercise takes. Instead he says, 'What did you think about our vicar?'

'OK. He seemed fond of his mum. He looked a bit shifty when he saw the picture of Chloe, I thought.'

As ever, they are all on first-name terms with the victim. Only this time it seems especially poignant to think of that glowing girl – immortalised in so many photographs and in oils above her parents' fireplace – lying dead in the morgue. Tim supposes that he will be the one to attend the funeral.

'He did look shifty,' he agrees.

'Shall we pop into Fakenham for some chips?' asks Clough.

'I've got something to tell you,' says Tim.

He tells Clough about wanting a transfer. Clough listens in silence and takes the turning back to King's Lynn and the station. He doesn't mention chips again.

# CHAPTER 12

Ruth calls in to see Cathbad and Judy on her way home. Gone are the days when Cathbad resided in a caravan on Blakeney Beach. Now he and Judy and their two children live in a fisherman's cottage in Wells-next-the-Sea. Judy's Fiat is parked outside and there are spring flowers growing in tubs on the steps. You'd be forgiven for thinking that this was a conventional family home, that is until Cathbad answers the door in his wizard's robes, accompanied by a bull-terrier wearing a bandana.

'Ruth. Lovely to see you.'

'I said I'd pop in. Kate!' This last as Kate rushes past Cathbad shouting 'Mikey! Mikey!' She loves Judy and Cathbad's four-year-old son Michael and recently announced to Ruth that she is going to marry him whether he wants to or not. Thing, the bull-terrier, follows her.

'Where's Michael?' asks Ruth.

'Hiding,' says Cathbad, standing back to let her come in.

'I don't blame him.'

'But he wants to be found.'

Whether Cathbad is right or not, no sooner have Ruth, Cathbad and Judy sat down at the kitchen table than Kate enters triumphantly, holding him captive by the hand.

'Got him. We're going to play being teenagers.'

'Why don't you ask Michael what he wants to play?' asks Ruth. She feels quite faint at the thought of Kate being a teenager.

'He wants to play it too.'

'Do you really, Michael?' Ruth wants to hug the solemn-faced little boy – she has always had a soft spot for Michael – but she knows that he is an intensely private person who will hug you only if he feels like it.

'Oh yes,' he says now with his rare, sweet smile, and Kate drags him away.

Judy settles the baby, Miranda, in her rocker, and puts on the kettle. 'Or would you rather have a glass of wine?'

'I can't. I'm driving.'

'What about my home-made elderberry wine?' says Cathbad, pulling faces at Miranda to make her laugh. 'That's practically non-alcoholic.'

'You know that's not true,' says Ruth.

'Cathbad thinks that natural ingredients don't make you drunk. Or fat,' says Judy.

Ruth has long since ceased to marvel at the union (unofficial, so far, unless you count a druid hand-fasting ceremony) of efficient policewoman Judy and fey wizard Cathbad. It works, that's all you can say for it. They seem blissfully happy together and have two gorgeous children. If some of their arrangements are unconventional (Michael, for example, has two fathers, Cathbad and Judy's ex-husband Darren), then that's no one's business but theirs. Now, sitting in the tiny kitchen lit by fairy lights and candles, their home seems an oasis of safety and comfort.

Judy pours the tea and Cathbad pushes the rocker with his foot. Thing comes back into the room and sits by Ruth's chair, leaning on her legs.

'I could make some pancakes later,' says Cathbad. 'It's Shrove Tuesday next week.'

'What's the point of Shrove Tuesday?' says Ruth. She's beginning to feel slightly sleepy. It will be an effort to gather up Kate and embark on the dark drive over the marshes. She thinks of Hilary saying 'It's not Lent yet'. Isn't Shrove Tuesday the start of Lent?

'It's a way of using up all your flour, eggs and milk before Lent,' says Cathbad. 'In Latin American countries they have carnivals on Shrove Tuesday. The word "carnival" means "giving up meat", or something like that.'

'I'm not giving up meat,' says Judy. 'I'm always a real carnivore when I'm breastfeeding.'

'I'll take you to the carnival in Brazil one day,' says Cathbad. 'We'll dance in the streets.'

They smile at each other. Ruth is beginning to feel left out. 'I was in Walsingham earlier today,' she says. 'I've never heard so many people talking about Lent.'

'What were you doing in Walsingham?' asks Judy. 'I remember going to the Slipper Chapel shrine with my school. Slightly weird, I found it. Cathbad loves it, of course.'

'I was visiting a friend who's at a conference there,'

says Ruth. 'We went to see the snowdrops in the abbey grounds.'

'I've been house-sitting in Walsingham,' says Cathbad, 'and I'm not sure I love it any more.'

'Tell her about the woman in the churchyard,' says Judy.

'I've heard about it from Nelson,' says Ruth. 'He says he thinks it was the girl who died.'

'Yes,' says Cathbad. 'Poor soul. I can't stop thinking that she was asking for my help in some way. I keep seeing her standing there by the gravestone. So beautiful and so sad. Like a visitor from another world.'

Ruth shivers but she notices that Judy accepts this statement with equanimity. She also notes that Cathbad is always susceptible to a pretty face, and Chloe Jenkins, whose modelling shots have been plastered all over the papers, was very beautiful indeed. She also reminds Ruth of someone. She thinks of the letters. *She stands before you, clad in blue, weeping for the world.*

Aloud, she says, 'I've been looking up archaeological digs in Walsingham. There was one in 1961 to find the site of the original holy house.'

But Cathbad's sixth sense is on alert. 'Is there an archaeological link to Chloe Jenkins' murder then?'

'No . . .'

'So you're just researching archaeology in Walsingham for fun?'

'No . . .' Ruth ends up telling Cathbad and Judy about the letters, as she had always known she would. After all, Cathbad is already involved in the case, and Judy is still a police officer.

'So Nelson thinks this letter-writer could have killed Chloe?' says Cathbad.

'It's just a line of enquiry,' says Ruth.

'There'll be prints on the letters,' says Judy, 'maybe DNA too, if the envelopes are the sort that you lick. Nelson could get an enhanced search done.' Ruth knows that Judy is itching to get back to work as soon as her maternity leave is over. She sounds every inch the police professional, an impression that does not diminish even when Miranda starts crying and Judy picks her up to feed her.

'She's such a good baby,' says Ruth. 'She only cries when she's hungry.'

'Which is all the time,' says Judy. She arranges the baby with practised one-armed ease. Cathbad puts a cushion in the small of her back. 'You look like a Madonna,' he says.

'I feel like a bottle of stout,' says Judy. 'There are some in the larder. Don't bother about a glass.'

Nelson is about to leave the station when he gets the call from Tanya, who is still with the scene-of-the-crime team.

'Boss. I think we've found something.'

He can hear the excitement in her voice but tells himself to be cautious. Tanya is so keen to contribute to the case that she could be making something out of nothing.

'What is it?'

'Some blue fabric. Looks like it came from Chloe Jenkins' dressing gown.'

'Where did you find it?'

'On a hedge by the Slipper Chapel. About a mile from where the body was found.'

'Stay there. I'll be with you in fifteen minutes.'

The Slipper Chapel is a small stone-and-flint church facing directly onto the road. With its stained-glass windows and stone saints in alcoves, it looks somehow too important for its size, like a miniature cathedral. Beside it is a bigger, more modern church. Nelson parks in the car park, empty now but obviously designed for busloads of the faithful. Tanya and Mike Halloran, from the SOCO team, are standing by the visitors' entrance. It seems to have got darker in the last few minutes and Nelson can only pick them out by Mike's fluorescent jacket.

'Right,' says Nelson. 'What have you got for me?'

Mike leads the way. It's a lonely stretch of road, open to the fields on one side, with a tall hedge on the other. Mike shines a torch. A few yards along, fluttering on the dark hedge, is a tiny piece of material, hardly more than a few threads. The fabric looks white in the torchlight, but when he goes closer Nelson sees that it is unmistakably blue.

'Can't be sure before we do the tests,' says Mike, 'but it looks like material from the dressing gown. We've taken photographs, but I wanted you to see it in situ.' Carefully, reminding Nelson of Ruth in archaeologist mode, he removes the material with a pair of tweezers and seals it into an evidence bag.

'At that height,' says Nelson, 'she might have been being carried.'

'That's what I thought,' says Mike, 'more likelihood of an unconscious body brushing along the foliage.'

'Unless she was hiding in the hedge,' says Tanya.

'Then she'd be crouching down,' says Nelson. 'This is about waist height on a tall man.'

'But why would he carry her down the road to leave her in a ditch a mile away?' says Mike.

'I don't know,' says Nelson. 'And we shouldn't speculate too much until we get some tests done. Have you spoken to the people at the chapel?'

'Yes,' says Tanya. 'I spoke to the custodian before they closed for the night. I said I'd be interviewing him tomorrow.'

'I'll be interviewing him,' says Nelson. Then, relenting slightly, he says, 'You can come too, Fuller. What do we know about the chapel place?'

It's Mike who answers. 'It's the Catholic shrine. Called the Slipper Chapel because pilgrims used to leave their shoes here and walk the last mile into Walsingham in their bare feet. That was when the shrine at Walsingham was Catholic, of course. Now it's Anglican, so the Catholics come here.'

'Why do you know so much about it?'

'With a name like Halloran, you don't have to ask. Lapsed Catholic at your service.'

There are a lot of them about, reflects Nelson. The thought doesn't make him feel exactly comforted.

# CHAPTER 13

Nelson and Tanya are back at the Slipper Chapel first thing in the morning. Already the road has been cordoned off and plastic sheets cover the section of the hedge where the material was found. A defiant 'Open As Usual' notice is stuck onto the sign for the car park.

'It's coming up to our busiest time of year,' says the custodian apologetically to Nelson. 'Easter, you know.'

Nelson is a bit vague about Easter now that his daughters are no longer at home demanding Creme Eggs. When he was at school – a Catholic boys' grammar in Blackpool called St Joseph's, but inevitably known as Holy Joe's – Lent loomed large in his life. Ash Wednesday, the itchy grey dust on your forehead all day, 'Remember, man, that thou art dust', giving things up – sweets usually – and failing on the first pocket-money day, Stations of the Cross, Good Friday Mass, the statues shrouded with purple drapes, Easter Sunday and the glory of that chocolate that tastes like no other.

'It's Ash Wednesday next week,' the custodian, Father Bill, is saying. 'A lot of pilgrimages start then.'

Pilgrimage, like Lent, is now almost a foreign word to Nelson. But a thought comes to him that maybe that was what Chloe Jenkins was doing, walking over the fields towards the Slipper Chapel. Going on a pilgrimage. And she hadn't been barefoot, she had actually been wearing slippers. He thought of the body in the ditch, the little feet in the white slippers. One way or another, he would catch the bastard who had done that to her.

'You probably know,' he says, 'that we're investigating the death of a young woman, Chloe Jenkins.'

'Yes. Poor soul.' Father Bill crosses himself. He's an elderly man, stick-thin, but with a certain wiry strength to him. He looked anxious when the two police officers arrived, but has been hospitable, offering them coffee and making them comfortable in his office, a tiny space spilling over with boxes and stacked chairs and a large statue of the Virgin Mary. Most of the boxes are marked 'Votive candles'.

'We have reason to believe that Chloe came this way, perhaps into the shrine itself. Would anyone have been here between eight o'clock and midnight on Wednesday 19th February?'

Father Bill shakes his head. 'No. We close at six unless there's a vigil mass or something.'

'Do you have CCTV?'

The priest sounds apologetic. 'Yes we do. It's a sad fact but people sometimes steal from churches and we've got a lot of valuable objects, icons and relics, that sort of thing.'

'That's good from our point of view. Can you give Sergeant Fuller –' he nods at Tanya – 'access to the tapes from the 19th?'

'It's all digital now,' says Father Bill. 'But that shouldn't be a problem.'

Tanya nods importantly and makes some swipes at her iPhone. Nelson knows that she's dying to ask some questions.

'In the weeks preceding the 19th,' he says, 'did you notice anyone suspicious hanging around the chapel? Anyone at all?'

Father Bill looks more worried than ever. The statue of the Virgin seems to be looking down on him, almost with embarrassment. She's a definite presence in the room, over six foot of painted plaster, blonde hair, blue cloak, outspread arms. One of her bare plaster feet is stepping on a snake. Nelson wonders why she's been relegated to the back office.

'We get a lot of strange people,' says Father Bill. 'This is a shrine after all. People come here because bad things have happened in their lives, because they want to forget or ask for forgiveness. And people come to the church for sanctuary. That's why I always feel a bit bad about it being locked at night.'

Had Chloe gone to St Simeon's for sanctuary? wonders Nelson. Tim said that Larry Westmondham hadn't known that his mother's former charge was a member of his congregation. But was it the Westmondham connection that made Chloe feel safe there, even in the graveyard in the night?

'Do you have a record of who visited on the 19th?' asks Tanya, determined to get a word in.

'I can tell you which parties were booked in,' says Father Bill, 'but other people are free to visit. We don't take a register.'

'Is it free?' asks Tanya.

'Of course it's free,' says Father Bill, sounding rather acerbic. 'You never have to pay to enter a Catholic church. Even St Peter's Basilica at the Vatican is free. Unlike the Church of England.'

The Counter-Reformation is alive and well, thinks Nelson. Aloud, he asks if they can look round the chapel and the grounds. 'Now we know it's free,' he can't help adding.

'Donations are always welcome,' says the priest hopefully.

The visitors are starting to arrive. A bus is pulling up in the car park: a handwritten notice on the back window proclaims 'Our Lady, Queen of Peace, Portsmouth. On Tour'. Inside the bus excited OAPs can be seen jostling to be first out.

'We get a lot of young people too,' says Father Bill, rather defensively. 'We have a youth pilgrimage every year. And we have Student Cross in Holy Week.'

'What's Student Cross?' asks Tanya.

'It's a pilgrimage,' says Father Bill. 'Students walk from London, taking turns to carry a heavy cross. It's to seek forgiveness for the sins of students everywhere.'

'That's a tall order,' says Nelson.

To his surprise, the priest laughs. 'Yes, when I think of my own student days ... Still, the walk does them good. The Milky Way, that's what they call the pilgrimage route.'

The chapel is surprisingly small. 'It used to be a wayside chapel en route for Walsingham,' explains Father Bill. 'It fell into disrepair after the Reformation – it was even a cowshed for a time – but was restored in the nineteenth century by an amazing woman called Charlotte Boyd. She was an Anglican, but converted to Catholicism. Do you want to look inside?'

Nelson says yes, more from curiosity than because he thinks it will help the case. Even if he visited the shrine the murderer is unlikely to have left any clues behind in the chapel, although, as Ruth is always telling him, we always leave some trace of ourselves behind. Still, it might give him some insight into the sort of person who would spend the time to trek halfway across the country just to see a church that isn't even the original.

The inside is beautiful, though. All reds and golds, like an expensive cigar box. Even though it is only just after nine o'clock many candles have been lit and people are kneeling in front of the altar, which is draped in blue and white. The church is high and narrow, with arched windows that let in very little light. The air smells of candlewax, incense and flowers. Father Bill points at a box in front of the altar. 'You write your intention and put it in the box. It'll stay on the altar all day.'

'Why would anyone do that?' says Tanya, too loudly. One of the praying pilgrims gives her a distinctly un-Christian look. Next door is another chapel, filled entirely with candle-holders.

'This is the Holy Ghost Chapel,' says Father Bill. 'By the end of the day it'll be blazing with light.'

Outside, pilgrims are wandering in the garden or heading for the Shrine Shop. Nelson notes that Father Bill's principles do not extend to the banning of commercialism altogether. He thinks of the rosary found on Chloe's body. Was it bought here?

The shop is a treasure house of angels and crucifixes and

sundry glittery objects. There are endless replicas of Our Lady of Walsingham sitting rather stiffly on a throne with the infant Jesus on her knee. You can, if you wish, buy an Our Lady of Walsingham fridge magnet. Nelson briefly considers getting one for his mother. There are CDs of devotional songs and Benedictine chants. There are books and postcards and soaps made from Norfolk lavender. One wall is entirely given over to rosaries.

'These are pretty.' Tanya fingers some blue and green beads. 'What do you do with them?'

'Pray,' says Nelson. 'You say a Hail Mary for each bead with an Our Father in between.'

'But there are so many beads.'

'Exactly. It's not meant to be fun. Have you got a photograph of the rosary found on Chloe's body?'

'Yes.' Tanya was given the job of tracing the origins of the rosary and she bristles slightly now. 'I followed it up and it's sold here and at the Shrine Shop.'

'Let's ask again. They might remember Chloe.'

'I thought the idea was that the perpetrator left the rosary on her body.'

'It could have been Chloe's. We shouldn't rule anything out. We know she liked angels and that sort of thing.'

The shop assistant is a surprisingly alternative-looking young man with dreadlocks and multiple piercings. But he's extremely polite and helpful. He looks closely at the pictures of Chloe and the rosary.

'I'm pretty sure I didn't serve her,' he says. 'I would have remembered. And the rosary is one of our standard designs.

It's popular because it's got an icon of Our Lady at the end rather than the traditional cross.'

Nelson peers at the tiny figure: blue dress, yellow hair, golden crown.

'You wouldn't be able to remember who you sold this rosary to?'

The man looks apologetic. 'I'm sorry. It's just that we have so many people in here. Hundreds on a Sunday or a feast day.'

As if to prove him right, the shop is steadily filling up. Nelson thanks the man and makes for the exit. He holds the door open for a group of Filipino nuns, who thank him shyly. Tanya stares at them as they pass.

Outside preparations are obviously under way for an open-air mass. Four men walk past, carrying a statue on a kind of bier. Rows of seats face a wooden platform where a table is being draped with an altar cloth. As the men walk past Nelson notices ordinary-looking barrels with a sign above them saying 'Holy Water'.

'There was a holy well at Walsingham once.' Father Bill has appeared at their side again. 'You can see the site in the Anglican shrine.'

Nelson doesn't ask the source of the water in the barrels. He wonders if it gets sprinkled over the pilgrims or if they have to buy their own container from the shop.

'Is there anything else I can help you with?' says Father Bill. 'It's just I ought to be getting ready . . .' He gestures towards the activity behind them.

'No. We've taken up enough of your time,' says Nelson.

'Can you email the CCTV footage to Sergeant Fuller? Have you got her card? Thank you very much.'

Tanya looks a bit sulky as they head towards the car.

'Can't someone else do the tapes, boss? I'd like to be more involved with the interviewing.'

Who exactly do you want to interview? thinks Nelson. But he doesn't want to discourage Tanya, so he says that she can come with him to talk to Hilary Smithson. She brightens immediately. In the distance, voices have started singing 'Morning has broken'.

Hilary Smithson meets them at St Catherine's Lodge, where the conference is being held. At first sight it looks like a private house, a charming flint cottage like many others on the high street, but as soon as Nelson steps through the door he knows at once that he's in an institution. It's the carpet, for one thing, green and hard-wearing, but it's also the noticeboards, the shiny cream paint and a sense of practicality over beauty. He thinks of the moment when the Sanctuary morphed from country house into hospital. St Catherine's even has the same hand-sanitisers. How dirty are your hands going to get on a theology course?

Hilary, who is waiting in one of the meeting rooms, is a surprise too. At first Nelson sees an old woman with grey hair, neatly but unfashionably dressed in a blue trouser suit. Can this person really have been at university with Ruth? Then Hilary stands up and Nelson sees that she's probably his age. In fact, her face is remarkably unlined and her eyes are bright. It's just the hair that deceived him. He tries to imagine Michelle letting herself go grey. If she's ever found a white hair, it's hidden in her streaky gold mane (she is a hairdresser, after all), and Nelson would be the last person to see it. But he supposes a priest is above such vanity.

But Hilary's handshake warns him not to underestimate her. She's friendly enough ('I've heard a lot about you from Ruth'), but she looks at him shrewdly, sizing him up. He introduces Tanya and she too gets the treatment.

'Doctor Smithson,' says Nelson. 'You know why we're here. It's about the anonymous letters that you've been receiving.'

'I don't want to make too much of them,' says Hilary, sitting on the orange sofa that, too, is functional, with square cushions that manage to be both hard and spongy at the same time. 'It's probably just some lost soul reaching out.'

In that case, why show them to Ruth? thinks Nelson. He's not fooled by the whole 'lost soul' business. He thinks Hilary was worried by the letters. And rightly too, from what he's seen.

'The letters may be nothing to be concerned about,' he says, sitting opposite her. 'But recent events in Walsingham have made us extra cautious.'

'Ruth said there might be a link between the letter-writer and the man who murdered that poor girl.'

'Did she now?' says Nelson.

'She was just speculating.'

Nelson is not mollified. Ruth had no business to be speculating, especially not to Hilary. That's the problem with civilians getting involved in police work. One minute they're an expert witness, the next they're Sherlock Holmes.

'We're interested in the letters because they mention Walsingham directly,' he says. 'Have you no idea who could have written them?'

'No,' says Hilary. 'There's no return address and I don't recognise the handwriting.'

'Postmark?'

'London, most of them. One is from somewhere in the Highlands.'

'Your parish is in London, isn't it? So it could be someone close to home.'

'London is a melting pot, Detective Chief Inspector. Half the world passes through London.'

But they don't stop to post anonymous letters, thinks Nelson. Hilary's condescending tone irritates him, even though she has a point.

'Have you ever had letters like this before?' he asks. 'It's my understanding that not everyone is delighted by the idea of women priests.'

'You're right, Detective Chief Inspector,' says Hilary. 'Not everyone is delighted. What are your own views?'

'It's not my business to have views,' says Nelson. 'Let's get back to you. So no one has ever written to you complaining about women priests?'

'I may have had the odd letter,' Hilary admits. 'A few emails, especially when I started as parish priest, but nothing too bad. I'm not on Twitter so I've escaped the trolls.' She smiles at Nelson, who doesn't smile back. He barely knows what Twitter is.

'It must be hard,' Tanya butts in, 'being a woman priest. Especially when you've got a child.'

Nelson wants to strangle her. Now is not the moment for misguided attempts at empathy. Judy would have known exactly when to say this sort of thing.

It's too late for Tanya. 'What do you mean?' snaps Hilary. 'My husband is a father and a priest. What's the difference?'

'The difference is that you've been receiving threatening letters,' says Nelson. 'Now is there anything in these letters that gives you a clue about the sender?'

'Not really,' says Hilary. 'I mean he seems to have some biblical knowledge and a very traditional view of the sacraments.'

'It might not necessarily be a man,' says Nelson. 'Never assume, that's what I tell my team.'

'It's certainly someone who dislikes and fears women,' says Hilary.

'Again, that might not mean it's a man. Can I ask you, what do you think the phrase "She stands before you, clad in blue, weeping for the world" could mean?'

'I don't know,' says Hilary, 'apart from the obvious.'

'Which is?'

'Oh, the Virgin Mary, weeping for mankind, Our Lady of Sorrows, that sort of thing.'

Nelson thinks of Cathbad's reaction to the words 'Our Lady'. 'Do you think the writer is a Catholic?' he asks.

Hilary looks curious, as if Nelson has succeeded in surprising her for the first time.

'I'm not sure. That's what I told Ruth too. There's a lot of veneration for Mary in the letters, but Anglicans venerate her too – just look around you. The ballad that he quotes is about the dissolution of the monasteries, though, so that might point to him being a Catholic.'

'The dissolution of the monasteries being when all the monks were chucked out and the gold melted down for Henry and his cronies?'

'That's a rather simplistic way of looking at it. The monasteries did help the poor, but there was a lot of abuse of privilege too. The monks hardly lived lives of poverty, chastity and obedience.'

Nor do you, thinks Nelson. He doesn't have any views about married clergy in general, but he does feel that the monks got rather a raw deal. There had been a monk who taught at his school, Brother Dominic, and he'd been a gentle soul, the focus of a lot of schoolboy teasing.

'Well,' says Nelson, getting up, 'I must ask you to be vigilant while you're here. The writer obviously knows you're in Walsingham. I'll have my officers keep a watch on the place. Probably nothing to worry about, but you'd be as well to keep on your guard. Try not to go out on your own too much.'

'There's a group of us going out for a meal tonight,' says Hilary. 'Ruth's joining us.' Is it his imagination or does she say this in a rather combative way?

'Would you like some police protection?'

'Oh no,' she laughs. 'It's just a girls' night out.'

Nelson tries and fails to imagine Ruth on a girls' night out. 'I hope you have a pleasant evening,' he says. 'Have you spoken about the letters to the other women on the course? They are all women, I take it?'

'Yes. They're all women priests.'

'And none of them have had letters?'

'I haven't asked, though Ruth suggested I should.'

Well done, Ruth. A good suggestion at last. 'I think it might be an idea,' he says. 'Again, there's no point in worrying them, but it might be significant if someone else has been receiving letters. Have you mentioned this to anyone else?'

'Only Robin Rainsford, who's running the course.'

'Can I speak to Mr Rainsford?'

'Yes, he's in the small sitting room, preparing for this afternoon's session. And it's Doctor Rainsford actually.'

Of course it is.

'I'll have a word with Doctor Rainsford now,' he says. 'Good day, Doctor Smithson, and thanks for your time.'

'Goodbye, Detective Chief Inspector. Goodbye.' This last is to Tanya.

'Goodbye,' says Tanya cheerily, unaware of any animosity.

Despite telling Nelson that she's intending to go out to dinner with the women priests, Ruth fully intends to cancel. She wakes up determined to cancel, and, when she drops Kate at school, she doesn't mention to her daughter that Clara might be coming to babysit that evening. It's always essential to warn Kate of these things beforehand because, although she loves Clara, if she's suddenly faced with an evening without Ruth she's likely to cling onto her legs and wail 'Don't leave me'. This clinginess is something new and something to add to Ruth's daily list of worries as she takes the road for the university. She won't go out, she'll get some work done, spend quality playing time with Kate (not trying to read the *Guardian* at the same time) and get an early night. This resolution survives Phil telling her – apropos of nothing much – that she should 'Get out more' and that he and Shona are quite worried about her. Shona is Phil's partner and one of Ruth's closest friends. Even so Ruth can just imagine her saying this. Shona won't be happy until Ruth is shackled to some gruesome Phil lookalike. But Ruth is definitely not going to Hilary's girls' night out. She doesn't care if she turns into a hermit and starts to knit clothes out of Flint's fur, she's not going to a restaurant with a lot of women who will talk about God as if He's sitting at the next table.

Mid-morning, Hilary rings.

'Hi, Ruth. I'm not interrupting, am I?'

'No. I'm just marking some mid-sessional papers.'

'What's the topic?'

'Field techniques in archaeology.'

'I do envy you sometimes. Still being in archaeology.'

'Really?' Then why, thinks Ruth, go to all the trouble – seven years wasn't it? – of becoming a priest? Especially if, by the end of it, people hate you for it.

'Ruth . . .' Hilary's voice changes. 'Your friend Detective Nelson came to see me just now.'

'He's not . . .'

'Seems a nice chap. He had this policewoman with him, glasses, very keen.'

That must be Tanya. She must be delighted to be doing interviews with Nelson. Judy would be spitting if she knew.

She wouldn't like the word 'policewoman' either, any more than Hilary would like 'priestess'.

'He seems to be taking the letters very seriously.'

'Well, he's very thorough.'

'He even offered us police protection for our dinner tonight.'

God, she had thought that was a joke. Please don't let Nelson send Clough. Or Tim.

'I said I'd thought we'd be safe enough at Briarfields. I booked there because I thought it was near you. Can't wait for you to meet the girls. We're getting cabs, so we can drink. Shall we swing by and pick you up?'

'It's OK,' says Ruth weakly. 'I'll drive myself.'


Nelson dispatches Tanya back to the station after the interview with Hilary. He says that he wants her to get going on the CCTV footage, but really he's had enough of her company for one day. When he's working with Clough they know each other so well that he has no need to telegraph when he wants his sergeant to cut in or keep silent. And, whilst Clough can be a bit un-PC sometimes, Nelson knows that his heart is in the right place because that's been tested many times. With Tim or Judy it's different, they are professionals and he can rely on them to be conciliatory or confrontational as the occasion demands. Judy, in particular, is excellent at empathy, letting the suspect think that she alone understands them and what led them to do this thing. Tim, with his good looks and quiet demeanour, gets results too. But Tanya, she's too keen to make her mark, to show how clever she is. And she *is* intelligent and a good officer, it's just that a suspect or any person of interest is not going to give you marks for cleverness; most of the time you just need to listen. The time for cleverness comes later.

Leaving Tanya to take a minicab back to King's Lynn, Nelson heads for the small sitting room. It's not as cosy as the name suggests; another institutional-looking room with the same orange armchairs and hard-wearing carpet. But someone has obviously been trying to make the room more welcoming. The chairs are clustered in a circle around a fireplace, dreamy chanting music is being played and there is a smell of something like incense in the air. A man in a pink jumper is sitting in one of the chairs, fiddling with what looks like a mobile phone.

'Doctor Rainsford?'

The man looks up: he has round glasses and looks rather like a grown-up Billy Bunter.

'I'm Detective Chief Inspector Nelson from the King's Lynn police. I wondered if I could have a quick word?'

Robin Rainsford stands up. He's taller than he first appeared. 'Of course,' he says. 'Is anything wrong?'

'Nothing to be concerned about,' says Nelson. He wonders if he's saying this too much. In his opinion, there's nothing wrong with putting the public on their guard. 'Shall we sit down?'

They sit in the orange armchairs. Rainsford puts his mobile down. 'I've succeeded in syncing iTunes to the sound system,' he says. 'Isn't it incredible?'

'Congratulations,' says Nelson. He still has a phone that

doesn't take pictures. 'Any chance you could turn it off now?'

Rainsford clicks his phone and the chanting stops.

'Thank you. I've come to talk to you about one of your delegates, Doctor Hilary Smithson. I believe she's told you that she has been receiving anonymous letters?'

'She did mention something about it. But she said they were probably just from some troubled soul and not worth worrying about.'

'That might well be true,' says Nelson, 'but nevertheless the police are taking them seriously. Did Doctor Smithson show you the letters?'

'No, but she told me something about the contents. The usual diatribe about a woman's place being in the home and not on the altar.'

'The usual? Have you seen letters like this before then?'

'Not anonymous letters, but there's always plenty of this kind of abuse on chat forums and the like. A lot of people get very exercised about the idea of women priests.'

'I take it you're in favour?'

'Of course I'm in favour!' Rainsford jumps to his feet and waves his hand at the window, where there's a rather fine view of the priory and grounds. 'The Church needs renewing and that's what women priests are doing. The Church is our mother, we can't let her die.'

'Plenty of people don't agree with you.'

'We'll convert them. That's what priests like Hilary are doing. "By their fruits you will know them." You can't convert by words, only by deeds.'

'Doctor Smithson doesn't seem to be converting the letter-writer.'

'No.' Rainsford seems to deflate slightly.

'Are you a clergyman, Doctor Rainsford?'

'No. I'm a layman. I was an RE teacher first, but I found teaching in secondary schools very tough. I did a further degree in theology and started teaching undergraduates. Then I got involved in the fight for women priests. And bishops.' He gives Nelson a toothy, earnest smile.

'What sort of people come on these courses?' asks Nelson. He can't imagine what it must be like sitting in rooms like this listening to dreary music and talking about becoming a bishop. He went on a course last year, something about the community and twenty-first-century policing. He'd lasted about two hours.

'We've got a wide range of delegates,' says Rainsford. 'Some with a lifetime's experience in the Church, some who got the call later in life. We've only had a few sessions so far, but there's a real energy in the group. I think we're going to achieve great things.'

'And none of the other delegates have mentioned receiving anonymous letters?'

'No. As I say, the mood has been very positive.'

'Do you live in Walsingham, Doctor Rainsford?' asks Nelson.

'Not far away,' says Rainsford. 'I went to school in Sheringham and just drifted back, I suppose. I love Norfolk. I just love walking through the fields and along the beaches. The sense of peace, those huge skies. Well, you know how it is.'

Nelson doesn't know how it is. Unlike Ruth, he feels no particular fondness for his adopted county. What sort of place has only the sky to recommend it? Everywhere has sky. He ploughs on.

'Do you ever attend St Simeon's Church?'

'Yes, sometimes. It's a beautiful old building, but it doesn't get the congregation it should.'

Nelson produces the picture of Chloe in the buttercup field. 'Did you ever see this woman at St Simeon's?'

Robin looks closely. As well he might. Like Tim, Nelson is struck by the contrast between Chloe's golden beauty and the drab ecclesiastical surroundings.

'I don't think so . . . no, wait. I've seen her on the news, haven't I?'

'Yes,' says Nelson grimly. He disapproves of the glamorous pictures that have accompanied reports of Chloe's murder. 'She was murdered last week. Very near here, in fact.'

'I remember. Such a terrible story. Poor girl.' There's a pause, during which Nelson can almost see the thought bubbles forming over Rainsford's head.

'The letters sent to Doctor Smithson,' says Nelson at last. 'They mention Walsingham specifically.'

Rainsford's eyes grow large behind his spectacles. 'You don't suspect that the letters have anything to do with the murder, do you?'

'I'm keeping an open mind,' says Nelson. 'But there are some references in the letters which cause us to take them very seriously.'

'Hilary must be more worried than she seemed, then. Poor child.'

Nelson can't quite see Hilary Smithson as a 'poor child'. He doesn't know how old Rainsford is – he has receding hair, but probably isn't much more than thirty, which makes him at least ten years younger than Hilary Smithson.

'I'm going to tell you what I told Doctor Smithson,' says Nelson. 'There's probably nothing to worry about, but it's as well to be on your guard. If you see anyone or anything suspicious, don't hesitate to give me a call.' He hands Rainsford his card.

'I will,' says Rainsford, staring at the card.

'Goodbye then, Doctor Rainsford.'

'Goodbye.'

As Nelson walks towards the front door, he hears the chanting starting up again.

Outside, it has started to rain. Despite this, there's a steady stream of people walking down the high street, some in clerical robes and some in more touristy garb, carrying cameras and picnic baskets. The pilgrimage has begun.

# CHAPTER 14

'Don't leave me, Mum!'

It's pitiful, like a child being wrenched from its mother's arms at the pit head, or the prison gate or on board the sinking *Titanic*. When, in truth, all Ruth is doing is going out for a meal at a hotel a few miles away. With any luck, she'll be back by ten.

'I won't be long, sweetheart.' She crouches down. 'And Clara's going to play Sylvanians with you and watch a DVD.'

'*Frozen*?' says Kate hopefully.

'What about something else?' Ruth feels she's had enough of *Frozen*'s faux feminist message. How come, when Elsa sings about letting go and the cold not bothering her, she suddenly gets an hour-glass figure and a plunging neckline? Ruth thinks that both female characters could benefit from wearing anoraks, to be honest. 'What about *The Jungle Book*?'

'*Frozen!*'

'Oh, all right then.'

When Clara arrives, all smiles and home-made fudge, Ruth

tells her that she has promised to let Kate watch *Frozen* before bedtime.

'Oh great! I love that film.' Both Kate and Clara launch into 'Let it Go'. Ruth is glad that Kate has cheered up, but she suddenly feels a hundred years old. All she wants to do is go to bed with the latest Ian Rankin and *Book at Bedtime* on the radio. Well, with any luck the priests won't want to make a night of it.

'I won't be late back,' she tells Clara.

'Don't worry,' says Clara. 'I'll be quite happy. I've brought my books with me.' Clara is studying for an Open University degree. She already has a degree in law, but dropped out of law school, saying that she wanted to do good in the world. Since then, as far as Ruth can see, she has been living at home and accumulating qualifications. Ruth sometimes feels that she should advise Clara to travel and see the world, but she doesn't because she's such a good babysitter.

Hilary and her friends are meeting at Briarfields, a popular hotel on the edge of the marshes. Ruth likes Briarfields, it's smart without being intimidating, the food is delicious and it's only a few miles from her cottage. She'll have a nice meal, chat politely and come home. She imagines that all the priests will be fasting anyway and drinking water. She does hope they won't say grace before eating.

When she gets to the hotel the first thing she sees is a group of smartly dressed women in the bar. They are shrieking with laughter and drinking cocktails. She is about to back out, but she sees that one of the women, wearing tight jeans and a black lace top, has grey hair in a smooth bob.

'Ruth! Come and meet the girls.'

The 'girls', who are in their thirties, forties and fifties, greet Ruth warmly. They commiserate with her for not being able to drink alcohol. 'Have a Virgin Mary,' says one, without apparent irony. Ruth accepts a non-alcoholic cocktail and is soon engrossed in a discussion about archaeology with a woman called Paula.

'I wanted to be an archaeologist,' says Paula, who is extremely attractive, with long, blonde hair. 'But I couldn't do the physics.'

'There isn't much physics in archaeology,' says Ruth. 'It's a mixture of history, geology and guesswork.'

'Bit like the priesthood,' says Paula, 'minus the geology, I suppose.'

'What did you do . . . er . . . before?'

'I was an actress,' says Paula, accepting another Manhattan. 'Not a very good one although I did get to play Third Prostitute in *The Bill*.'

'Not even First or Second Prostitute,' says a woman called Sydney, taking a swig of her drink. 'That's rough.'

Ruth's mind is reeling. Who are these women, talking about prostitutes and drinking strong liquor? It's worse than going out with the field archaeology team. Her heart sinks when she hears the talk turn to relationships.

'I'd like to find a man,' says Sydney, 'but Christian dating sites are so dull.'

'Oh, I met Simon on a Christian site,' says another woman. 'He posted a video of himself playing the ukulele.'

'Surprised that didn't put you off for life,' says Sydney.

'What about you, Ruth?' asks Hilary.

'What about me?'

'Do you ever want a man in your life?'

Ruth hesitates. Should she tell Hilary to mind her own business (religious people can be very nosy) or explain the whole complicated story of her relationship with Nelson? Or should she tell her about Frank? On evenings like this she misses Frank – confident, gregarious Frank – very much.

'I don't need a man,' she says at last. 'I've got a daughter and a cat.'

This is met with universal approval. It turns out that, if there's one thing women priests love more than cocktails, it's cats.

Nelson has had a frustrating afternoon. The road blocks and door-to-door have failed to bring forth any new witnesses. The CCTV footage from the Slipper Chapel shows nothing between the hours of eight and midnight on the 19th apart from a dark and deserted car park. At one point a large animal stalks across the screen and there's some discussion in the station about whether it's a 'big cat'. There are always dozens of these big cat sightings in Norfolk; Nelson supposes that it gives the locals something to do.

At six o'clock Nelson is in his office reading Tanya's report on angel healing courses. The one she considers most likely to have appealed to Chloe is an online qualification in angel therapy, promising a certificate via PDF at the end of it. It has a comforting pseudo-academic feel, with each of the seven modules based on one of the archangels. Some of the names Nelson recognises – Gabriel and Michael, for example – others, like Uriel, Chamuel and Zadkiel, sound frankly made-up. He reads on, with increasing incredulity. The course promises to help the participant tap into 'vibrational energies' which will aid healing. Did Chloe really believe in this stuff? Tanya has added a note to say that the company running the course has no record of receiving payment from a Chloe Jenkins. So either Chloe thought better of studying angel healing or she booked under an assumed name. Nelson Googles and, under the coy heading 'Remuneration', he finds that the course costs a hundred and fifty pounds, including complementary angel oracle cards. Jesus wept. Purely for the pleasure of disapproving, he clicks on the link 'Angel gifts' and finds an array of crystals, bracelets, pendants and colour-therapy scarves. He's about to switch off when he notices the last item in the celestial shopping basket. 'Beautiful angel brooch, solid gold. Provides protection wherever you go.' Nelson thinks of Jean pointing out the ornament pinned to her grey tracksuit. Whether she had completed the course or not, Chloe had clearly thought enough of her friend to buy her this gift. In solid gold no less.

He is still browsing the angel healing sites (who knew there were so many?) when Tim knocks on his door.

'Boss? I've had a call from Larry Westmondham. You know, the vicar. Doreen's son. He said he has something to tell us. A matter of conscience, he said.'

'And he couldn't tell you on the phone?'

'He said he'd rather talk face to face.'

Nelson sighs and rings Michelle to tell her that he'll be late home. Or rather, he tells her answering service because she's still at the salon.

'She's always working late these days,' he says to Tim.

Tim doesn't answer. Nelson supposes that old married couples are of no interest to him.

Larry Westmondham says he'll see them at seven 'after Evensong'. Now they're sitting in the beautiful old church of St Simeon's waiting for the vicar to emerge from some shadowy space behind the high altar. The church seems very bare after the Slipper Chapel. Like all churches, it smells of incense and candlewax. It's also freezing cold.

Nelson picks up a hymnbook. 'Fancy a sing-song to pass the time?'

'I only know "Jesus loves you".'

'"Soul of my Saviour". That's the one I remember. Depressing as hell.'

'We should have Cloughie here. He loves karaoke.'

'Jesus. Do you remember all those Elvis songs at the Christmas party?'

A faint cough signals that the vicar is in their midst. Nelson is faintly embarrassed that he was caught saying 'Jesus'.

It's his first meeting with Larry Westmondham, and his immediate impression is that this is a man with the cares of the world on his shoulders. The vicar is fairly young, despite being almost bald, but his face has already settled into lines of worry. He's dressed in a black shirt and trousers and doesn't seem to feel the cold.

'Detective Chief Inspector Nelson. Good of you to come.'

'Sergeant Heathfield said that you had something you wanted to tell us.'

'Yes.' The vicar sits in the row in front and twists round to face them. Nelson feels oddly awkward, childhood memories of Confession fighting with his police officer's instinct to conduct interviews in properly regulated circumstances, not sitting in an icy church at seven p.m.

Westmondham, too, seems to be finding it difficult. He runs a hand over his smooth skull. 'I've wondered whether I should tell you this. I've prayed about it. It goes against my instincts, but there's a chance that it might have a bearing on the murder of Chloe Jenkins.'

Nelson and Tim exchange glances. 'Then you should definitely tell us,' says Nelson, trying not to sound impatient.

'Sergeant Heathfield told me that Chloe used to come to Sunday services here. I didn't know. I mean I didn't know that she was the same girl that Mum used to look after. But I did know that there were some patients from the Sanctuary. One of them I recognised.'

Another pause during which the priest seems to be fighting with his conscience.

'Stanley Greenway. He used to be a vicar at a neighbouring parish to mine. Before I came here. He had to leave.'

'Because of problems with drink?' asks Nelson.

Larry Westmondham looks at him squarely. 'No. Because he was a convicted sex offender.'

The surprise strikes Nelson and Tim momentarily dumb. Westmondham carries on: 'Almost every priest has a sex offender in the parish. It's logical. It's where you come when the rest of the world rejects you. And mostly we manage it. We have safeguarding guidelines. We can make sure they're never left alone with children, for example. But, apart from that, we leave them alone. After all, they need God as much – if not more – than the rest of us.'

'Stanley Greenway's offences,' says Nelson, 'were they against children?'

'Technically, yes,' says Westmondham. 'I think the girl was seventeen. It's still abuse – abuse of power for one thing – but it's obviously not the same as if she was a very young child. Greenway claimed to be in love with her. The mother found out and called the police. Terribly sad business.'

'What happened to the girl?' asks Nelson. He is thinking of Stanley, sad and stooped in the visitors' room at the Sanctuary, saying 'She was like an angel'. Had he been in love with Chloe too? Had that led him to kill her?

'She wasn't named,' said Larry. 'And I think the family moved away. I hope she's put it behind her now.'

'Why didn't you tell us this before?' asks Tim.

'Well, at first I didn't link Stanley Greenway to the dead girl. But then you showed me her picture, and I remembered that he used to come to services with her.'

'But why didn't you tell me then? When you remembered?'

Now Larry Westmondham looks really uncomfortable. 'I thought . . . well, there was nothing to link Stanley to the murder. And being a sex offender – especially in his circumstances – doesn't necessarily make you a killer. And he was in rehab, obviously getting help. I suppose I didn't want to be the one to cast the first stone.'

'What made you change your mind?' asks Nelson.

'I prayed about it, as I said. And Sergeant Heathfield seemed a decent man. I didn't think he'd hound Stanley or anything. And I thought Mum would want me to do everything I could to help the police.'

Thank goodness for a guilty conscience and the power of mothers, thought Nelson. As he stands up, he says, 'Your mother sounds a remarkable woman.'

Larry's smooth, worried face seems to come to life. 'Oh, she was. She fostered over a hundred children, you know, and still always had time for the three of us. A lot of her foster children still keep in touch. They're nurses, teachers, social workers, all sorts. There's even a priest. They're her memorial, not the stone outside.'

'Talking of the gravestone,' says Nelson, 'I think Chloe had been cleaning it.' He describes the discovery of the cleaning materials hidden behind a bush.

Larry's face works like a child about to cry. 'That's very touching. Poor girl. To think she was still so attached to Mum. I wish she'd come and talked to me.'

It's pitch dark when they leave the church. Larry Westmondham locks up with a huge, archaic-looking set of keys. He lives at the top of the village, he tells them.

'Don't you live in the vicarage?' Nelson asks. He remembers seeing a rather grand house of this name, set back from the road near the church.

Larry laughs. 'The vicarage is worth a million or thereabouts. The Church sold it long ago. I live in a modern semi-detached.'

They walk through the graveyard, the frost crunching under their feet. A night bird calls from the trees, but otherwise everything is silent. At the lych-gate in the passage under Justin's house, Larry says goodbye and heads off into the night. They can hear him whistling as he walks. It sounds like a hymn.

'We need to talk to Stanley Greenway in the morning,' says Nelson.

'OK,' says Tim, 'but, like Larry said, there's nothing to link him to the murder.'

'He was obsessed with one young girl, he might have been obsessed with Chloe too. Didn't he tell us that he loved her? We need to get fingerprints and a DNA sample. If his DNA's on Chloe's nightclothes then we've got him.'

Their cars are parked on the road outside the cottage. Nelson calls goodnight to Tim then starts the engine of his Mercedes. But, instead of the satisfying throaty roar that he's used to, there's a feeble click and then silence. He tries again, but the engine is completely dead.

Tim appears as Nelson is looking under the bonnet.

'Is it the battery? I've got jump leads in my car.'

'No, it's not the battery. I think the starter motor's gone. Can't believe it. I've had this car ten years with no trouble.'

'Do you want me to drive you home?' says Tim. 'You can get the AA to pick it up.'

'Don't worry,' says Nelson. 'I'll call Michelle. She's not far away. She just texted to say she was leaving the salon.'

'I'll wait with you,' says Tim. 'Keep you company.'

Nelson would have thought that Tim had better things

to do of an evening than wait in a car with his boss. But he supposes it's a kindly thought.

'All right then,' he says, somewhat ungraciously. 'As long as we don't have to play I Spy.'

# CHAPTER 15

When their table is ready, the party repairs to the dining area. As soon as they sit down Hilary orders some wine: 'A bottle of each.' Ruth starts to get nervous. What are her chances of leaving at nine now? She puts in a plea for some water.

'You can have a glass of wine, surely?' says Hilary.

'I'd rather not drink at all,' says Ruth. 'The roads round here are so dark at night.'

'Do you live near here?' asks Sydney.

'About ten minutes' drive away.'

'But there's nothing here!' Sydney waves a rather uncoordinated arm towards the window, which is completely black, no street lights, no signs of human habitation. But Ruth knows that out there are the marshes, that treacherous zone between land and sea. There are other things too: sea spirits (according to Cathbad), archaeological treasures (to Ruth's certain knowledge) and endless layers of the past compressed into the uncertain, peaty soil. She doesn't feel able to explain this to the table full of priests.

'I live on New Road,' she says. 'There are two other houses

there.' She doesn't add that one is owned by weekenders who seldom visit their holiday home, and the other is occupied by a nomadic poet, currently on a tour of New Zealand.

'Don't you get lonely?' asks Paula. She doesn't say it in a judgemental way, rather as if she really wants to know. In return Ruth tries to give an honest answer. 'It's lonely sometimes, but I love the landscape and most of the time I like my own company. It's crowded places that make me nervous, not being on my own. Besides I've got Kate and Flint, my cat. Friends visit, my brother comes with his sons in the summer. It's beautiful in the summer.'

'I know,' says Paula, 'I spent some time here as a child. I remember swimming at Wells-next-the-Sea. The miles of sand and the little railway.'

'My daughter Kate loves that train,' says Ruth.

'It's an ungodly place to my mind,' says a woman called Freya. Ruth has already marked her out as the most ascetic of the women. She has a pinched, intense face, and is the only one, apart from Ruth, to be drinking water.

'How can you say that?' says Paula. 'Look at lovely Walsingham, the most holy place in England.'

'There's still a pagan feel to it,' says Freya. 'They say that there are a lot of those New Age thinkers in Norfolk.'

There certainly are, thinks Ruth. She could put Freya in touch with a fully-fledged druid in one easy phone call. Aloud she says, 'Well, archaeologists think Walsingham was a pagan shrine first, probably sacred to the Roman god Mercury. When they did an archaeological dig they found quite a few relics from that time, including a bronze figure of Mercury.'

'That's what I mean,' says Freya. 'It has an unwholesome feel.'

'Doesn't that just mean that people have worshipped there for thousands of years?' says Ruth. 'I'm not a Christian, but I would have thought that made it more special.'

'You sound like Erik,' says Hilary, with a smile. 'The sacred landscape.'

'Well, he was very knowledgeable,' says Ruth. And completely mad, she adds to herself.

'Who's Erik?' asks Freya, rather rudely, Ruth thinks.

'Our tutor at university,' says Hilary. 'Now who's having red?'

'So then I took the graduate fast-track course . . .'

Nelson tries to suppress a yawn. He supposes it is kind of Tim to stay while they wait for Michelle, but really he would have preferred to sit on his own in the car with the radio playing undemanding drive-time music. Instead of which, he is having to listen to what sounds like Tim's life story. Who knew the self-contained Tim could talk so much?

'So how did you get into the force?' Tim is asking.

'Joined as a cadet at sixteen,' says Nelson. He sees, with relief, that he has a call from Michelle. He clicks on the green 'accept' button.

'Hallo, love. Where are you? Oh, we're the other side, by the high street. I'm with young Tim. No, that's OK, I'll come to you. It's just through the graveyard. I know. That's Walsingham for you.'

He turns to Tim. 'That was Michelle. She's parked in

front of the church. I'm going to meet her now. Thanks for stopping.'

Tim gets out of the car, then he stands there, in the street, looking uncertain.

'Bye, now,' says Nelson firmly.

He takes the quickest route, via the passageway under Justin's house. His hand is on the lych-gate at the end when a terrible scream fills the air. A woman's scream. Michelle's scream.

'Michelle!' Nelson starts running, but he is knocked aside by someone rushing past him. Someone also shouting 'Michelle!'

Nelson used to be a fast runner, but he's older and heavier now. He runs blindly, stumbling over gravestones and cursing. By the time he reaches Doreen Westmondham's gravestone he finds his wife lying on the ground, sobbing in Tim's arms.

'Michelle! What happened?'

Michelle looks up at him. Her face looks white in the darkness, almost luminous. She starts to say something about someone attacking her from behind, but Nelson is distracted by Tim, who seems to be saying, 'Darling, are you hurt?'

'Why the fuck are you calling my wife darling?'

Tim stands up and Nelson thinks he hears him say 'Sorry'. But there's no time to give shape to the thoughts that are crowding, unwelcomed, into his head. Michelle stretches out her hand to him. 'Harry?'

Nelson helps his wife to her feet. He tries to force himself to think clearly.

'What happened?'

'I decided to come to meet you. You said through the grave-yard. It was so dark I stopped to put on my torch app. Then someone . . .' She stops, breathing hard.

'Someone?'

'Someone grabbed me by the throat. He . . . he pushed me to the ground. He was standing over me and he leant forward as if he was about to strangle me. Then I screamed and he ran away.'

Nelson turns to Tim. 'Don't just stand there. Get on to all units. Looks like this is our man and he might not be far away. Search the church and the grounds. Get one of the dog-handlers out.'

'Yes, boss.' They listen to Tim's footsteps retreating and Nelson says, 'Did you get a good look at the man?'

'No. It was dark and it all happened so quickly.'

'You're sure it was a man?'

'Yes. He seemed so strong and he smelt like a man.'

Nelson knows that Michelle is famous for her sense of smell.

'What did he smell of?'

'BO and soap and something else. Something like those sticks you burn.'

'Joss sticks?'

'Yes, something like that.'

Michelle is shaking. Nelson puts his arm round her. She is only wearing a thin jacket and she seems smaller than usual. Her hair has come loose from its complicated plait.

'I've lost my shoes. And I dropped my phone.'

'Let's get you to the car, and I'll come back with a torch.' He has a good solid one in his car, useful as a weapon too.

They walk back through the lych-gate and the dark passageway, Michelle leaning heavily on him. He thinks that she's crying. He helps her into the Mercedes and gives her his phone. 'Lock the doors. I'll be back in a minute.' He hears Tim radioing all units from his car. The silent village will soon be waking up.

He soon finds Michelle's high-heeled shoes and her iPhone. Then he swings the torch's powerful beam round the graveyard. The stones lean towards each other, as if they have just stopped moving, but there is not a living soul to be seen. He tries the church door. It's still locked. He remembers Larry Westmondham walking off into the night, whistling. Where is the vicar now?

As he heads back through the passageway he sees flashing lights. That was quick. He takes back everything he has ever said about the control room; this is impressive. They might even be in time to catch the attacker. Then the lights stop beside his Mercedes and a voice says, 'Did you call the AA?'

'Yes.' Nelson steps forward. 'It's this car here. Think it's the starter motor.'

He opens the door and gives Michelle her shoes. 'I need to stay here. I'll get a car to drive you home.'

'I can drive myself.'

'Are you sure?' He ought not to let her, but it would be awkward to have both their cars stuck in Walsingham.

'Yes. I just want to get home.'

'Call me when you get in. And take off the clothes you're

wearing and put them in a sealed plastic bag. We ought to get a doctor to look at you too.'

'I don't want a doctor.'

'It's for evidence. I'll get the on-call police doctor.'

'Not that Chris Stephenson please.'

'No. I'll make sure it's a woman. I'll walk you back to your car.'

As they walk back round to the front of the church they see more flashing lights. Back-up has arrived. Nelson has to get to work.

Michelle gets into her car. 'Remember, call me when you get home,' says Nelson.

'I will.' She turns to him. 'Harry. About Tim . . .'

'We'll talk later.' And he heads off towards the squad cars.

The table is getting raucous. They have finished the main course and every woman apart from Freya and Ruth is having pudding and a liqueur. Well, Ruth is only having pudding, but she makes up for it by choosing the most fattening thing on the menu, chocolate cake with home-made toffee ice cream. The priests are talking about the course, about someone called Robin and a 'dishy bish' called Peter.

'There'll never be a woman bishop,' says someone rather woozily.

'Yes there will,' says Hilary firmly. 'After all, they already have them in America.'

'The synod will vote yes,' says Freya. 'I'm sure of it.'

'But there'll be people who will vote against,' says Paula, 'so the Church will be divided. That makes me really sad.'

'Why do you want to be bishops?' asks Ruth. Her question came out louder than intended. 'I mean, what can a bishop do that a priest can't?'

'It's the purple,' says Sydney. 'Such a lovely colour.'

'It's a matter of principle,' says Hilary. 'Imagine if someone said to you that, however hard you worked, you could never be head of department. How would that make you feel?'

Effectively this is what Phil has already said, but Ruth takes the point.

'You're brave to keep persevering in the face of so much opposition,' she says. 'I don't know if I could.'

'Oh, you would,' says Hilary. 'I know you, Ruth. You never give up when you really want something.'

She's looking at Ruth rather hard, which is uncomfortable. What's she getting at?

'Hilary told us about the letters that were sent to her,' says Paula. 'It's awful to think that people hate us so much.'

It's the first time that anyone has mentioned the letters. Ruth, who didn't want to be the first to bring the subject up, asks, 'Have any of you had similar letters?'

A chorus of voices answers her. From what she can make out, although almost all the women have had abusive letters about women priests, none of them have been the victim of a sustained campaign like Hilary.

'I feel sorry for the letter-writer,' says Paula. 'He's a soul in torment really.'

'I feel compassion for him,' says Hilary, which is not the same as feeling sorry for him. 'I just wish he would leave me alone.'

'No one smelts a feeble metal,' says Freya. 'If God gives you trials it's because He knows you can survive them. You are being tested as fire tests and purifies gold.'

'Peter 1:7.' Hilary supplies the reference briskly. 'Well, I think I've been tested enough. Who's having another drink?'

Ruth looks at her watch. God, how is it already nearly eleven?

'I've got to get home,' she says.

In Walsingham, lights are flashing and the road has been sealed off. Some inhabitants have come out of their houses to see what's going on, but, mostly, blinds remain drawn and doors remain closed. Tim is organising door-to-door enquiries. He's keeping out of Nelson's way, and Nelson is glad of this. He's more relieved than he can say to see Clough striding towards him, crumpling a chocolate wrapper in his hand.

'What happened, boss?'

'Michelle was attacked in the graveyard. We think it's likely to be the same person that killed Chloe.'

'Same time, same place,' says Clough. 'And Michelle and Chloe look an awful lot alike.'

You can always rely on Clough to say the obvious. It's quite comforting really.

'Is Fuller with you?' Nelson asks.

'Are you joking? Couldn't keep her away from something like this.'

'I want her to go to see Michelle and get a proper statement. Also we need a doctor to see her.'

'Don't you want to get back to her?'

'No. I'm needed here.' Nelson looks at his phone. A text message from Michelle flashes up. One word: *'Home'*. 'Michelle's home,' he tells Clough. 'She's fine. Just get Fuller over there, will you?'

He thinks that Clough is looking at him oddly. 'OK, boss.'

'DCI Nelson?' Nelson is glad to see a handler and her dog coming towards him. He recognises the woman as Jan Adams, famous in Norfolk for having won several medals for bravery. Her dog, a beautiful long-haired German Shepherd, is a bit of a celebrity too. What was his name again?

'Barney,' says Jan, in answer to his question. 'What's going on?'

Nelson explains about the attack. Barney looks at him, head on one side, as if he too might be about to ask a question.

'So I need you to look in the graveyard. See if our attacker dropped anything.' He knows that police dogs are trained to search out evidence but not to touch it. They sit by it until it can be seized by someone wearing gloves. He wishes his team were as meticulous. 'It's pretty dark, I'm afraid.'

'Dogs work better at night,' says Jan. 'Fewer distractions, fewer people to contaminate the scene.'

'Can you search the lane and the surrounding area?' says Nelson. 'He can't have gone far.'

'Perpetrators normally hide somewhere quite close,' says Jan. 'They wait until they think the police have gone away. But if he's nearby, we'll find him.'

Barney nods intelligently. Nelson can see Tim coming towards him. He wishes that he could carry on talking to

Jan and her dog, but he knows that he has to get on with the investigation. He says goodbye and watches as Jan and Barney disappear through the lych-gate. Then he turns to face his sergeant.

Tim is accompanied by a man in a leather jacket and woollen cap. Nelson sees the flash of a white collar.

'You said you wanted to talk to the Reverend West-mondham,' says Tim.

'Yes,' says Nelson. 'This way, Reverend. Is there somewhere we can talk?'

'In the church,' says Larry Westmondham. 'I've got the keys. What's going on?'

'I'll tell you in a minute.'

They walk back through the graveyard. Nelson can just make out Jan and Barney moving steadily along by the outer wall. Larry opens the heavy oak door and they sit in the porch, opposite notices for Frugal Lent Lunches and Alpha courses.

'Reverend Westmondham,' says Nelson. 'A serious assault has occurred. I need to find out if anyone was in the church or churchyard this evening.'

'An assault?' says Larry. 'What happened?'

'A woman was attacked,' says Nelson. 'Now, I saw you lock the church at about eight o'clock. Did you go back after that?' Tim and Nelson were sitting by the lych-gate entrance, but Larry could easily have gone in the front way. Nelson looks down at the keyring in the vicar's hands. So many keys, so many doors.

Larry is still looking shocked, but he answers calmly

enough. 'I went straight home,' he says. 'Like I told you, it's only a short walk.'

'Does anyone else have the keys?'

'The verger, but he lives a few miles away.'

'Is there anywhere round here where a person could hide?'

'All the buildings are locked,' says Larry, 'but I suppose someone could hide in the churchyard. It's very dark at night.'

'You didn't see or hear anything suspicious as you were going home?'

'No. I didn't hear anything until Sergeant Heathfield knocked on my door.'

'OK. Thank you. Someone will be round to take a statement in the morning.'

'Can I go home now?'

'Yes.' Larry locks up again and walks quickly away through the graves. As Nelson watches, a rectangle of light appears in the darkness, like an Advent calendar door being opened. A man is standing in the back doorway of St Simeon's Cottage.

'What's going on?' It's Cathbad's friend, Justin. He's wearing some kind of velvet dressing-gown affair and he has the cat in his arms. As Nelson approaches, the animal narrows its eyes and hisses quietly.

'There's been a serious assault in the graveyard,' says Nelson. 'Did you hear or see anything?'

'I didn't hear anything,' says Justin. 'I was listening to music with my headphones on. But then I saw all the lights and people hurrying to and fro. No, Chesterton, you can't get down.'

The cat is struggling to escape. Nelson remembers that it was the cat who first led Cathbad to Chloe Jenkins. He wishes that he could ask it a few questions.

'Someone will be round to take a statement tomorrow,' he says.

'Always delighted to see a policeman,' says Justin, 'but I don't really think I'll be able to add anything. I'd better take Chesterton in now. I saw a big, rough dog going past.'

The door shuts, and the churchyard is dark once more. Nelson is about to go back through the passageway when he hears a noise behind him. Jan is standing by the gate to the lane. Doreen Westmondham's tombstone gleams white in the darkness. Nelson can't see Barney, but he knows he's nearby.

'Any luck, Jan?' he asks.

'There's a track,' says Jan. 'Someone has walked over this grass recently. They probably went out by this gate, but there's no one in the lane.'

She calls softly. A few seconds later Barney appears at her side.

'He's a good dog,' says Nelson.

'The best.'

'Go on searching, will you, Jan? I've a feeling our man is still around here somewhere.'

'Will do. Come on, Barney.'

Nelson watches as the woman and her dog disappear into the night. For the first time in years he misses his dog, Max, who looked a bit like Barney. Max died ten years ago and Nelson has sometimes thought about getting another dog.

If a dog were waiting for him at home, maybe he wouldn't be dreading going back there.

By eleven-thirty Ruth is desperate. The women seem in no hurry to leave and several of them have ordered more liqueurs. Ruth doesn't want to go before the bill comes (however much cash you leave, it always looks as if you're trying to get out of paying your share), but she really needs to be getting back to Kate. She escapes to the loo and texts Clara. 'Still at Bfields. Sorry! Leaving soon.' Clara texts back reassuringly. 'No prob all well here x.' On her way out of the cloakroom Ruth bumps into Hilary.

'Hilary. Look, I'm sorry. I've got to go. The childminder can't stay too late.' This isn't true, Clara never minds staying late, but with any luck Hilary will think it's all part of Ruth's tragic life as a single mother.

'Of course,' says Hilary. 'I'm sorry. You should have said. I'm afraid the others are well away.'

There are two doors between them but they can still hear the women's voices. All the other diners have gone home.

'Actually, Ruth –' Hilary says and puts her hand on her arm – 'Could you give me a lift back? I've got a bit of a headache and I don't want to break up the party.'

'Of course,' says Ruth, glad to have a cast-iron excuse to leave. Come to think of it, her friend does look rather pale. She hopes she won't be sick in the car.

Ruth and Hilary leave cash with Freya (the self-appointed treasurer), and then Ruth is free, driving through the dark roads, headlights on full. It's a clear night with a full moon, but that doesn't help much around here. As she drives along the raised-up road there's no way of knowing whether the space on either side is land, sea or marshland. She hears Erik's voice, perfectly preserved in the peaty depths of her brain. 'Marshland is a liminal zone, neither land nor sea, neither life nor death, a bridge to the afterlife.' Hilary's voice: 'You sound like Erik. The sacred landscape.'

A fox or some other animal runs out in front of her and she brakes sharply. The new car has stronger brakes than her old one, and she skids slightly.

'Sorry,' says Ruth, as Hilary pitches forward.

'It's OK,' says Hilary. 'I wouldn't like to drive on these roads at night.'

'You get used to it,' says Ruth. Though you don't, really. She waits for Hilary to say that she doesn't know how Ruth manages it, living alone in the wilds of Norfolk without a man. But Hilary is silent for a while, as the liminal zone gives way to trees and hedgerows. When she speaks again her voice sounds thin, almost as if she's trying not to cry.

'I envy you, Ruth. You've got your life sorted out. A job that you love, a place that you love.'

'So have you,' says Ruth. 'You're doing what you wanted to do. You're a priest. You might even be a bishop one day.'

'But people hate us. How can we minister to people if they hate us?'

'People change,' says Ruth. 'Women used not to have the vote. Everyone got used to that.'

'Eventually,' says Hilary. 'I'm just not sure I've got the patience to wait.'

'Of course you've got patience,' says Ruth. 'You were an archaeologist, weren't you?'

Hilary laughs. 'You're right. Sorry, Ruth. I'm just feeling a bit melancholy. Too much wine probably.'

Walsingham is quiet. Just a security light by the abbey gates and a black cat strolling down the centre of the road. Ruth drops Hilary at her guesthouse and watches as she lets herself in. Somehow it seems important to see Hilary safely inside. Somewhere, quite close by, a clock is striking midnight. The moon is round-faced and baleful above the gateway to the ruined priory. Ruth does a three-point turn and heads back the way she came. The cat watches from the side of the road.

As Ruth passes the church she notices something that she hadn't seen the first time. There's a light on in the porch and it illuminates police tape across the entrance. Why is that there? She slows down and, as she does so, she sees something else, a man walking slowly along the lane by the church. He's tall, wearing a long black coat and a hat. But as he passes the porch she sees his face quite clearly. It's Father Hennessey.

# CHAPTER 16

It's past midnight when Nelson gets home. The AA have towed his car away and he gets a lift in a squad car. He's grateful that the driver is the taciturn sort who doesn't like to chat.

'You can stop here,' he says, at the entrance to the cul-de-sac. 'Save you turning round. Goodnight.'

The lights are on downstairs. His heart sinks and he realises that he'd been hoping Michelle was upstairs, asleep, and that any talking could wait until morning. Don't be a wimp, he tells himself. He was less scared when a madman pulled a gun on him last year.

Michelle is in the sitting room watching one of those programmes where celebrities talk about themselves and their films. She's wearing her white dressing gown and her hair is loose.

'Did Tanya come?' he asks.

'Yes. She brought a lady doctor with her. She was very nice.'

Nelson switches on the overhead light. In its unforgiving glare he can see the bruises around his wife's neck. She shields her eyes with her hand.

'Harry, please. You know I hate that light.'

She does too. She thinks it shows the little lines that are starting to appear around her eyes. She's still beautiful, though. Never more so than at this moment.

Nelson moves to stand in front of her.

'Are you having an affair with Tim?'

Even now he expects her to deny it, to be angry, to laugh at the absurdity of the idea. Instead she says, in a flat voice, 'It wasn't exactly an affair.'

'What the hell does that mean?'

'We didn't sleep together.'

'What did you do?'

Michelle sighs and starts plaiting the tassel on one of the cushions. 'We went out, we kissed, we talked. He listened.'

'How long has this been going on?'

She pretends to think. 'For about a year.'

'A *year*! Jesus Christ.'

'But we stopped seeing each other in December. After that Blackstock Hall affair.'

After Tim saved his life. Why the hell had he done that? Why hadn't he pushed Nelson into the path of the bullet and buggered off with his wife?

'Jesus Christ,' he says again. 'Why?'

So suddenly that it is almost terrifying, Michelle flares up. She tosses back her hair and her eyes flash.

'You can't talk! I didn't sleep with Tim. You slept with Ruth and she had your baby. How dare you pretend to be the one in the right? You betrayed me.'

'Is this what this is about?' says Nelson. 'Getting back at me?'

She looks at him with what is almost contempt. 'Not everything is about you, Harry.'

'What is it about then?'

'It's about me!' He can't remember the last time that he heard Michelle shout but now her raised voice makes the glasses in the cabinet ring. 'It's about me. You cheated on me and then you forgot all about it. You went on seeing Ruth. And Katie. Everyone knows about it. You humiliated me.'

'You agreed that I could see Katie.'

'Yes,' says Michelle bitterly, 'shows what a mug I am.'

'I suppose Tim told you that. I suppose he played on you, saying what a bastard I am. Jesus. The sneaking little swine.'

'It's not his fault. He listened to me. He loves me.'

'I suppose he told you that.'

'Yes, he did! He still loves me.'

And Nelson, remembering Tim's voice as he cradled Michelle in his arms, thinks that she is probably right. Doesn't stop him wanting to tear the little bastard limb from limb though. And, tomorrow, that's just what he'll do.

Ruth leaves Walsingham behind and drives home, Bruce Springsteen on full blast. The country roads with their high hedges seem like a maze, nightmarish and unending. Surely she's seen this crossroads before? If only she had her sat-nav plugged in, at least it could tell her if she was going the right way. She's just wondering if she should stop and consult her phone when the landscape opens up and she's driving over the Saltmarsh, the moon silver on the sea. Nearly home. It's been an unsettling evening one way or another: the discussion about Norfolk and the sacred landscape, Paula describing the letter-writer as a 'soul in torment', the panic of wanting to get back to Kate, the dark drive with a strangely sombre Hilary and, finally, that sighting of Father Hennessey in the graveyard. Why was he standing by a church in the middle of the night? And why was there police tape over the entrance to the church? What has been happening in Walsingham?

Clara is asleep when she gets in, dozing on the sofa with her textbooks around her. Ruth asks if she wants to stay the night, but Clara says that she ought to go because she's starting a new course in the morning. After Clara has left and the sound of her car engine has died away, Ruth stands by the door and listens to the silence. Sometimes nights on the Saltmarsh can be noisy affairs, with the wind howling and the sea roaring away in the distance. But tonight everything is deathly quiet, as if the dark is a muffling hand. Ruth gets herself a glass of water and climbs the stairs to bed. She checks on Kate, who is sleeping peacefully, spread-eagled on her Dora the Explorer duvet. Ruth tucks her in and goes into her own room. She switches on her bedside radio and soothing Radio 4 voices tell her about financial disaster and fiscal catastrophe. For the first time that evening, Ruth starts to relax.

She dreams of marshland, of bones and silence, of ancient relics washed up like flotsam and jetsam on an incoming tide. She dreams of a woman in a blue cloak, of the god Mercury, of the voices of lost children beneath the waves. She wakes suddenly while the sky outside is still dark. Her phone is ringing. It says 6.15 and 'Hilary'.

'Hilary? What's up?'

There's a silence and, for a moment, she thinks that Hilary may have called her number by mistake. Then there's an intake of breath and Hilary says, in a voice quite unlike her own, 'Ruth. Something awful has happened.'

'What is it?'

'It's Paula. She's dead. Someone's killed her.'

# CHAPTER 17

Nelson is already up when he gets the call. He hadn't slept well although Michelle, annoyingly, seemed to sleep peacefully all night. He had lain awake at four a.m., listening to her regular breathing, and wanting to shake her awake. Didn't she feel at all guilty about seeing another man for almost a year? Was it really all his fault? Yes, he had slept with Ruth and that was unforgivable, but Michelle had forgiven him, or so she said. And that one sexual act had occurred at a time of great emotional strain for him and Ruth. And afterwards, from the moment he knew she was pregnant, he really had tried to act in the best way possible, trying to be fair to all of them – his wife, the woman who was having his baby and the baby herself – even though he knew that it wasn't really possible. Was he really such a bad guy? At five he is drinking coffee downstairs and thinking that he is definitely ill-used. Some men would have run a mile if a woman got pregnant after a one-night stand. Some men would have tried to pressure her to have an abortion. He has done none of those things. He has tried to be a father to Katie and be true to Michelle and his other daughters. Except, except ... Was Ruth really no more to him than the mother of his child? What about that other time, that other night he had spent with Ruth, with no excuse except that he had wanted her badly? No, he's not the good guy. He really wanted to have them both, Michelle and Ruth, and all three daughters. He has behaved like some back-woods patriarch who wants several wives waiting on him and bearing his children. No wonder Michelle has sought sanctuary in the arms of Tim, good-looking, polite Tim who has listened and told her that she was beautiful and that he loved her. When did he, Nelson, last say these things to his wife? He deserves to lose her, he really does. And if he does lose her ... What if she left him for Tim, if the two of them disappeared into the sunset (or Essex)? Would he then be able to live with Ruth and bring up Katie with her? Don't think like that, he tells himself. But, sitting in the dark kitchen as the microwave clock ticks towards dawn, it is impossible to stop.

The phone call is a relief, even though a call from police control at six a.m. is unlikely to be good news.

'Nelson.'

'DCI Nelson. You're needed in Walsingham. A woman's body has been found in the abbey grounds. It looks like she's been strangled.'

Nelson goes upstairs. Michelle is still fast asleep, her hair spread out on the pillow. Nelson shakes her shoulder gently.

'Michelle? I've got to go out.'

'Why?' says Michelle, not opening her eyes.

'Someone's been killed. The thing is, I'll have to take your car. Is that OK?'

Michelle sits up. Nelson can see the bruises on her neck, darker than they were last night.

'It's OK,' she says. 'Debbie can give me a lift into work.'

'You're not going to work? After what happened last night?'

Michelle's eyes flash. 'Why not? My job's important, although you never think so.'

'You've had a shock. You should take it easy.'

'I'll be fine,' says Michelle. 'You get back to your case.' She turns away. Nelson knows he should say something more, but he's still angry after last night and, besides, he's itching to get to work. He heads for the shower, but when he's at the door, Michelle says, 'You won't do anything stupid, will you, Harry? You know, with Tim.'

Nelson has the satisfaction of not answering this question.

It is just getting light when he reaches Walsingham. A uniformed policeman whom he knows by sight is waiting for him at the visitors' centre.

The man introduces himself: 'PC Bradley Linwood. The body's through here, sir. In the grounds.'

'Who found her?'

'The groundsman. He's in the visitors' centre. He's very shaken.'

'Do we have an identity for the dead woman?'

'We rang St Catherine's Lodge because that's the nearest place. A couple of people came out and identified her as

Paula Moncrieff, a delegate at a conference being held at St Catherine's. They're in the centre too.'

'Have next of kin been informed?'

'Not yet, sir.'

'I'll do that myself once I've had a look at her. Are SOCO on their way?'

'Yes, and Doctor Stephenson.'

'Good. You've done well, Linwood. Now show me.'

They walk through the door into the grounds. The early morning sun is shining through the trees and illuminating a vast archway standing on its own in the middle of the park. To Nelson it looks both absurd and sinister. A few yards further on and a woman's body lies on the lawn, guarded by another police officer. From the distance, she could be asleep, but, as Nelson gets closer, he sees the marks on her neck and the awkward sprawl of her limbs. He thinks of the bruises that he saw on his wife's neck less than an hour earlier.

Nelson kneels next to the body, careful not to touch her. He is struck by two things. The dead woman is beautiful, and she looks very like Chloe Jenkins – and Michelle. Her long blonde hair is spread out on the grass and it glitters with what look like spiders' webs. She is wearing a black sparkly jacket, white silk vest and smart-looking trousers. Her feet are bare, but high-heeled black shoes lie a few feet away. Unlike with Chloe Jenkins, this time the murderer has made no attempt to hide the body. The dew-drenched grass is flattened as if someone has walked over it, but Nelson doubts if any footprints can be found. Standing up, he sees a small brass cross, like a stepping stone embedded in the ground.

A few yards away is a sign: 'Site of the 11th-century, Anglo-Saxon shrine of the holy house of Nazareth (excavated 1961).'

He turns to PC Linwood. 'I'd better talk to the groundsman. Let me know when Stephenson gets here.'

In the visitors' centre, under framed posters advertising pilgrimages in 'England's Nazareth', sit a young man in a heavy jacket and two people Nelson recognises as Hilary Smithson and Robin Rainsford. Hilary stands up as soon as he comes in.

'DCI Nelson. What's happening? We've been here hours.'

'Forty-five minutes,' says Linwood.

'I'm sorry Doctor Smithson,' says Nelson, 'but a serious crime has occurred. We're working as fast as we can. I need to speak to this young man first. Can we get you a hot drink or something?' By 'we' he means PC Linwood and is pleased to see that the young officer is quick to offer tea or coffee, saying that there's a machine in the office. Hilary, who is wearing a coat over what are obviously pyjamas, accepts gratefully. Rainsford, who is fully dressed, seems in a daze and doesn't seem to understand the question. 'What? Yes. Tea. No, coffee. Thank you. Yes.'

'I've phoned Ruth,' says Hilary.

Nelson looks accusingly at Linwood. 'Well, you shouldn't have. Please don't contact anyone else until such time as I give you permission. Now –' he turns to the groundsman – 'if I could have a word, Mr . . .?'

'Peters. Lee Peters.'

'This way please, Mr Peters.' He pushes a door at random and finds himself in a sort of museum full of glass cases.

There's nowhere to sit, so they stand by a display of agricultural machinery.

'Mr Peters. Can you describe how you discovered the body?'

The young man looks nervous but speaks fluently with a strong Norfolk accent. 'I do a tour of the grounds at five, just to pick up any litter and check that nothing's happened overnight like. I were just crossing the main lawn when I saw her . . .' He pauses, wiping his brow with one of his gardening gloves.

'Take your time,' says Nelson. 'What did you do then?'

'Well, I thought she might be sleeping. Sometimes people break in to sleep in the grounds. You know, hippies and that. So I called out to her and, when she didn't answer, I shook her. I probably shouldn't have touched her. I've seen on TV . . .'

'Don't worry about that. Then what?'

'I called 999.'

'Police or ambulance?'

'Police. I were pretty sure she were dead.'

'Why?'

'When I touched her she were cold. Like a statue.'

That places time of death at a few hours back, even accounting for the cold night. Nelson must have left Walsingham at nearly midnight. How long afterwards did the killer strike, having been deprived of his victim in the graveyard?

'What time did you start work?' asks Nelson.

'Five.'

'And you didn't see or hear anything suspicious? No signs of a break-in?'

'No. I come in through the side gate as usual. It were locked.' He brandishes a key ring very like the one Larry Westmondham used to lock the church.

'Thank you, Mr Peters. I may need to speak to you later, but you can go home now. You acted very responsibly. Thank you.'

The young man looks surprised at this praise. He nods and then says, 'It were horrible. I mean, she were so pretty. Poor lady.'

'Yes, it's horrible,' says Nelson grimly.

When he goes back into the visitors' centre, Clough and Stephenson have both arrived. Hilary is sipping a cup of coffee, still looking argumentative. Rainsford is staring into space.

'Cloughie,' says Nelson. 'You go with Doctor Stephenson. We'll need to secure the site. I just need to talk to these witnesses, then I'll call the next of kin.'

'OK,' says Clough. 'Is Tim on the way?'

'No. I didn't call him.'

Clough looks both surprised and pleased. He knows better than to ask why, though. Stephenson greets Nelson heartily ('We have to stop meeting like this, Admiral') and he and Clough pass through the door marked 'To the Abbey Grounds'.

Nelson sits down next to Hilary and Robin Rainsford.

'I'm sorry,' he says. 'This must be a terrible shock.'

'Awful,' says Rainsford. He looks ashen and, when he takes off his glasses, his eyes are pink-rimmed. Hilary is made of stronger stuff. 'Is it the same man who killed the other girl, the model?' she says.

'We don't know yet,' says Nelson, 'and let's not presume

anything. Now, what time did PC Linwood contact you this morning?'

'At about five-thirty,' says Rainsford. 'He called at the house and the housekeeper woke me.'

'And you woke Doctor Smithson?'

'I was already awake,' says Hilary. 'I often wake up early. It's a good time to pray. I was in the kitchen making tea.'

'So the two of you went with PC Linwood?'

'Yes,' says Rainsford. 'I must say, I was glad of Hilary's company.'

'And you identified the dead woman immediately?'

'Yes,' says Hilary, with a shudder, 'it was definitely Paula.'

'Did you know her well?'

'I just met her this week on the course but she was a lovely person, lovely. Why would anyone . . .'

'When did you last see Paula?' asks Nelson.

'Last night. We went out for a meal. I had a headache, so I left early. Ruth drove me home.'

Nelson realises, with a slight shock, that this was the dinner that Ruth had been planning to attend. Maybe that was why Hilary was so quick to ring her.

'Do you know what time that was?' he asks.

'Midnight. I heard the clock striking. The others got back about an hour later. I heard them come in but I didn't go downstairs to join them.'

'Are you sure that Paula was with the others?'

'I think I heard her voice, but I can't be sure.'

'Doctor Rainsford, did you hear the other delegates come in?'

'Yes. I was in bed too. I didn't go down either. I thought it might spoil the party, seeing the course leader. And everyone sounded, well . . . jolly.'

'We'd all had quite a lot to drink, I'm afraid,' says Hilary.

Nelson is quite shocked. Women priests going out and getting drunk like a gang of rugby players. He wonders what Ruth made of the evening.

'Do you know what could have made Paula go out again?' he asks.

'She may have gone for a walk,' says Hilary. 'When we . . . when we saw her, she was still wearing what she wore to the restaurant. She may have just felt like a moonlight walk.'

'Is that the sort of thing she was likely to do?'

'I don't know.' Hilary blushes, very noticeable on her pale skin. 'As I say, we were all a bit drunk, DCI Nelson.'

'I'll need names of everyone who was at the dinner,' says Nelson. 'Can you provide that?'

'Of course.'

'And I'll need next-of-kin details for Paula.'

'I'll have the details on file back at St Catherine's,' says Robin Rainsford.

'I'll come with you,' says Nelson. 'And I'll need somewhere quiet to make the phone call.'

When Nelson gets back to the abbey grounds he sees that a small tent has been erected over the body and the SOCO team are searching the area nearby. He also sees Tim, deep in conversation with PC Linwood. He breaks off when he sees Nelson.

'I've organised door-to-door, boss. Cloughie's getting all the CCTV together.'

'Good,' says Nelson. 'We need to talk to everyone who was with the dead woman last night.' He waves a list.

'What do we know about her?'

'Paula Moncrieff, aged thirty. She was a priest. Lived in Kent, married with one child. I've just spoken to her husband and I've sent a car to pick him up.'

'I've fielded the press, but Superintendent Whitcliffe wants you to give a statement.'

'I bet he does. Tell him midday at the station. Then I'm going to see Stanley Greenway.'

'Do you really think he's involved?'

'He's got a motive for Chloe Jenkins. I'll be interested to see where he was last night.'

'Do you want me to come with you?'

'No. I'll take Cloughie. You keep going door-to-door, appeal for witnesses. Someone must have seen something.'

'OK.' Tim hesitates. Then he says, 'Boss, we've got to talk.'

'No,' says Nelson. 'We're not teenage girls. We don't have to talk. Michelle tells me that you didn't sleep together, which is the only reason you're still in one piece. As it is we've got to catch a murderer. When we've done that I'll approve your transfer and then I never want to see your fucking face again. Understood?'

'Understood,' says Tim. And he walks quickly away across the grass.

\*

Ruth listens to the radio all morning, but there's nothing about Paula's death. When she got Hilary's call she'd asked if her friend wanted her to come to Walsingham. She hoped she'd say no; it would be a hassle getting Kate up and off to Sandra's so early and she didn't really know what help she could be to Hilary. Hilary had said no. 'Thanks, Ruth, but there's nothing you could do. I'm just waiting to be interviewed by DCI Nelson. Robin's with me.' 'OK,' Ruth had said, 'I'll call later.' The mention of Nelson had disturbed her, though she couldn't have said why.

But, as she is getting Kate ready for school, dropping her off and driving through the morning traffic to the university, Ruth keeps thinking about Paula. She'd liked her best out of all the women there last night. She'd seemed interesting and not frighteningly pious. Ruth remembers the Third Prostitute conversation. Paula hadn't taken herself too seriously, but there was no doubt that she had looked more like an actress than a priest. Ruth remembers her saying that they should reach out to the letter-writer, that he was a 'soul in torment'. Had that tormented soul now killed her?

When she reaches her office she can feel her phone buzzing in her bag. She swipes open her door and searches in her organiser handbag. Why can she never find anything in any of the compartments? Why doesn't this seem to happen to other women? When she finally unearths the phone it says: Missed call. Nelson.

'Nelson. Hi.'

'Were you at this Briarfields dinner last night?'

'I'm fine, thank you,' says Ruth in her head. But she forgives him. He's in the middle of a murder enquiry, after all.

'Yes. I can't believe that Paula's dead. What happened?'

'We don't know yet,' says Nelson. 'She got back to her lodging house at about midnight last night. The women stayed up having coffee. Apparently they were all a bit drunk.'

'They were,' says Ruth.

'At some point this Paula Moncrieff must have decided to go for a walk in the grounds. The gardener found her body this morning.'

'God. How awful.'

'I'm on my way to the station now,' says Nelson, 'but I'll be speaking to all the women later. I'd like to talk to you too.'

'Of course. Do you want me to come to the station?'

'No. I'll come to your house tonight. It might be quite late, though. Is that all right?'

'Of course.'

'Good. See you later.'

He rings off without saying goodbye, but Ruth stays staring at her phone for a long time.

# CHAPTER 18

Giles Moncrieff, Paula's husband, arrives at the station at midday. Nelson has just finished giving a statement to the press ('No, we haven't found the murderer yet') and he finds Tanya sitting with Giles in his office. There's a box of tissues on the desk which reminds Nelson of the Sanctuary. It's times like this when Nelson misses Judy the most. She's very good with the bereaved, empathetic and caring, but also professional enough to stop the situation collapsing into tears and breakdown. Tanya is saying all the right things, but she is staring at Giles as if he's an exhibit in the zoo. Giles, a tall man in his thirties who looks like he'd be more at home in cycling shorts, has the shell-shocked look of someone who is hoping that the last few hours have been a particularly nasty dream.

Nelson greets him. 'I'm so sorry for your loss. Can I get you anything?'

Giles shakes his head. 'No. Sergeant . . . er . . . the sergeant has been very kind.'

'Sergeant Fuller,' says Tanya unnecessarily.

'You'll want to see your wife's body,' says Nelson. 'Sergeant

Fuller will take you there in a minute. You can take as long as you want.'

Giles stares at him blankly. 'I just can't believe it. Paula. I mean, she was just here for a conference. I encouraged her to go. "It'll be a break for you," I said. It's hard work with the parish and a young child. Christ, I wish she hadn't come.'

Nelson pulls round his chair so that the desk isn't between them. 'This must be very difficult for you,' he says, 'but you'll appreciate that we have to find the person that did this to Paula. I promise you that we won't rest until we do. So, anything that you can tell us about Paula now will be invaluable. Anything that might be relevant.'

'What do you mean?'

'Well, for example, had anyone been threatening her? Sending her abusive letters, for example.'

Giles looks more nonplussed than ever. 'No. Everyone loved Paula. Her parishioners adored her. When Jack was born they threw a surprise party for her. On her birthday we had so many cakes we had to give them to a shelter for the homeless. Oh God . . .' He looks helplessly at Nelson and Tanya. 'How am I going to tell Jack?'

'How old is Jack?' asks Nelson.

'He's four. He'll be starting school in September. He was so happy. Paula had already bought his uniform.' He rubs his eyes but can't stop the tears. Tanya hands him the box of tissues. 'Who's looking after Jack now?' she asks.

'My parents. They're devastated too. They loved Paula.'

'What about Paula's parents?' asks Nelson.

'They're dead,' says Giles. 'They died when she was a child.

Paula had a terrible childhood really, she was in children's homes, with various foster parents, in and out of care. But it never made her bitter. She was extraordinary.'

'How long had she been a priest?' asks Nelson.

'Only two years. She was still a curate when Jack was born. That's why it was such a big thing for her, being invited on this course. Paula was an actress when I met her. She used to joke that she wasn't very good, but she was, she could have gone a long way. I mean, she was beautiful too. Beautiful and talented. But she wanted to do good in the world, she said. Look where that got her.'

'I'm sure she did do good in the world,' says Nelson.

Giles looks at him. 'Do you believe in God, Inspector?'

'I'm not sure,' says Nelson honestly. 'Sometimes I think I do.'

'Well, I don't,' says Giles. 'How could a just God let this happen?'

Nelson has no answer to this and, after a few more desultory questions, Tanya leads Giles Moncrieff off to the morgue.

All in all, Nelson is glad of the distraction of the drive to the Sanctuary. The only problem is that he's a passenger, which he hates. He usually insists on driving (in defiance of the protocol that it should be the junior officer who takes the wheel), but he doesn't think that Michelle's little Matiz is quite suitable for the job. Besides they need room in the back for Stanley Greenway. Nelson is determined to bring him back to the station to get DNA and fingerprint samples.

Clough is obviously relishing being at the wheel. When he turned the engine on, Bastille had blasted from the CD player. Nelson recognises the group because they are one of his daughter's favourites and rightly suspects the influence of Clough's girlfriend, Cassandra. Left to himself Clough is strictly a rock ballads man.

'So,' says Clough, pulling out to overtake a tractor, 'do you think Greenway is our man?'

'Never assume,' says Nelson mechanically. He is thinking about Michelle. He had rung her from the station, but the phone had gone through to answerphone. At least she can't be with Tim because he's still going door-to-door in Walsingham. Nelson fully plans to keep him employed there for several days. Weeks, if necessary.

'But a convicted sex offender . . .' says Clough.

'Being obsessed with a young girl doesn't make you a killer,' says Nelson.

'Doesn't hurt, though,' says Clough.

'I admit I'll be interested to see where he was last night,' says Nelson. 'Whoever attacked Michelle obviously hung around and got lucky when Paula went walking in the grounds.'

'How is Michelle?' says Clough. 'Must have been bloody frightening for her.'

'She's OK,' says Nelson. 'Insisted on going in to work today.'

'Probably the best thing. Take her mind off it.'

'Yes,' says Nelson. They are stuck behind another farm vehicle. Nelson drums his fingers on the glove compartment. 'You can overtake here.'

'Better not,' says Clough, 'it's a tricky bend.'

A BMW powers past them, proving Clough right, which

doesn't improve Nelson's mood. On the next straight stretch, Clough pulls out smoothly to pass.

'That Paula didn't look like a woman vicar, did she?' says Clough.

'How many women vicars have you met?' asks Nelson. But he knows what Clough means. Seeing Paula's picture stuck up on the board beside Chloe's had been startling. Although the two women hadn't been identical – Paula was older, for one thing – the resemblance was striking. Both had long blonde hair and classically beautiful features. When Nelson had added a snapshot of Michelle – taken from home that morning – there had been gasps in the room. Not just because she was the boss's wife, but because the three women could have been sisters.

'The scene wasn't the same, though,' he says now. 'Chloe's body was hidden in the ditch. It was positioned there with care, the rosary on her chest. Paula's body seemed to have been left where she fell. No rosary, no arrangement of the body.'

'Could just be that the killer didn't have time. Maybe he was interrupted.'

'Who would have interrupted him in the abbey grounds in the middle of the night?'

'I don't know, but the murders look pretty similar to me. Same method, for one thing.'

Chris Stephenson has confirmed that Paula died from manual strangulation. 'Would have had to be someone fairly big and strong. She was a tall woman.' She was a tall, beautiful woman – like Chloe, like Michelle – but she hadn't been expecting an attack. She had been wandering in the grounds, slightly drunk, probably thinking lovely thoughts about heaven and angels and fluffy clouds. It wouldn't have taken a very strong person to have overpowered her. Only someone determined.

They drive on in rather uncomfortable silence.

Doctor McAllister is definitely less friendly than before.

'Have you got a good reason for wanting to see Stanley? He's in a rather vulnerable state just now.'

'He's a person of interest in our inquiry,' says Nelson. 'So it's very important that we speak to him. You can sit in on the interview if you like.'

The doctor looks at him squarely through her intimidating glasses. 'Is this because of his previous conviction?'

'That's part of it,' says Nelson, 'as is his relationship with Chloe Jenkins.'

'But you can't suspect him for last night's attack? He was here.'

'Are you sure of that?' says Nelson. 'Because Chloe Jenkins got out without you or your staff being any the wiser.'

Fiona McAllister shoots him an unfriendly look, but she seems to take the point. She picks up the phone. 'I'll get someone to bring Stanley here,' she says. 'It's probably better if we talk in my office.'

Stanley is wearing his usual tracksuit, and he looks thin and stooped and nervous. There's no sign, though, that he looks any more nervous than usual. He blinks at Nelson in surprise, but takes the seat offered by Doctor McAllister and awaits questions calmly, as if this is just another group session.

'Mr Greenway,' Nelson begins. 'When we came to see you last, you told us that you sometimes went to church with Chloe Jenkins. To St Simeon's. Is that right?'

'Yes,' says Stanley. 'I went a few times.'

'Did you know the vicar, Larry Westmondham?'

Stanley swallows but answers quietly. 'I think I met him before. In my former life.'

'Talking of your former life,' says Nelson, 'you didn't tell us the reason that you left the priesthood.'

'I'm still a priest,' says Stanley. 'Technically.'

'But you didn't tell us that you served a jail sentence for having sex with a minor.'

Fiona McAllister cuts in. 'Is this relevant, Inspector?'

But Stanley raises his hand, curiously dignified. 'It's all right, Doctor McAllister. No, I didn't tell you that, Inspector, because I knew you wouldn't understand. I loved Shelley and she loved me.'

'And did you love Chloe Jenkins?'

'What are you getting at?'

'Where were you on the night of 19th February?'

'Here, of course.'

'And last night?'

Stanley looks around the room. 'Why are you asking me that?'

'Just answer the question please.'

Nelson expects Stanley to say, again, that he was at the Sanctuary, blamelessly in his room. But, instead, he looks apologetically at Fiona and says, 'I went for a walk.'

It's hard to say which of the three people listening is more surprised by this. But it's the doctor who exclaims, 'What do you mean, you went out for a walk?'

'It was a lovely night,' says Stanley, 'so I went for a walk over the fields.'

'But you're not allowed out of the house at night. You have to sign out.'

'I know. I'm sorry.'

Nelson has had enough. 'Mr Greenway, I'm going to have to ask you to come to the police station with us.'

'Am I under arrest?' Stanley's voice is gently curious.

'No. This is purely voluntary. However, I would like your permission to take fingerprints and DNA swabs.'

'Do I need a lawyer?'

The question is addressed to Doctor McAllister, but Nelson answers, 'You are entitled to call a solicitor but I must stress that you're not under arrest.' Yet, he adds to himself.

'I'll need my coat.'

'I'll come to your room with you,' says Fiona McAllister.

Nelson and Clough wait in the hall with the looming fireplace and the waxy flowers. The grandfather clock ticks importantly, but Nelson notices with irritation that it's half an hour slow. He paces to and fro while the receptionist eyes him anxiously.

'Think he's made a run for it?' says Clough.

'You can catch him, if so. You're always telling me how fit you are.'

'I could beat Tim in a race.'

'I don't doubt it.' Nelson turns as he hears someone descending the stairs. But it's not Stanley. It's a tall man in clerical black. A man with white hair and broad shoulders.

'Father Hennessey?'

'Harry. My dear boy.'

'What are you doing here?'

'Visiting the sick. There are a lot of troubled souls in these places.'

'Ruth said she saw you in Walsingham the other day.'

'Yes. I'm here on a private visit. Ruth looked well. I can't believe the little one is at school.'

Nelson is never sure what Father Hennessey knows about Katie. Once, at a very low point in his life, Nelson confessed to the priest that he had slept with a woman, who then got pregnant. A year later Father Hennessey had baptised Katie, and Nelson knows that he is capable of putting two and two together. He remembers the priest saying, 'A child is always a blessing.' Well, he was right there. But, today, Father Hennessey doesn't seem inclined to talk.

'I'd better be on my way. Lovely to see you, Harry. And you too, David. God bless you both.'

And he hurries out of the door, leaving Clough staring after him.

'How did he know my name?'

'He's met you before. Remember, six years ago, when we found that body in the old children's home? He was the priest that used to run the home.'

'I remember,' says Clough. 'I never trusted him. He looked pretty shifty just now.'

And Nelson, although he both likes and trusts the priest, has to admit that Clough has a point.

*

There is a small group of reporters at the front of the station so Clough drives round to the back entrance. Stanley Greenway still seems in a dream, hardly noticing his surroundings, but Nelson dreads to think what will happen when the press pack find out about his previous conviction. He can see the headlines now.

Tanya meets them at the door, eyes wide with excitement.

'Sergeant Fuller,' says Nelson, 'can you take Mr Greenway and organise fingerprints and a DNA swab? He's not under arrest and is free to leave at any time.'

'Yes, boss.' Despite Nelson's words, Tanya grasps Stanley's arm firmly. 'This way, Mr Greenway.'

Nelson and Clough shut themselves in Nelson's office.

'What do you think?' asks Nelson.

'I don't like him,' says Clough, somewhat predictably. 'He's a convicted sex offender and he hasn't got an alibi for last night.'

'He hasn't got a motive either.'

'She looked like Chloe. Didn't he say that he loved Chloe? When you interviewed him before?'

'Yes. They both said it. Stanley and Jean, the older woman who had befriended her. At the time I thought she was a substitute child for them.'

'Stanley didn't sound very paternal towards the other girl. What was her name? Shelley. He said he loved her and she loved him.'

'No,' said Nelson, remembering the shambling figure in the tracksuit. 'There's no fool like an old fool.' And he's a fool too, he thinks. He's a fool for trusting his wife. How many times over the last year had Michelle told him that she was working late or at the gym? And he'd believed it every time, wrapped up in his work and his own life. But, curiously, it's Tim's betrayal that hurts most. He had brought Tim down from Blackpool, made him one of the team, one of the family. He had thought that Tim liked him and looked up to him. Well, you live and learn.

'Boss?'

He had been so deep in thought that he hadn't heard Tanya coming into the room.

'Where's Greenway?' he asks. 'You can't have finished taking prints yet.'

'He's with the duty sergeant. I want to show you something.'

Nelson looks at Clough, who shrugs. 'OK. What is it?'

Tanya leads them to her computer, which has a video window open. 'This is the CCTV footage from the Slipper Chapel on Wednesday 19th.'

'Thought it didn't show anything.'

'Apart from the big cat,' says Clough.

'No, but I looked earlier on in the day,' said Tanya, her glasses glinting. 'Then, when I saw that man, Greenway, I recognised him.'

Nelson leans in, interested now.

'There was a service at six o'clock in the evening,' says Tanya. 'Here are the people coming out. Look there. Next to the man in the waistcoat.'

Nelson looks. Grainy and indistinct, the man in the shabby raincoat is nonetheless definitely Stanley Greenway.

## CHAPTER 19

Ruth had almost given up hope. She managed to get Kate to bed fairly early, came downstairs, poured herself a glass of wine and tidied up by putting the books in piles and shoving everything else under the sofa. By nine o'clock she has drunk half the bottle and is convinced that Nelson won't come. He has probably had a long day at the station and has gone home to Michelle and a cooked supper. Then, just when she's considering getting into her pyjamas, car headlights illuminate the sitting room. Flint sits up, eyes popping as if he's expecting an axe murderer, and then a hand that can only be Nelson's hammers on the door.

'I thought you weren't coming,' says Ruth, ushering him towards the sofa. Flint jumps off, orange tail fluffed up in outrage.

'I said I would, didn't I?' Nelson looks exhausted, thinks Ruth. His eyes are shadowed and she can see the clenched muscles in his jaw. He hasn't shaved either and this gives him a rather desperate and piratical appearance.

'Do you want a cup of tea?' she says. Then, seeing his eyes

flicker towards the bottle on the coffee table, 'Or a glass of wine?'

'A glass of wine would be grand.'

This is a surprise. Nelson rarely drinks when he's on duty or driving. Also he prefers beer to wine. She pours them both a generous glassful.

'It's so awful about Paula,' she says. 'I've been thinking about it all day.'

'How well did you know her?' asks Nelson.

'I only met her that evening. But she seemed nice. Not at all like a priest.'

'That's what everyone says,' says Nelson. 'But her husband says that she was dedicated to her job. Her parishioners loved her, he says.'

'So she hadn't had any threatening letters?'

'No. I asked him and he seemed shocked at the idea. Mind you, the poor bloke was in shock anyway. His wife went away for a week's conference, and now she's dead. Suddenly he's a widower with a four-year-old child. Fuller said he was in pieces when he saw her body.'

Ruth shivers, imagining the scene. 'When I asked, most of the women priests said that they had had some abuse,' she says, 'but no one had received letters like Hilary's.'

Nelson smiles faintly. 'Nice to see you're doing some detective work, Ruth.'

Ruth can feel herself blushing. 'I only asked a question,' she says.

'The questions are more important than the answers. That's what you told me once.'

Ruth looks at Nelson. He seems to be behaving rather oddly this evening. Arriving late, drinking wine, remembering past conversations. For some reason, she feels it's important that they get back to the topic in hand.

'What happened after Paula got back to Walsingham last night?' she asks.

'Apparently they all had coffee and chatted in the sitting room. They all admitted to drinking too much. You wouldn't expect it of a group of priests, would you? Or maybe you would. I don't know. Anyway, one of the women – Sydney something – said that Paula decided to walk in the abbey grounds. She wanted to see them by moonlight, she said. This Sydney almost went with her, but she was tired and went to bed. She felt pretty bad about that.'

'Hilary said that she felt bad too. But they couldn't have known, could they?'

'They could have been more careful,' says Nelson, 'knowing that there was a killer on the loose. But there's no point saying that now.'

'Do you think it was the same person? The same person who killed the other girl. What was her name?'

'Chloe,' says Nelson. 'Chloe Jenkins. It certainly looks like the same modus operandi. Both women were strangled. And there are other similarities. The women looked alike, for one thing.'

'Did they?' says Ruth in surprise. 'But Chloe was so glamorous. I saw the pictures in the paper.'

'Paula was glamorous too,' says Nelson. 'And the same

type. Long blonde hair and all that.' He hesitates, then says, 'Michelle was attacked last night too.'

'Michelle?' Ruth can hardly believe she's heard right. 'Michelle was attacked?'

'Yes.' Nelson is speaking quickly now. 'She came to meet me. My car had broken down outside St Simeon's. She walked through the graveyard and someone jumped on her from behind.'

'Oh, my God. Was she hurt?'

'Just shocked. Tim and I got to her in a few minutes. The attacker got away. We had police everywhere – sniffer dog, the lot – but he must have hidden, bided his time, and attacked Paula later.'

'Lucky you and Tim were there.'

'Yes.' Nelson looks at her, his eyes very dark. 'Did you know that Michelle and Tim were having an affair?'

'*What?*' For the second time in a few minutes Ruth doubts her own hearing. Please don't let him say what I think he's said, she prays.

'So you didn't know? I thought everyone must know.'

'I don't believe you.'

'They both admitted it,' says Nelson, draining his glass. He picks up the bottle, 'Want some more?'

'No thanks.'

There's not much left in the bottle, but Nelson pours it all in his glass.

'They admitted it?'

'Well, they said that they hadn't slept together, but that's irrelevant.'

Is it? thinks Ruth. It doesn't sound very irrelevant to her. But she says nothing.

'They've been seeing each other for over a year. Christ, what a mug I've been. When you think how guilty I've felt about you and me.'

Nelson is a great one for guilt, Ruth knows, but she doesn't quite like how he puts this.

'I've felt guilty too,' she says defensively.

'Well, we needn't have worried. We could have been having an affair all this time.'

'Could we?' says Ruth.

They stare at each other. Ruth feels as if the very air is charged, as if she can see the little pluses and minuses hovering around them.

'Haven't you sometimes wanted to?' says Nelson.

'Yes,' says Ruth. 'Yes, I have.'

Nelson reaches out and touches her cheek. She can see his eyelashes, the black stubble on his chin.

'Don't, Nelson.'

'Why not?'

'Because you're just doing it because you're angry with Michelle. You need to talk to her. She hasn't had an affair if they didn't sleep together. A few meetings at the gym doesn't constitute an affair.'

'What did you say?'

The change in his tone is almost frightening. For a second he looks like a stranger.

'I said . . . I said they weren't really having an affair if they . . .'

'You said "a few meetings at the gym". How did you know they met at the gym?'

'I didn't . . .'

'Yes, you did. You knew.'

Nelson stands up. He looks very big and very threatening. Flint jumps back on the sofa as if to protect Ruth.

'I didn't know,' she says.

'You're lying, Ruth.'

Ruth stands up too, angry now. 'OK. I saw them together at the gym once. I didn't know that they were seeing each other, though. Michelle was hardly likely to confide in me, was she?'

'Why didn't you tell me?'

'Tell you what? That your wife was seen at the gym with another man? You would have thought I was mad.'

Nelson looks as if he is about to say something. Then he looks as if he's going to come towards her. Then, with a gesture as if he's pushing something away, he makes for the door.

'Where are you going?'

'I'm going to the bloody gym,' says Nelson. 'What do you think?'

And he's gone, slamming the door behind him.

# CHAPTER 20

Nelson fully intends to drive round all night. When he gets back into the car there are three messages on his phone from Michelle, but he ignores them. He heads for the sea, parking by the sand dunes at Hunstanton. He gets out of the car and takes the path to the beach. The sand is silver in the moonlight and the sea is breaking in smooth black waves. He thinks of the wooden henge with the body buried in its circle, the case where he first met Ruth. He thinks of their night together, the night Katie was conceived. It's true that Michelle has had much to forgive, because, since that night, Ruth has barely been out of his thoughts. The salt wind stings his face. He has always hated the Norfolk landscape, but tonight the sea and the sky are strangely suited to his mood, the long unforgiving miles of sand, the endless tide of water.

He walks back to Michelle's car. There's a message from Ruth too, but he doesn't read it. He heads for home because, really, where else is he going to go?

Michelle is waiting up for him. She is in her dressing gown again, her hair tied back. She should look less glamorous than normal, but, to Nelson, she looks as beautiful as ever. More so, perhaps, because he is the only person who sees her like this, her eyelashes pale, her lips slightly chapped.

'Where have you been, Harry? I've been really worried.'

'I was working late. A woman was killed yesterday, remember?'

'I'm not likely to forget, am I, considering it was nearly me?'

Nelson looks at the marks around her neck. They are greenish-yellow now. The people at the salon must think he's a wife beater.

'How are you feeling?' he asks.

'All right. Harry, we have to talk.'

'That's what Tim said to me. Stupid bastard.'

Nelson goes to the drinks cabinet and pours himself a whisky. 'Do you want one?' he asks grudgingly.

'No thank you.' From the cup beside her Nelson can see that his wife has been drinking one of her disgusting herbal teas. She's never been a big drinker.

'Harry, have you been with Ruth?'

The acuteness of her guess takes him by surprise. 'Why would I go there?' he blusters.

'I thought you'd go to her. That you'd think it would be OK to be with her now.'

Nelson looks at her curiously. 'Is that what you think I want?'

'Sometimes.'

'Is that why you had an affair with Tim?' He raises a hand. 'OK. I know you didn't sleep with him. But you were seeing him behind my back.'

Michelle fiddles with the end of her ponytail. 'Partly. Partly just to prove that someone still found me attractive. It's hard, you preferring someone like Ruth to me.'

'I don't prefer her.'

'Really?' Michelle looks at him squarely. 'Really?'

'Really. Do you prefer Tim to me?'

'No!' Her response is so immediate, so genuine, that he is touched. 'You're the only man I've ever loved.'

He makes a move towards her and she flings herself, weeping, into his arms. After a few moments he bends his head to kiss her. There are tears in his eyes too.

In the morning, he wakes before the alarm. He lies there for a few moments, letting the events of yesterday run through his mind. He can't help feeling that he's messed things up in some subtle but catastrophic way. Yesterday he had felt betrayed by Michelle, and, at the same time, drawn to Ruth. He hadn't gone round to Ruth's house determined to carry on their affair, but, all the same, he can't deny that the thought hadn't been far from his mind. But also, Ruth's little house had suddenly seemed a place of refuge, a sanctuary if you like. Ruth had turned him away, that's what it feels like anyway. And now he feels betrayed by Ruth, but – by some strange marital alchemy – reunited with Michelle. Last night they had made love and he knows that Michelle thinks that this has set the seal on their reconciliation. Soon Tim will be gone and he and Michelle can continue to mend their marriage, adjusting to life without the girls, enjoying their mid-life years. So why isn't he feeling happier?

Enough soul-searching, he tells himself. He doesn't like talking about emotions, not even to himself. There's a murderer to catch. Tanya's CCTV footage has upgraded Stanley Greenway from a 'person of interest' to a suspect with a number in the case files. But, all the same, he didn't think there was enough to arrest the man. The footage didn't place Greenway at the Slipper Chapel at the time of the murder, though it did leave him with some questions to answer about his movements that night. He'd let Stanley Greenway go back to the Sanctuary. 'After all,' he told Clough, 'he's as safe there as anywhere.' But, if Greenway's DNA is found anywhere on Chloe or Paula's clothing, then Nelson will be round at the Sanctuary gates with an arrest warrant faster than you can say 'Innocent until proven guilty'.

So, his first job today is to hassle the lab about the DNA results. It's possible to get them back in twenty-four hours, though this is expensive and, therefore, frowned upon by Whitcliffe. He also wants to go back to the Slipper Chapel with a photograph of Stanley Greenway. They need to go through all the witness reports from Walsingham too. He looks at the clock. Six o'clock. Time to get going. He'll have to take Michelle's car again, but hassling the garage will also be on his list. He gets out of bed, careful not to wake Michelle, and heads for the shower.

He's at work by seven. King's Lynn is deserted, mist rising up from the quay, everything grey and dreamlike. On the steps outside the police station there's a rough sleeper who greets him with an ironical, 'Morning, Inspector Morse.'

'Didn't I give you money to go to a shelter last time?'

'Yes, you did, God bless you.'

'Well, go and get yourself some breakfast.' Nelson slips the man a fiver and watches him hurry off down the road throwing 'God bless yous' over his shoulder. He's pretty sure that the breakfast will be entirely liquid.

Inside, there's only the night sergeant yawning over a cup-a-soup.

'Morning, Shane.'

'Morning, sir. You're early today.'

'Lots to do.' Nelson is conscious of his mood lightening the further he gets into the building. He climbs the stairs two at a time, makes himself a cup of instant coffee and sits at a computer in the incident room to go through the previous day's reports.

Tim comes in at eight, carrying his sports bag. He says good morning to Nelson, who nods at him.

'Is this all the CCTV we have? The abbey grounds and the gift shop?'

'Yes. There's a camera outside the farm shop, but it doesn't work.'

'Anything from the door-to-door?'

'I'm going to type up the reports now. One possible sighting. A woman walking her dog saw a man walking along beside the church at midnight. Said he looked furtive.'

'Description?'

'Not a very good one. But we could show her pictures of Stanley Greenway. Or have an identity parade. The CPS loves identity parades.'

Nelson knows that this is true. He doesn't want to grant Tim the satisfaction of agreeing, though.

'What are you going to do now?'

'It's Chloe Jenkins' funeral. You said that I should go. To represent the force.' Tim holds up his bag. 'I'm going to change as soon as I've done the reports.'

'All right,' says Nelson grudgingly. 'Pick up anything you can from the family. This case isn't over yet.'

'It'll be tough for them, hearing about Paula being killed.'

'Yes, it's tough,' says Nelson. 'And we haven't got time to chat about it. There's a team meeting at nine.' He can't help feeling aggrieved that Tim is in before Clough.

Clough arrives at eight-thirty, still chewing his McDonald's breakfast. Tanya is already making a health-food smoothie in the tiny kitchen. She has brought in her own blender and everything.

'Much better for you than all those carbs,' she says. 'Kale's a super-food.'

'Count me out,' says Clough, chucking the greasy wrappers in the bin.

'If you've finished chatting about food,' says Nelson, who is having his fifth cup of coffee, 'I'd like to have a meeting.'

'Do you want a smoothie?' asks Tanya, waving a container of sludge-green liquid.

'No, you're all right,' says Nelson. 'What is it?' This last to Tom Henty, the desk sergeant, who has appeared in the doorway.

'Someone to see you, boss. He says it's important.'

'Who is it?'

'He's a priest. I think I remember him from the children's home case.'

Nelson's first thought is that Father Hennessey looks as bad as he does. The priest is still an intimidating presence, with his rugby player's shoulders and boxer's nose, but his eyes are shadowed and he looks as if he hasn't slept. He puts his hat on the floor and accepts a cup of coffee.

'I'm giving up coffee for Lent,' he says. 'Better make the most of it.'

'This stuff's enough to make you give up coffee for life,' says Nelson. 'I should know. I've drunk about a gallon of it.'

Father Hennessey smiles and drinks his coffee in silence for a few minutes. Just as Nelson is wondering if the priest is ever going to speak, if he's waiting for Nelson to make the first move ('Bless me, Father, for I have sinned'), Hennessey says, 'Fiona . . . Doctor McAllister . . . tells me that you called Stanley Greenway in for questioning.'

'I can't discuss ongoing investigations,' says Nelson.

'But that much is common knowledge.'

'All right,' says Nelson, 'he did come into the station yesterday.'

'The thing is,' says Hennessey and, uncharacteristically, he looks away as he speaks, 'I can give him an alibi for Wednesday night.'

'Go on.'

'I left the Sanctuary at about eleven o'clock on Wednesday,' says Hennessey, speaking rather fast. 'It was a lovely clear night so I thought I'd walk back across the fields to

Walsingham. When I was still in the Sanctuary grounds, though, I saw a man lying on the ground. My first thought was that he might be hurt but, when I went over, I saw that it was Stanley. He was just lying there, staring up at the stars. I asked if he was all right and he said that he just liked lying there, thinking. It helped him "make sense of things", he said. He wasn't in distress of any kind, so I left him.'

'You didn't think to tell Doctor McAllister?'

'No. I knew that, strictly speaking, patients weren't allowed out at night, but Stanley seemed so peaceful. Sometimes we all need a bit of silence, a bit of time with God.'

'What did you do after you saw Stanley?'

'I walked back to Walsingham. I wanted to go and pray in the church, but it was locked, so I went back to my pilgrim house.'

The alibi isn't perfect. Paula was probably killed some time in the early hours of Thursday morning and it wouldn't have been impossible for Stanley to have stopped star-gazing, walked to Walsingham, and killed her. Not impossible but, Nelson has to admit, not that probable either. He looks curiously at the priest.

'I have to ask you, Father, what you were doing at the Sanctuary so late at night?'

He expects Hennessey to come up with some line about visiting the sick, but, to his surprise, the priest runs a hand through his white hair and utters something very like a groan. When he speaks, his words are the very last thing that Nelson expects. 'Celibacy,' says Father Hennessey, 'is very hard. A real sacrifice. Especially for a young man.'

'It must be,' says Nelson.

'When I was a young priest I was sent to a parish in Glasgow. I loved the place. It's a great city.'

Father Hennessey loves cities, Nelson remembers. It's the countryside he can't stand. He waits for the priest to continue.

'I loved Glasgow,' says Hennessey, 'but the work was hard, working in the tenements amongst the very poorest of the poor. This was the sixties. Exciting times, but lots of gang violence, lots of suffering.'

Nelson says nothing. He assumes that Father Hennessey has not come here to give him a lecture on Scotland in the swinging sixties.

After a few minutes, Hennessey says, speaking very fast now, 'None of that is any excuse, of course. I fell prey to temptation. I had an affair. It sounds terrible, put like that. I fell in love. But I loved God too. What matters is I broke my vows. I slept with a young woman and she became pregnant. I offered to leave the priesthood and marry her, but she said no. She was very strong, far stronger than me. She knew that I had a vocation and that I'd be miserable if I didn't fulfil it. So we parted. She had the child and eventually married someone else. I moved down to Norfolk and started the children's home, trying to give those children a good life even if I couldn't acknowledge my own.'

'That's a sad story,' says Nelson, 'but how is it relevant here?'

'My child, my daughter, eventually found out that I was her father. Her mother told her on her deathbed. And she got in contact.'

Nelson thinks he can guess the rest, but he asks, 'And your daughter is?'

'Fiona. Doctor Fiona McAllister. She's a wonderful woman, very like her mother. I've been getting to know her, spending time at the Sanctuary.'

Nelson remembers Jean saying that Fiona was an atheist. He supposes that it's enough to make you an atheist, having a Catholic priest as a father. But, then again, he thinks that Fiona is probably more like Father Hennessey than she realises. She has inherited his crusading zeal, for one thing.

'I understand that this might come out in the course of your investigation,' says Father Hennessey, 'but I'll leave that to your discretion.'

'I'll try to keep your relationship with Doctor McAllister out of it,' says Nelson. He doesn't really see why the priest should suffer for his former mistake. Hennessey is still a principled man who has done a lot of good in the world. And, if he were a C of E priest, he could have had any amount of children. Larry Westmondham has four, he seems to remember.

'Thank you, Harry,' says Father Hennessey. 'You're a good man.'

'I'm not a good man,' says Nelson. 'I do try to be a good policeman, though.'

'You're a better man than you think,' says Father Hennessey, 'and you're a better father than I am. At least you're involved in your daughter's life.'

So he does know about Katie.

# CHAPTER 21

Ruth wakes up knowing that she's worried about something. Is it Kate? Always her first thought. She runs through her list of Kate worries: illness, developmental delay, friendship problems at school. But no. Kate had seemed in rude health yesterday, her teacher says she's the best reader in the class, and she seems extremely popular, her book bag always full of invitations to parties and play dates. Ruth had friends at school, but she was never one of those children who is effortlessly top dog, the arbiter of playground fashions, the one everyone fights to sit next to at lunchtime. It seems amazing to her that she has given birth to one of those alpha pupils. So it isn't Kate. Is it work, her parents, the state of the world? No – as she rises from sleep it all becomes clear. It's Nelson.

What actually happened last night? Ruth ponders this, and other Nelson-related matters, as she showers and dresses, wakes Kate and supervises her washing and dressing. 'I need white socks with frills today,' says Kate informatively. 'It's too cold,' says Ruth, 'you should wear your woolly tights.' 'It's white socks with frills day,' counters Kate. 'Who says so?

Mrs Mannion?' asks Ruth. Kate narrows her eyes, wondering how far she can go with this – 'I expect Mrs Mannion thinks it's a good idea.' Ruth lays out the tights.

Making breakfast, Ruth wonders whether she should ring Nelson, just to clear the air. She dismisses this at once. What is there to say anyway? Nelson came over to tell her that his wife was having an affair, Ruth had suggested that he talk to Michelle about it and Nelson had stormed out in a temper. But that's without the subtext, without the moment when Nelson had touched her cheek, had leant towards her, the moment when she knew that he was going to kiss her. Why had she pulled away? Why had she wanted to make sure that this – this thing that she had wanted for so long – wasn't just a reaction to Michelle and Tim, but something that Nelson actually wanted too? She had spoken up, like an idiot, and in doing so had given herself away.

She makes breakfast for herself, Kate and Flint. Flint is the only one who eats heartily. Kate is a picky eater in the morning, and Ruth doesn't feel hungry. Hooray. At this rate she'll be thin, albeit with a broken heart. Is her heart broken? She thinks about it as she cuts Kate's lunchtime sandwiches into triangles (squares are unacceptable). Her heart isn't broken but only because she has immunised herself against this eventuality, building herself up with little doses of heart-break every now and again. Every time that Nelson goes home to his wife, every time he says 'we' and means him and Michelle, every time he talks about their shared past, every Mother's Day, every birthday, every Christmas. So she isn't in pieces. She just feels numb and rather scared, terrified that the fragile relationship she and Nelson have built since Kate's birth might be shattered. That can't happen. She owes it to Kate to keep on civil terms with her father. She adds an apple to Kate's lunchbox, hoping that she won't notice that it's green instead of the more socially acceptable red.

As she drives over the marshes (silver-grey with frost this morning) Ruth makes a decision of sorts. She has a morning without lectures; she'll go to King's Lynn Museum and look up the Walsingham digs from 1961 and 2011. There might be something there that links to Hilary's letters. And, if she finds anything, then she'll have to steel herself to ring Nelson and tell him about her discovery. After all, the letter-writer might be the person who killed Chloe and Paula. She thinks of Paula's family. Hilary said that she had a husband and son. What must they be feeling this morning? How Paula would love the chance to be arguing about woolly tights (or the male school uniform equivalent). Ruth really must count her blessings.

Hilary is going home today. She has asked Ruth to meet her at the Anglican shrine at five to say goodbye. Ruth wanted to find an excuse (she never wants to go to Walsingham again), but knows that's only cowardice. She owes it to Hilary to meet. After all, they might never see each other again. All the same, the thought of the encounter makes a morning in the museum seem even more appealing.

At the school she zips into a parking space made available by some monster people carrier. As she walks Kate to the gate she sees several little girls wearing white frilly socks, their legs blue with cold.

*

Tim gets caught in a hold-up on the M25 and so only just makes it to the crematorium on time. It's a plain room, aggressively tasteful, with bleached wood and lavender-painted walls. Tim finds himself feeling nostalgic for St Simeon's with its stained glass and high altar, even for the clashing primary colours of his mother's church. But, unlike St Simeon's, this place is full to bursting. Tim has to stand at the back, next to a group of mourners who could have stepped from the *Vogue* fashion pages ('Funeral Chic Special'). Tim has attended a few funerals, both as a policeman and his mother's son, and remembers the congregations consisting mainly of old people, some clearly just looking forward to the food afterwards. But today the crowd is overwhelmingly young and beautiful. He can't see Chloe's family, but assumes that they are at the front of the room. A burst of recorded music, and people start to stand up. The girl next to Tim is crying so hard that she looks about to collapse. 'Are you all right?' he whispers. A singularly stupid question.

The coffin is carried in, a wreath of white roses on top. And following behind are Chloe's family. Julie, in a smart black dress, leaning heavily on Alan. And, behind them, a beautiful blonde woman who can only be Lauren, Chloe's sister. She is accompanied by a handsome young man with a designer goatee. Is this Thom Novak or another male relative, a cousin perhaps? An elderly couple complete the family party. Chloe's grandparents, Tim assumes. What a terrible thing it must be to outlive your granddaughter.

The service is brief, ecumenical and – to Tim – heartbreaking in its lack of certainty. Chloe was a beautiful young woman, taken too soon, who is now in some hazy location 'with the angels'. Lauren takes the pulpit to say that Chloe was the best little sister anyone could have had. A schoolfriend (Kelly or Kylie, Tim doesn't quite catch the name) remembers the fun they used to have. 'Chloe was the best friend ever. She'd do anything for anyone.' Isn't that what Alan had said, with rather more sinister overtones? *Chloe always found it hard to say no.* But Chloe wasn't killed by drink or drugs, she was murdered. The manner of her death is never mentioned, and Tim doesn't blame the family for that. This is a time for remembering Chloe in life. By the end, when Robbie Williams' 'Angels' fills the room, there's not a dry eye in the place.

As the music swells and the sobs abound, the curtains open and Chloe's coffin is borne smoothly away. What a horrific moment this is, thinks Tim, and nothing Robbie Williams can say about loving angels instead is going to change that. Chloe was alive and now she's dead. Soon, all her parents will have of their daughter is an urn full of ashes.

Robbie has finished and something classical is playing as the congregation files out, by a back door this time. Tim is one of the last to leave and he finds Alan, Julie and Lauren standing in a sea of flowers still shaking hands and managing to smile.

They don't recognise him at first.

'Detective Sergeant Tim Heathfield from King's Lynn CID,' says Tim. 'The whole team send their condolences. We're all thinking of you today.' This isn't perhaps strictly true but the team will be doing the next best thing; trying to find Chloe's killer.

'It's so good of you to come, Sergeant Heathfield,' says Julie.

'Tim, please. I wanted to pay my respects.'

'That other girl who was killed yesterday,' says Alan. 'Do you think it's the same person?'

'We're not jumping to any conclusions,' says Tim, 'but there are similarities, yes.'

'She even looked a bit like Chloe, we thought,' says Julie. 'Poor woman. We feel for her family, we really do.'

'I know you do,' says Tim, thinking that the Jenkins family are really the only people who know what today will be like for the Moncrieffs. Today, tomorrow and all the days afterwards.

'There are some refreshments at the golf club,' says Julie. 'We hope you'll join us.'

'I ought to get back to work.'

'Just for a cup of tea. Before you have to drive back. It's a long way.'

'That would be very kind.'

But Tim isn't the only person making the drive back to Norfolk. In the car park he sees Fiona McAllister getting into a smart Range Rover. Stanley and Jean are in the back seat.

King's Lynn Museum is a modern state-of-the-art establishment, brimming with the best of old and new. The timbers from the henge are there, and Ruth often visits them for old time's sake, wondering what Cathbad and the other druids who complained about their removal would think about this new chapter in the life of these ancient oaks. But today Ruth is far from the glass cabinets and interactive displays. She is in the basement, going through the archaeological finds from Walsingham. It always gives her a strange feeling to be in these subterranean rooms, surrounded by hundreds of labelled boxes. How many treasures are here, identified and catalogued, but hidden from sight? She knows that there's not room to display everything but, even so, she sometimes wonders if it wouldn't be better to leave these objects in the ground – part of the natural world, as Cathbad would say – instead of bagging them up in acid-free paper, putting them in a box and forgetting all about them.

The Walsingham finds are conveniently marked WS. As Phil said, the bronze Mercury and some of the more interesting pieces are on display in the museum, but there's plenty here: some flint tools and axe-heads, a Bronze Age knife, pieces of quern-stones, fragments of pottery, a few Late Saxon coins and a rather interesting Viking buckle. But it's the more recent finds that she's interested in, the ones relating to the medieval shrine. She finds the ampullae and the copper alloy reliquary thought to be meant for a fragment of the True Cross, plus a medieval leather boot (preserved because it was apparently found in a sewer). Most of these finds come from the 1961 dig which excavated the remains of the original holy house. But there are some objects from the dig Ruth attended a few years ago which concentrated on land just outside Walsingham, on the way to the Slipper Chapel, in fact. At the time, she remembers that the team had been disappointed, a week's digging, and all they had found were a few pieces of pottery, impossibly broken up by ploughing. There had been some flints too and a few coins, nothing that justified further excavation. She looks down the list now:

WS1025 Fragment of Roman pot
WS1026 Fragment of Roman pot
WS1027 Flint implement
WS1028 Coin, Roman: 43–409 AD
WS1029 Coin, Roman: 43–409 AD
WS1030 Lead ampulla with scallop shell design
WS1031 Medieval gilt, possibly from horse harness
WS1032 Fragment from neck of hand-blown glass phial

The scallop shell design is quite interesting. The scallop shell is the symbol of pilgrimage; Ruth seems to remember that it comes from Santiago or Saint James. She went to Santiago de Compostela with Shona once, and there had been scallop shells everywhere, including (Ruth had been pleased to see) on their dinner plates. Coquilles St Jacques, one of the great pleasures of earthly life. She and Shona had travelled by bus, but Ruth remembers seeing pilgrims, dusty and sunburnt, staggering along by the side of the road with their backpacks and staffs. At each stage you had to have the scallop shell stamped in your passport, and then you got a free meal at the end of the pilgrimage. Ruth wonders whether the same system applied in medieval times.

She looks at the last item on the list. *WS1031 Fragment from neck of hand-blown glass phial.* There's no picture, but the notes describe it as 'Early Medieval, possibly mid-to-late

12th century'. With some difficulty, she locates the correct box. She finds the pieces of Roman pottery and the lead ampulla and the horse harness, but, although she looks several times, there's no sign of the piece of hand-blown glass. It's not unknown for objects to go missing – perhaps taken for display elsewhere – but why would anyone want to show a broken piece of old glass? Ruth stares at the sheet of grid-references, troubled by a memory that's buried in some forgotten storeroom of her brain.

The golf club has put on quite a spread. Tim accepts a cup of tea and a biscuit. He looks around at the room, which is now making the kind of upper-class roar more suited to a cocktail party. Still, people have to unwind somehow after the stress of the funeral. The whole thing has made him want to write a will specifying that he wants to be buried at sea with no mourners present. Planning her own funeral is one of Tim's mother's favourite pastimes. Recurring themes include a horse-drawn hearse (with plumes), a gospel choir and internment in a proper grave with a proper headstone. 'A cross or an angel. Or one of those books like the Bible. White marble.' 'Where are we going to get the money for all this?' Rick, Tim's eldest brother, had asked after the last such conversation. 'Save it,' their mother had said darkly. 'Go without.'

Who would attend *his* funeral? thinks Tim, standing on the outskirts of the room, drinking his tea. He hopes for her sake that he will outlive his mother. His brothers, presuming they are both out of prison at the time? His sisters? His nephews and nieces? Michelle won't be there because, when this case is over, he will have to go away and never see her again. To his horror, he feels tears pricking behind his eyes.

'Detective Heathfield?' Tim puts the cup down and blinks rapidly. It's Lauren and the goatee man. He knows from their faces that they saw the tears and were touched by them. He feels oddly guilty about this.

'I'm Lauren, Chloe's sister. This is my boyfriend, Jake.'

So it's not Thom Novak. Where is Chloe's mysterious boyfriend today?

'You spoke really well,' says Tim. 'That must have been difficult to do.'

'I thought someone from the family should say something,' says Lauren. 'Mum and Dad couldn't have managed it.'

'How are they doing?' asks Tim.

'All right. Mum threw herself into arranging the funeral. I think it will hit her afterwards. Dad's been in pieces, though. I've never seen him cry before, but now he can't stop.'

It's terrible when a man like Alan Jenkins finally gives in to grief. Tim has seen it before. He asks if the family are getting counselling.

'Mum and Dad have seen someone. Mum said she was really good.'

'Maybe you should see her too,' suggests Tim gently.

'That's what I said,' says Jake.

'Maybe.' Lauren twists a strand of hair in a way that reminds him agonisingly of Michelle. 'Can I ask you something, Sergeant Heathfield?'

'Do call me Tim. Yes, of course.'

'Those people that were here from the Sanctuary. The old man. Someone told me that he was a suspect.'

There's no sign of Fiona, Stanley and Jean at the wake. They must have driven straight back to Norfolk. A good move, thinks Tim. He wonders who could have told Lauren that Stanley is a suspect.

'We've interviewed Mr Greenway,' he says carefully. 'But no charges have been brought.'

'If you've interviewed him,' says Lauren, 'then he must be a suspect.'

'I can't really say,' says Tim. 'I'm sorry.'

'I suspect him,' says Jake. 'He looks the type.'

That's the trouble, thinks Tim. Stanley Greenway *does* look the type. The trouble is that there isn't really a type. Tim has met charming, respectable murderers, people who wouldn't look out of place at a Surrey golf club. It would help a lot if they were all seedy-looking loners.

As soon as he can, he asks about Thom Novak.

'Oh, Thom,' says Lauren, sounding half-affectionate, half-exasperated. 'Goodness knows where he is.'

'What do you mean?'

'Oh, he checked out of the clinic in Switzerland two days ago. No one has any idea where he is now.'

Ruth knows that something is up as soon as she gets to the Archaeology department corridor. As she stands by her door, trying to dig her keycard out of her organiser handbag, Zita, the department secretary, pokes her head out from Phil's office.

'Here she is.'

Phil himself emerges. 'Ah Ruth, there you are.' As usual, he makes Ruth feel as if she's late, although, as she has no lectures or tutorials that morning, her time is her own.

'Hi, Phil.'

'Ruth, there was a man asking for you.'

His words take Ruth back to another day. The day, almost seven years ago, when she arrived at work to find a strange man waiting for her. Nelson, wanting her help in dating bones found on the Saltmarsh. She realises that Phil is still talking to her.

'A man?' she repeats.

'No, not a man,' says Zita, appearing at Phil's side. 'A priest.'

'He's waiting in the canteen,' says Phil.

As Ruth only knows one priest (one male priest, that is) she's not that surprised to find Father Hennessey waiting for her at one of the long tables, a cappuccino in front of him.

'Hallo, Ruth. Sorry to call in on you like this.'

'That's OK.'

'Are you going to get yourself a drink? This coffee's really very good. It's truly terrible, the stuff they serve at the police station.'

'I know.' Ruth has had her own experience of Nelson's coffee. She often wonders if it's a way of torturing suspects until they confess. In contrast, the coffee at the university is excellent. Ruth gets herself an espresso. She thinks that she might need the energy. She has a feeling that, like the visit from Nelson all those years ago, this conversation is going to complicate her life.

They sit opposite each other. It's nearly lunchtime and the canteen is filling up, but the undergraduates give them a wide berth. Perhaps it's the clerical collar.

'Ruth, I've just been to see Nelson.'

'Oh?' That's the best she can do.

'I had a story to tell him and I'd like, if I may, to tell the same story to you.'

He tells her about Glasgow, the tenements, the deathbed confession, Fiona McAllister. Ruth listens in silence.

'Last night, after I left the Sanctuary, I walked back to Walsingham. I think you saw me outside St Simeon's. I recognised your car going past.'

'Yes. I was dropping off my friend Hilary.'

'I heard what happened to that poor girl. I'm so sorry.'

'She wasn't a girl,' says Ruth, suddenly irritated. 'She was a woman. And a priest.'

'I know. I'm sorry.'

'Why did you come here and tell me all this?'

'I thought that seeing me might have raised some questions in your mind. I wanted to tell you the truth.'

'What if I tell other people?'

'You won't, I'm sure. Besides I'm going to make a clean breast of it to my bishop. That's one of the things I have decided on this trip.'

'I won't tell anyone.'

'Thank you, Ruth.'

Ruth looks at the priest, one of the few people she had believed to be genuinely good and incorruptible. He looks the same: grey hair, broken nose, bright blue eyes. Who knows what secrets people are hiding? The thought makes her feel afraid, as if the brightly lit canteen has been suddenly plunged into darkness.

'It's been a strange time,' says Father Hennessey, stirring the remains of his coffee. 'It's been wonderful to get to know Fiona, but such terrible things have happened. Fiona was so upset about that young girl . . . woman . . . Chloe. And now this other death. Places like Walsingham can be dangerous.'

'What do you mean by that?'

'Pilgrimages can be very fulfilling, spiritually fulfilling, I mean. This trip has been a pilgrimage for me too. But, by their very nature, pilgrimages make people think about the past. And that can be dangerous.'

'Don't people go on pilgrimage to ask for forgiveness?'

'That's true. But forgiveness is a powerful thing.'

After Father Hennessey has gone, sweeping through the undergraduates like Gandalf on a visit to Hobbiton, Ruth wonders whether that was what the priest was doing today. Asking forgiveness, or at least understanding, from her and Nelson. Why he should want her forgiveness she doesn't know, but she gives it anyway. Fathering a child doesn't seem like such a terrible sin. She wonders what Nelson thought and whether he made his own confession in return. He was raised a Catholic, after all.

'Hallo, Ruth.'

She's not really surprised to see Phil and Shona bearing down on her. Phil always wants to know everything that happens in the department and it's not every day that one of his colleagues gets a visit from a priest complete with dog collar.

'So,' he says as soon as he sits down, 'who was the mysterious visitor?'

Ruth considers telling Phil that Father Hennessey is a long-lost uncle/serial killer/emissary from the Pope. Instead she says, 'I got to know him when we excavated that house in Norwich a few years ago. You remember, the one with the skeleton under the door. The foundation sacrifice.'

'I remember,' says Phil, losing interest slightly.

'Gosh, Ruth,' says Shona, 'you do live, don't you?'

Ruth agrees that she does. Shona starts to eat her salad and Ruth feels her mouth watering (though not for salad). She usually tries to avoid eating in front of Phil because he always has to make some comment about her menu choice. 'You do love your carbs, don't you, Ruth?'

There is something she wants to ask him, though.

'I was at the museum today,' she says, 'going through the Walsingham finds.'

'Oh, is this for your friend's dig?'

Ruth has almost forgotten the lie she told Phil at the start of Hilary's visit.

'Er, yes,' she says. 'Sort of. I wanted to ask you something. You know about old glass, don't you?'

'It's one of my areas of expertise,' says Phil modestly.

In fact Phil has a few of these rather dull specialisms. Ruth often suspects it's a way of getting maximum media attention. Looking for an expert in eighteenth-century lustreware? Phil Trent is your man. Even now he has his TV face on, head on one side, eyes crinkling encouragingly. Ruth shows him a copy of the print-out from the museum.

'This piece of glass. Could it be important, do you think? It's quite early for glassware in Britain, isn't it?'

'Not really. You sometimes get glass beads in Anglo-Saxon funerary contexts and glass was fairly common in the Roman era. Glass goblets have been found in Viking graves too. Post Roman occupation, glass-making went into decline, but it was still manufactured in monasteries using wood furnaces. They were banned eventually, because the process used too much timber. Then you get a post-medieval boom when they started using coal furnaces.'

'So this could be a rare piece?'

Phil shrugs. 'It could be Venetian. You got a lot of Venetian glassmakers coming over in the Middle Ages. Hard to tell without looking at it. But this sort of find is fairly common. The monks would have had glassware, or it could be from an apothecary or used to carry holy oil and what have you. Why are you asking?'

'I was looking through the Walsingham finds at the museum today. This one is missing.'

Phil shrugs again and takes a piece of cucumber from Shona's salad bowl. 'Things go missing all the time.'

'Not at the museum. They're very organised.'

'Why are you so interested? Is this to do with the police?'

'Oh no,' says Ruth. 'I was just curious, that's all.'

'Curiosity killed the cat,' says Phil. A singularly tactless thing to say to Ruth.

Apart from police tape over the entrance to the abbey, there's little sign that Walsingham has been the scene of a violent crime only forty-odd hours ago. The shops are still selling vestments and holy pictures; groups of pilgrims are still wandering up and down the high street taking pictures of the pump-house and the pub. Ruth sees a woman priest dressed in purple like a bishop, and a man with a long beard who looks like a Greek Patriarch. She also sees Clough sitting in his car outside St Simeon's Church eating a Crunchie bar. The car is unmarked, and Clough isn't in uniform so maybe he's undercover. Ruth is just wondering whether to approach when Clough leans out of the window and shouts, 'Hi, Ruth!' So much for the Secret Service.

'Hi, Dave.' Ruth crosses the road to talk to him. She's known Clough for years, one way and another, and is rather surprised how fond she is of him.

'Bad business, isn't it?' says Clough, nodding towards the church with the abbey behind it.

'Awful.'

'The boss said you knew her, the woman who died.'

'I didn't really know her, but I went out to dinner with her once. She was very nice.'

'That's what everyone says. Good-looking too.'

Ruth reflects that the death of someone attractive (Chloe Jenkins, Paula Moncrieff) is always considered borderline more tragic than the death of someone aesthetically displeasing. But there's no point saying this to Clough.

'Did you hear that Michelle was attacked too?' Clough is saying. 'Must have been the same bloke. She had a lucky escape.'

'I did hear, yes.'

'Lucky Tim and the boss were close by. Did you know that Tim has applied for a transfer?'

Ruth thinks it's best to pretend that she doesn't know this. She expresses surprise.

'Everyone's deserting me.' Clough sounds really aggrieved. 'First Judy, now Tim.'

'Judy'll be back.'

'So she says.' Clough's voice is gloomy. 'She'll probably bring the baby with her and insist on breastfeeding all over the office.'

That's the thing about Clough, thinks Ruth, as she says goodbye and follows the signs to the Anglican shrine. Just when he's being human, he says something that reminds you what a Neanderthal he can be. Except that the Neanderthals probably had a more enlightened attitude towards breastfeeding.

The Anglican shrine is round the corner from The Bull. Ruth almost walks straight past it because the front is modern and glass, with automatic doors. When she passes through the doors (which make a sinister swooshing sound) she finds herself in a rather charming garden. Brick paths take slow serpentine routes through the spring flowers and, apart from the occasional visitor sitting quietly on benches, the place is deserted. Along the path there are brick pillars inlaid with brightly coloured frescoes. Ruth peers at one, 'Jesus falls for the second time.' What are these called? Stations of the Cross, something like that. Underneath is a small sign saying 'Mother Mary, Pray For Us'. Ruth hurries on.

Hilary had said that she would meet her in the cafe, but instead Ruth finds her sitting on a bench near an outdoor altar covered with a sort of sail. They embrace awkwardly.

'I thought I'd wait for you here,' says Hilary. 'I couldn't cope with the cafe somehow.'

'It's nice here,' says Ruth, sitting beside Hilary on the bench. 'Peaceful.'

'Yes,' says Hilary. 'I really felt that I needed some time here before I left.'

'I'm so sorry about Paula,' says Ruth.

'It's horrible.' Hilary looks like she hasn't slept. Her hair is lank and her eyes deeply shadowed. Ruth remembers Hilary at the dinner on Wednesday night, sleek and attractive in her black top. She thinks of Paula too and feels again the shock at the finality of death. Two days ago Paula was sitting in the Briarfields bar, funny and animated, talking about her acting career, and now she isn't anywhere. She has gone. Completely, irrevocably. Except that Hilary, presumably, thinks that she's in heaven. Sometimes Ruth thinks that she'd do anything to share this belief.

'Her husband came to identify her body,' says Hilary. 'I thought he might come to St Catherine's, but he didn't.'

Ruth thinks that Paula's husband probably doesn't want to come within a million miles of Walsingham. What was it that Father Hennessey said? Places like Walsingham can be dangerous.

'The last two days have been terrible,' says Hilary. 'The police interviewing us, everyone crying. You'd think a group of priests would be able to cope better, that we'd be able to pray, to comfort each other, but everyone just seems stunned.'

'Surely that's natural,' says Ruth. 'You're only human after all.'

By mutual consent they start walking along one of the brick paths. The birds are singing and the air suddenly seems soft and springlike. They walk past a raised piece of ground with three crosses on it and more brick pillars with brightly coloured scenes of death and suffering.

'Are you going home tonight?' asks Ruth.

'Yes,' says Hilary. 'Inspector Nelson said we could go. He took all our names and addresses, though. He can be quite abrupt, can't he?'

'Sometimes,' says Ruth. 'He's got a lot on his mind at the moment.'

'The police don't seem to have any idea who did it,' says Hilary, idly crushing a piece of lemon-balm between her fingers. Ruth wonders if that's why her friend has requested this meeting, to pump her about the police investigation. She's come to the wrong place, if so.

'It's early days,' Ruth says, thinking what a meaningless phrase this is.

'Nelson asked me about the letters again. He can't really think that my letter-writer killed two women.'

'I don't know,' says Ruth. 'I really don't know what he thinks.'

'He says he's assigned me police protection. I told him that the police in Streatham have better things to do.'

'Well, be careful all the same,' says Ruth.

They stop by steps that lead to a courtyard with a fountain. A sign says sternly, 'Silence in the courtyard. People are praying.' Ruth feels that this is a message telling her not to go any further.

'Come and have a look at the church,' says Hilary. 'It's very ornate, very beautiful. They've got a replica of the holy house.'

'I'd better be going,' says Ruth. 'I need to collect Kate.'

Hilary seems to know not to push it. 'It's been good to see you again, Ruth,' she says. 'Despite everything. Do keep in touch, won't you?'

'I will,' says Ruth. It's an easy promise to make, after all.

'I'll be praying for you,' says Hilary. 'This Lent is going to be a very difficult time for all of us.'

'Thank you,' says Ruth, who feels that some response is called for.

Hilary smiles. 'You think it's all nonsense, I know. But I'll pray for you all the same.'

Somehow it sounds like a threat.

Later that evening, after Kate is in bed, Ruth makes a determined effort to dredge up the memory that's bothering her. She once saw a programme about memory that said you ought to see it as a house; everything's there, it's just that it's all folded into drawers, or shut up in cupboards, or (in Ruth's case) shoved under the sofa. Sitting at the table by the window she looks out over the blackness of the Saltmarsh and takes a trip through her memory house, which appears to be a cross between this cottage and her parents' semi in Eltham. The Walsingham dig, pottery, glass, Cathbad, St Simeon's, Clough, Nelson (Don't go there), Kate, Michael, Judy . . . She has a feeling that she's very near. Maybe some wine would help. She pours herself a glass and goes back to the window.

*'She'll probably bring the baby with her and insist on breastfeeding all over the office.'*

*'You look like a Madonna.'*

*'The holy house was panelled in wood and contained a statue of the Virgin and a phial of her breast milk.'*

And the letter-writer: *'You may have borne a child (O sacrilege that anyone calling themselves a priest should do so!), but you have not suckled from the Virgin's breast.'*

She thinks of the medieval glass. Is this what it was? A phial containing the Virgin Mary's breast milk? And, if so, why has it gone missing?

# CHAPTER 22

Ruth always knew that it would be a difficult conversation.

'So you think a bottle of breast milk has gone missing. And that's somehow relevant to the case?'

'A phial that may have contained something claiming to be the Virgin Mary's breast milk.'

'Oh, that makes all the difference.'

Ruth counts to ten; her usual practice with Nelson.

'The letter-writer refers to the "true treasure" of Walsingham. What if this is it? If you find out who took the glass you may find out who wrote the letters.'

'That easy, is it? How am I supposed to track down a bit of broken old glass?'

'I don't know. Check who was on the original dig, who had access to the museum. You're the detective.'

'Yes, Ruth.' Nelson is trying out his patient voice. 'I am.'

'Are you going to follow this up?'

'I'll put my special medieval-glass team on to it right away.'

Sod you, thinks Ruth. She hadn't wanted to ring Nelson. She'd wanted to let a few days go by after that awful evening at her house. But she had genuinely thought that she had uncovered something that might be relevant to the case. Now Nelson is making her feel stupid, as if she's an unworldly academic or – worse – an amateur detective. She wants to yell at him but she can't; she isn't his wife.

'See you around,' she says.

'It was good of you to call.' Nelson now sounds almost conciliatory. 'How are you doing? How's Katie?'

'We're both fine.'

'I'm taking Katie out at the weekend, remember?'

'I remember.'

'We thought we might take her to Redwings. She loves horses, doesn't she?'

Ruth notes the 'we'. 'Yes,' she says, 'she'd like that. See you on Saturday. Good luck with the case.'

'I'm going to need it,' says Nelson.

Nelson puts the phone down feeling rather ashamed of himself. Ruth was only trying to help, he shouldn't have been sarcastic to her. But, the truth is, deep down, he is still angry with Ruth. Why didn't she tell him that she had seen Michelle and Tim together at the gym? He brushes aside the thought that he would hardly have welcomed this information, or been very well disposed towards the informant. As it is, it feels as if Ruth and Michelle have both been deceiving him and, whereas Michelle is being particularly loving at the moment, Ruth remains cool and aloof, only ringing him with some ridiculous theory about the Virgin Mary's breast milk. He doesn't want to remember the moment when Ruth had looked at him in a way that wasn't cool and aloof. He doesn't like to think about what might have happened.

Nelson walks out into the incident room. Tanya is going through CCTV footage from Wednesday night. The screen is split into four. He can see the priory wall, a ruined archway and two sections of complete blackness.

'Fuller?'

'Yes, boss.' She turns round eagerly.

'Have we heard from the lab about Stanley Greenway's DNA?'

'Not yet.'

'Well, hassle them. I want it checked against DNA from Chloe's clothes and from Paula's. Where's Clough?'

'At the Sanctuary. You sent him.'

Clough is interviewing security staff. Apart from Father Hennessey's sighting in the field, Greenway has no alibi for the early hours of Thursday morning. Clough is talking to the night watchman and anyone else who may have been on duty at the time. Nelson knows it's unreasonable to be irritated that this is taking so long. It doesn't stop him, though.

'And Heathfield?'

'Talking to Interpol.'

The news of Thom Novak going AWOL has added an unwanted complication to the investigation. He checked out of the Swiss clinic two days ago, and no one has seen him since. 'We tried to stop him,' the staff had said. 'We could see that he was in a bad state. But he was free to leave when he pleased. There was nothing we could do.' 'Bloody Swiss,' Nelson had said when he heard that. 'Always so bloody neutral.' Tim (who, until a few days ago, Nelson would also have had down as one of life's neutrals) is liaising with Interpol in the search for the missing male model. It's not that he's a suspect exactly. Novak has an alibi for Chloe's murder and it's unlikely that he came to Norfolk and killed Paula on the spur of the moment just because she resembled his dead girlfriend. 'Unlikely,' Nelson reminded the team, 'but not impossible.' In any case, they need to find him.

'Have you got the witness statements from the conference delegates?' Nelson asks now.

'Yes.' Tanya brandishes a file.

'Give it here then.'

He sits opposite Tanya, under the map of Walsingham and the photographs of the two dead women, and reads through the printed witness statements. There were eight women present at the meal, including Ruth. By all accounts the meal was convivial and lasted a long time. Staff at Briar-fields confirm that five bottles of wine were consumed, as well as several liqueurs. The mood, they said, was 'lively, but good-humoured'. They were nice women, the waiting staff said, and left a generous tip. Ruth and Hilary left first, at about eleven-forty, and arrived at St Catherine's Lodge at midnight. The other women called a taxi and got back around one. They had made coffee and chatted until about one-thirty. Then most of the women had gone to bed. Paula Moncrieff, Sydney Bowen and Freya Drew-Hayes had remained down-stairs. At about two o'clock Paula Moncrieff expressed her intention of going for a moonlight walk. 'I almost went with her,' said Sydney Bowen, 'but I was tired and went to bed.' The written statement does not convey the guilt and pain in Sydney's voice when she said these words. Nelson also has a statement from Robin Rainsford, who was woken by the housekeeper at approximately five-thirty a.m. He had dressed, gone downstairs and spoken to PC Linwood. Hilary Smithson was also there, making tea in the kitchen. Rainsford and Smithson had then accompanied PC Linwood into the abbey grounds, where they had found Paula's body. 'She was such a lovely woman,' said Rainsford, 'she had a difficult start in life, but that hadn't made her hard or bitter. She saw the best in everyone.' Her husband had said something similar. Nelson leafs through the file until he finds his notes on the interview with Giles Moncrieff.

*'Paula had a terrible childhood really, she was in children's homes, with various foster parents, in and out of care. But it never made her bitter.'*

'I'm going out,' Nelson tells Tanya.

'Where?' she asks, though it isn't strictly speaking her place to do so.

'Walsingham. I'm going to talk to Larry Westmondham.'

Nelson enjoys the drive to Walsingham. He has his Mercedes back and it's a joy to feel it purring through the narrow lanes rather than bouncing around like Michelle's car. He drives through the village. A couple of uniforms are standing by the entrance to the abbey, which is still sealed off. They'll have to open it soon. Nelson is getting hassle from the local bishop as well as the Norfolk Tourist Board. They'll want the abbey grounds open by Ash Wednesday, which is next week. Never let it be said that death got in the way of tourism.

He remembers Larry Westmondham's amusement at the idea that he might live in the grand Victorian vicarage by the church. As Nelson drives past the timbered cottages towards the modern estate on the edge of the village, he realises that he's entering a very different world. The garden of the Westmondhams' house is full of bicycles, punctured footballs and the remains of a rusting swing set. There are even a few chickens pecking dispiritedly behind a wire fence. The sign on the door says, helpfully, 'Ring here for the vicar', but the bell seems to be out of order. Nelson knocks loudly and, after a few minutes, the door is opened by a woman wearing the kind of apron Nelson has only seen in fifties' films. She has the face to go with it, round and cheerful, completely free from make-up. Her dark-blonde hair is pulled back into a ponytail.

'Is Larry – the Reverend Westmondham – in?'

'He's picking the girls up from school,' says the woman. 'He won't be long. Do you want to come in and wait?'

'Thank you,' says Nelson. The woman seems to expect that people will come to her door demanding to see her husband. She doesn't even ask for his name. Nelson gives it anyway and shows her his warrant card for good measure.

'Oh, is this about those poor women who were killed? Larry was so upset. We both were. To think of it happening here, in Walsingham.' She wipes her hands on her apron and holds out her hand. 'I'm Daisy. Larry's wife.'

'Pleased to meet you,' says Nelson.

'Come through to the kitchen. I'm just putting some scones in the oven.'

Scones? Oven? Has he really gone back fifty years in time? Michelle is a good cook, but he can't imagine her making scones in the middle of the afternoon. Don't all women work these days? Or, if they're not at work, they're out meeting their lovers at the gym.

In the kitchen is one reason why Daisy Westmondham is not out cracking the glass ceiling in the City or breaking the pain barrier at the gym. A large baby sits in a highchair. He's either worryingly pale or covered in flour.

'This is Samuel. He's always filthy, I'm afraid.'

'Hi, Samuel.' Nelson waves from a safe distance. The baby beams at him.

Daisy puts a baking tray in the oven. 'Can I get you a drink? Tea? Coffee?'

'Only if it's no trouble.'

'Oh no. I always make a pot when Larry comes home.' Of course she does. Other women would use teabags, but not Mrs Domestic Harmony 1952. Nelson is not at all surprised when Daisy gets out a large brown teapot complete with knitted tea cosy.

Nelson sits at the table opposite Samuel. After the emotional traumas of the last few days Daisy Westmondham's kitchen is a rather restful place to be. The radio is playing, not Radio 1 (Michelle's choice) or dull people talking on Radio 4 (Ruth), but something tuneful and undemanding. Daisy hums along as she puts out cups and saucers (cups and saucers, not mugs), and Samuel beats time with a spoon.

'It was so awful about Paula Moncrieff,' says Daisy, measuring out tea leaves. 'Awful about the other girl too, but I'd actually met Paula, which made it worse somehow.'

'Had you?' This is news to Nelson.

'Yes. I had all the delegates round for supper on their first night in Walsingham. I always try to do that for all the people who go on courses at St Catherine's. Nothing special, just a big lasagne or shepherd's pie. Paula was lovely, really chatty and friendly.'

'Everyone says what a nice person she was,' says Nelson. His mind is still boggling at the sort of woman who thinks that having eight people for supper (plus her family, presumably) is 'nothing special'.

'Did all the women priests come that evening?'

'Yes, and Robin too. They were a really nice bunch. Sometimes the delegates can be very serious. Women priests especially. Somehow they seem to feel that they have to be more . . . well, pious than the men. But this group were really good fun. Paula had been an actress, you know. Freya had been a teacher and Sydney used to work in a circus.'

'A circus?'

'Yes, she was an acrobat or something like that. Anyway, they were all so interesting. We stayed talking until past midnight. Usually I'm in bed at ten, what with this one –' she nods at Samuel, who is now dreamily eating flour – 'keeping me going all day.'

'How old are your other children?' asks Nelson.

'Becky's ten, Lizzie's eight and Victoria is six. They're all at the local primary. It's walking distance, which is great. I don't drive. I know it's ridiculous in a grown woman, but I've just never got round to it and I couldn't afford the lessons. Larry's always offering to teach me, but he's so busy.'

'Have you lived here long?' asks Nelson.

'Five years,' says Daisy. 'We lived in Croydon before this. It was a great parish, but we had a tiny flat with no garden. Not much fun with three kids. I was delighted when this came up. I've always wanted to live in the country. And this is where Larry's from. He was brought up in Houghton St Giles.'

'He must have been pleased to move back here.'

Daisy wrinkles her nose. 'Ish. The thing is, I think Larry felt that he was doing more good in an inner-city parish. Here it's all retired colonels and people who think that the church is their personal fiefdom. I mean St Simeon's is a beautiful old church, but people get furious if Larry tries to change any-thing. Even when he put in a hearing loop for the deaf. Half of them can't hear, but they're against anything that means drilling holes into the precious walls. And Walsingham's a funny place. I've got a friend, Janet – she's a historian – and she says that it has a dark atmosphere, something to do with a curse and the dissolution of the monasteries.'

'Do you believe that?'

'No. I mean, anywhere that's a centre for pilgrimage arouses really strong emotions. It's a beautiful place and I've met some lovely people. It's a wonderful place to grow up. Larry had a really happy childhood here.'

'Did you know Larry's mother, Doreen?'

'No.' Daisy looks genuinely regretful. 'She died just before I met Larry. He was still mourning her really. I wish I'd known her. She sounds like a wonderful woman. Larry and his brothers have all sorts of stories about her. That's her, on the noticeboard.'

She points to a cork board which is so covered with pictures, invitations, shopping lists and certificates saying 'Star Pupil: ten ace points for sitting quietly at story time' that it resembles one of those pieces of modern art collected by Juan, the co-owner of Michelle's salon. It takes Nelson a few moments to pick out a photograph of a smiling woman standing by a caravan with a surly-looking youth at her side.

'That's Doreen with Larry. They all used to go on holiday in that caravan. They had it specially adapted because Eddie, one of the long-term foster children, was in a wheelchair. You know she fostered over a hundred children?'

'I've heard.'

'I wish I could do something like that, but I find it hard to cope with four.'

'I'm not surprised. My wife and I found it hard to cope with two.'

She gestures at Samuel. 'This one was my present to myself. A boy after three girls. Now, I keep thinking, what about another baby to keep him company?'

Michelle had wanted another baby after Rebecca, Nelson remembered, but he had thought two children were enough. Well, now he has three. No wonder Michelle resented him for it. He's about to say something when there's a noise outside and Daisy's face lights up.

'In here, darlings.'

There is a lot of crashing in the hall and then three children and a dog burst into the room, followed by the Revd Larry Westmondham.

There is such a din of children shouting, the baby beating a tattoo on the tray of his highchair and the dog barking that it's a few moments before Larry registers Nelson's presence.

'Detective Chief Inspector. I'm sorry. I didn't see you there.'

'Don't worry. You've got your hands full.'

Daisy puts a cup of tea in front of her husband. 'Detective Inspector Nelson came to see you, Larry.'

'Do you want to see my picture?' asks one of the girls, the youngest, he thinks.

'Yes, please,' says Nelson.

'It's a friendly shark,' says the girl.

The picture shows a blue sea with what looks like a floating smile in it. The paper smells strongly of primary-school paint and brings back memories of Laura and Rebecca waving similar masterpieces at him.

'I like his teeth.'

'It's a lady shark.'

'Leave Inspector Nelson alone, Victoria,' says Daisy. 'He's here to talk to Daddy.'

'Are you to do with the church?' asks Victoria.

'No.'

'I didn't think you were,' she says, peeling away to play with the dog, a large excitable spaniel. One of the older girls has taken Samuel out of his highchair and there's a move towards the garden. Daisy puts a plate of scones in front of Nelson and Larry.

'I'll go out into the garden too,' she says, 'then you can talk in peace. Be careful, they're a bit hot.'

It's a few minutes before Nelson realises that she's talking about the scones.

Larry Westmondham drinks his tea with the abstracted air of one whose mind is far away from domestic minutiae, in inner-city Croydon, perhaps.

'Sorry to bother you at home,' says Nelson. 'I bet you don't get much time to yourself.'

'No,' says Larry, crumbling a scone into his saucer. 'That's the only thing about being a priest with a family. Your wife and children miss out really. There are hundreds of people out there who call you "Father" and your real kids come second a lot of the time. Sometimes I think there's something to be said for a celibate clergy.'

Nelson is glad that Daisy is not here to hear this endorsement of family life. He thinks of Giles Moncrieff going home to break the news to his son of his mother's death.

'Must be difficult for husbands of female clergy too.'

'Yes. I often think that. It's hard to share your spouse with a whole parish.'

Giles had said that Paula's parishioners had adored her. Had he found it hard to share her with them? It's a new line of thought.

'I actually wanted to talk to you about your mother,' says Nelson.

'Really?' Larry's eyebrows seem to rise into his bald head. 'Why?'

'Paula Moncrieff, the woman who died, she had been fostered. I just wondered – I know it's a long shot – if your mother had had a foster child called Paula?'

Larry's forehead wrinkles. 'I'm not sure. There were so many, and some only stayed a few weeks. They would know at the council, wouldn't they?'

'Yes. I'm going to look at the local authority records. I just thought it might be quicker to come to you. When I spoke to you in the church you said that one of your mother's foster children had become a vicar. I thought that might be Paula.'

'I heard that one of them was a vicar,' says Larry. 'I don't know who told me, but I assumed it would be a man.'

'Not a safe assumption these days.'

'No.' Larry looks at Nelson. 'Paula and the other women priests came here for a meal at the start of their course. You'd think that Paula would have mentioned it if she'd been fostered by Mum.'

'You would,' admits Nelson. 'But sometimes people don't like to talk about their childhood. Especially if it hasn't been very happy.'

'The other girl that died was looked after by Mum. Do you think that's the link then?'

'I don't know,' says Nelson. 'It's just a line of enquiry.'

Larry still looks troubled. He's about to speak when the back door opens and Victoria bursts in to demand that he plays football with them.

'We need someone who can actually kick the ball. Mum and Samuel are in goal.'

'I'm busy, sweetheart.'

'You've got a few minutes to play football, surely,' says Nelson. 'I'll join you. I once had a trial for Blackpool Juniors.'

'Oh,' says Larry vaguely. 'Have Blackpool got a football team?'

When Nelson gets back in his car, still out of breath (partly from the shock of Larry's remark) he puts in a request to Intel, asking for the names of all the children fostered by Doreen Westmondham. Could this really be the link between Chloe and Paula? That they had both been cared for by the kind-faced woman in Daisy's photograph? But, if that was the case, why was Michelle attacked? Was it simply because the killer had mistaken her for Paula? He's just about to ring the station when his phone buzzes. Clough.

'What is it?'

'We've got the DNA results. Stanley Greenway's DNA matches semen found on Chloe Jenkins' dressing gown.'

'Meet me at the Sanctuary,' says Nelson. 'We're going to bring him in.'

# CHAPTER 23

Fiona McAllister insists on accompanying Stanley Greenway to the police station.

'It's all right, Dr McAllister,' says Stanley, 'I'm sure this is all just routine.'

'I'll come anyway,' says Fiona grimly.

Nelson, looking at Fiona McAllister in the driving mirror, tries to see if he can see any resemblance between the doctor and Father Hennessey. On the surface they couldn't be less alike. Hennessey is heavily built, with strong, irregular features; Fiona McAllister is slim and attractive, radiating coolness and poise. But there is something there all the same: maybe it's just the crusading expression or the sense of certainty. Nelson knows that he must play this interview by the book.

'I want to make a statement,' says Fiona, 'stating that Stanley Greenway is on drugs which can cause paranoid delusions and blackouts.'

'You can make a statement at the station,' says Nelson.

'I've called my solicitor,' Fiona is saying now. 'She's meeting us there.'

'What's her name?'

'Khan. Nirupa Khan.' That figures. Nirupa Khan is one of the smartest lawyers around. What's more, she's no fan of the police.

Nelson drives round to the back entrance. Nirupa Khan is waiting at the front desk.

'Have you charged him with anything?' she says.

'No,' says Nelson. 'Mr Greenway is just here on a voluntary basis to answer some questions.'

'I'll sit in on the interview,' she says.

'Is that what you want?' Nelson asks Stanley.

Stanley looks confused. 'I strongly advise you to have Ms Khan with you,' cuts in Fiona.

'All right then. If you say so, Doctor McAllister.'

'It's going to be quite a party,' murmurs Clough as Stanley, Nelson, Nirupa and Fiona file into Interview Room One. Clough takes his seat beside Nelson as Nelson explains that this is an interview under caution and Greenway doesn't have to answer the questions but that anything he says may be taken as evidence. Greenway stares at him vacantly.

Nelson introduces himself and DS Clough for the tape. Then he says, 'Mr Greenway, what was the nature of your relationship with Chloe Jenkins?'

Nirupa stirs, but allows the question.

'We were friends,' says Stanley.

'Is that all?'

'We were fond of her, Jean and I. She was almost like a daughter to us.' Stanley is gaining in confidence now, sounding almost angry. 'She was such a sweet, gentle soul, very spiritual. She believed in angels. To think that someone could . . .' He dabs his eyes.

'Mr Greenway,' says Nelson, 'we have had forensic tests done on Chloe Jenkins' nightclothes, the clothes she was wearing when she was killed, and we found traces of your semen on them. How do you explain that?'

Nirupa Khan says, 'You don't have to answer, Stanley. Remember you can leave at any time.'

Nelson ignores her. 'Can you explain that, Stanley?'

Stanley stares at the ceiling. Eventually he says, in a gentle voice, as if he is explaining something to a child, 'I used to go into her room when she wasn't there and try on her clothes. I liked her dressing gown because it was big. It fitted me. I used to walk round in it. And sometimes I got excited.'

Nelson stares at him. 'You masturbated in her clothes?'

'If you want to put it like that, yes.'

'A perfectly reasonable answer,' says Nirupa. 'Now if I could have a few minutes with my client.'

'Jesus wept.' Nelson and Clough are having a hasty meeting in Nelson's office. Rather reluctantly, Nelson has asked Tim to join them. 'Can you believe it?'

'I can believe anything of him,' says Clough. 'He gives me the creeps.'

'The trouble is,' says Nelson, 'it is an explanation for his DNA being on Chloe's clothes. Being a creep doesn't make you a murderer.'

Clough looks unconvinced.

'Does he have an alibi for the night of Chloe's murder?' asks Tim.

'Says he was in bed at the Sanctuary but no alibi to confirm this. And, given his fondness for sneaking out at night, I think we could have a good go at breaking that down. We've got to be careful though. Nirupa Khan will be down on us like a ton of bricks if we ask anything approaching a leading question. Stanley's obviously quite vulnerable mentally too. That's why it's good that his doctor's here.'

'I think we'll get a confession,' says Tim. 'He's that type.'

Would you have confessed, thought Nelson, if you hadn't given yourself away with Michelle in the graveyard? Aloud he says, 'Greenway isn't a Catholic. It's Catholics who like confessing.'

'Anglo-Catholics do too,' says Tim. 'I've been reading up about it.'

At any other time Nelson might have been impressed by this, but now he just says, sourly, 'Nirupa Khan will try to stop him coming over all confessional in the interview.'

'We'll just have to press the right buttons,' says Clough. 'What an angel Chloe was, how no one understood their relationship. That sort of thing.'

'Blimey,' says Nelson, 'have you been going to empathy classes in night school, Cloughie?'

Clough looks modest. 'I've learnt a thing or two in the past few years.'

'We all have,' says Nelson. 'Come on, let's get back in there.'

*

Ruth is in a very different environment, the Humanities library at the university. Yet she too is primarily concerned with bodily fluids. She is immersed in a heavy hardback book with hand-cut pages. It is called *Relics of the Medieval Saints*. It's all here: vials of blood, St Anthony's tongue, St John the Baptist's head, the finger of Doubting Thomas, even something called the Holy Foreskin (a prized relic in medieval times apparently). There are also enough pieces of the True Cross to build an ark. Ruth reads on, turning the pages with care. Occasionally she writes in her notebook. It's quite soothing, reminding her of her student days and the slower pre-Internet world.

It's far quieter here than in the Natural Sciences library, where there's a constant whirr of photocopying and low-level chatting. The windows look out onto the ornamental lake, currently as still and smooth as glass. Faint shouts can be heard from the tennis courts behind the octagonal lecture theatre, but, in the library, there is a heavy scholarly silence. Ruth is not even sure that the woman opposite her is breathing.

'Ruth! What are you doing here?'

It's Shona, scattering the dust motes with her carrying voice and her glowing face and hair. The woman opposite wakes up with a start and glares at them.

'I thought you never came to the Humanities block,' Shona is saying.

'I managed to get past the checkpoint.'

'What are you reading?' Shona reaches out to look at the cover of Ruth's book. The title is embossed in gold. Shona peers at it. 'Relics of the Medieval Saints . . . Are you getting religious in your old age, Ruthie?'

'Come for a coffee,' says Ruth, 'and I'll tell you. I'll just put this book back. You're not allowed to take it out of the library.'

'I bet there's a waiting list a mile long,' says Shona.

Just to give himself some thinking time, Nelson checks his emails before he goes back into the interview room. There's one from Intel listing Doreen Westmondham's foster children. Nelson scans down impatiently. There's a Pauline Berry on the list, also a Paula White. He calls, 'Fuller!'

Tanya appears at the door. 'Yes, boss?'

'Can you do something for me? Check Paula Moncrieff's maiden name. Be sensitive, mind, if you speak to the husband.'

'Of course. How's it going with Stanley Greenway?'

'If he confesses,' says Nelson, 'you'll be the first to know.'

Tanya clearly doesn't get the irony and leaves the office looking complacent.

Shona is actually a very good audience. Ruth doesn't tell her about the possible link to the letters, only that she is on the trail of the missing piece of glass. Even so, Shona listens wide-eyed, letting her cappuccino get cold.

'Those old relics are really interesting. Have you seen St Etheldreda's hand in Ely?'

'No. I love Ely, though. Is it in the cathedral?'

'No, in St Etheldreda's Church. It's apparently the oldest

Catholic church in England, but it's tucked away in a back street. You'd miss it if you didn't know where to look. The hand's in a glass case and it lights up if you put a coin in. There's a pretty good provenance to it, though.'

'That's more than can be said for these breast-milk relics.'

'Are there a lot of them around?'

'Yes. Apparently there's quite a tradition of the nursing Madonna, especially in the Greek Orthodox Church. There's a church called the Church of the White Grotto, built on white stone in Bethlehem where a drop of Mary's milk is meant to have fallen. There's also St Bernard of Clairvaux who had a vision of the Virgin Mary where he got squirted in the eye with her breast milk.'

'That's quite a vision. Did he go blind?'

'No. It cured his eye infection apparently.'

'Is there a breast-milk tradition connected to Walsingham?' asks Shona.

'Well the original holy house apparently contained a phial of the Virgin's breast milk. It's shown on some of the pilgrim badges. And the pilgrim route used to be called the Milky Way.'

'It's a funny thing,' says Shona. 'The Catholic Church is meant to be against the sins of the flesh, but it's obsessed with these corporal objects. I always remember reading that Robert Browning poem, "The Bishop Orders His Tomb", and there's a line about something being "as blue as the vein o'er the Madonna's breast". I found that quite shocking – I was a good little Catholic schoolgirl at the time – but then there are all these churches with bits of wrinkled flesh kept as holy objects. It's all very odd.'

Ruth thinks about the letter-writer and his preoccupation with the masculinity of the scriptures. Maybe the cult of the nursing Madonna is a way to combat this. She wonders what Hilary would think of it all. She also realises how much she has missed Shona and her literary take on events. She has seen far less of Shona since she moved in with Phil, and her life feels poorer for it.

Maybe Shona has been thinking the same thing.

'We could go to Ely and see the hand, if you want. Take the kids. Make a day of it. Louis would love to see Kate.'

Since Shona's little boy Louis spends most of his time beating Kate up, Ruth rather doubts that this feeling will be mutual, but the thought of a day with Shona is very enticing.

'I'd love that,' she says. She catches sight of the clock over Shona's head. 'Oh God, it's five o'clock. I've got to pick Kate up from the childminder.'

'I've got to get Louis from the nursery. They make you feel so terrible if you're late.'

That's one problem the Virgin Mary didn't have, thinks Ruth, as the two mothers hurry out of the canteen.

Time is moving on for Nelson too. Nirupa Khan is looking at her watch, and Stanley Greenway has been answering questions for over an hour. Despite Nelson's constant references to the angelic qualities of Chloe, Stanley sticks to his story pretty well. He was in bed at the Sanctuary, he didn't hear about Chloe's death until Doctor McAllister told him the next day. Yes, he'd been at the Slipper Chapel earlier in the evening. He likes to attend different churches and there's a statue he likes at the Catholic shrine. He was devastated when he heard about Chloe, had to take a tranquilliser. Dr McAllister drove him and Jean to the funeral. It was so sad, there were white roses on the coffin, and they'd played a song about angels. On the night of Paula's death he had gone for a walk, just strolling around aimlessly looking at the stars and trying to pray. He'd been back at the Sanctuary by two because he remembered the grandfather clock striking in the hall.

That clock was slow, remembers Nelson. Even so, if this is true, Stanley was back at the Sanctuary by two-thirty. Paula was killed between one-thirty and three-thirty. It's still possible.

At six o'clock Nelson takes a break. He knows that he hasn't got much time left and he doesn't think that the DNA on its own is enough for an arrest. If he doesn't get a confession soon he will have to let Greenway go and the momentum will be lost. Going back up to his office, he meets Tanya on the stairs.

'You still here, Fuller?'

'Of course. And I found out about Paula Moncrieff. Her maiden name was White and her husband said that she was fostered by a lovely woman who lived in Houghton St Giles. He remembered the name because it was like his.'

'Well done.' Nelson stands still on the stairs, thinking. If the link is Doreen Westmondham, then surely that lets Stanley Greenway off the hook. Maybe the ex-priest really is just a slightly creepy man who likes dressing up in young girls' clothes and not a murderer after all. As Nelson debates with himself, Tom Henty calls from downstairs.

'DCI Nelson? Ms Khan wants a word.'

Nirupa Khan is looking thoroughly irritated. Nelson assumes this is because he has been questioning her client for so long, so he is stunned when she says, 'My client wants to make a statement. I must tell you that this is against my advice and that of his doctor.' She shrugs. Nelson feels almost sorry for her.

Stanley Greenway's statement is brief. 'I killed Chloe. I'm very sorry. It was just that I loved her so much.'

# CHAPTER 24

*17th April 2014, Maundy Thursday*

The arrest of Stanley Greenway for the murder of Chloe Jenkins takes some off the pressure off Nelson and his team. The press jump eagerly onto the idea of a defrocked vicar as a killer, helped, Nelson thinks cynically, by the fact that Stanley Greenway looks like everyone's idea of a sinister predator. 'Police Arrest Paedo Priest,' screams the *Sun*. The only problem is that there is still nothing to link Stanley to Paula Moncrieff's murder. There were no traces of his DNA on her clothes and, though his clothes (retrieved from the Sanctuary laundry) were stained with mud and grass, that could easily have come from lying in the field looking up at the stars. Nelson is also slightly worried by Stanley's confession. Apart from saying constantly that he loved Chloe, Stanley can't come up with any other motive. His statement, transcribed verbatim by the police stenographer reads:

'And I was just lying there in the grass the birds blackbird thrush robin looking at her so pretty then she was dead I loved her but she was dead I prayed at the chapel mea culpa mea culpa mea maxima culpa . . .'

Nirupa Khan is talking about entering a plea of insanity.

Nelson hasn't forgotten the Doreen Westmondham link, but that too has proved to be a dead end. He has looked into the background of everyone involved in the case and none of them were in care. Larry Westmondham seems infuriatingly vague about his mother's foster children. 'Daisy probably knows more than me. She's been going through all the old pictures.' Nelson went to see Daisy, cunningly timing his visit for tea-time. Over Victoria sponge ('Named after me,' said the youngest girl), Daisy laid out the pictures on the kitchen table. Doreen smiled into the camera, accompanied by a variety of children, of all ages and ethnic groups, one in a wheelchair. That must be Eddie, for whom the camper van had been adapted. In some of the photographs, she was in the company of a mild-faced man who looked some years older than her. 'Larry's father,' said Daisy, 'he only died a few years ago. He was a sweet man, but somehow he doesn't come into the family stories much.' There was only one picture of Doreen and her three sons: Steven, Kevin and Larry. The three boys had stared sullenly into the camera, much less beguiling than the foster children. But, then again, maybe they had less to smile about.

There was no way of knowing if any of the pictures featured Chloe or Paula. Was Chloe the little blonde girl holding on to Doreen's skirt on Cromer beach? Was Paula the awkward-looking teenager pictured building a tent in the garden? So many children, so many lives. Nelson showed

Daisy a picture of Stanley Greenway and she examined it closely. 'I think I might have seen him at Sunday services. At St Simeon's.' 'Do you think you've seen a younger version in any of the old photographs?' asked Nelson. 'I don't think so,' said Daisy. 'But people change so much, don't they?'

Nelson had interviewed Steven and Kevin Westmondham, but they too were less than enlightening. Steven, an older version of Larry, said that he didn't really remember any of his mother's foster children. 'There were so many, they all merged into one really.' 'Do you recognise this man?' Nelson showed him the photograph. 'No,' said Steven. 'Oh, wait. I've seen him on the news. Isn't he the vicar who killed those two girls?' 'Looks like a pervert to me,' said Kevin, the other brother. 'No, I've never seen him before.'

So, more than a month after Stanley's arrest, Nelson is still trying to firm up the case. He's in Walsingham to meet the woman who claimed to see a lurking figure near the church on the night of Paula's murder. The witness, Bella Hendred, has not been terribly helpful so far. She failed to pick out Greenway in an identity parade and the description in her witness statement is vague in the extreme. But maybe he'll be able to get something better out of her.

Nelson has rather lost count of the days, so he's surprised when he arrives in Walsingham to see the village so full of people. When he cuts through the abbey grounds to have another look at the murder site, he sees that two men are erecting a huge wooden structure in front of the ruined arch. There are other such structures spaced at intervals around the park. One looks like the dock in a magistrate's court, another like a cave. The largest edifice, in front of the arch, looks disconcertingly like a gibbet with an upright and a crossbar being hammered into place.

'What's going on?' Nelson asks a passing workman.

'It's for the play tomorrow,' says the man. Then, seeing Nelson's blank look he adds, 'The Good Friday Passion Play. They act out Jesus being killed and all that.'

Nelson looks back up at the gibbet. He sees now that it's a massive cross, silhouetted against the pale-blue sky. He shivers, thinking, not for the first time, that it's a weird thing to be celebrating torture and death. Religious people might as well wear little electric chairs around their necks. Only a few yards away is the spot where Paula Moncrieff had the life choked out of her. Nelson hurries on, head down against the wind which is rattling the instruments of torture. Today must be Maundy Thursday then. A more convivial feast, the meal in the upper room, the sharing of bread and wine. But then, the agony in the garden, betrayal and death. It's a wonder they tell children these stories, though Nelson remembers taking part in a Passion Play at his primary school. He had played Judas because, as Sister Anthony kindly explained, he was good at looking angry. Blond-haired, blue-eyed Joseph O'Malley had played Jesus.

Bella Hendred lives in a cottage off the high street. The walls are pale pink and the front door is green, the knocker in the shape of a hand. Nelson fears the worst.

And he's proved right. The room contains wind chimes, statues of Buddha and the Virgin Mary and, on every surface, crystals, scented candles and tiny carved objects. The air smells of incense and over the fireplace is a sampler informing Nelson that 'The best and most beautiful things in the world cannot be seen or even touched – they must be felt with the heart'. Want a bet? thinks Nelson. He takes his seat on the blue-draped armchair and says no thank you to a glass of cranberry juice. A small fluffy dog stares at him stonily from the adjacent chair.

He has only seen Bella once before, at the identity parade, and he supposes that she had made an effort to look conventional on that occasion. Today she is wearing an orange kaftan emblazoned with silver suns and moons. Enough, in Nelson's mind, to make her lose credibility with any jury in the land.

'I'd like to ask you again about the man you saw on the night of the 19th February,' he says. 'I know it's a long time after the event, but sometimes things do occur to us when some time has passed.'

'That's so true,' says Bella. 'I think it's because those events have been in the universal subconscious for longer and so we gain greater understanding.'

'That's an interesting viewpoint,' says Nelson. 'Could I just take you through your witness statement from that night?'

'Of course.' Bella sits opposite him, and the dog gets out of its chair to sit on her lap. Two pairs of eyes stare at Nelson expectantly.

'You were walking your dog by the church at approximately ten past midnight on the 19th February . . .'

'Yes.' Bella pats the animal in question. 'I always take Francis out then. There's less chance of meeting other dogs.'

'Doesn't he like other dogs?'

'He doesn't seem to,' says Bella sadly. 'I think he must have had a trauma in a former life.'

Nelson decides to skate over this. 'So you were walking beside the church, past St Simeon's Cottage, and you saw a man. What was he doing?'

'That was it,' says Bella, 'he wasn't doing anything. He was standing in the graveyard looking up at the church. I'm the last one to stop people communing with the spirits, but it seemed an odd thing to be doing in the middle of the night. Francis barked. He could tell something wasn't right.'

Nelson suspects that Francis barks quite a lot. Though he's a fraction of the size of Jan's dog, Barney, he seems far more aggressive.

'You described the man as being "quite tall, wearing dark clothes". Is there anything else you can add now, thinking back?'

Bella shuts her eyes, Francis, though, continues to stare at him. Eventually Bella says, 'He was wearing a hat. A black hat. Like the one that Pat O'Brien wore in *Angels with Dirty Faces*. People don't seem to wear hats so much these days. My dear father . . .'

Nelson interrupts. 'Did he look at you? Respond to your presence?'

'No. He didn't even look round when Francis barked. He seemed lost in his own thoughts.'

Larry Westmondham was wearing a hat on the night that Michelle was attacked, Nelson remembers. He has a clear picture of the vicar wearing a heavy coat and black woolly hat.

Then another picture comes into his head. Catholic youth club, a black-and-white film, Jimmy Cagney on the way to the electric chair.

'Pat O'Brien in that film you mentioned. He played a priest, didn't he?'

'Yes,' sighs Bella Hendred. 'It was so affecting that last scene, where he convinces James Cagney to pretend to be afraid so as not to be a role model for those tearaways.'

And Nelson thinks of Father Hennessey sitting in his office, drinking coffee and talking about his illegitimate daughter, his black trilby hat on the floor beside him. Father Hennessey had been in Walsingham that evening. He had gone to the church to pray and found it locked. Nelson had watched Larry lock it only a few hours earlier.

'And you'd never seen this man before?' he says. 'Around the village, for example?'

'I don't think so. He was an unfamiliar presence.'

So the mysterious lurking man may have been Father Patrick Hennessey. Nelson thanks Bella and stands up to leave. On the way out she tells him that she's not a churchgoer, but she likes the spiritual energies of Walsingham. She gets strength from the Buddha as well as her guardian angel and various Christian saints.

Nelson thinks to ask who Francis is named after.

'St Francis of Assisi, of course. Patron saint of animals.'

Francis barks shrilly.

On his way back to the car Nelson makes a detour to look at St Simeon's Church and the place where Bella saw her mysterious man. On that occasion the lane had been deserted, but today it is rather more crowded than Nelson would like. Standing by the door of Justin's cottage are the house owner himself (resplendent in embroidered waistcoat), Cathbad (in cloak), Ruth, Hilary Smithson, Robin Rainsford and another of the woman priests. What's her name? Something outlandish. Freya something.

Nelson stops and considers backing away, but Cathbad has seen him.

'Talk of the devil,' he says brightly.

There's been far too much talk of angels and devils already for Nelson's liking. Also, he doesn't relish the idea that the group have been discussing him. He has seen Ruth a few times since their argument at the cottage, mostly when he has dropped off or collected Katie. On those occasions Ruth has been polite and coolly friendly. Nelson wants to apologise for losing his temper, but he doesn't know how to. Perhaps because he's still angry.

Now Ruth shoots him a distinctly hostile glance. Cathbad says, 'We were just saying that we're sure that poor vicar is innocent.'

'Really?' says Nelson. 'Well it's always nice to hear an informed viewpoint, but the CPS are happy that we've got sufficient evidence against him.' He doesn't add that this evidence is mostly in the form of a rambling, often incoherent, confession.

'There's nothing to tie him to the murder of the other woman, though, is there?' says Justin. 'What was her name?'

'Paula,' says Freya tightly. 'Her name was Paula.'

'Does this Greenway man have any links to Paula?' asks Hilary.

'That's not something that I can share with the general public,' says Nelson. 'I'm surprised to see you here, Reverend Smithson. I wouldn't have thought you'd want to come back to Walsingham.'

Hilary Smithson's face doesn't change, but she can't stop herself turning a particularly bright shade of pink, like vestments on a feast day.

'Freya and I came for the Good Friday Passion Play,' she says. 'I won't let Paula's death stop me practising my faith.'

But there's nothing to stop you practising it at home, thinks Nelson. The woman's manner strikes him as furtive.

'I'll be at the Passion Play too,' says Cathbad. 'I love a good Passion. What about you, Justin?'

'Oh, I'll be there,' says Justin. 'I'm playing Pontius Pilate.'

Ruth had been very surprised to get an email from Hilary at the beginning of April. Despite their promises to keep in touch, the two women hadn't been in contact since Paula's murder. Ruth had sent flowers to Paula's funeral, but honestly thought that would be the last she would hear from any of the women priests. But two weeks ago there had been this email:

Hi, Ruth,

Hope you're well. I've been having a peaceful and fulfilling Lent, despite everything. Paula's funeral was beautiful. Sydney led the service and all the women from the course came. Robin read the

lesson and little Jack read out a prayer he had written. He was so brave. Giles was too upset to speak. Anyway, Ruth, I'm coming to Walsingham for the Good Friday Passion Play. Could we possibly meet at the Blue Lady at 11 o'clock on Maundy Thursday? There's something I want to show you.
Love and prayers,
Hilary

Ruth had turned up at the Blue Lady to find the place deserted and a sign on the door saying 'Spring Cleaning for Easter'. She had walked back through the village, following the Abbey wall, and found Hilary, Freya and a large man in glasses chatting with Cathbad outside a cottage attached to the church. A man in a waistcoat was standing in the doorway, also deep in conversation with them.

'Here's Ruth now,' said Cathbad as she approached.

'Hi, Ruth.' Hilary came forward to fold her into a warm embrace. 'The cafe was closed so I was just looking for somewhere else to go, and I ran into Cathbad. He says he's a good friend of yours.'

'I've never seen him before in my life,' said Ruth.

Cathbad laughed, but Hilary looked troubled. 'Sorry, I . . .'

'It's a joke,' said Ruth. 'Cathbad and I go back a long way.'

'Have you met Justin Fitzroy-Jones?' said Cathbad. 'It was his cottage I was looking after when I saw Chloe Jenkins in the graveyard.'

'If it was Chloe,' said Justin with a slightly foxy smile, 'and not the Blue Lady herself.'

'You know Freya, of course –' Hilary carried on with the

introductions as if she was at a cocktail party – 'Freya and I are taking part in the Good Friday Passion Play tomorrow. We've just come from a rehearsal.'

Ruth felt out of her depth. She had only the vaguest idea what a Passion Play entailed. 'What are you doing in the play?' she asked.

'We're apostles,' said Hilary. 'And Robin is an apostle too. Have you met Robin Rainsford? He was running the . . . well, the course that I was on.'

Ruth thought that Robin looked rather embarrassed at the mention of the fateful course. He blushed pink, matching his jumper.

'We were talking about the case,' said Cathbad. 'I'm really worried about the police arresting this Stanley Greenway fellow. He looked very vulnerable to me. Do you know anything about it, Ruth?'

Ruth was quick to deny any inside knowledge, but they had got into an enjoyable discussion about wrongful arrests and general police brutality when Nelson spoilt it all by strolling up looking like a thundercloud. He hadn't addressed a word to Ruth, but sparred briefly with Cathbad and expressed surprise at seeing Hilary in Walsingham. Hilary replied that she was there for the Passion Play, but she coloured when she said it, confirming Ruth's suspicions.

Now Hilary, Cathbad and Ruth are in The Bull, which is filled to the brim with Easter pilgrims. Hilary seemed anxious to shake off Freya and Robin ('I know you'll want to rest') and now Ruth sees why. As soon as they sit down,

Hilary rummages in her voluminous handbag and pulls out a handwritten letter.

'I wanted to show you this.'

Ruth's first thought is that, if Hilary has had a new letter, this proves that Stanley Greenway can't be the killer. Then she remembers that the letter-writer and the killer aren't necessarily the same person. She and Nelson have been fooled that way once before.

Cathbad takes the letter. Ruth isn't quite sure how Cathbad has inveigled his way into Hilary's confidence, but it seems that he has; maybe because he appeared to be so sure of himself with Nelson earlier. Or maybe it's just the cloak.

Ruth reads over Cathbad's shoulder.

Dear Jezebel [nice to see that the letter-writer's salutation has not changed, she thinks],

You would not heed my warnings. If you want to know why those two fallen women had to die, meet me at the holy house on Good Friday at 3 p.m., the hour Our Saviour died for our sins. Do not tell the police, especially Harry Nelson, for he is a sinful man, guilty of the sin of adultery. Come on your own, and I promise that all will be made plain to you. For now we see through a glass darkly, but then face to face.

Yours in God –

Ruth stares at the letter. The phrase 'for he is a sinful man, guilty of the sin of adultery' seems to be growing bigger

and bigger, almost pulsating on the page. How can the letter-writer know about her and Nelson? Only a few people
know, and they are the people closest to them: Michelle,
Judy, Cathbad, Clough, Shona. Even her parents don't know
who Kate's father is. How can this person know? Or maybe
it's just a shot in the dark. She mustn't give herself away.
She is grateful to hear Cathbad's voice, sounding uncharacteristically serious. 'Hilary, you aren't planning to meet this
character, are you?'

Hilary takes a sip of her tomato juice. 'I certainly am.'

'But it's madness. If you really suspect that this man is
the murderer, you must tell the police at once. Let me ring
Nelson.'

'No,' says Hilary, pointing at the letter, 'he says not Nelson.'

'When did you get this letter?' asks Ruth.

'A few weeks ago.'

'A few weeks . . . And you didn't tell anyone?'

'No.' Hilary has her martyr's face on again. 'He wrote to
me. It's up to me to see this thing through.'

'You can still meet this person,' says Cathbad, 'but the
police can be nearby, watching, ready to pounce if he attacks
you.'

'Where would they hide? The site of the holy house is out
in the open. By three o'clock tomorrow the grounds will be
full of people watching the Passion Play.'

'They can mingle with the crowds,' says Cathbad, 'or you
can wear a mike. Seriously, they have ways of doing these
things.'

It's quite amusing to hear Cathbad, the man who once

hated the police, sounding like an expert on their procedure. Ruth weighs in too.

'You have to tell the police, Hilary. If this man is the killer, you'll be in terrible danger.'

'I'm not afraid,' says Hilary, sounding stubborn. 'I'm a black belt in taekwondo.'

Nelson is back at the station when he gets the call from Cathbad. He listens impatiently, then with mounting incredulity.

'Do you mean to say that Hilary Smithson was planning to meet this person and not inform the police?'

'That's right. But Ruth and I talked afterwards and thought that you should know. Even if Hilary asked us not to tell you.'

'Very kind of you both. Why on earth didn't Hilary want to tell the police?'

'The letter says not to. In fact it mentions you by name.'

'Does it? What does it say?'

There's a slight pause then Cathbad says, 'Something about you being a sinful man.'

'Go on.' Something tells Nelson that there's more.

'Oh, more Old Testament stuff. Something about you being an adulterer.'

'I see.' Nelson is beginning to understand why Ruth didn't make this call.

'It's very over the top,' says Cathbad. 'About looking through a glass darkly – though that's a beautiful phrase – and all being revealed. But it's worth taking seriously, don't you think?'

'Yes, I do,' says Nelson. 'I'll make sure I have people at the site of the holy house tomorrow. Three o'clock, was it?'

'Yes. The hour that Jesus was crucified.'

How the hell do they know that? thinks Nelson. He has trouble getting his team to fill in their timesheets correctly, let alone keep count from two thousand years ago.

'We'll be there,' he says. 'Thank you for telling me.'

'That's OK,' says Cathbad. 'Perhaps now you'll let that poor priest go.'

'Goodbye, Cathbad.'

Nevertheless, thinks Nelson as he puts down his phone, Cathbad might have a point. Greenway is in custody, but someone claiming knowledge of the killings is still out there. And there's nothing to link Stanley Greenway to the letters, although the biblical knowledge could point to someone with theological training. A handwriting expert has concluded (as far as these people ever conclude anything) that the writing in the letters does not match Stanley's. Is it possible that there are two killers out there, that a different person murdered Paula Moncrieff? Never assume, that's what Nelson tells his team, but is he guilty of assuming that the two murders were committed by the same person? There were some differences, as he pointed out at the time. Chloe's body had been laid out carefully, the rosary on her chest; Paula's left where it had fallen. These details have never been released to the press. Could Paula's even be a copycat crime, based on what had actually made it to the papers? Are there two murderers in Walsingham?

He thinks of Justin saying that there is nothing to link

Stanley Greenway to the murder of Paula Moncrieff. Not that he wants to take policing lessons from some waistcoat-wearing . . . Nelson stops. Something is chiming in his brain, a tiny alarm bell somewhere. What is it? Stanley Greenway, Chloe Jenkins, Paula Moncrieff, Cathbad, Justin . . .

Nelson goes into the incident room. Tim and Tanya are both there, glued to screens.

'Fuller,' says Nelson. 'Can you find the CCTV footage of Stanley Greenway at the Slipper Chapel?'

'Sure,' says Tanya. She clearly wants to ask why, but doesn't dare to. Tim looks up from his work.

Tanya clicks on various icons and a grainy window appears on the screen.

'There he is,' says Tanya, 'on the left.'

But it isn't Stanley Greenway that Nelson is looking at. He has remembered Tanya's words when she first spotted Greenway in the footage. 'Look there,' she'd said. *'Next to the man in the waistcoat.'* And the man next to Greenway is none other than waistcoat-wearing Justin Fitzroy-Jones.

# CHAPTER 25

*Maundy Thursday, afternoon*

Ruth drives home, feeling that her hard-won serenity is, once again, under threat. Over the last few weeks she has concentrated on work and looking after Kate and has almost succeeded in not thinking about Nelson. Well, not much anyway. When he arrives to pick up Kate she manages to chat to him pleasantly enough, not rising when he reminds her about new child car-seat regulations or reminding him how to pronounce his daughter's name. She hopes that he quakes before the new ice-queen Ruth and feels shrivelled inside but she has a nasty feeling that he hasn't noticed any difference.

Still this last month hasn't been without its pleasures. She and Kate went to Ely with Shona and Louis. They visited St Etheldreda's Church and were shown the relic by the charming parish priest, Father Tony. The hand itself, enclosed in a small curtained niche, was surprisingly ungrisly. It was just a grey object, made innocuous by its surroundings.

Shona, of course, had crossed herself and genuflected madly, partly for Father Tony's benefit (he was a man, after all, and all men are susceptible to Shona). But it had been a lovely day. Louis didn't attack Kate once. They visited the soaring cathedral and had tea by the river. Perhaps there is life after Nelson.

But now Hilary's visit has brought everything back: the murder, the sinister letters, the row with Nelson. Ruth and Cathbad agreed to tell Nelson about the latest missive, despite Hilary asking them not to. 'You ring him,' Ruth said to Cathbad. 'It'll sound better coming from you.' Cathbad had looked quizzical, but hadn't asked any questions. They have arranged to meet at the Passion Play tomorrow. 'That way we can keep an eye on things,' said Cathbad, clearly desperate not to miss any of the action. Ruth had agreed, but now she has a feeling of dread in the pit of her stomach. She doesn't feel that an afternoon spent watching the re-enactment of a violent death will help matters very much. Besides, she's dreading seeing Nelson again.

She collects Kate from Sandra, the childminder, at two. At least it's the holidays, which means she can spend some quality time with her daughter. Unfortunately Kate has had a great morning doing potato prints with Sandra and doesn't want to come home. It's at times like this, when Kate actively prefers the company of her childminder to that of her mother, that Ruth feels her whole life – all the juggling of work and childcare and school parents' evenings – is a complete failure.

'Come on, Kate,' she says, trying to keep a happy 'fun

mother' smile on her face. 'We can go to the beach and dig in the sand.'

'I hate sand,' says Kate. 'And digging,' she adds, perhaps knowing that this is what would hurt Ruth most.

'Well let's go and see Flint then,' says Ruth, keeping the smile plastered on.

Kate eventually allows herself to be shepherded to the car and Ruth drives off, waving cheerfully.

Ruth keeps up a merry flow of chat as far as the turn-off for New Road. Then she lapses into silence. The tide is out and the sand stretches forever, interspersed with cool blue lakes and patches of wind-blown grass. Even Kate cheers up a bit at the sight. 'We *could* go and dig in the sand,' she says, as if making a huge concession.

'Not if you don't want to,' says Ruth. Honestly, she thinks, what kind of person scores points off a five-year-old?

But, as they get nearer the house, they see a car parked outside.

'Is it a visitor?' asks Kate. Such apparitions are rare in her life, but usually mean that fun is cancelled in favour of Mum sitting on the sofa chatting and drinking glasses of wine. Her lower lip starts to protrude.

Ruth is no less apprehensive. She doesn't recognise the car, so it can't be Cathbad or Nelson, her only two regular callers. Maybe it's just someone going for a walk over the Saltmarsh. But there's a perfectly good car park about half a mile away and bird-watchers are never scared of walking. As Ruth comes to a halt behind the car she sees that the driver is still in their seat. Again, she doesn't recognise the person's back view. She takes her phone out of her bag and clicks on Nelson's number. One false move from her caller and she'll summon the cavalry.

But, as Ruth gets out, so does the other driver and Ruth recognises her. It's Freya. Why is she here when Ruth only saw her a few hours ago? Besides, they hardly know each other. At the Briarfields dinner Freya had seemed rather humourless and intense. She was the one who said Norfolk had an 'unwholesome feel'. Ruth had felt insulted on behalf of her adopted county. And, if Freya hates the place so much, what's she doing here now? Ruth seems to remember that she lives in Wiltshire.

Still, the woman doesn't seem to be actually dangerous, so Ruth gets Kate out of the car.

'Hallo,' she calls. 'Have you come to see me?'

'Yes,' says Freya, walking towards her. 'I hope it's not an intrusion.'

'Not at all,' says Ruth. 'Come in and I'll make a cup of tea.'

Kate sighs heavily.

When Ruth last saw Freya she was very smart and controlled. Whippet-thin, with short dark hair and a penchant for neutral clothing, she had seemed like the sort of woman who made Ruth feel more than usually untidy and inadequate. But, today, something is different. Freya is still neatly dressed in jeans and a black windcheater, but there's something about her face that looks slightly hysterical. She sits bolt upright on Ruth's sofa and places her hands carefully on her lap, as if this is the only thing that will stop her wringing them together. Flint wanders over nosily, but something in Freya's rigid stance seems to repel him and he meanders off again. Kate gets out her Sylvanians and starts a rather bad-tempered game with them.

'I'm sorry if I'm intruding,' says Freya again.

'You're not,' says Ruth. 'It's fine. Tea or coffee?'

'Just water, please.' Ruth remembers Freya drinking water at the Briarfields evening. Well, she had been too, but only because she was driving. Freya's choice, then and now, seems more of a moral standpoint. Only bread and water for me, please. The rest of you carry on with your gluttonous eating and drinking. Just don't expect me to bring you a glass of water while you're burning in the everlasting fires of hell. Ruth goes to the kitchen and makes herself a cup of tea, whilst running the water so it's cold enough for Freya. She's certainly not going to offer biscuits.

When she gets back, Freya is watching Kate lining up her Sylvanian babies in front of the schoolhouse.

'I used to have some toys like that when I was young,' says Freya. 'Whimsies, I think they were called.'

'Do you have children?' asks Ruth.

'No,' says Freya. 'I don't have a husband either. I suppose I'm married to the job.' She gestures at her neck as if she's wearing her dog collar. And, even though she isn't, her plain black sweatshirt still looks like some sort of uniform.

'I haven't got a husband either,' says Ruth. 'They're rather hard to come by, aren't they?' She remembers the conversation about Christian dating sites. Hadn't one of the priests met her husband that way? Ruth dreads the day that her mother learns how to work a computer; she'll be sending Ruth the hyperlinks in a nanosecond.

'I suppose you're wondering why I came,' says Freya.

'I know you're here for the Passion Play,' says Ruth. Although this doesn't explain why Freya is here, in her house, drinking water and watching Kate play with her miniature woodland animals.

'Yes,' says Freya. 'Hilary suggested it. She thought it might be a way to come to terms with Paula's death. Visiting the place where it happened and praying for her.'

It occurs to Ruth that her old friend is very fond of managing people. Meet me here, do this, read that. Hilary might say that it's all for altruistic reasons, but it's rather bossy all the same.

'I've never been to the Passion Play,' she says, 'but Cathbad and I are going to watch it tomorrow. We'll look out for you.'

'The thing is,' says Freya as if Ruth hadn't spoken, 'do you remember Hilary talking about those anonymous letters?'

'Yes,' says Ruth.

'Well, I've had one,' says Freya, twisting her hands together.

'Have you?' Ruth's heart sinks.

'Can I show you?'

Please don't, screams Ruth silently. But Freya is already getting a piece of paper out of her backpack.

Dear Jezebel [the old ones are the best],

Good Friday is the day of Our Lord's Passion and Death. We kneel before the True Cross and know that we are not worthy. Beware, for the Lord sees into your soul. He will strike you down in your wickedness. You strut and fret your hour upon the stage, but then you will be heard no more.

There's no signature. Even so, Ruth is pretty sure that this is the same person who wrote to Hilary. There are too many similarities: Jezebel, the True Cross, the threatening suggestion that the Lord (and, by association, the letter-writer) is watching at all times. Only the last line sounds different somehow. That's not the Bible, is it? It sounds like Shakespeare.

'*Macbeth*,' confirms Freya, 'I read English at university. It's the "Tomorrow and tomorrow" speech: "Life's but a walking shadow, a poor player, That struts and frets his hour upon the stage, And then is heard no more. It is a tale, Told by an idiot. Full of sound and fury, Signifying nothing."'

As Freya quotes the lines, she suddenly reminds Ruth of Shona, who has an encyclopaedic knowledge of Shakespeare. It's not a comparison that would have occurred to her before, what with Shona being a Titian-haired beauty and Freya being a priest who wears windcheaters and sweatshirts. It's more the rapt look that came over Freya's face when she said the words. She might not love Shakespeare more than God, thinks Ruth, but it's a close thing.

'When did you get this?'

'After I saw you in Walsingham I went back to my B&B. This was waiting for me. Hand-delivered.'

So the letter-writer is someone who lives in or around Walsingham, thinks Ruth. Aloud, she says, 'Have you shown this to Hilary?'

'No,' says Freya. 'I thought I'd come to you first.'

Of course, thinks Ruth, that makes perfect sense. Accost a woman you've hardly met, but don't consult your friend and colleague who has actually received similar letters herself. But she doesn't think this is the most important issue here.

'You need to show this to the police,' she says.

'They won't be interested.'

'I think they will. Please tell DCI Nelson about it.'

'DCI Nelson interviewed us after Paula died,' says Freya. 'I can't say I took to him much. He was rather brusque.'

'He can be like that,' says Ruth, thinking, *Tell me about it.* 'But he's a good policeman. He'll take it seriously.'

'The reason I'm showing it to you,' says Freya, 'is because of the True Cross reference. Hilary said that a relic of the True Cross had been found near Walsingham. I thought you might know something about it, being an archaeologist.'

'A holder, supposedly meant to contain a relic of the True Cross, was found at Walsingham,' says Ruth. 'I've been doing some research, though, and apparently there were loads of such relics about at the time.'

Freya doesn't ask why she was doing the research. Instead she says, 'I've got no patience with that sort of thing. Icons and relics and angels and incense. It saddens me that some of my fellow women priests seem to have a weakness for ritual.'

'I'm not a believer,' says Ruth, 'but there's evidence that even the earliest human societies practised some forms of ritual. There are Stone Age bodies buried with animal bones and special stones, for example.'

'What do you mean, special stones?'

'There are fossils called shepherd's crowns,' says Ruth, 'you can find them on the beach here. Well, they've also been found in Palaeolithic graves.'

Freya looks less than interested in Palaeolithic burial practices. Ruth remembers that Freya has no time for so-called 'New Age' thinking.

'You're an old friend of Hilary's, aren't you?' she says.

'Yes,' says Ruth, wondering if this is really true. 'We were at university together.'

'Both studying archaeology?'

'Yes.'

'You must have been surprised when she decided to become a priest.'

'Yes, I was,' says Ruth. 'But we hadn't been in contact for quite a few years. People do change. I know I have.'

'I haven't changed,' says Freya. 'I've wanted to be a priest for as long as I can remember. Of course, at first it seemed impossible, as if the Church of England would never change its position. But I prayed. I prayed fervently. And it came to pass.'

Freya says this with a certain smugness, as though her prayers alone have changed the mind of the General Synod. Ruth thinks it's time to get the conversation back on track.

'Are you going to take this letter to the police?' she asks. 'I really think you should. It's quite threatening. All that stuff about striking people down in their wickedness.'

'It's not worth it,' says Freya, gathering up her backpack. 'It's like the *Macbeth* quotation. "Full of sound and fury, Signifying nothing."'

But *Macbeth*, thinks Ruth after Freya has left, is not the best omen. Not only is the play notoriously unlucky, but she seems to remember that quite a few people get murdered in it. Why did Freya want to show her the letter? After all, they had only spoken a few words at that fatal dinner. Was it really because of the vague archaeological reference or was it something altogether more sinister? Should she, Ruth, tell Nelson, even if Freya refuses to? The fact that the letter was hand-delivered must be significant, after all.

She sits on the sofa and Kate, miraculously sunny again, comes and sits on her lap. 'I do like you, Mum,' she says. 'I love you,' says Ruth, giving her a fierce hug. She is certain of one thing. Kate will not be coming to the Passion Play with her tomorrow. Kate will stay safely with Sandra making potato prints or playing in the sandpit. Places like Walsingham can be dangerous.

Justin Fitzroy-Jones greets Nelson politely, with just a hint of a raised eyebrow.

'How can I help you, Inspector?'

'Could I have a few minutes of your time?' says Nelson. 'There's something I'd like to clear up.'

'Of course.' Justin stands back to let Nelson in. He has to duck under the low beam. 'I warn you, I haven't got long. I've got a meeting at three. We're protesting about the plan to build new houses on Badger's Copse.'

'This won't take long,' says Nelson.

He takes a seat in the low-ceilinged sitting room. The room exudes order and comfort. Like Bella Hendred, Justin obviously enjoys collecting *objets d'art*, but his are minimalist and tasteful: a china vase on a low table, a collection of watercolours, a single orchid on the mantelpiece. Chesterton, the black cat lying on the white brocade sofa, seems to be placed there purely for aesthetic impact. A bowl of white hyacinths on the coffee table fills the room with a subtle yet heady fragrance. An ornate clock ticks above the fireplace.

Justin offers tea or coffee, both of which Nelson declines. Justin sits beside Chesterton on the sofa. Without looking at his owner, the cat gets up and moves away.

'Mr Fitzroy-Jones,' says Nelson, 'Can I ask your whereabouts on the 19th February?'

Justin raises both eyebrows now. 'I was in Ireland. I'm surprised you ask. Cathbad was house-sitting for me and I know you two are friends.'

The word 'friends' is said slightly maliciously.

'The thing is,' says Nelson, 'I have CCTV footage that places you at the Slipper Chapel that evening.'

He keeps his eyes on Justin and is rewarded by a tiny flicker of fear on the neatly whiskered face. Eventually Justin says, 'What do you mean, CCTV footage?'

'As part of our investigations we looked at the CCTV from the chapel. We've got a picture of you leaving a service with Stanley Greenway, the man charged with the murder of Chloe Jenkins.'

Justin looks from left to right, a cornered woodland animal now.

'I don't know the man.'

'Oh, come on,' says Nelson, 'you can do better than that.'

'You wouldn't understand.' More nervous eye movement.
'Try me.'

Justin adjusts a coaster on the spindly table beside him. 'It's
a brotherhood,' he says. 'The Brotherhood of the Madonna
Lactans. We meet at the Slipper Chapel because there used to
be a statue there which belongs to the brotherhood. Father
Bill has hidden it in his office now. He's suspicious of us,
thinks we're a dangerous cult. He doesn't understand our
deep love for the Madonna. When you lose your mother as a
child, like I did, you turn to the Holy Mother. She nourishes
us, she cares for us.'

'What is the Madonna Lactans?'

'The nursing Madonna,' says Justin. 'The brotherhood
started in the twelfth century. There's a fresco showing the
breastfeeding Virgin in Santa Maria Trastevere in Rome and
on several Greek and Russian icons. It was revived by the Cis-
tercians in this country. There was a phial containing Mary's
milk above the high altar at Walsingham. Women would pray
to the relic for help with conception or childbirth.'

This account seems to have given Justin confidence. He
even over-pronounces the Italian in a way that strikes Nelson
as deeply pretentious. Nelson himself is still trying to get
over the fact that Ruth's ridiculous idea about the phial of
breast milk seems to have some basis in reality.

'Who else is a member of this . . . brotherhood?' he asks.

'I can't tell you. I swore a vow.'

'You'd better, unless you want to be arrested for obstructing
a police enquiry.'

Justin rolls his eyes heavenward. 'Stanley Greenway is a

member and Larry Westmondham, the vicar here. Also Robin Rainsford, a theologian.'

'Why did you pretend to be in Ireland that week?'

'I wanted to go on retreat. There's a retreat house near the Slipper Chapel. I couldn't tell Cathbad, though I think he'd understand. We're sworn to secrecy, you see. I gave Cathbad a glow-in-the-dark statue and told him it came from Ireland. In fact I bought it at the Shrine Shop.'

'There's a piece of glass missing from the museum,' says Nelson. 'Is that anything to do with you?'

Now Justin looks really amazed. 'How did you know about that?'

'I have my methods,' says Nelson.

'I volunteer at the museum,' says Justin, 'and I found the glass in the basement, just stored in a box with bits of old stone and pottery. I thought it was possible that it was from a phial that had contained the Virgin's milk. Perhaps it was even the very phial that had sat on the high altar at the priory. And to see it kept in such a way, with no reverence, no respect! I took custody of it. We worship it as a holy relic.'

Nelson thinks 'I took custody of it' sounds a lot better than 'I stole it'. It never ceases to amaze him, the way people find comfortable language for uncomfortable actions. Justin has relaxed slightly, but he and the cat are both still looking at Nelson warily. As far as Nelson is concerned, Justin still has some explaining to do.

'What did you do after you left the service at the chapel?' he says.

'I went back to the retreat house,' says Justin. 'I had a simple meal and went to bed early.'

'And did you see Stanley Greenway during that time?'

'I said goodbye to him at the Slipper Chapel. I think he was going to walk through the fields back to the Sanctuary.'

Stanley Greenway certainly likes walking through fields, thinks Nelson. Was he walking home when he saw Chloe and attacked her? The material found on the hedge suggests that, at some point, Chloe was brought back to the chapel. Did Stanley bring her there to commune with the Madonna Lactans? He remembers Stanley saying that there was a statue that he liked at the Slipper Chapel. Justin had mentioned a statue too. He asks Justin.

'Yes,' says Justin. 'It's a beautiful work of art. It shows the Virgin Mary with blonde hair. I don't hold with all those modern depictions of her looking swarthy and dark. She was golden-haired, like an angel.'

And like Chloe Jenkins too, thinks Nelson. And Paula Moncrieff. He thinks of Stanley saying that Chloe used to meet her guardian angel at St Simeon's. But, of course, on that night, she had met someone else entirely.

It's just that he's still not sure who it was.

Nelson drives straight from St Simeon's Cottage to the Slipper Chapel. In contrast to his last visit, the place is absolutely heaving. The car park is jammed with tour buses, and there's an open-air mass going on. Nelson stands at the back, remembering bits of it: the sitting and the standing, the responses, the incense, the readings, the odd little ritual before the gospel reading when you are meant to trace a cross on your forehead, lips and chest. Nelson has to stop himself doing it with the rest of the congregation. He spots Father Bill at the altar. He's not the main priest, but seems to be assisting. In fact the altar is as crowded as the car park. Nelson counts five priests and ten altar servers (a job he once did, earning himself a bronze Guild of St Stephen medal). He wants to talk to Father Bill, so decides to stay for the rest of the service. It's quite soothing, standing there amongst the swaying crowd, feeling the soft early evening breeze as it ripples the altar clothes and the white robes of the priests.

After the homily, there is a movement amongst the congregation and several men rise and make their way to the altar. A vague memory starts to take shape in Nelson's mind and, as the men sit on a bench in front of the altar table and start to take off their shoes and socks, the memory crystallises and hardens. The Washing of the Feet. Before the Last Supper, Jesus is meant to have washed the disciples' feet. Peter, who gets everything wrong, protests, and Jesus promises him: 'One day you will understand . . . I have given you an example so that you may copy what I have done to you.' It's in the words of the reading that they have just heard. And, on Maundy Thursday masses, the priest washes the feet of twelve members of the congregation, in remembrance of this act of humility. Nelson remembers the ritual as embarrassing; the men with their callused, often dirty, feet, Father O'Brien fastidiously patting at them with a snowy white towel. The altar servers had to carry the bowl of water, not that any real washing was done. Pope Francis apparently went into a prison and washed the inmates' feet. He washed women prisoners' feet too. No women on the altar today, just as there are no women in the Brotherhood of the Madonna Lactans.

Finally the mass is over and the participants surge towards the car park. Nelson manages to catch Father Bill as he processes out.

'Can I have a word, Father?'

The priest looks round at the crowds, at the new pilgrims now taking their places at the benches in front of the altar.

'It won't take a minute,' says Nelson, 'but it could be important.'

'All right, but we've got another mass in twenty minutes. I'm concelebrating.'

'I'll be quick,' promises Nelson.

In Father Bill's office, under the gaze of the plaster Madonna, Nelson explains about the brotherhood that meets at the Slipper Chapel. Father Bill doesn't look surprised, and Nelson remembers that Justin implied that the priest knew about the group and didn't approve.

'I did know about it,' Father Bill confirms. 'You do often get things like this. Odd little devotions and so on. But this seemed a bit . . .' He pauses, looking up at the dusty ceiling.

'A bit what?'

'A bit extreme, I suppose. It's dangerous to make Our Lady into a living and breathing woman. It's dangerous to see her as our actual mother.'

'Dangerous?' says Nelson. 'That's an odd word to choose.'

'A woman is dead.' Father Bill looks at him steadily. 'Two women. I'd say it was dangerous.'

'Justin Fitzroy-Jones and Stanley Greenway were both here on the 19th February,' says Nelson. 'Did you see them?'

'I can't be sure, but it's fairly likely. They often come to early evening mass.'

'We've got footage of them leaving the service at five past six. Did you see them leave?'

'No. Sometimes, after mass, they go into one of the smaller chapels to pray.'

'And you don't go with them?'

'No.'

'You know that Stanley Greenway is under arrest for the murder of Chloe Jenkins?'

'Yes, I'm praying for him.'

'Did he ever say or do anything that made you feel that he could be a danger to women?'

'No. I knew that he was troubled, but I thought that he was a dreamer, a fantasist. I never would have thought that he could be violent.'

Fantasists can kill, thinks Nelson. In fact, they often kill when real life disappoints them by not living up to their fantasies. Was this the case with Stanley and Chloe?

'What about Justin Fitzroy-Jones?'

'He's an odd man, but I believe that he has a sincere faith.'

'He says he was at a retreat on the 19th.' Nelson will have to get this checked.

'It's possible. There is a retreat house near here.'

'What about the other men in the so-called brotherhood? Larry Westmondham and Robin Rainsford?'

'Larry I know slightly. He's a traditionalist, but his heart's in the right place. His wife is a very pleasant woman. She invited me to Sunday lunch once. Roast lamb and all the trimmings.'

Father Bill's voice is wistful as he says this. Is he regretting the absence of Sunday roasts in his life or something fundamentally more substantial, the right to a wife of his own?

'And Robin Rainsford?'

'He's a layman, a moderniser. Very committed to the cause of women priests.'

'Seems an unlikely person to be obsessed with the Madonna.'

'When you've been a priest for as long as I have, you cease to be surprised by people's obsessions.'

'You said that too much devotion to Our Lady was dangerous. Do you think that one of these men killed Chloe Jenkins?' Nelson notices himself using the title 'Our Lady'. Half an hour in the Slipper Chapel and he's turning back into a Catholic.

Father Bill looks up at the statue. 'I can't say,' he says slowly. 'But I do think that the Madonna is at the heart of it somehow.'

Nelson is looking at the statue too. 'Justin and Stanley both mentioned a statue that was important to them. Was it this one?'

'Yes,' says Father Bill. 'It's a fairly undistinguished Victorian work, but they fixated on it for some reason. Maybe because Mary has golden hair. Of course, most depictions of Mary nowadays show her with dark hair, which is ethnically more convincing. There was a real outcry when they put up a modern statue of a fair-haired Mary in Ely Cathedral recently.'

But the brotherhood liked the blonde Mary. Was this covert racism or something even more sinister? Nelson doesn't think that Father Bill can answer this question. The bells are ringing and mass is starting again. Nelson leaves Father Bill to prepare. But, instead of going straight back to the car park, he takes a detour to the Slipper Chapel. It's empty, perhaps because everyone is at the open-air mass. But Father Bill was right; the tiny room is blazing with light from hundreds of candles, some of them newly lit, some burnt almost to their wicks. Nelson takes a piece of paper from the pile by the door. After a second's thought, he writes the names of his daughters. Laura. Rebecca. Katie. Then he puts the paper in the box in front of the altar, offering up his intentions.

When he gets back to his car, his phone is still plugged in and he has a missed call from Ruth.

'Ruth. It's Nelson. You called me.'

'What's that noise in the background?'

'Just some hymns.'

'Some *hymns*?'

'I'm at the Slipper Chapel in Walsingham.'

'Oh.' He hears Ruth digest this. 'I hope this isn't a bad time. It's just that something's come up.'

'Is it about that letter sent to Hilary Smithson? Cathbad already told me about it.'

'No. It's about another letter actually.'

'Hilary's had another letter?'

'No. This one was sent to Freya Drew-Hayes. Another one of the women priests who was on the course at St Catherine's.'

'Freya . . . The miserable-looking one I met yesterday?'

'I don't know what you mean.' Nelson suspects Ruth knows exactly what he means, but she's not going to admit it in her present mood. 'Anyway Freya's in Walsingham for the Passion Play. A letter was hand-delivered to her today. It looks to me like it was sent by the same person who wrote to Hilary.'

'Does he want to meet her at three o'clock tomorrow too?'

'No, but he says God will strike her down in her wickedness.'

'And she didn't think to call the police? What's wrong with these people?'

'What do you mean, "these people"? Women or women priests?'

Nelson thinks it's best to ignore this. 'What else did the letter say?'

'Something about Good Friday and not being worthy. And there's a quote from *Macbeth*.'

'But you think it's from the same person.'

'Yes, I do. It was addressed to "Dear Jezebel".'

Nelson is silent for a few minutes and Ruth says, 'So this must mean that Stanley Greenway can't have written the letters.'

'Leave the policing to me, Ruth.'

'I'm only too happy to.'

Another silence. Nelson tries for a conciliatory tone. 'Do me a favour, Ruth, stay away from Walsingham tomorrow.

It's probably nothing, but there's obviously someone rather disturbed wandering around.'

Ruth laughs and, for a moment, Nelson thinks that it's all right again. Ruth has forgiven him and they can go back to their previous spiky but affectionate relationship. Then Ruth says, in a hard, tight voice, 'Why would I want to do you a favour?'

# CHAPTER 26

*18<sup>th</sup> April 2014, Good Friday*

Walsingham is already buzzing with activity by the time that Ruth arrives at one o'clock. The streets are full of robed people, not just priests, monks and nuns, but also sundry apostles and residents of first-century Jerusalem. Ruth has to park her car some way out of the village and, as she walks, she sees more men with tea-towels on their heads than she would have thought humanly possible. Women too, and children, some with wings and halos, and even a patient-looking donkey or two. But even the thought of how much Kate would enjoy seeing a real-life donkey does not make her wish she had brought her daughter with her. She thinks of the line in the last letter that was sent to Hilary: 'You would not heed my warnings', and of the threat wrapped up in the quotation from *Macbeth*: 'then you will be heard no more'. No, Kate is much safer with Sandra.

She is meeting Cathbad at The Bull Inn, where they are having lunch. Cathbad has booked a table, knowing that the place will be heaving. 'We don't want to end up with no room at the inn,' he said, 'although that has a biblical precedent, of course.'

Ruth has to fight her way through a regular army of apostles to get into the pub. Inside she can see more tea-towels, as well as a man apparently dressed as Herod. Does he even come into this bit of the story?

Cathbad is sitting at a corner table under a noticeboard crammed with Technicolor saints and sepia photographs of priests. The whole place is beginning to make Ruth feel rather anxious. She was never, for one moment, going to stay away because Nelson told her to, but, all the same, it is a rather frightening feeling that somewhere amongst the robed hoards there is the person who wrote to Freya 'Beware, for the Lord sees into your soul. He will strike you down in your wickedness'. Don't be stupid, she tells herself. The letter-writer is probably not the same person as the murderer and Nelson knows all about it: the place will be swarming with police. But, looking around, she can see disciples, angels, Mary and Joseph – but nobody in police uniform.

Still, Cathbad has already got her a glass of red wine, which does help. He fights his way through the disciples to order them two roast beef sandwiches.

'I thought there were only twelve apostles,' says Ruth, when he gets back.

'There are twelve apostles in the Passion Play,' says Cathbad. 'This lot are just the audience. They like to come dressed up.'

'Are the rest professional actors?'

'Some of them. I think Jesus and some of the main people are professionals. The rest are just keen amateurs. You heard Justin saying that he was Pontius Pilate.'

'That's a good part.'

'The best. Some great lines. "Truth? What is that?" Fabulous stuff.'

That's not quite how Ruth would describe it, but she knows that the crucifixion makes terrific drama. Even in the Nissen hut where her parents get to grips with being 'born again', they can't deny the power of the story. She remembers, as a child, watching Zefferelli's *Jesus of Nazareth*. It probably delayed her coming out as an atheist for a few years. Who played Pontius Pilate in that?

'Rod Steiger,' says Cathbad. 'He was incredible. I remember watching it in Ireland. Of course, Robert Powell was far too western-looking to be Jesus. There's no way He would have had blue eyes.'

'Rather lovely blue eyes, as I remember,' says Ruth. 'That intense stare. I was still nominally a Christian at the time and it had a great effect on me. Mind you, I was probably going through puberty, which didn't help.'

'It's all connected,' says Cathbad. 'Religion and sex. Birth and copulation and death. Speaking of which, I've been reading the letters.'

Ruth had been rather surprised when Hilary had given Cathbad the letters yesterday, saying that she would value his opinion. She wasn't surprised that the two had got on so well – religious people always liked Cathbad – but it seemed odd that Hilary, who refused to involve the police, was so willing to involve a part-time druid whom she had only just met. Ruth wonders what Hilary would say if she knew that Cathbad had told Nelson about her plan to meet the letter-writer today.

'What did you think?' she asks.

'I found them very disturbing,' says Cathbad. 'All that hatred, both towards Hilary and towards women in general. All that religious feeling, which should be a force for good, turned inwards.'

'Is religion ever a force for good?' asks Ruth.

'Well God is love,' says Cathbad, 'and love is always good.'

Is it? wonders Ruth, thinking of the times when she has witnessed crimes committed in the name of love. Thinking, too, of the times when love has led her to places that she would rather not revisit. She doesn't say this to Cathbad, though, and they are both momentarily distracted by the arrival of their sandwiches. It might not be as powerful as love, but food is pretty important too.

'Look who's here, scoffing away in a dark corner.'

Ruth looks up, embarrassed, as ever, to be caught in the act of eating. (*Scoffing?*) They are being addressed by a tall man in a dark-blue robe and a red headdress. The costume is professional in the extreme – not a tea-towel in sight – and it is a few minutes before Ruth recognises DS Dave Clough.

'Dave! What are you doing here?'

'I'm undercover, aren't I?' says Clough, pulling a chair over to their table. 'I'm an apostle.'

'Which one?' asks Cathbad.

'The most important one,' says Clough. 'Who's the most important apostle?'

'Peter,' says Cathbad. 'On this rock I will build my church.'

'I can't be Peter,' says Clough, 'they've got a proper actor for him. John too. I'll be one of the others.'

'Andrew?' suggests Cathbad. 'Matthias? Philip? Bartholomew?'

'Bartholomew,' says Clough. 'I like that.'

'So what are you doing, Bartholomew?' asks Ruth. In the background a woman in purple robes is looking vainly for her chair.

'Keeping an eye on your friend Hilary,' says Clough. 'Apparently she's meeting some nutter at three o'clock. The boss told me to stick to her like glue. She's an apostle as well, so it's easy. Cassie got me the gear, her theatre company's involved in this malarkey. Cassie's Mary Magdalene.'

That figures, thinks Ruth. She's only met Cassandra a few times, but she looks the type who would grab the only glamorous part in the gospels.

'Is Nelson coming?' she asks.

'He said he'd be here,' says Clough. 'Of course, we've got the killer, but we still want to catch the letter-writer bloke.'

'What if you've got the wrong man?' asks Cathbad.

'Oh, you would think he's innocent,' says Clough. 'You always think everyone's innocent. Greenway's the killer, mark my words.'

Cathbad is about to answer, but a diversion is caused by

Mary Magdalene appearing and enfolding Bartholomew in a passionate embrace.

Nelson is planning to set out for Walsingham when he gets a message that Stanley Greenway wants to speak to him. Clough and Tim are already mingling with the crowds at the Passion Play. Clough had assured Nelson that Cassandra would provide costumes for the two policemen.

'You can be the only black apostle,' Clough told Tim.

'Simon of Cyrene was black,' said Tim.

'Who was he when he was at home?'

'The man who helped Jesus carry His cross.'

Nelson remembers what Tim had said about his mother, that her life revolved around the church. Clearly some biblical knowledge has rubbed off.

Despite it being a bank holiday, the team are working full strength. They still haven't made an official arrest for Paula's murder and all non-essential leave has been cancelled. Nelson finds Tanya in the incident room.

'Come on. We're going to prison.'

Stanley is being held in a remand prison just outside Norwich. It's a Victorian building, not unlike the Sanctuary in appearance, and not unpleasant on this bright spring day. As they pass through the two checkpoints the guards nod at Nelson, but give Tanya covertly appraising glances. He sees her noticing and wants to apologise for this sexist behaviour, but doesn't know how to start the conversation. Better leave it. Tanya's a professional, after all.

Stanley is sitting with Nirupa Khan in the visitors' room.

He's still wearing his tracksuit – remand prisoners are allowed to wear their own clothes – and actually looks calmer and better fed than he did in the Sanctuary.

'I've remembered something,' he says in greeting.

'I'll be looking for some recognition of my client's co-operation,' says Nirupa.

Nelson ignores her. 'What have you remembered?' he asks Stanley.

'I went to the service at the Slipper Chapel,' he says. 'There's a group of us and we have a special relationship with the Madonna.'

'The Madonna Lactans,' says Nelson.

Nirupa looks at him in surprise, but Stanley just smiles and nods. 'Exactly so. Well after the service I went to walk back to the Sanctuary across the fields. I love walking in the open air. Then, I don't know, it all went black and Chloe was lying there at my feet.'

Nelson shifts impatiently. He's heard all this before. *Then it all went black.* Does Stanley take him for an idiot?

'What's this new information you have for us, Stanley?' he asks. 'I haven't come here for the good of my health.'

Stanley smiles his vague, irritating smile. 'There was a smell.'

'A smell?'

'Yes, like incense. I always use incense in my services. The smoke rising up, like our prayers rise up to God. Some of my parishioners complained. They thought it was too High Church . . .'

His voice drifts away, perhaps thinking of other things that his parishioners complained about. Nelson's mind is racing. Michelle said that the man who attacked her smelt of body odour, soap and joss sticks. Joss sticks are a kind of incense. But these aromas could have come from Stanley himself. After all, he had just come from a Catholic service where, presumably, incense was being wafted all over the place. What's the incense thing called? Memories of his altar-serving days come back to him. The thurible. He'd enjoyed swinging the thurible.

'Anything else?' he asks. 'Anything about Paula Moncrieff, for example?'

Stanley blinks at him. 'Paula who?'

Nelson gives up.

Cathbad and Ruth follow the crowds towards the abbey gate. Clough and Cassandra have gone for a last-minute cast briefing in the church.

'I don't envy the person who explains the Stations of the Cross to Dave Clough,' says Cathbad.

'Or tells him that he can't be Bartholomew.'

There are so many people at the gate that it takes a few minutes to pass through. Once inside, Ruth thinks how different the grounds look from that day in February when she walked amongst the snowdrops with Hilary. The snowdrops have gone, and the grass is already being churned into mud by the footsteps of the faithful. The vast archway still dominates the scene, but now, in front of it, there's a platform with a huge wooden cross. The cross casts a shadow over the crowd as they gather by the platform where the first station is due to be enacted.

'So dramatic,' breathes Cathbad. But the whole thing seems rather nightmarish to Ruth: the cross, the crowds, the gloomy music that is blaring out from loudspeakers high in the trees. She can't shake the thought that something awful is about to happen – apart from the crucifixion, that is.

'The first station is right by the site of the holy house,' she says. 'How is the letter-writer going to meet Hilary with all these people about?'

'They'll have moved off by then,' says Cathbad. 'The stations are dotted all over the grounds.'

'But they come back here at three,' says Ruth. 'For that.' She gestures at the cross.

'Maybe everyone will be so caught up in the drama that they won't notice one of the disciples slipping away,' says Cathbad. 'Of course, in the scriptures the whole lot of them up and run.'

'You know a lot about scripture for a druid.'

'I was brought up a Catholic, as you know. And I love the stories. It's an essential human act, telling stories.'

As long as you don't make the mistake of believing them, thinks Ruth, as she follows Cathbad to the first station.

Nelson and Tanya drive straight to Walsingham. Well, straight isn't quite the word, as the journey across Norfolk is convoluted and frustrating. Every time Nelson takes a side road, it is blocked by a tractor or slow-moving holiday traffic. His temper isn't helped by Tanya yacking on about the case. 'Does he think Stanley Greenway is insane? Could Greenway have had an accomplice? What about Justin Fitzroy-Jones? Or that woman, Jean Something, in the Sanctuary?' Eventually, to shut her up, Nelson switches on the radio. It's R.E.M, a band he likes, but Tanya starts singing along so he turns it off.

'Was that the first time you've been to the prison?' he asks.

'No,' says Tanya. 'I've been there to conduct post-arrest interviews.'

'The atmosphere can be a bit intimidating,' says Nelson, thinking of the guards and the way they'd looked at Tanya.

'I don't care about men staring at me,' says Tanya. 'If they keep on, I just tell them that I'm gay.'

'Why would you say that?' asks Nelson.

'Because I am.'

Nelson knows he should say something, to show that he's not embarrassed (he is embarrassed), to show that this is all in a day's work for the modern, twenty-first-century policeman.

'Have you got a . . . a partner?' That's the best he can do.

Tanya beams. 'Yes. Her name's Petra. She's a PE teacher. We're thinking of getting married next year. Perhaps Hilary Smithson could conduct the service. It would be nice to have a woman priest.'

That's not a view shared by everyone, thinks Nelson. Someone out there thinks women priests are a very bad idea indeed. And it's not necessarily Stanley Greenway.

'If you don't want this known at work,' he says, 'you can count on my discretion.'

'Oh, I think they've all guessed,' says Tanya. 'Apart from you and Clough.'

The rest of the journey passes in silence.

It's nearly two o'clock when they arrive in Walsingham. The Passion Play is due to start at two and people are pouring through the main gates into the abbey grounds. Nelson parks on a double yellow line and hurries to join them. Like Ruth, he is slightly thrown by the number of people in costume. He'd assumed that only the participants would be dressed up, and that it would be easy to spot Hilary as one of the disciples. But almost everyone seems to be in robes and some sort of headdress. They are all moving in the same direction, so Nelson follows, feeling uneasy. He hates crowds. So much potential for crime in a crowd – even a holy one like this.

Tanya veers off and comes back with a printed sheet. 'Apparently we walk around the grounds for the different scenes,' she says. 'It's called the Stations of the Cross. Does that make sense to you?'

'I think so,' says Nelson. He remembers walking in a procession around the sooty church where they had worshipped in Blackpool. A prayer at each station, wood-carvings so crude that it was hard to tell which was Jesus and which was the cross. A swing of the thurible, a bit of chanting. He thinks of Stanley Greenway saying, 'I always use incense in my services. The smoke rising up, like our prayers rise up to God.' There's something here that he's not quite getting. What is it?

'I think the first one's over here,' says Tanya. 'Where the platform is. It's called "Jesus is Sentenced to Death".'

'How many stations are there?' It's quite a few, he remembers that much.

'Fourteen.'

A large crowd has already gathered around the raised platform. It's very near the site of the holy house, notes Nelson, and close to the giant cross where – presumably – the procession will end. Tanya and Nelson stand at the back, Tanya on tiptoe, anxious not to miss anything, Nelson looking around for potential murderers.

'After this,' he tells Tanya, 'you move on with the rest of the crowd. I'll stay here.'

'OK, boss.'

He has told Clough not to let Hilary out of his sight, so, if she tries to slope off for her assignation, Clough should be close behind. Tim won't be far away either. It's hard to see how anyone can manage to have an assignation in the middle of such a crowd, but Nelson doesn't want to take any chances. He texts Clough: '*R u in place?*' In a few seconds he gets a text back: '*Yes. Feeling holly.*' He hopes this is a predictive-text misspelling of 'holy'.

He scans the crowd, searching for familiar faces. He thinks he sees Father Bill, the custodian of the Slipper Chapel, as well as people he vaguely recognises from his daughters' schools and Michelle's work. Then, standing on the very edge of the crowd, he sees a tall grey-haired figure. Father Hennessey. Is Fiona McAllister with him? It doesn't seem so. The priest appears to be on his own; his face is sombre, deep in thought.

'Nelson!' Nelson swings round to see two very familiar, but definitely not welcome, faces. Cathbad and Ruth. Cathbad is wearing a purple robe, but, of course, in this setting he blends in nicely. Ruth is wearing jeans and an embarrassed expression.

'I thought I told you two to keep away.'

'We're not living in a police state yet,' says Cathbad serenely. 'We're here to see the Passion Play.'

'Bollocks. You're interfering in my investigation.'

'We felt compelled to be here,' says Cathbad.

'Bollocks,' says Nelson again. A mother with two young children gives him a reproving look. 'Stay away from Hilary Smithson or you could ruin everything. I've got it covered.'

'Yes, we know,' says Cathbad. 'We've seen Clough in costume.'

Nelson turns to Ruth. 'I wouldn't have thought that this was your idea of a fun day out, Ruth.'

Ruth raises her eyebrows, but her retort is silenced by a sudden blast of trumpet music. 'Shh,' says the mother with the children, 'it's starting.'

The music stops and the crowd parts to allow a group to pass through. 'The disciples,' says someone. The disciples pause near Nelson and Peter and John start speaking. You can tell who the professional actors are. John, dressed in pinkish robes, is almost ridiculously handsome, and Peter is emoting away as he denies Christ three times. The extras are less convincing. They include Hilary Smithson and Robin Rainsford, as well as Clough and Tim. Nelson also spots Freya Drew-Hayes, the woman who received a poison-pen letter yesterday. Obviously, this is a progressive group of disciples that admits women. Freya looks grim, but Nelson suspects that this is her usual expression. Does the fact that she received a letter – hand-delivered, no less – mean that the writer is very close, amongst this crowd in fact? After all, he or she is planning to meet Hilary Smithson in less than an hour's time.

Nelson does a quick disciple count. Why are there only eleven of them? Oh yes, Judas must already have betrayed Christ and deserted the cause. He commits suicide, Nelson seems to remember. Sister Anthony used to say that Judas's worst crime was not believing in the possibility of forgiveness. But then she said a lot of things. The loudspeakers blare out with the sound of a cock crowing. Peter falls to his knees. John turns away, covering his face. The other disciples attempt to look concerned/frightened/sad. All except Clough, who is grinning and has his mobile out. Still, at least he is still close to Hilary. Tim, in dark robes, looks the most serious of the lot. Pity he's not playing Judas. Now that would be good casting.

Peter, his big scene done, disappears into the crowd. The other apostles process to the platform and arrange themselves on the steps. Only John, his face anguished, is still acting. Hilary is smiling at someone in the crowd, and Clough is taking pictures with his phone. A trumpet blast, and a man in purple appears on the stage and takes his seat. It's a few seconds before Nelson recognises Justin playing Pontius Pilate. There's a moment's silence, and then a man in white robes steps onto the stage. This must be the actor playing Jesus. Nelson is too far away to hear the words, but he's surprised at how effective it is: the man in white standing in front of the seated Roman prelate, the crowds, the birds singing.

Then Pilate points, and Jesus is led away. He walks back through the crowds between two Roman soldiers. The apostles follow, and then, at a discreet distance, the audience. On to the next station, where it says: 'Jesus Is Given His Cross to Carry'.

Tanya, Cathbad and Ruth all move away, but Nelson stays where he is. He doesn't want to leave the holy house site. It feels oddly peaceful now that the crowds have gone.

'Hallo, DCI Nelson.' Nelson turns and sees a woman with a pushchair. She has a dog on a lead and is accompanied by another robed man. Daisy and Larry Westmondham.

'Hallo,' says Nelson, bending to pat the dog. He turns to Larry, who seems uncomfortable in brown robes that look like they were meant for someone bigger. 'Aren't you part of this affair?'

'I'm Joseph of Arimethea,' says Larry. 'I don't come in until the end.'

'I love the Passion Play,' says Daisy. 'Becky, our oldest, is in the children's choir, but I thought I'd better keep my distance. Samuel can be a bit noisy and Lulu gets overexcited in crowds.'

Lulu's the dog, Nelson remembers. She always seemed slightly mad to him and is now panting enthusiastically, straining at her leash.

'Why are you here, Inspector?' asks Larry. 'I wouldn't have thought this was your sort of thing.'

This is effectively what Nelson has just said to Ruth, but that doesn't stop him feeling obscurely offended. 'I thought it would be worth seeing,' he says. 'I was brought up a Catholic.'

'I didn't know that.'

'I'm going to catch them up,' says Daisy, 'I don't want to

miss the singing. You won't forget to bring Becky home, will you, darling? I have to leave early to collect Lizzie and Victoria.'

'I won't forget,' says Larry. Nelson thinks that he wouldn't bet on it.

Daisy says goodbye and sets off, bumping the pushchair over the grass, the panting spaniel at her side.

'Your wife,' says Nelson, 'is a very nice lady.'

'Yes,' says Larry, 'she is. Funny thing, she reminds me of my mother sometimes.'

Larry hurries off after his wife, his brown robes billowing, leaving Nelson wondering why he finds this last remark quite so unsettling.

As he watches the vicar rounding the corner by the trees, Nelson's phone rings. It's Michelle.

'Harry! Please come home. I think he's back. The man who attacked me.'

# CHAPTER 27

*Good Friday, afternoon*

It's half an hour's drive from Walsingham to Nelson's house on the outskirts of King's Lynn, but he does it in twenty minutes, siren on, lights flashing. He screeches to a halt outside his house to find Michelle waiting in the doorway.

'What is it? Have you seen someone hanging around the house?'

As he speaks he scans the cul-de-sac. It's a sunny afternoon, so several of his neighbours are outside, mowing their lawns and getting barbecues out of garages. It's hard to see how any sinister stranger could infiltrate this cosy, suburban scene.

'Look at this.' Michelle is holding out her phone. There's a message on the screen. *I'm coming back for you.*

'Who's it from?'

'Caller unknown.' Michelle, who was so brave about an actual physical attack, is white and shaking.

'I can trace the number,' says Nelson. 'Mobile phones have a unique number that they send out when they make a call.

I'll be able to trace it to its local base.' He's already dialling the station.

'He's coming back for me.' Michelle grabs his arm. 'I'm sure it's the man in the graveyard.'

'It's OK, love.' Nelson steers her to the sofa. 'I'll look after you. I'll get someone to stay with you.'

Michelle grabs hold of him again; her eyes look almost wild. 'No! I want *you* to stay.'

Nelson is talking to Tom Henty. 'I need a trace on a phone. Here's the number . . . and I need someone to come here and guard my wife. Really? Are you sure? There's no one else? OK. Send him at once.'

Nelson crouches down in front of his wife. 'I'm getting a policeman to come and stay in the house.'

'Why can't you stay?'

'I'm in the middle of an undercover operation. But I won't leave until he gets here.'

Michelle seems to accept this. She leans back against the cushions, her eyes closed.

'I'll make you some tea,' says Nelson. 'A proper cup, not that crap you like.'

Michelle smiles faintly. 'Just some water would be nice.'

In the kitchen Nelson checks that the back door is locked. Then he goes upstairs and does a quick sweep of all the rooms, shutting all the windows. Going back into the kitchen, he pours water from the purifier into one of Michelle's favourite glasses. When he comes back into the sitting room, Michelle is replaiting her hair. He takes this to be a good sign. Her face has lost some of its pallor too.

'Who's coming from the station?' she asks. 'Anyone I know?'

'Roy Taylor.'

'Is he the one you call Rocky?'

'That's right.'

'Isn't he meant to be stupid?'

'No,' lies Nelson. 'That's someone else.'

Thank God Michelle never pays attention when Nelson talks about work, otherwise she would have heard him describe Rocky as 'proof that evolution works both ways'. Nelson just prays that he's smart enough to watch a house.

After her initial doubts, Ruth is surprised to find herself enjoying the Passion Play. It is pleasant to walk through the abbey grounds with Cathbad at her side. It's nice to be with such a good-natured, friendly group of people, moving back to let children get to the front, listening to the actors in respectful silence. And, though this is harder to admit to herself, she is finding the play itself rather moving. It's one thing to hear – in her parents' Nissen hut, for example – that Jesus carried His own cross, quite another to see the actor lifting the heavy piece of wood and carrying it, with obvious difficulty, through the watching crowds. When Simon of Cyrene steps forward to help him bear the weight, an audible sigh runs through the audience. And when the actor takes his place in front of the cross, arms uplifted, and the children's choir sings 'There is a green hill far away', their voices sweet and fragmented in the open air, she has to turn her head away so that Cathbad won't see the stupid tears in her eyes.

They are nearly at the end now. She looks at her watch. Ten to three. Saint John, the Virgin Mary and Mary Magdalene (Cassandra, wearing a dress that owes much to the character's origins as a prostitute) stand at the foot of the cross. The actor playing Jesus still has his arms outstretched, and the choir sings something about Jesus remembering us. Ruth looks across at the apostles standing a little way away. Although the gospels tell a different story, in this version Jesus's followers are all present at His death. Clough is easy to recognise in his red headdress. He's also the only disciple looking at his iPhone. Tim is there too, in dark-green homespun, his eyes downcast. What is he thinking? wonders Ruth. Is he regretting everything that has happened with Michelle or is he just concentrating on the job in hand? Tim is hard to read at the best of times. She suppresses the ignoble thought that it's hard to see what two complex, intelligent men can see in Michelle. She must have hidden depths, that's all. Ruth sometimes suspects that she, herself, has hidden shallows.

Hilary is standing near Clough. As Ruth watches, she too glances down at her wrist. Then, with a quick look around her, she starts to walk away.

'Jesus remember me,' sings the choir, 'when you come into your kingdom.'

Ruth looks at Cathbad, and they start to make their way out of the crowd. It's hard to do this surreptitiously. The play is nearing its climax and people are standing, or kneeling in prayer. Ruth apologises as she trips over one pair of legs after another. She hears someone say 'Jesus!' in a distinctly unreligious way. When they are finally free they hurry to the place where the holy house once stood. It's only a few hundred yards from the main stage, but the neat square of grass is completely deserted.

Clough runs towards them, holding up his skirts. 'Did you see where she went?'

'No.' Ruth looks around helplessly, but they are in the open, there's nowhere to hide.

Suddenly a bell rings and people in the crowd start to fall to their knees. Three o'clock. The bell continues to toll, and, appropriately enough, a cloud passes over the sun. Tim appears from a southerly direction. 'She was seen going out of the gate,' he says.

'Which way did she go?' says Clough.

'She turned left, they thought.'

'Come on!' Clough pulls off his headdress and starts towards the exit.

'Hang on,' says Cathbad. The bell stops suddenly, and his voice carries further than he intended. Several of the crowd look round disapprovingly.

'The holy house,' says Cathbad, in a lower voice, 'it could be somewhere else.'

'Where?' says Clough. 'Almost everywhere in this bloody place is holy.'

'I remember Justin saying something to me about his cottage. You know, the place next to St Simeon's. "This is a holy house," he said.'

'Justin?' says Tim. 'The man who owns the cottage? Isn't he in the play?'

'He was here at the beginning,' says Cathbad. 'He's not here now.'

Ruth looks back towards the stage. The characters are still frozen in tableaux. Pontius Pilate is nowhere to be seen.

'Do you really think it could be Justin?' says Ruth.

Cathbad nods. 'That was the thing that really disturbed me about the letters. They sounded like they were written by someone I knew.'

Nelson reaches Walsingham just as the bell starts ringing. The high street is deserted, but, as he parks, he sees a woman with a pushchair hurrying up the road, tugging a reluctant spaniel behind her. Daisy Westmondham, obviously late for her two younger daughters. As he watches, she takes the track by the farm shop. Nelson has a ridiculous urge to call after her, to tell her to be careful. Why? It's broad daylight in a Norfolk village. Anyway, she has the dog to protect her. Not that Lulu seems much of a guard dog. As he thinks this, another dog approaches, a small furry creature barking angrily. Francis, patron saint of animals, taking Bella Hendred for a walk. Anxious to avoid talking to her, Nelson hurries towards the abbey entrance. With any luck, Clough will have intercepted the letter-writer by now.

But, as Nelson passes the gift shop, he sees his two sergeants, still in their robes, running through the archway. They are followed by Cathbad and Ruth.

'What the hell . . .?'

'St Simeon's Cottage,' says Clough, not breaking stride.

'Where's Hilary Smithson?' says Nelson. But the three men

have run past him, and he is forced to address the question to Ruth.

'She got away,' pants Ruth. 'Cathbad thinks she might be at the cottage. With Justin.'

Nelson opens his mouth to speak, but, thinking better of it, turns and follows his officers. Ruth trots after him.

In the background the crowd are chanting the Lord's Prayer.

Daisy doesn't know why she is so worried. Lizzie and Victoria are spending the afternoon with their friends Grace and Ella and won't mind at all if she's a bit late. Grace and Ella's parents are the laid-back type too. They are probably all out in the garden, enjoying the bank holiday sunshine. There's a treehouse and a swing; Lizzie and Victoria won't be in any hurry to leave. In fact, last time Victoria had said, embarrassingly, 'I wish our house was like yours.' Grace's mother had been understanding: 'All children say things like that. I'm sure you like your home best.' Daisy wouldn't bet on it. Victoria's views on lifestyle are already diametrically opposed to her mother's. Victoria announced the other day that, when she was grown up she was going to have a 'flat with glass all round and no children in it'.

So why is Daisy hurrying along the lane behind the farm, bumping poor Samuel over the ruts and potholes? Partly because she doesn't want to hear, as she hears so often, 'Daisy's late again', or see the look that goes with this statement, half-affectionate, half-irritated. She's going to be the kind of calm, composed mother who's always first at the school gates and always has plasters and wet wipes in her bag. She stops because she's lost a shoe. Lulu whines and pulls at the lead. Daisy would like to let her off the lead, but, last time, Lulu ran four miles across country and had to be brought back by a farmer in his trailer.

'Stop it, Lulu. We're nearly home.'

She gets her shoe on and looks at her watch. Ten past three. Damn, she told Victoria that she would be there at three, and, even if Victoria is enjoying herself in the tree-house, she'll still have one eye on the clock.

'Come on, Lulu.' At least Samuel has, miraculously, fallen asleep. Daisy opens the gate to the field and shoves the push-chair through. Then she follows with Lulu and turns to shut the gate. As she does so, she sees a figure hurrying along the path by the farm. Nothing strange in that – it's a public foot-path, after all – but for some reason the approaching figure makes Daisy feel uneasy. She watches as the person (it's too far away to tell if it's a man or woman) skirts the farm build-ings and continues on the track she has just taken, moving quickly. Daisy grips the wooden bars of the gate, the clouds are scudding over the grass, giving her the odd feeling that the world is moving and she is standing still.

She takes hold of the pushchair. This field is full of rape-seed, stinging yellow against the blue sky. But, there's a path running through it and, at the far side, she can see the back of her house and, further up the hill, the palatial garden belonging to Grace and Ella. She can even hear children's voices, very clear on the still air. It reminds her of the choir, earlier. 'There is a green hill far away, without a city wall.'

How beautifully they had sung. She sets off again, almost running now, Lulu silent at her side.

Ruth knew she should have carried on going to the gym. There's a slight hill towards St Simeon's, but even that's enough to make her slow to a walk. By the time she gets to the cottage the door is swinging open and all four men are inside. She has no idea whether Clough and Tim kicked the door down, but, as she stands for a second on the doorstep, she can hear raised voices and a rather sickening thump. She dreads what she will find inside.

What she finds are Clough, Tim, Cathbad and Nelson standing almost helplessly as Hilary kneels in front of them, pinning Justin's head to the floor. On the sofa a black cat is washing itself, oblivious.

'You see,' Hilary says, when she sees Ruth, 'I told you I was a black belt in taekwondo.'

'I think you might be killing him,' says Ruth.

'No. He can still breathe.'

Ruth is not so sure about this. Justin's face is turning blue. Nelson obviously thinks the same thing because he says, 'Let him go now, Doctor Smithson. We've got this.'

With obviously reluctance, Hilary loosens her grip and stands up. Justin remains on the floor, gasping and choking. Tim kneels beside him and helps him onto the sofa. Cathbad disappears and comes back with a glass of water.

'Now, Doctor Smithson,' says Nelson. 'Perhaps you could tell us what's happening here.'

Hilary sits on an armchair, looking perfectly composed.

She holds out her hand for the water, although Ruth is pretty sure that Cathbad meant it for Justin.

'I had a letter asking me to meet the writer at the holy house at three,' she says. 'I was pretty sure that meant here. It's often called the holy house in medieval records. But I let Ruth and Cathbad think that it meant the site of the holy house in the abbey grounds. Sorry,' she says to Ruth.

'You could have been killed,' says Ruth.

'Oh, I was almost certain that he wouldn't kill me,' says Hilary. 'When I got here, Justin was sitting in this chair. I asked him if he wrote the letters, he said yes, and I got him in a headlock.' She smiles sweetly, smoothing out her robes.

Nelson turns to Justin. 'Did you write the letters?'

Justin massages his throat for a minute, and then he says, 'It's sacrilege for a woman to call herself a priest. Women are called to motherhood, not the priesthood.'

'The Church is our mother,' says Hilary. 'A loving, gentle mother.'

'With a black belt in taekwondo,' suggests Ruth. Nelson gives her a look.

'You should be at home with your child,' Justin tells Hilary, still rubbing his neck.

'I'm called to serve God,' says Hilary, 'why can't you understand that?'

'Let's get this straight,' says Nelson. 'Mr Fitzroy-Jones, you wrote a series of malicious letters to Doctor Smithson.'

'I met her when she came to a talk at the museum,' says Justin. 'She seemed to represent everything that I deplore about women priests.'

Ruth thinks that Hilary looks rather proud to hear this. She takes a thoughtful sip of water.

'So you sent her threatening letters?' says Nelson.

'They weren't threatening,' says Justin, 'they were meant to point out the error of her ways.'

'I've read them,' says Nelson. 'They sounded pretty threatening to me. You also sent her a letter asking her to meet you today. In that letter you said you'd explain why Chloe and Paula had to die.'

Hilary looks reproachfully at Ruth. 'You told him about the letter.'

'I told him,' said Cathbad. He is sitting on the window seat. As Ruth watches, the cat comes up to him and rubs against his legs.

'What did you mean by saying you'd explain about the murders of Chloe and Paula?' says Nelson.

'I know why they died,' says Justin, 'but I didn't kill them.'

'You don't have an alibi for either murder,' says Nelson. 'I'd start talking if I were you.'

'He has an alibi for Chloe's murder,' says Cathbad. 'He was in Ireland.'

'No, Cathbad,' says Nelson. 'Justin lied to you. He was in Walsingham that night. We've got CCTV footage of him at the Slipper Chapel. He belongs to a secret society called the Brotherhood of the Madonna Lactans. They meet at the chapel.'

Lactans, thinks Ruth, that's breastfeeding isn't it? Is it possible that her hunch about the glass phial was correct?

Justin is looking apologetically at Cathbad. 'I'm sorry for lying to you,' he says.

Cathbad says nothing. He looks very shocked. The cat is still purring against his legs, and he strokes it mechanically.

'What did you mean by saying that you knew why the women had been murdered?' says Nelson again.

'I can't tell you.'

'You'd better,' says Nelson, 'if you don't want me to arrest you for the murder of two women.'

There's a silence, and then Justin says, looking out of the window, 'They were murdered because they were sinful. The first woman was a drug addict, the second was an actress.'

He says 'actress' like it is the most wicked profession imaginable. Ruth sees Clough stir angrily. She thinks about Freya, ascetic, severe Freya, with her dark clothing and hatred of ritual.

'Why did you write to Freya too?' she asks.

'She was like Doctor Smithson,' says Justin. 'She thought herself worthy to be a priest. The two of them came to the rehearsal yesterday, wanting to play apostles. Sacrilege. There were no female apostles.'

'What about Mary Magdalene?' cuts in Hilary. 'Most theologians concede that she was an apostle. She stood with the Virgin Mary at the foot of the cross. She was the first to see the risen Christ. And she was a prostitute. Jesus loves the outcasts of society. The drug addicts, the prostitutes.'

Ruth glances at Nelson, expecting him to break into this theological debate. Instead she is surprised to see that he is looking out of the window, towards the graveyard. His face has a look of frowning concentration that Ruth knows well.

'Boss?' says Clough at last.

Nelson turns. 'Tim, do you know where Doreen West-mondham was a dinner-lady?'

'I can't remember,' says Tim. 'But I think I made a note.' He gets out his phone. 'Yes, it was a boarding school in Sheringham.'

'Come on,' says Nelson to Clough. 'You come with me. Heathfield, you stay here. Ruth and Cathbad, go home.'

Ruth is still trying to find the words to protest at being spoken to in such a way when the door slams behind Nelson.

# CHAPTER 28

Daisy hears the field gate open and shut. Lulu turns and barks loudly. 'Come on,' says Daisy pulling at her lead. Now is not the time for Lulu to develop bravery. Daisy keeps moving. Samuel's head lolls as the pushchair rattles along. Could she take a short cut across the field? But the rapeseed grows high on either side, almost shoulder-height in places. She'd never get the pushchair through. She must just keep on the track. Keep right on till the end of the road. She contemplates singing, but, when she opens her mouth, only a croak comes out. She met Larry when she was singing in the choir at the church in Croydon where he was a deacon. On his days off they used to get a bus to the South Downs or the Pilgrims Way. They'd take a picnic and they'd walk for miles. Sometimes they'd sing as they walked, harmonising naturally, pop songs and favourite hymns. 'O lord my God, when I in awesome wonder consider all the works Thy hand has made.' In those days the countryside had seemed like heaven.

Daisy starts to jog. She always claims that walking everywhere has made her fit, but now she's out of breath in seconds, a stitch like a knife wound in her side. One of the soldiers plunged his spear into Jesus's side and at once blood and water poured out. The Passion Play seems years away. She stops. Silence, just a bird singing somewhere very high up. Blue sky, yellow flowers, like one of Victoria's paintings. Has her pursuer taken another path? Is she safe? Or have they stopped too? This last is somehow the most terrifying thought of all. She wants to look round, but finds she can't turn her head. She starts to run, faster than before, oblivious to the pain in her ribs. And, behind her, the footsteps start to run too.

For a few minutes Hilary, Cathbad, Ruth and Justin all stare at each other. In some ways, thinks Ruth, there is so much to say; in other ways, nothing at all. It is Tim who says, slightly apologetically, 'I expect you'll all be wanting to get on your way.'

Ruth looks at her watch. It's twenty past three. She has to collect Kate at four.

'I'd better be going,' she says. 'Cathbad?'

Cathbad is looking at his friend. 'How could you lie to me?' he says.

'I'm sorry,' says Justin. 'I didn't think you'd understand about the Madonna Lactans.'

'Don't I usually understand things like that? I'm a druid, remember. I understand the mystical.'

'You say you do,' says Justin, 'but underneath I think you're pretty hard-nosed, Cathbad. You're more like your friend Nelson than you think.'

Cathbad looks deeply hurt and doesn't reply.

'Goodbye, Justin,' says Hilary serenely, standing up. 'I hope we meet again.'

Justin stands too. As the two of them are still in biblical dress, it gives the moment a strange solemnity.

'I'm sorry if the letters frightened you,' says Justin.

'I wasn't frightened,' says Hilary. '"The Lord is my strength."'

And, with that, the three of them file out of the door.

Outside, they stand, uncertain, in the lane. People are streaming out of the abbey grounds, returning to cars and lodgings. The mood seems oddly cheerful, considering the drama that has just been re-enacted. Hilary too seems almost elated, humming under her breath. Ruth can't be absolutely sure that it isn't 'Onward, Christian Soldiers'. Cathbad, on the other hand, seems extremely depressed. For the first time since Ruth has known him, he looks too slight for his druid's robes, as if he's merely dressing up.

'I should have known,' he says. 'The cat's called Chesterton, after all.'

'You couldn't have known,' says Ruth. 'We can never know what people are really like.' She's thinking of Michelle and Tim, of Father Hennessey and Hilary. Of everyone, really.

'I'd better get home,' says Cathbad. 'Can I have a lift, Ruth?'

'Of course,' says Ruth. She notices that he brightens up at the thought of home. 'Let's fight our way through the pilgrims.'

Nelson and Clough are caught up in the crush at the main gates. 'Police,' shouts Nelson. 'Let us through.' This causes consternation as people try to get out of their way and end up creating more of a bottleneck.

'Call Fuller,' Nelson tells Clough. 'Find out where she is.'

Nelson pushes his way through and finds that the grounds are almost empty. The grass has been trampled into mud, and men in overalls are picking up litter. Clough is still trapped at the gate. Where the hell is Tanya? As he stabs impatiently at his phone he sees a familiar figure in brown coming towards him. It's Larry Westmondham, bald head gleaming, holding a girl of about ten – presumably his daughter – by the hand.

'There, you see,' he says to Nelson. 'I didn't forget her.'

'Yes, you did, Dad,' says the girl. 'Miss Lewis had to remind you.'

'Larry,' says Nelson. 'Have you seen Robin Rainsford?'

'Robin who? Oh, the teacher. Wasn't he one of the apostles?'

Thank God. Tanya is on the phone.

'Fuller. Where's Rainsford? Remember, I told you to keep an eye on him.'

Tanya sounds flustered. 'He left just before the end.'

'Didn't you follow him?'

'You told me not to leave the grounds.'

'Jesus.' Nelson turns back to the rather shocked Larry. 'Have you heard from your wife?'

'Daisy?' Larry's forehead crinkles. 'No. But she'll be collecting Lizzie and Victoria.'

'They're at the Hendersons',' says his daughter. 'Lucky things. They have ice pops in their freezer.'

'Do you know which way she will have gone?'

'She had the pushchair so she probably went by the road.'

'No,' says the daughter. 'She had Lulu, so she would have gone over the fields behind the farm. It's quicker that way too.'

'Can you show me?'

'Of course.' She skips forward happily, followed by her father, Nelson and, seconds later, a red-faced Tanya.

Tim is left alone with Justin. Of the two of them, Tim feels that he is the most embarrassed. Justin just sits there on the sofa. The cat jumps up and sits next to him. Tim finds the animal rather creepy, with its jet-black fur and green eyes. He is sure that his mother would say that a pure black cat was bad luck.

Tim looks out of the window, at the strange view of the graveyard with its tilting stones. St Simeon's is in the background, a solid grey shape surrounded by blossoming trees. It all seems a million miles away from the abbey grounds, where a killer might still be at large. Why did the boss go charging off like that? And why did he tell Tim to wait at the cottage? Was it just to keep Tim out of the action or to make sure that Ruth and Hilary got away safely? Tim looks at Justin, still sitting serenely on the sofa, stroking the demonic cat. It's hard to see this man as dangerous. Weird, certainly, with some pretty nasty views about women. But not dangerous.

'I'm going now,' says Tim. Justin doesn't look up, and Tim feels an urge to jolt him.

'You'll be hearing from us,' he says. 'About the letters.' He doesn't know if this is true. Hilary may well not want to press charges now that she has succeeded in half-strangling the perpetrator. In fact, Justin might want to bring charges of actual bodily harm against Hilary. But he suspects that neither of these things will happen. The letters will be forgotten, especially as it seems they weren't written by the murderer.

Justin turns his head towards Tim. 'I meant what I said in the letters, you know.'

'Which bit in particular?' asks Tim.

'About DCI Nelson being an adulterer. He's had an affair outside wedlock.'

'Who told you that?'

'Cathbad. In confidence.'

'Well, you don't seem to have respected the confidence,' says Tim. One way or another he's not really in the mood to talk about Nelson's marriage.

'Those girls were killed because they were sinful too,' says Justin. 'That's what I think.'

'They were killed because there's a murderer out there,' says Tim, moving towards the door. 'You'll be hearing from us again.'

Justin stays sitting on the sofa, the cat at his side.

Outside Tim takes off his robe, folds it neatly and leaves it by Justin's front door. Then he walks quickly towards the abbey grounds, hoping to catch up with Nelson and Clough. If there's a race to find the killer, he wants to be involved. He wonders where Ruth and Hilary have got to. With any luck, they will have gone home.

But, when he reaches the grounds, he finds that almost

everyone has gone home. It seems amazing that a place that was so full only ten minutes ago is now almost deserted. Discarded prayer sheets litter the grounds and two men with black sacks are picking them up. Someone else is loading music stands onto a trolley. The Stations of the Cross remain in place: the stage where Pilate (a.k.a. Justin Fitzroy-Jones) sentenced Jesus to death, the tomb where His body was laid and, towering above the rest, the cross on its raised platform. As Tim looks towards the platform, he sees something hanging from one of the arms of the cross. Is it a discarded costume? No, it looks too bulky for that. Tim starts to run across the grass. One of the litter-collectors shouts at him, but he keeps on running.

When he gets closer he sees what is hanging from the cross. A man's body, dressed in pink robes. Something in the way it twists and turns tells Tim that it's too late, but he calls the ambulance anyway, shouting into his phone as he gets closer. The litter-collectors look in his direction and soon they are running too. Tim climbs onto the stage and fumbles with the rope around the man's neck.

'Here, use this.' One of the litter-collectors is proffering a dangerous-looking knife. Tim must remember to question him about it afterwards.

The knife does the trick, though. The rope gives way and the body sags into Tim's arms. He lays it on the platform. The man is clearly dead. Despite the distorted features, Tim recognises him immediately as the handsome actor who had played John, the disciple Jesus loved.

'Who is it?' says one of the litter-men. 'He's dead all right. Poor bastard.'

'One of the actors,' says the other. 'Do you know his name?' he asks Tim.

Tim shakes his head but, in his heart, he is certain of the dead man's identity. He thinks that he has found Thom Novak.

The hymn is still echoing in Daisy's head as she runs. 'When through the woods and forest glades I wander, And hear the birds sing sweetly in the trees . . .' She can see the houses now, the white gate leading to the Hendersons' garden, that paradise of treehouse and swings. She's nearly there – in a few seconds she'll be with her darling daughters. She'll tell the Hendersons about her fears and they'll laugh together, they'll give her tea and biscuits and offer her a lift home.

The next minute she is on the ground. There's a heavy weight pressing her into the mud and hot breath on the back of her neck. She has let go of the pushchair and she hears Samuel give a startled shout as it topples over. Lulu is barking. Protect Samuel, she sends a thought message to the dog. Protect Samuel, don't worry about me. She struggles, but her assailant is too strong for her. Now his hands are round her neck. Lulu's barking seems to be coming from a long way away. She tries to pray, to say an act of contrition, but all she can think is how unfair this is, she's only thirty-five, she has four children, how will Larry ever be able to cope on his own?

Darkness. Is this it, the promised land?

Led by Becky, Nelson, Clough and Tanya take the path behind the farm buildings. Becky sets a good pace, obviously a child used to walking. It's Larry who stumbles, hampered by his long robe, and almost falls several times. Nelson thinks of the Stations of the Cross, 'Jesus Falls for the Third Time'. He has already telephoned the station asking for back-up and circulating a description of Robin Rainsford.

'Why do you think he's our man?' asks Clough, as they approach the gate to the rapeseed field. At least Clough has discarded his costume. Nelson doesn't think he could cope with two people in fancy dress.

'Something Stanley Greenway said,' says Nelson. 'It all fell into place back in the cottage. I think that Robin was befriended by Doreen when she was a dinner-lady at his school. It made him pathologically jealous of her foster children – and her actual children. That was the link between Chloe and Paula. Not that they looked alike, it was because they were Doreen's children.'

'But, even if that's true,' pants Larry. 'Why would he go after my wife?'

'It's a hunch,' says Nelson. 'And I hope I'm wrong. It was when you said how like your mum Daisy was. I think Rainsford's jealousy might be at work again. He met Daisy when she made supper for the delegates. Daisy seems like such a perfect wife and mother. She's Doreen's daughter-in-law. And killing her, of course, would be the perfect way to get at you.'

'Dear God,' says Larry. 'I hope you're wrong.'

They see the pushchair first. It's lying on its side, wheels spinning. Samuel is still strapped inside and he's crying in an exhausted way, as if he's been doing so for a long time.

'Daisy!' Suddenly Larry gets a burst of energy and he runs

along the path, Clough close behind. But it's Tanya, who never misses a day at the gym, who sprints past them both. Nelson suddenly grabs Becky's hand, unwilling to let her see what might be ahead.

'She's here,' shouts Tanya.

Nelson lets go of Becky and runs forward. Daisy is lying in the yellow flowers just off the track. Tanya and Clough are leaning over her. Larry has fallen to his knees and is crying.

'Look after your daughter,' Nelson shouts at him.

Plant stalks are flattened all around as if a struggle has taken place; the scent of the flowers is acrid and unpleasant. Nelson fully expects to see a dead body but, instead, Clough is phoning an ambulance and Tanya is briskly turning Daisy into the recovery position.

'She's alive, boss.'

Nelson goes back to the pushchair and frees Samuel, lifting him up into his arms. Larry is sitting on the ground with tall Becky in his lap and Nelson doesn't think he could cope with the baby as well.

'Daisy's alive,' he says. 'The ambulance is on its way.'

Larry looks at him blankly. 'Where's Lulu?' he says.

Who the hell's Lulu? Oh, the dog. Still holding the baby, Nelson sets off through the flowers. A few yards away he finds Robin Rainsford lying on the ground, with Lulu growling on his chest.

# CHAPTER 29

Tim's hunch proves correct. A search through the dead man's pockets (he is wearing jeans under the pink robes) produces a driving licence and a passport in the name of Thomas Novak. Tim calls the station and sits with the body until the coroner's van arrives, trundling self-importantly over the grass. It strikes him as immeasurably sad that this young man, with all his life ahead of him, preferred to die rather than to live it without the woman he loved. Love, he thinks, is a very frightening thing.

Back at the now deserted station he rings the next-of-kin number given in the passport. Thom's mother answers, and he gives her the news as gently as he can. What strikes him most is that she isn't in the least surprised. 'When he left the rehab place we were worried that he might . . . that he might do something stupid.' Was it stupid to kill yourself? Tim supposes so, but Novak's action has a tragic logic nonetheless. Mrs Novak seems comforted to hear that Thom had attended a religious ceremony before he died, so Tim makes a lot of this without expanding on the horror of the giant cross and the body hanging from it. 'Thom was brought up a Catholic. I hope he got some help from that . . . at the end.'

'I'm sure he did,' says Tim.

Next he rings Chloe's parents. Julie Jenkins listens in silence and then she says, 'Poor Thom. He did love her really.' 'I think he did,' says Tim. He can't bring himself to say (as his mother would) that they are together again now. 'I'll speak to his parents,' says Julie. 'Maybe we can have his ashes buried with Chloe's.'

'That's a nice idea,' says Tim.

He feels rather depressed after the phone calls and could do with someone to talk to but the incident room is empty. Surely the boss and the others should be back by now? Tanya's computer is on, its low insistent hum filling the silent room. Tim clicks on the screen and sees a journey planner app showing a route from the remand prison to Walsingham. Clough's emergency Mars bar is still on his desk. Where is everyone?

Rainsford's trousers are torn and there seems to be blood on the grass. But he's alive and, when he sees Nelson, he shouts 'Help' in a feeble voice. Nelson gives the baby to Larry, grasps the spaniel's collar and pulls her off. Becky comes forward to take Lulu from him, bending down to bury her face in the dog's hair.

Rainsford struggles to sit up. 'That dog,' he pants, 'it's mad. It attacked me. Bit both of my ankles.'

'Robin Rainsford,' says Nelson, pulling the man to his feet. 'You're under arrest for the murders of Chloe Jenkins and

Paula Moncrieff and the attempted murder of Daisy West-mondham. Do you understand the nature of the charge?'

'It drew blood.' Rainsford seems to be asking for sympathy.

'You do not have to say anything,' says Nelson. 'However it may harm your defence if you do not mention when questioned something which you later rely on in court. Anything you do say will be taken in evidence.'

Clough is at his side. 'She's OK, boss. More shocked than anything. Tanya's with her now.'

'And the ambulance is on its way?'

'Yes, but we ought to get to the road. They'll never find us in the middle of a field.'

'Where's Daisy?' says Larry. He too seems in shock. He gazes at Rainsford as if he's never seen him before.

'I'm here,' says a voice. It's Daisy, leaning on Tanya's arm, shoeless, her skirt ripped but her smile miraculously intact.

Larry wraps his arms round his wife, sobbing. Samuel, in danger of being crushed between his parents, starts crying too. Becky stands silently, holding the dog in her arms. Nelson puts his arm round her. 'It's all right, love. Let's get out of here. Where's the nearest road?'

'Our friends live there.' Becky puts down the dog and points to a white gate, about a hundred yards away.

'OK. Clough, have you got cuffs?'

But Clough has already handcuffed Rainsford, who is still trying to look down at his injured ankles.

'Let's go then.'

Tanya has recovered the pushchair and Larry puts the baby into it. Daisy reaches out to her daughter and gives her a hug. Together they walk towards the gate, with Larry following, pushing the buggy. Tanya hovers protectively at Daisy's shoulder. Nelson and Clough bring up the rear with the handcuffed Rainsford between them. Lulu circles them excitedly.

'That dog should be put down,' says Rainsford. 'It's quite out of control.'

'You should be put down,' growls Clough.

Back at the cottage, Ruth finds it hard to settle. Kate, over-excited after a day of arts and crafts with Sandra, is whiny and irritable. Ruth cooks supper, plays several games where the Sylvanians go to prison and/or boarding school, gives Kate her bath, reads two Josie Smith stories and still Nelson hasn't rung. What is going on? Why did Nelson and Clough rush off so suddenly? Nelson asked Tim something about a school. What did that mean?

When Kate is finally asleep, Ruth opens her computer and Googles Madonna Lactans. 'A depiction of the Virgin Mary,' she reads, 'where the Virgin is shown breastfeeding the infant Jesus.' So she was right about the breast milk. She hopes that Nelson remembers how scathing he had been about the missing glass phial. Why doesn't he ring so she can say 'I told you so'?

Ruth paces around her tiny sitting room, watched impassively by Flint. She thinks of Hilary forcing Justin to the ground. Hilary was certainly telling the truth when she said that she wasn't afraid of her stalker. In fact she had seemed positively to enjoy the encounter. Cathbad, on the other hand, had seemed to feel that he had been personally betrayed by his friend, the man whose cat he had looked after. Thinking of the cat, Ruth goes back to her laptop.

'G. K. Chesterton, English writer and Christian apologist. Best known as the creator of the Father Brown stories, Chesterton converted to Roman Catholicism in 1922.'

So that was why Cathbad had said that the cat's name should have given him a clue. Scrolling through a selection of G. K. Chesterton quotations, she reads, 'Reason is always a kind of brute force, those who appeal to the head rather than the heart . . . are always men of violence.' She thinks of Justin's letters, of the attempts to justify his views by twisted reasoning and quotations from scripture. She thinks of Hilary's own arguments, so measured and confident. Perhaps it's better just to believe things, as Cathbad does, without attempting to explain them.

Maybe Nelson won't ring her at all. After all, she's not involved in the case. She's neither a colleague nor a wife. Nelson is under no obligation to tell her what happened today. She supposes she'll hear it on the news, just like everyone else.

At nearly ten o'clock her phone rings.

'Ruth. It's Nelson.'

'Nelson. I was hoping you'd ring. What happened after you left Justin's cottage?'

'A whole lot happened,' says Nelson. 'For one thing, we've arrested Robin Rainsford for the murders.'

'Robin Rainsford? Oh . . . the man who led Hilary's course. Why did you arrest him?'

'Well, we caught him trying to murder Daisy West-mondham, for one thing.'

'Who?'

'She's the vicar's wife. Rainsford was obsessed with his mother.'

'Whose mother? The vicar's?'

'Yes, a woman called Doreen Westmondham. She was a dinner-lady at Rainsford's school. Apparently she befriended him, and he became jealous of her children and the children she looked after – she fostered hundreds of children, including Paula Moncrieff.'

'What about Chloe Jenkins?'

'Doreen was her childminder. When Rainsford met Chloe at the church, the whole thing started up again. He kept tabs on all of them. It seems that he asked Paula to come on the course specially. I remember her husband saying that she was surprised to be invited. She hadn't been a priest very long.'

'God. Poor woman.'

'Yes. It just clicked when we were at Justin's house. I remembered that Rainsford had been at boarding school near Walsingham. Then I thought about Daisy and realised that she might be in danger.'

'Why didn't he go after the vicar? After all, he was this Doreen's actual child.'

'He only attacked women, and I think it helped if they were blonde. It's all very nasty. Uniform went round to his house, and it's full of pictures of blonde women. He was also obsessed with a golden-haired statue of the Virgin Mary.'

'When Justin confessed to writing the letters I really thought it might be him.'

'Yes. The letters were a distraction really. All that stuff about the Madonna dressed in blue, weeping for the world. It turns out that it wasn't the Virgin Mary that Rainsford was obsessed with but his own substitute mother, Doreen.'

'I was right about the breast-milk link, though, wasn't I?'

Nelson laughs. 'Yes, you were right, Ruth. Is that what you wanted me to say?'

There's a small silence while Ruth thinks about what she really wants Nelson to say. 'I'd better go,' says Nelson at last. 'It's been a long day.'

'Yes. It was very kind of you to ring me. I was going mad wondering what was going on.'

Another silence, then Nelson says, 'Ruth, I'm sorry about the other evening . . . the things I said.'

'That's OK,' says Ruth. 'Have you spoken to Michelle?'

'Yes,' says Nelson. 'We've . . . well, we've straightened things out.'

'I'm glad,' says Ruth. 'I really am.'

As she clicks off the phone she thinks that, if Hilary's God can make those words come true, she might even start believing in Him.

# CHAPTER 30

*20th April 2014, Easter Sunday*

'Will he be all right on his own?'

'He'll be fine. He's got his blanket.'

'I'm not sure. He's so little.'

Nelson and Michelle both look fondly at the puppy. He looks back up at them, head on one side, stumpy tail wagging. He has no idea that they're planning to abandon him for the morning. Nelson feels his heart contract.

It was Lulu's bravery on Good Friday that had finally convinced Nelson to get a dog, but the thought had been forming in his mind ever since his last meeting with Jan Adams and Barney. He'd rung Jan late on Good Friday evening and she'd said that she knew of a rescue place that had some German Shepherd puppies. 'They're all vaccinated and chipped, ready to go to new homes.' Nelson and Michelle had driven over to the rescue centre on Saturday and had fallen in love at first sight.

Nelson had wanted to call the puppy Jimmy, after Jimmy

Armfield, a legendary Blackpool player. If he'd had a son he would have insisted that the name Jimmy featured somewhere on the baptismal certificate. But Michelle had said that the puppy just didn't look like a Jimmy, though Nelson is sure that she would have had the same reservations in the case of a son. Nelson's previous and much-loved dog was called Max, but now he dislikes the name. Michelle suggested Rocky, but, although Nelson likes the idea of naming the dog after a boxer, it still reminds him too much of PC Roy 'Rocky' Taylor. 'Roy was really sweet,' Michelle had told him after the policeman had steadfastly guarded her on Friday afternoon. 'I don't know why you're always so nasty about him.'

It was Laura who christened the new pet via her weekly Skype call from Ibiza. 'He's so fluffy and gorgeous. He looks like a bear. Let's call him Bruno. Bruno the bear.' Nelson had acquiesced. It could have been worse, knowing his daughters. Rebecca once had a hamster called Fluffykins. At least there was a boxer called Frank Bruno.

Robin Rainsford has confessed to the murders of Chloe and Paula and to the attempted murder of Daisy. He confessed while still in hospital having his dog bites treated. Perhaps he knew that DNA evidence would link him to the crimes; perhaps it was being caught attacking Daisy or perhaps he was just too tired of lying. 'How did you guess it was Rainsford?' asked Tim, when Nelson finally arrived back at the station. 'I remembered he'd been at school in the area,' said Nelson, as he had to Ruth, 'and it just clicked suddenly.' But, in fact, it was something else, words that had been running in Nelson's head ever since Stanley Greenway's taped confession: 'And I was just lying there in the grass the birds blackbird thrush robin looking at her so pretty then she was dead I loved her but she was dead . . . ' The unintelligible babble had, in fact, contained a witness statement. Some time on Good Friday Nelson's brain had unscrambled this and added punctuation:

'And I was just lying there in the grass, the birds: blackbird, thrush. Robin looking at her, so pretty, then she was dead.'

Stanley had actually seen Robin Rainsford looking down on Chloe's dead body, but, in his drug-addled state, hadn't been able to connect this with her murder. Stanley's first conscious memory was of finding himself beside Chloe's corpse and this convinced him that he must be the killer. He had carried Chloe back to the Slipper Chapel, intending to pray to his beloved Madonna. But the chapel had been closed and, in terror, Stanley had laid Chloe's body in a ditch, placing his rosary on her chest. He had then staggered back to the Sanctuary and managed to block out the whole thing.

'It's fairly typical of the drugs he was on,' said Fiona McAllister. 'They can cause blackouts and paranoid delusions. I told you that at the time.'

Yes, she had told them, but they hadn't listened. Stanley had confessed to the crime and Nelson can't acquit himself or his team of the assumption that Stanley must have been the killer because he simply looked the type. He knew that he had doubts – there was never anything linking Stanley to Paula, for example – but he had suppressed those feelings. And he hadn't trusted Robin Rainsford from that first meeting in the room smelling of incense. Robin must have been at the Slipper Chapel that evening, along with Justin and Larry. And, walking back through the fields, he had encountered Chloe Jenkins, wandering back from a visit to her beloved childminder's grave. Robin, recognising Chloe from church and knowing her to be linked to Doreen, had killed her, leaving her body where it lay. Paula, too, was a marked woman from the moment she was invited on the course. Robin had attacked Michelle in the graveyard, thinking she was Paula. But Paula was out with the other priests and all Robin had to do was to wait for her to come back to St Catherine's. He had heard her return, had heard her announce her attention of walking in the grounds and he had gone to meet her. Then he had returned to his room and, by his own account, slept peacefully until the police came to rouse him in the early hours of the morning.

Father Bill was right, in a way, Nelson thinks. The clue was the Madonna. Not Our Lady or the Virgin Mary or the Madonna Lactans. It was the mother, the foster mother, the extraordinary, ordinary Doreen Westmondham, who had enough love in her heart for her own children and for a hundred foster children, yet still had time to befriend a little boy at boarding school. As an adult, Robin Rainsford championed the cause of women in the Church, perhaps because he remembered the kindness of his surrogate mother. But, unlike the millions of pilgrims who flock to Walsingham every year, he was not willing to share the love of his mother. He was jealous of anyone she had cared for. Even Daisy Westmondham, who had never met Doreen, wasn't immune. She was her daughter-in-law, and had had the temerity to have a photograph of Robin's ideal mother stuck to her kitchen noticeboard. Robin must have seen it when he came to dinner at the start of the course.

And now Larry Westmondham has invited them to this Easter service. 'Please come, Detective Chief Inspector. All of you. It'll be a way of putting the past behind us and making a new start. That's what Easter morning is all about. Resurrection, new life, a new start.'

Nelson passed the message on to the team. Clough and Cassandra will both be there. Tim, who is leaving after Easter, was vague about his plans. Tanya, on the other hand, was keen. She's keen about everything these days, especially since Nelson has recommended her for a permanent promotion to detective sergeant. It was well deserved, too. It was Tanya who had spotted Stanley Greenway and Justin Fitzroy-Jones on the CCTV. And it was Tanya who, running like the wind through the rapeseed fields, found Daisy first. Nelson wonders if Tanya will bring her partner to the church. If so, Nelson prays that Clough won't say anything too embarrassing.

But Michelle is clearly having second thoughts. 'I don't think we should both go, Harry. Look at Bruno's little face. He'll be so sad.'

Nelson looks at Bruno's little face. He knows that he is going to the service on his own.

Ruth, too, is on her way to church. In her case, it was Hilary who did the emotional blackmail. 'Please come, Ruth. It would mean so much to me.'

'I don't believe in God,' said Ruth. 'You know that.'

'I understand,' said Hilary, though she still sounded as

if she didn't. 'But come for me, for all of us. It was such a shock about Robin. It feels important to leave Walsingham on a positive note.'

'What about Kate?'

'Bring her too,' said Hilary. 'I'd love to meet her. They're giving out Creme Eggs after the service.'

Ruth had sighed and given in. Maybe Hilary's right and they do need some sort of ceremony to mark the occasion. And you might see Nelson, says that unwelcome, but insistent voice in Ruth's head.

It's a blustery morning, and, as Ruth drives over the marshes the wind makes the long grass undulate like the sea. Kate is eating a chocolate egg (Ruth hopes she's remembered wet wipes) and clutching a woolly lamb, an Easter present from Nelson and Michelle.

'Why are we going to this place?' she asks, rather indistinctly.

'Because it'll be fun,' says Ruth. 'There'll be singing and . . . er . . . candles and . . .'

'Candles? Is it a birthday party?'

'Not exactly.'

'Christmas is Jesus's birthday, isn't it?'

In a way, thinks Ruth. She remembers Cathbad saying the Christians picked the date of the 25th December for Christmas because it coincided with a pagan feast. 'And it's traditional, of course, to have a feast in mid-winter. Light in the dark, warmth in the cold.' At least Cathbad will be at the church today and then Ruth and Kate are going back to his and Judy's house for lunch.

'Easter is celebrating life,' she says, 'and spring and lambs and all that.'

'And chocolate,' says Kate.

'And chocolate,' agrees Ruth. She hopes that there will be enough Creme Eggs for the adults.

Michelle listens to Nelson's car driving away; he's accelerating too much as usual and has to brake noisily at the entrance to the cul-de-sac. But Nelson will always drive like he's involved in a pursuit, even when he's doing something as innocuous as going to church.

Michelle looks down at Bruno, who crinkles his nose engagingly. 'You're going to like me best,' Michelle tells him, 'be a real mummy's boy.' 'We mustn't start referring to ourselves as the dog's mummy and daddy,' Nelson had said last night, 'that really would be the beginning of the end.' Too late, thinks Michelle, the process has already started in her head. 'Mummy loves you,' she says defiantly to the puppy, who looks back at her with absolute adoration.

Michelle takes out her phone. '*He's gone*,' she texts. No need for more words. A guilty text if there ever was one. Except she's not guilty, she tells herself, as she goes into the kitchen to prepare the lamb joint for lunch. She is going to do everything she can to save this marriage, it's just that she thinks she owes herself this meeting first.

Tim arrives ten minutes later. She watches him walking to the house, having left his car at the top of the road as instructed. Her next-door-neighbour is mowing his lawn, but he doesn't look up as Tim, sober and unremarkable in jeans and a grey jumper, goes past. A people-carrier parks across the road bearing her opposite neighbours' grandchildren and, under the cover of their joyful exclamations of welcome, Michelle lets Tim into the house.

He hasn't been inside the house since the time, three years ago, when Michelle cooked him lunch to welcome him to the team. She wonders if he'll think of that now, smelling the garlic and rosemary from the lamb. She always lays the table for Sunday lunch, even if it's just for two of them, but she hasn't done it today. She thinks that seeing the two places, the wine glasses, the mats showing Norfolk scenes, would be too much for both of them.

'Do you want a drink?' she asks. 'Tea? Coffee? Something stronger?'

'No, thanks,' says Tim. 'Is this the puppy?' He bends down to talk to Bruno, who flattens himself onto the carpet, in a posture that's half-welcome, half-abasement. 'Clough was telling me about him.'

'He's called Bruno,' says Michelle. 'We only got him yesterday but he's been so good. He didn't cry at all last night.' She doesn't add that this was because they took him into their bedroom at the first sign of a whimper.

Tim straightens up. He looks out of place in her sunny sitting room; too tall, too serious, too intense. He's not as big as Nelson, but he's still a rather intimidating presence. He also looks, Michelle realises with a shock, too young for a room that has matching sofas and a dining alcove. Tim is ten years younger than her, but it has never seemed to matter before. Now he almost looks like he could be one of her daughters' friends.

'Nice house,' he says.

Michelle shrugs, though, in truth, the house is her pride and joy.

'Be careful the dog doesn't chew the furniture,' says Tim. 'My brother had a German Shepherd that did that. Mind you, I think that was because it was bored. Rick didn't take him out much.'

'I'm going to take Bruno for a long walk every day,' says Michelle. 'It'll be better than going to the gym.'

They stare at each other. Eventually Tim says, 'I'm sorry my text scared you.'

'That's OK. It was just that it was an unfamiliar number.'

'I always used to call you from my other phone. In case the boss saw the texts.'

The message, '*I'm coming back for you*', had turned out to be from Tim. When Michelle found out she was almost more frightened than when she believed it was from a madman threatening to kill her. What did Tim mean, he was coming back for her? What if she didn't want him to? What if she did and the knowledge meant that she could never again live happily with Harry? Michelle hadn't slept at all last night, lying awake, listening to Harry and Bruno snoring in unison.

Now she says, 'What did it mean? The text.'

Tim spreads out his hands. 'I still love you, Michelle. I'm sorry, but I do. I know you want to stay with Nelson and I respect that. It's just . . . well, if you ever need me, you know where I am.'

It occurs to Michelle that she actually has no idea where Tim will be. She says so.

'My transfer has come through,' says Tim. 'I'm starting with Essex CID after Easter. The boss has been very fair, given me a good reference.'

'I'll miss you,' says Michelle. At that moment she wants, more than anything else, to fling herself into Tim's arms, to drag him upstairs so he can make love to her on the king-sized marital bed with French Colonial-style duvet. Why not? she thinks wildly, I might never see him again. Why shouldn't I have this to remember? But she doesn't move.

'Goodbye, Michelle,' says Tim.

'Goodbye, Tim.'

She doesn't go with him to the door. She stands still in the middle of the room, listening to the metallic hum of next-door's lawnmower. After a few minutes Bruno comes to her side and she buries her face in his fur.

The first person Nelson sees is Clough. He looks unusually smart in a blue suit and is standing with Cassandra by the church porch. Nelson is early as usual, but he's surprised to see a stream of people walking through the graveyard and into the church. Out of the corner of his eye he can see Doreen Westmondham's tombstone, very white in the spring sunshine.

'All these people,' he says to Clough. 'It'll be standing room only.'

'It's Easter,' says Cassandra. 'If you only go to church once a year, you go at Easter.' She's looking beautiful in a flowery dress and pink cardigan. Clough, as always in her presence, seems about to burst with pride.

'Is Michelle coming?' asks Cassandra. Rather to Nelson's surprise, the two women get on well.

'She stayed at home,' says Nelson. 'She didn't want to leave the puppy.'

'That dog will rule your life,' says Clough. 'You mark my words.' Clough had a dog when he was with a previous partner, Nelson remembers. He once told Nelson that he missed the dog more than the girl.

'I'll go and save us a seat, shall I?' says Cassandra. She disappears into the gloom of the church. Nelson goes to follow her but Clough puts a hand on his arm.

'Just a minute, boss. Something I want to tell you.'

Nelson looks at him in surprise. For one awful moment he thinks that Clough, too, is about to ask for a transfer. But Clough is looking too happy for it to be bad news.

'Just wanted you to know before it's all round the station. Cassie's pregnant. I'm going to be a father.'

'Congratulations,' says Nelson, shaking Clough's hand. 'Are you getting married? No, forget I said that. It's the sort of thing my mum would say.'

Clough laughs. 'That's OK. My mum said it too. Bit rich, coming from her, seeing as she didn't marry my dad or Mark's. But, yes, we want to get married. We're going to have the baby first, though. Cassie says she doesn't want to look fat on her wedding day.'

'Congratulations,' says Nelson again. 'It's wonderful news. You'll be a great dad.'

'I'm going to try.' Clough suddenly looks serious. 'I really am.'

Fatherhood changes you, thinks Nelson, as he follows Clough into the church. It makes you the sort of person who gets emotional about news like this, for a start. Nelson rubs his eyes. He hadn't cried, but it had been a dangerously close thing.

Ruth had intended to sit a long way away from Nelson but, before Ruth can stop her, Kate runs across the church to sit next to him. Ruth follows, aflame with embarrassment. The congregation smile benignly and move up to make room. After all, Ruth can see them thinking, it would be a shame to break up this happy family. Kate sits on Nelson's knee and Ruth is squashed uncomfortably between Nelson and Clough.

'This is cosy,' says Clough. His girlfriend, an irritatingly glamorous actress, gives her a superior smile. Ruth, unable to take off her jacket, can feel herself getting red in the face all over again.

The first hymn starts almost as soon as they have sat down. They scrabble to their feet again, looking for their places in the hymnbooks. Clough sings loudly in a fine tenor. Nelson mumbles the words, keeping his arm around Kate.

'Christ the Lord is risen today . . .'

It is the first time that Ruth has seen the Reverend Larry Westmondham, and she finds him rather an uninspiring speaker. He obviously feels it all very deeply, his round face gets quite anguished when he talks about purgatory, but he seems rather embarrassed about imparting any insights that he might have. Ruth is left with a general mumble of thoughts about life, death and rebirth, together with a vague idea that it might be good if we were all nicer to each other. The church is lovely, though, possibly twelfth century, with a rood screen and some beautiful stonework. There are flowers everywhere and incense swirls from a silver orb on a chain which is being swung enthusiastically by one of the altar servers. Kate flaps her hand, but doesn't say anything. Cassandra coughs and Clough pats her on the back, whispering solicitously.

Ruth doesn't see Hilary until they are all filing out at the end after another rousing hymn ('Thine be the glory'). Hilary is with Freya, and they are both wearing dog collars. Some of the congregation are looking at them suspiciously, but Larry, passing them on his way out, makes a point of shaking their hands. Bearing in mind his membership of the Brotherhood of the Madonna Lactans and the incense, Ruth assumes that Larry is fairly High Church and may be opposed to women priests. If so, he's making a pretty good job of appearing welcoming. Behind the priests, Ruth sees Janet Meadows, resplendent in a patchwork velvet coat, and Tanya, who is accompanied by a blonde woman whom Ruth doesn't recognise.

There are so many people leaving the church that Ruth, Clough and Cassandra get trapped in their pew. Nelson has managed to escape, but Ruth holds Kate firmly by the hand. Opposite them, a similarly trapped woman smiles and waves.

'That's his wife,' hisses Clough. 'The one who was attacked.'

When the crowd shuffles forward Ruth finds herself next to a pretty, fresh-faced woman in jeans and a blue jacket. She's holding a baby and has a girl of about six by the hand. Two slightly older girls hover behind her, one of them wearing a choirgirl's surplice.

'Hi, Daisy,' says Clough, behind Ruth. 'You're looking good for someone who was strangled the day before yesterday.'

Daisy laughs. She doesn't seem fazed by this typical Clough humour.

'I'm fine,' she says. 'The hospital discharged me that night. I just had a few cuts and bruises. Thanks to you and DS Fuller and DCI Nelson getting to me so quickly.'

'Thanks to your little dog,' says Clough. 'Where is she?'

'Daddy says she can't come to church,' says one of the older girls resentfully.

'What does Daddy know?' says Clough. 'Daisy, let me introduce my fiancée, Cassandra, and my friend Ruth.'

Daisy shakes hands with them both, while Ruth thinks *fiancée*?

'I've heard lots about you,' says Daisy to Ruth. 'I'm a friend of Janet Meadows. You must come to tea one day. Bring your daughter.'

'I'd like to,' says Ruth. Kate and the youngest girl smile warily at each other.

'Happy families,' says Clough, who seems in a weirdly ebullient mood. He kisses Cassandra on the cheek, and they laugh together quietly.

Outside Ruth finds another happy family: Cathbad, Judy and Michael, with Miranda in the buggy. Kate runs up to Michael.

'Did you get me an Easter egg?'

'Kate!' Ruth wonders if it's possible to die of shame.

'We're going to have an Easter egg hunt in the garden,' says Cathbad.

'Easter egg hunt!' Mad with surplus energy Kate runs off through the gravestones with Michael following. The wind has stripped the cherry trees of their blossom and the grass is full of white petals. Like confetti, thinks Ruth, although most churches seem to forbid confetti these days.

'Watch she doesn't run in the road.' Ruth doesn't have to look round to know that this is Nelson.

'I am watching.'

Kate and Michael are now playing hide-and-seek around Doreen Westmondham's gravestone. Ruth tells Kate to stop.

'Don't worry,' says a voice behind them. It's Larry Westmondham, still in his vestments, holding a basket full of Creme Eggs. 'Mum loved to have children round her.'

'Creme Eggs,' says a voice, 'my favourites.' Hilary is sailing towards them. Larry proffers the basket rather nervously.

'Thank you,' says Hilary. 'I'm going to do the same in my parish next year.'

'Where is your parish?' asks Larry.

'Streatham,' says Hilary, unwrapping silver paper.

'I know it well,' says Larry, with what Ruth, a south London girl, thinks of as misplaced enthusiasm. 'I used to live in Croydon. I hope to go back there one day.'

'Funny thing to hope for,' says Ruth, and she and Hilary walk through the graveyard together. Kate and Michael are playing a complicated game of jumping over the flat stones instigated by Larry Westmondham's youngest daughter. The curtains are drawn in Justin's cottage. According to Cathbad, he has gone away on retreat. The police, at Hilary's request, aren't pressing charges. Chesterton has been booked into a cattery; Cathbad doesn't think he'll be asked to cat-sit again.

'I feel bad,' Hilary says now. 'I felt so angry with Justin. When I got him in that headlock I really wanted to hurt him. That's a terrible thing for a priest to say, isn't it?'

'It just shows you're human,' says Ruth. 'Priests are allowed to be human. Male priests and female priests.'

As she says this, she thinks of Father Hennessey. She hasn't spoken to the priest since that day in the canteen, but she did see him in the distance at the Passion Play. She hopes that, even if he does confess, the bishop will let him carry on being a priest. It's not a job that would appeal to Ruth, but some people, Hilary included, really do seem cut out for it.

She stops to call Kate, but Nelson has already got to her and is leading her back to Ruth.

'Thanks,' says Ruth, when they reach her. Hilary has wandered away to talk to Cathbad.

'What are you doing for the rest of the day?' says Nelson.

'We're going to Cathbad and Judy's for lunch. There's an Easter egg hunt apparently.'

'Katie will enjoy that.'

'Yes, she will. Well, goodbye, Nelson. Happy Easter.'

'Happy Easter.'

She moves away, but somehow she knows that he is watching her. She has the oddest feeling that they are alone in the world, and everyone else, even Kate, is just part of a dream. Is it a dream, then, when Nelson catches up with her and, just briefly, takes her hand? She thinks he says something, but she doesn't catch the words and, before she can ask him to repeat it, Nelson is striding away through the tombstones.

# ACKNOWLEDGEMENTS

As always in my books, I have made the real Walsingham into my own fictional version of the place, including real and imaginary elements. The priory, the abbey grounds, the Anglican shrine and the Slipper Chapel are all real. There is a beautiful Russian Orthodox Chapel in the old railway booking office. The snowdrops in February are justly famous and well worth a visit. However, St Simeon's Church and Cottage are imaginary, the cottage owing much to my father-in-law's house in Smarden, Kent. St Catherine's Lodge is also imaginary, although similar religious institutions established to host conferences and retreats do exist. Most importantly, with one exception, the people are all completely made up. The Slipper Chapel does have a custodian, but Father Bill is a fictional character.

Last year, a woman called Jan Adams took part in a fund-raising auction for the young people and children's cancer charity CLIC Sargent. The prize was the chance to appear as a character in these pages. When I found out that Jan had been a police dog-handler I was determined that she should feature in that role. I also wanted to include her dog, Barney. Thanks to Jan, both for bidding and for all the fascinating information about the work of police dogs.

Several people have been very generous with their time and advice. These include Francesca Lewington, Andrew Maxted and Julie Williams. However, I have only followed the experts' advice as far as it suits the plot, and any resulting mistakes are mine alone. I'm also grateful to Emma Bryant for the information about Renault key cards. Thanks to Tracy Stickland for inviting me on a pilgrimage to Walsingham, and to Father Kevin O'Donnell for sharing his knowledge of the place and explaining some of its mysteries. Thanks also to Father Kevin for recommending a wonderful book, *Walsingham: Pilgrims and Pilgrimage* by Michael Rear (St Paul's Publishing, 2011).

Special thanks, as always, to my editor, Jane Wood, and my agent, Rebecca Carter. Thanks to everyone at Quercus and Janklow and Nesbit for working so hard on my behalf. Love and thanks always to my husband, Andrew, and our children, Alex and Juliet.

This book is for my sister, Giulia, with love.

# WHO'S WHO
## IN THE DR RUTH GALLOWAY
## MYSTERIES

# Dr Ruth Galloway

Profession: forensic archaeologist

Likes: cats, Bruce Springsteen, bones, books

Dislikes: gyms, organized religion, shopping

Ruth Galloway was born in south London and educated at University College and Southampton University, where she met her mentor Professor Erik Andersen. In 1997 she participated in Professor Andersen's dig on the north Norfolk coast which resulted in the excavation of a Bronze Age henge. Ruth subsequently moved to the area and became Head of Forensic Archaeology at the University of North Norfolk. She lives an isolated cottage on the edge of the Saltmarsh. In 2007 she was approached by DCI Harry Nelson who wanted her help in identifying bones found buried on the marshes, and her life suddenly got a whole lot more complicated.

Surprising fact about Ruth: she is fascinated by the London Underground and once attended a fancy dress party as The Angel Islington.

# Harry Nelson

Profession: Detective Chief Inspector

Likes: driving fast, solving crimes, his family

Dislikes: Norfolk, the countryside, management speak, his boss

Harry Nelson was born in Blackpool. He came to Norfolk in his thirties to lead the Serious Crimes Unit, bringing with him his wife Michelle and their daughters, Laura and Rebecca. Nelson has a loyal team and enjoys his work. He still hankers after the North though and has not come to love his adopted county. Nelson thinks of himself as an old-fashioned policeman and so often clashes with Super-intendent Whitcliffe, who is trying to drag the force into the twenty-first century. Nelson is impatient and quick-tempered but he is capable of being both imaginative and sensitive. He's also cleverer than he lets on.

Surprising fact about Nelson: he's a huge Frank Sinatra fan.

# Michelle Nelson

Profession: hairdresser

Likes: her family, exercising, socializing with friends

Dislikes: dowdiness, confrontation, talking about murder

Michelle married Nelson when she was twenty-one and he was twenty-three. She was happy with her life in Blackpool – two children, part-time work, her mother nearby – but encouraged Nelson to move to Norfolk for the sake of promotion. Now that her daughters are older she works as a manager for a hair salon. Michelle is beautiful, stylish, hard-working and a dedicated wife and mother. When people see her and Nelson together, their first reaction is usually, 'What *does* she see in him?'

Surprising fact about Michelle: she once played hockey for Blackpool Girls.

# Michael Malone (aka Cathbad)

Profession: laboratory assistant and druid

Likes: nature, mythology, walking, following his instincts

Dislikes: rules, injustice, conventions

Cathbad was born in Ireland and came to England to study first chemistry then archaeology. He also came under the influence of Erik Andersen though they found themselves on opposite sides during the henge dig. Cathbad was brought up as a Catholic but he now thinks of himself as a druid and shaman.

Surprising fact about Cathbad: he can play the accordion.

# Shona Maclean

Profession: lecturer in English Literature

Likes: books, wine, parties

Dislikes: being ignored

Shona is a lecturer at the University of North Norfolk and one of Ruth's closest friends. They met when they both participated in the henge dig in 1997. On the face of it Shona seems an unlikely friend for Ruth – she's outgoing and stunningly beautiful for a start – but the two women share a sense of humour and an interest in books, films and travel. They also have a lot of history together.

Surprising fact about Shona: as a child she won several Irish dancing competitions.

# David Clough

Profession: Detective Sergeant

Likes: food, football, beer, his job

Dislikes: political correctness, graduate police officers

David Clough ('Cloughie' to Nelson) was born in Norfolk and joined the force at eighteen. As a youngster he almost followed his elder brother into petty crime but a chance meeting with a sympathetic policeman led him into a surprisingly successful police career. Clough is a tough, dedicated officer but not without imagination. He admires Nelson, his boss, but has a rather competitive relationship with Sergeant Judy Johnson.

Surprising fact about Clough: He can quote the 'you come to me on my daughter's wedding day' scene from The Godfather off by heart.

# Judy Johnson

Profession: Detective Sergeant

Likes: horses, driving, her job

Dislikes: girls' nights out, sexism, being patronised

Judy Johnson was born in Norfolk to Irish Catholic parents. She was academic at school but opted to join the police force at eighteen rather than go to university. Judy can seem cautious and steady – she has been going out with the same boyfriend since school, for example – but she is actually fiercely ambitious. She resents any hint of condescension or sexism which can lead to some fiery exchanges with Clough.

Surprising fact about Judy: she's a keen card player and once won an inter-force poker competition.

# Phil Trent

Profession: professor of Archaeology

Likes: money, being on television, technology

Dislikes: new age archaeologists, anonymity, being out of the loop

Phil is Ruth's head of department at the University of North Norfolk. He's ambitious and outwardly charming, determined to put the university (and himself) on the map. He thinks of Ruth as plodding and old-fashioned so is slightly put out when she begins to make a name for herself as an advisor to the police. On one hand, it's good for the image of UNN; on the other, it should have been him.

Surprising fact about Phil: at his all boys school, he once played Juliet in *Romeo and Juliet*.